The Empire of the Self

The Empire of the Self

*Self-Command and Political Speech
in Seneca and Petronius*

CHRISTOPHER STAR

The Johns Hopkins University Press
Baltimore

© 2012 The Johns Hopkins University Press
All rights reserved. Published 2012
Printed in the United States of America on acid-free paper
9 8 7 6 5 4 3 2 1

The Johns Hopkins University Press
2715 North Charles Street
Baltimore, Maryland 21218-4363
www.press.jhu.edu

Library of Congress Cataloging-in-Publication Data
Star, Christopher.
  The empire of the self : self-command and political speech in Seneca and Petronius / Christopher Star.
       pages cm.
  Includes bibliographical references and index.
  ISBN 978-1-4214-0674-9 (hardback : alkaline paper) — ISBN 978-1-4214-0726-5 (electronic) — ISBN 1-4214-0674-8 (hardback : alkaline paper) — ISBN 1-4214-0726-4 (electronic)
  1. Politics in literature. 2. Latin literature—History and criticism. 3. Seneca, Lucius Annaeus, ca. 4 B.C.–65 A.D.—Criticism and interpretation. 4. Petronius Arbiter. Satyricon. I. Title.
  PA6029.P64S73 2012
  870.9'001—dc23   2012006338

A catalog record for this book is available from the British Library.

Special discounts are available for bulk purchases of this book. For more information, please contact Special Sales at 410-516-6936 or specialsales@press.jhu.edu.

The Johns Hopkins University Press uses environmentally friendly book materials, including recycled text paper that is composed of at least 30 percent post-consumer waste, whenever possible.

Contents

	Acknowledgments	vii
	Introduction	1
	PART I: Soul-Shaping Speech	
1	Senecan Philosophy and the Psychology of Command	23
2	Self-Address in Senecan Tragedy	62
3	Self-Address in the *Satyricon*	84
	PART II. Soul-Revealing Speech	
4	Political Speech in *De clementia*	117
5	Soul, Speech, and Politics in the *Apocolocyntosis* and the *Satyricon*	140
6	Writing, Body, and Money	171
	Epilogue	209
	Notes	215
	Bibliography	277
	Index	295

Acknowledgments

Redde quod debes, "pay back what you owe," write both Seneca and Petronius. I cannot hope to repay the friends, colleagues, and institutions that have aided me in completing this book. This expression of gratitude will have to stand as small recompense for the debts I have incurred. My forays into self-address in Seneca and Petronius began with my dissertation at the University of Chicago under the guidance of Shadi Bartsch, Martha Nussbaum, and David Wray. Since then those three have continued to support my work in a variety of ways. Susanna Braund and Niall Slater have also provided a great deal of encouragement and assistance for several years now.

Work on this book was supported by a generous grant from the Loeb Classical Library Foundation. My thanks go to Richard Thomas and the other members of the foundation. My sabbatical was spent as a visiting scholar at Harvard University. Thanks to John Duffy, chair of the Department of the Classics, and the other members of the department for allowing me to visit for the year.

Portions of this book were presented to audiences at Boston University, Dartmouth, Emory, Harvard, Temple, and Yale. I am grateful to all who have provided suggestions and encouragement, including Victor Bers, Pramit Chaudhuri, Margaret Graver, Wolfgang Haase, Jeffery Henderson, Albert Henrichs, Robin Mitchell-Boyask, Victor Nuovo, Michael Reeve, Steve Scully, Nancy Sherman, Steve Strange, Peter White, and Jack Zupko.

Further support was provided by a grant from Middlebury College to employ a research assistant at a crucial stage in the book's development. I am grateful to James Ralph, dean of faculty development and research, for awarding the grant and to Margaret Clark for filling that role so admirably. My colleagues in the Department of Classics at Middlebury College, Jane Chaplin, Randall Ganiban, Pavlos Sfyroeras, and Marc Witkin, welcomed me into the fold and encouraged me to develop new courses that helped to foster and explore several of the ideas contained in this book.

My editor, Matthew McAdam, is to be thanked for taking immediate interest in this book and for his guidance and support throughout the publication process. He and the staff at the Johns Hopkins University Press were remarkably efficient and helpful in seeing it through production. The anonymous reader for the Press provided numerous suggestions and critiques that greatly aided my final revisions. Joanne Allen was a skilled and careful copyeditor.

An earlier version of chapter 2 was published as "Commanding *Constantia* in Senecan Tragedy" in *Transactions of the American Philological Association* 136, no. 1 (2006): 207–44, copyright © 2006 The American Philological Association, used with permission from The Johns Hopkins University Press.

On a more personal note, my greatest debt of gratitude is to my family, both the Stars and the Robertses. I owe an incalculable debt to my wife, Sarah, who always was willing to leave her own important work to come to my aid and listen to my ideas. This book is dedicated to her.

The Empire of the Self

Introduction

The narratives of two travelers describing their journeys around the Bay of Naples—Lucius Annaeus Seneca and the fictional rogue Encolpius—have come down to us from the early Roman Empire. The account of Seneca, Stoic philosopher, tragedian, tutor, and adviser to the emperor Nero, can be found in letters 49–57 of his *Moral Epistles*, ostensibly missives sent to his younger friend Lucilius while en route.[1] That of Encolpius, whose adventures in southern Italy are preserved in the fragmentary *Satyricon*, which was likely written by another of Nero's advisers, Petronius.[2] The precise dates of composition are unclear, but most scholars agree that both were written during the reign of Nero, likely between 62 CE and 66 CE. Although these two travelers did not journey together, the form and content of their accounts are strikingly similar. Both authors pepper their highly polished prose with poetic quotations and compositions. Both narratives contain specific references to the environs, mentioning Baiae, Cumae, Misenum, Pompeii, and the tunnel that leads back to Naples, the Crypta Neapolitana. Both provide vivid descriptions of the local bathhouses and villas and the leisure activities of the inhabitants. The two travelers frequently see their own journeys in light of the epic tradition. They often mention the wanderings of Odysseus and Aeneas, who, according to tradition, themselves spent time in the area. Both have a difficult and eventful journey out of the region. In addition to their descriptions of the external world they encounter on their travels, both writers also provide vivid accounts of their own internal worlds. They attempt to understand and plumb the depths of those whom they meet as well.

To many readers a study of Seneca and Petronius would appear to unite two people who spent the final years of their lives sniping at each other and attempting to put as much distance between themselves as possible. According to the standard line of thought, the two were sworn enemies whose lives, deaths, philosophies, and literary output were incommensurable. Any engagement between the two exists on the level of negative criticism and parody.[3] Yet if we can de-familiarize Seneca and Petronius and move away from preconceived notions about Seneca's rigid Stoicism or the *Satyricon*'s chaotic "amorality," the deeper connections between the two become more apparent.[4]

To build further on the points of contact outlined above, both Seneca and Encolpius adopt an autobiographical, first-person perspective. These two authors position themselves similarly in relation to the leisure and peace provided by the Roman Empire. Both have the time to travel, study, and then construct a narrative of past adventures. Both present the lives of those who are living away from the center of the social community. Seneca is the philosopher who shuns the ideals of the masses. Encolpius is a rogue scholar who claims that he is living "outside of the law" (125.4). In addition, the works of Seneca and Petronius encompass many genres and are encyclopedic in character. Both authors are driven by a similar impetus to narrate, encapsulate, describe, and in short to conquer and domesticate as many varieties of human experience as possible. This "domestication," I argue, is based upon two key points of contact between Seneca and Petronius.[5] Both engage with the problems of self-construction and presentation. How can the self be conquered? How can the body, soul, and passions be brought into line with one's desires? How can the self obey the command? What are the means by which this construction can be displayed? How can one be sure that one's virtues are externalized and properly interpreted by others? The role of language in these processes is demonstrated in the works of both authors, from the histrionic monologues of Nero, Cato, and Medea written by Seneca to the mock tragic-heroic stances of Petronius' characters. The creation of the self, whether by the emperor, the Stoic *proficiens*, or Encolpius, and the creation of a literary work, whether it is a moral or political treatise, a tragedy, or prose fiction, are inextricably implicated. All are dependent upon a bricolage of literary forms and the appropriation of memorable texts, figures of speech, and production of great-souled utterances.

Although Seneca and Petronius have long been considered enemies, I argue for a more complicated literary, cultural, political, and intellectual engagement between them. By necessity, however, I spend more time investigating the works of Seneca. This is not only because more of his work has survived. In order to develop the intellectual project of this book, Seneca's "official" philosophical ideas must be established before we can view them through the lenses of tragedy and comedy. My analysis of Seneca is shaped by the growing interest in reading Seneca's corpus holistically rather than interpreting Seneca either as a philosopher or a tragedian.[6] Furthermore, as the debate about the "newness" of Seneca's concept of the self continues, his unique contribution to this topic may lie not in his work as a philosopher but rather in his combination of literary, cultural, rhetorical, and philosophical themes and ideas.[7] For example, as several scholars have noted, throughout Senecan philosophy traditional Roman ideals are reevaluated and internalized in order to develop the care of the self. Seneca writes of the court of the self, of self-censorship, of how the life of the philosopher is a military life.[8] Following this precedent, I investigate Seneca's focus on the new problem of political autocracy. I look at how empire structures the self and how it is internalized in the ideal of self-command (*sibi imperare*). In part 2 I consider the logical result, how empire is externalized on linguistic, psychological, and corporeal levels. By including Petronius, I further expand the project of understanding the complicated and contested notion of the self during the early Roman Empire. Indeed, reading Petronius in tandem with Seneca extends what Seneca himself does to his philosophy through his tragedies and the *Apocolocyntosis*. In addition, Petronius has the potential to make us more attuned to the satirical, Saturnalian, and corporeal aspects of Seneca's philosophy, opening new roads of inquiry into his work. Similarly, scholars have also demonstrated that the ancient novel must be included if we are to gain a fuller picture of the development of ancient ideas about the care of the self. Michel Foucault's portrait has been criticized for focusing almost exclusively on philosophical and medical works, so-called normative texts.[9] Thus, studies of Senecan tragedy have demonstrated how Seneca viewed the cracks and contradictions in his own project of Stoic self-shaping. A study of Petronius in this context augments our understanding that the care of the self and indeed the very concept of the self were not monolithic, nor were they simply the concern of philosophy or of "high literature."

I contend here that parts of the *Satyricon* provide the comic double to Seneca, just as Seneca's *Apocolocyntosis* engages similarly with the serious work performed by *De clementia* (*On Mercy*) and Senecan drama is the tragic double to his philosophy. Thus, Petronius extends the investigations that Seneca performs on his own ideas. These two authors look at self-construction and self-presentation from a variety of angles. At times Seneca deconstructs his own ideas; at other times Petronius breaks down the oppositions Seneca creates. The fact that the cracks and seams in the notion of the self are so readily subjected to scrutiny and parody both by Seneca himself and by Petronius does not suggest that the two are "negating" Senecan philosophy; rather, it suggests that these very cracks, paradoxes, and contradictions are under investigation. A holistic view is required. As William James notes, "The most complete philosophies must find some ultimate way of affirming that which has been rejected."[10] I contend that the literary works of Seneca and Petronius bring to center stage elements that have been underexplored or excluded by Seneca's philosophy. By looking at all of these works in tandem, we can see how the roles of the philosopher, of myth and literature, emperors and fool kings, rogues, freedmen, and slaves, are all subject to investigation. Seneca and Petronius consider the care of the self in a variety of contexts, ranging from the sublime to the horrifying to the ridiculous, from the imperial to the servile.

Before undertaking our investigation, it will be helpful to address some of the received wisdom concerning the nature of the relationship between Seneca and Petronius. This is a neglected topic, mostly treated by Petronian scholars. J. P. Sullivan provides the *locus classicus* for the idea of a "Neronian literary feud" and hostile relationship between Seneca and Petronius. He writes in his study of the *Satyricon* that "it is doubtful whether there could have been anything but a natural antipathy between the insouciant courtier, whose functions were aesthetic and social, and the earnest counselor, rapidly losing his influence and doomed to lose even more. Certainly the continuous moral posturing of the *oeuvre*, and the presumably genuine Stoic attitude to life and literature, would be antipathetic to Petronius' Epicureanism, which, from Tacitus' account, was the philosophically cruder if more elegant Roman version of the Master's hedonism."[11]

The portrait of the overtly hostile relationship rests on several assumptions that are heavily based on Tacitus' portraits of the deaths of our two authors in the final surviving books of the *Annales*. Seneca and Petronius are opposed not only philosophically, the Stoic versus the Epicurean, but also chronologically. As Seneca's influence at court wanes, Petronius rises in Nero's favor. Seneca's failed Stoic moralizing gives way to Petronius' aestheticism, hedonism, and literary amusements. According to this line of argument, Petronius was a literary and intellectual opportunist who helped provide Nero with the inverse of the life he had led under the tutelage of Seneca and Burrus. The final example of the genuine animosity Petronius bore toward Seneca even after his death is "confirmed" by Petronius' parody of the philosophical death. I shall discuss the relationship between Seneca and Petronius as presented in Tacitus' *Annales* later in this introductory chapter. For now, let us consider further Sullivan's notion of the antithetical relationship between Seneca and Petronius as evidenced by the text of the *Satyricon*.

In his book-length study of the *Satyricon* Sullivan points out the extensive connections between Seneca and Petronius.[12] Indeed, the connections that Sullivan treats have become standard points of reference for linking the two authors. To cite only examples from the *Cena*, Trimalchio's many foibles are seen as being based on anecdotes primarily preserved in Seneca's *Epistles*. For example, Trimalchio's garbling of mythological stories is related to Seneca's account of Calvisius Sabinus (*Ep*. 27.5–8). His mock funeral is paralleled in Seneca's description of the similar behavior of Pacuvius (*Ep*. 12.8; see also *Brev*. 20.3 on the mock funeral of S. Turranius). Trimalchio's disruptive and indiscriminate inviting of slaves to the table mocks Seneca's advice to Lucilius on how to live on friendly and familiar terms with his slaves in letter 47. Trimalchio's agnomen, *Maecenatianus*, which will be inscribed on his tomb, looks to Seneca's condemnation of Maecenas as a dissolute fop in letter 114.[13] Sullivan also claims that Seneca fired back at Petronius. He believes that Seneca's condemnation of the "troupe of night owls" (*turba lucifugarum*) in letter 122.15 refers to Petronius and his habit of inverting daytime and nighttime activities as described by Tacitus. In addition, Sullivan contends that the shift in Seneca's attitude toward Epicureanism in the *Epistles*, from generally approving in the early ones to hostile in the later ones, is a response to Petronius' elevated position in Nero's court.[14]

Sullivan cautions the reader against naively believing that Petronius' engagement with Seneca means that both authors can be classified as "moralists" and that Petronius is using the moralizing ideas of Seneca as "a serious indictment of contemporary Roman civilization."[15] Sullivan's portrait of Petronius as a literary opportunist is a response to "moralistic" interpretations of Petronius by Gilbert Highet (1941) and William Arrowsmith (1966).[16] Sullivan's study is, as his book's subtitle makes clear, "a literary study." Thus for Sullivan, and for others such as P. E. Walsh, Petronius' work is primarily a humorous, literary one.[17] It does not advocate for a return to traditional Roman morality or decry the vices of the age; it was simply written for the entertainment of Nero's court. Petronius references Seneca only to parody his philosophical ideas and his style of writing. For Sullivan, Petronian parody is negative. It engages with Seneca only to ridicule and reject him.[18] Seen in this light, the *Satyricon* attempts to push Seneca out while further ingratiating Petronius with Nero's new in group.

Soon after the publication of Sullivan's studies, Martin Smith evaluated some of his claims in an appendix to his commentary on the *Cena* (1975). Smith's main counterarguments are that where Sullivan sees direct borrowing from Seneca, Petronius may have been working from a common source or with ideas and turns of phrase commonly employed at the time. Smith does not think, however, that the search for connections between Seneca and Petronius should be abandoned. His main point is that readers should be more cautious than Sullivan. In fact, he warns against looking solely to Seneca's *Epistles*, to the exclusion of his earlier works. He also argues against Sullivan's overarching claim that Petronius almost exclusively ridicules Seneca. While he does not offer any specific examples, Smith states that there are likely several references to Seneca in which "no parody is intended."[19] Smith does not elaborate on what this nonparodic relationship between Seneca and Petronius might entail, but this brief statement is crucial for our understanding that the relationship between the two may not be exclusively negative.

More recently, in his *Companion to Petronius*, Edward Courtney combines the methods of Sullivan and Smith. Like Sullivan, he enthusiastically looks for parallels; but following the advice of Smith, he does not exclusively investigate Seneca's *Epistles*. He does acknowledge, however, that the letters provide "more grist to Petronius' mill than any other work of Seneca." Furthermore, Courtney states that Petronius does not simply parody Seneca. He notes that the portrait of the relationship between Seneca and Petronius as hostile "might well be over-simplified." In contrast to the standard vision of Seneca and Petronius attacking each other through their writing, with Seneca living on the periphery and Petronius at the center of Nero's court, Courtney suggests that the two may have interacted frequently and been willing to adhere to "the proprieties of social intercourse" when they did. He even proposes the admittedly unprovable hypothesis that Petronius listened to readings of drafts of Seneca's last works, the *Epistles* and the *Natural Questions*. In his brief discussion of Petronius' engagement with Seneca, Courtney notes several trends. He calls Eumolpus' poem on the destruction of Troy (*Sat.* 89) a "pastiche of Seneca's tragic style, which . . . surely betrays antipathy." Yet he also notes that only "seldom" does Petronius reference Seneca "in such a way as to parody or deflate the originals." He cites Trimalchio's discussion of his digestive problems (*Sat.* 47.6), his dining with his slaves (*Sat.* 71.1), and Encolpius' words spoken over the dead body of Lichas (*Sat.* 115.9–19) as examples of this method of engagement. Otherwise, according to Courtney, Petronius simply takes material from Seneca and uses it in "a neutral way" or "without prejudice to Seneca."[20]

For Sullivan, Smith, and Courtney, Petronian parody of Seneca is negative, intended to deflate Seneca's ideas and style. Smith and Courtney also admit that this is not the only way that Petronius engages with Seneca. According to them, when Petronius is not ridiculing Seneca, he simply uses him as source material. It is not the goal of this book to look at every passage where an echo of Seneca might be perceived in Petronius. Rather, I shall focus on passages that engage with ideas of self-shaping and self-revelation. In my view, Petronius does not simply negatively parody or otherwise remain "neutral" toward Seneca; and I argue that our understanding of the nature of Petronius' engagement with Seneca can be helped by turning to modern critical theory of parody and carnival. As Margaret Rose argues, and our critics confirm, parody has traditionally been seen as a solely negative and ridiculing practice. Its critical yet constructive and positive potential has been ignored. According to Rose, parody should be defined in a way that fully captures its ambiguous character. For her, parody allows an author to be both critical of and sympathetic to another author or group of texts or ideas. Parody is characterized by both nearness and opposition.[21] Following Rose's definition, I argue that Petronian parody does not negate Senecan philosophy any more than Seneca's tragedies do or any more than the *Apocolocyntosis* negates the ideas set out in *De clementia*. Instead, the laughter of Petronius and of Senecan satire serves as the comic double to Senecan philosophy; that is, it provides a critical commentary on and investigation of Seneca's ideas. My analysis is further influenced by the work of Mikhail Bakhtin and his modern critics on the role of Saturnalia and carnival in literature. Anticipating Rose's arguments, Bakhtin writes that "carnival is far distant from the negative and formal parody of modern times."[22] In fact, some of the main tenets of Bakhtin's theory of carnival, with its focus on laugher, feasting, and the grotesque body, in particular the stomach, bowels, and genitals, provide a powerful means for understanding the relationship between Petronius, the *Apocolocyntosis*, and the serious world of Senecan philosophy. Thus, reading these low, satirical texts together with the elevated works of philosophy gives us a more complete picture of the contestation of ideas concerning the nature of the self during the early Roman Empire. Seneca and Petronius address similar questions from opposite directions. Developing ideas from Bakhtin's notion of the carnivalesque, Peter Stallybrass and Allon White note the importance of treating comical and "low" texts alongside elevated, "official" forms of discourse.

> A recurrent pattern emerges: the "top" attempts to reject and eliminate the "bottom" for reasons of prestige and status, only to discover, not only that it is in some way frequently dependent upon that low-Other (in the classic way that Hegel describes in the master-slave section of the *Phenomenology*), but also that the top *includes* that low symbolically, as a primary eroticized constituent of its own fantasy life. The result is a mobile, conflictual fusion of power, fear and desire in the construction of subjectivity: a psychological dependence upon precisely those Others which are being rigorously opposed and excluded at the social level. It is for this reason that what is *socially* peripheral is so frequently *symbolically* central. The low-Other is despised and denied at the level of political organization and social being whilst it is instrumentally constitutive of the shared imaginary repertoires of the dominant culture.[23]

Following this line of reasoning, on one level Seneca and Petronius can be seen as existing at the vertical extremes of high and low. In simple terms, Seneca focuses on the soul, and Petronius on the body. As we shall see, however, this and other dichotomies are not easily maintained. In fact, the world of Senecan philosophy is not concerned solely with the purity of the soul. Laughter, feasting, and old, sick, and dying bodies are all important topics. While Seneca may frequently moralize against the carnivalesque, the grotesque, and Saturnalia, these modes continually work their way into his prose. On the other hand, we should not assume that the laughter and Saturnalia that characterizes the *Satyricon* and the *Apocolocyntosis* are opposed to official order and seeks a return to the golden age of Saturn, when all were equal. Both texts are concerned with the dangers of nondifferentiation. Both use laughter to establish boundaries and exclude outsiders.

While critics like Sullivan are correct in pointing out that Petronius is not a moralist in the manner of Seneca, the *Satyricon* does engage with moralization on a metalevel. That is, it points out the underlying paradoxes of taking a moral stance during the Neronian age, the age of decadence par excellence. This, as Jas Elsner argues, is one of the main contributions of Petronian satire.[24] The *Satyricon* laments the decline and excesses of the age at the same time that it portrays characters who revel in this decadence. By doing so, Petronius may outdo Seneca in terms of critical self-reflexivity. A further irony is that Seneca is credited with using reflexive language with a frequency and manner that is unprecedented in Latin, yet he is typically seen as lacking the self-reflexivity to engage with his own position as a moralist who enjoys the delights of Nero's court.[25] Hence the standard picture of Seneca as a hypocrite who extols the virtues of poverty while using his imperial position to actively, even avariciously, increase his personal fortune.

Recently, however, scholars have begun to move away from this portrait of Seneca as a millionaire courtier and hence bankrupt philosopher. Seneca's attitude toward wealth is considerably more complicated. He does not adopt the simple notion that poverty equals moral authority and the possession of wealth automatically leads to luxury and debasement. Indeed, economic themes and metaphors are central to Seneca's writing. Like Petronius' acquisitive freedmen, Seneca considers the ways in which money, exchange, and the proper attitude toward wealth can demonstrate one's virtues. Both Seneca and Petronius suggest that in the post-civil-war world of the Roman Empire, economic rather than military or political endeavor is a crucially contested means for self-display. In *De vita beata* (*On the Happy Life*) Seneca replies to those critics who "bark at philosophy" because philosophers do not live up to their ideals. At one point, Seneca repeats the attacks leveled against wealthy philosophers (17.1–4).

Interestingly, several points of this invective describing a lavishly living philosopher could also describe Trimalchio. Both dine according to fixed rules; their dinnerware shines; they drink wine that is older than they are; they set out gold; their wives wear costly earrings; they must be served artfully; their food must be skillfully carved; they possess lands across the sea, and more lands than they even know of; they have so many slaves that they do not know them all. These connections may seem like yet another example of how Petronius uses Senecan material, even examples from Seneca's own life, to mock him in the person of the boorish and nouveau-riche Trimalchio. Yet we should be wary of seeing the defenses that conclude *De vita beata* as autobiographical and Seneca's personal apology for his wealth. Instead, this connection may demonstrate further how both Seneca and Petronius deal with standard forms of invective against wealth and consider the ways in which wealth contributes to social dissonance. If philosophers are supposed to shun wealth, how does possessing it affect their authority? If freedmen possess a senator's fortune, what factors keep them out of the elite levels of society?

Let us take a look at another passage in which Petronius seems simply to degrade Senecan moralizing in order to show that their supposed incommensurability is more apparent than real. In the midst of his own hedonistic dinner party, Trimalchio recites a poem of "Publilius" that decries the alimentary and sexual indulgences of the age (*Sat.* 55.6). Although Trimalchio claims to be quoting lines from Publilius Syrus, the famous first-century BCE mimographer, several scholars believe that the real target here is Seneca, who cites several *sententiae* of Publilius and even claims that philosophers can strengthen the effect of their arguments by including his verses (*Ep.* 108.9).[26] Furthermore, after his recitation Trimalchio launches into a series of philosophical questions. Encolpius sums up Trimalchio's combination of poetry and philosophy by claiming that his host "was putting the philosophers out of business" (*Sat.* 56.7). This phrase has been connected with a similar one in Seneca's *Epistles* (88.44).[27] Even if we do not wish to view this passage as directly quoting Seneca's writings, we can see how Petronius launches an attack on moralizing in general. He demonstrates the incongruity of inveighing against luxury in the middle of a dinner party and thus shows the ease with which this stance can be adopted. Anyone can rattle off this sort of thing, regardless of context or character. Thus, Seneca's ideal of language being a reliable indicator of one's moral character, *talis oratio qualis vita*, the topic of letter 114, is shown to be simply naïve idealism. Trimalchio, the master of revels, and Eumolpus, the philosopher-poet-exegete, are masters of dissimulation. There is a continual dissonance between what Encolpius first expects from them and what they reveal themselves to be. At first he is told that Trimalchio is a "most refined human being" (*lautissimus homo*, 26.9). At the end of the feast, his host's drunken, mock funeral brings things "to the height of nausea" (78.5). Eumolpus' rough external appearance "promises something great" (83.7). But after inveighing against the present age's love of money and neglect of literature, Eumolpus reveals that he uses his ability to look and talk like a moral philosopher to seduce schoolboys after gaining their parents' trust (85–87). Thus, while Seneca blithely writes on the morally revelatory powers of language, Petronius responds with a book about deception in which reality and appearance never coincide.

Nevertheless, learning how to interpret appearances properly is a central project of Stoicism. Indeed, Seneca in particular focuses on the deceptiveness of appearances and continually exhorts his readers not to be deceived by outward show. He wants to strip things down to their essential core, the *animus*, and only then render judgment. Petronius, it would seem, gives the lie to this project. Trimalchio's "blessedness of soul" is determined by the regal colors with which his dining-room pillows are stuffed (38.5). Trimalchio himself seems only to be stuffed with food and foul, potentially deadly gasses. No immortal souls are to be found in this text. The *Satyricon* revels in the play of illusion and deception and the continual adoption of literary personae. The text speaks against the ideal of an unchanging, consistent Stoic self. As Fredrick Jones remarks, "It is hard to believe there is a center beneath the masks, and beyond this level, in the narrative itself there is no accessible reality, only layers of imitation, and only relative criteria to judge between different genres."[28] Yet Seneca also plays with shifting masks of authorial personae, as Catharine Edwards has demonstrated.[29] His message is much the same as that of Petronius' characters when he notes that we all take part in the "mime of human life, and play our parts badly" (*Ep*. 80.7).[30] Furthermore, Seneca himself is not dogmatically certain what lies at the core of each individual. The tyranny of the passions is ever present. The material soul runs the risk of contamination with baser matter. Indeed, when Seneca tries to locate the soul, he admits that we do not know where it hides and that its virtues are difficult to externalize. Even the emperor's appearance and soul can be easily misinterpreted.

Seneca and Petronius in Tacitus

As already noted, Tacitus' accounts have exerted enormous influence on our understanding not only of the relationship between the two courtiers but also of how each author's final moments encapsulate key themes in their literary corpus. Although Nero granted several of his victims the "free choice" to commit suicide, and even though Seneca was caught up in the paranoid bloodbath that followed the failed Pisonian conspiracy in early 65 CE and Petronius was a victim of Tigellinus' jealousy in the following year, their deaths as presented in Tacitus offer a diptych of attitudes toward life and death.[31] As also already noted, Tacitus' account is frequently used to illustrate the adversarial relationship between the two, both in Nero's court and in their writings. Petronius' death continues the parodic attack on Seneca, since even in his last moments he rejects all philosophical "flummery."[32] Tacitus does not mention Petronius as the author of any literary texts. The belief that Nero's *arbiter elegantiae* was also the author of the *Satyricon* rests in part on the hypothesis that Petronius' "learned luxury" and the ironic elegance of his life and death recalls the style and ambiance of the *Satyricon*.[33] If we accept the connection on these grounds, then we must also accept that Petronius, or at least Tacitus' presentation of Petronius, appropriated yet another favorite moralistic ideal of Seneca's to his own paradoxical ends, *talis oratio qualis vita*.

In Tacitus' account, despite their antithetical lives, both Seneca and Petronius are able to die and retain their sense of self in the face of tyranny. In addition, both continue to write even as their lifeblood leaves them (15.63.3, 16.19.3). This connection suggests that Tacitus wishes us to group together the textual legacies that Seneca and Petronius left behind. Their death scenes stage a contestation of key ideas and concepts in a manner similar to that of their writings. The two books in which Tacitus narrates the deaths of Seneca and Petronius can be related to each other in dramatic terms. Book 15, which contains Seneca's death scene, ends with Nero's tragic revenge against the members of the Pisonian conspiracy. Nero's power as dramaturge forces his subjects to offer thanks for his survival and to change the name of the month of April to *Neronis* (15.74.1). With the opening of book 16, however, the tragic atmosphere entirely vanishes. This book, as one scholar points out, "begins like a satyr-play).[34] Tacitus opens by stating that Fortune ridicules Nero (*inlusit dehinc Neroni fortuna*" (16.1.1). Believing the mad Caesellius Bassus' claim that he has discovered Dido's gold in Carthage, Nero promptly sends one of his ships on a treasure hunt (16.1). As Miriam Griffin notes in her biography of the emperor, during this year Nero escapes "more and more into a world of fantasy."[35] With Tacitus' tragic handling of the end of book 15 and his comic handling of the beginning of book 16 in mind, we can note how he stages both death scenes with reference to Campania. Seneca, "either on purpose or by chance" (*forte an prudens*), has just returned from Campania and is at his suburban villa, located four miles from the city, when Nero's soldiers deliver the emperor's orders (15.60.4). Petronius is caught in Cumae, after

Nero has "by chance" (*forte*) decided to journey to Campania (16.19.1). The feasts of both men turn into funerals.[36] Both die slowly. Yet here the straight correspondences end, and Tacitus contrasts how Seneca's death continually frustrates his desires, while Petronius' fulfills his.

Seneca's slow death may ironically be the result of his frugal, philosophical life.[37] Of all the suicides described by Tacitus, only in the case of Seneca's must the veins in both the arms and the legs be cut, since too little blood flows from his aged and ascetic body.[38] Indeed, Tacitus suggests that the effects Seneca's lifelong preparation for death have on his body threaten his Stoic tenets.[39] Although Seneca declares that his and Paulina's joint suicide will demonstrate the glory of their *constantia*, he soon worries that his wife's soul will waver at the sight of his pain and that he too will be unable to endure.[40] Petronius expressly eschews *gloria* and *constantia*, yet he never wavers. In contrast to Seneca's asceticism, Petronius lives a life of "learned luxury" (*erudito luxu*, 16.18.1), but he is able to retain control of his body and die as he wishes (*ut libitum*, 16.19.2).[41] Petronius has the power to play with reality and illusion. He makes his forced death appear to have happened by chance (*fortuitae similis*, 16.19.2). Tacitus states that Petronius avoids "seriousness" during his purposely protracted death (*non per seria*, 16.19.2). Yet by specifically mentioning Petronius' avoidance of "the glory of steadfastness [*constantia*]," talk of the "immortality of the soul," and "theories of the philosophers," Tacitus implies that Petronius does not so much negate or deny these concepts as he appropriates them. Petronius demonstrates that his manner of life and death is valid, perhaps even more successful than that of Seneca, and hence not to be ignored. Thanks to Tacitus, Petronius gains renown for his paradoxical version of consistency. Indeed, we should not think that Tacitus' Petronius rejects all forms of morality; his final codicil enumerates Nero's sexual deviance.[42] He also breaks his signet ring so that it cannot be used for harm after his death. In fact, after Petronius' death, Nero descends further into tyranny and resolves to kill some more pesky Stoics, Thrasea Paetus and Barea Soranus. This act is equivalent, according to Tacitus, to extinguishing "virtue itself" (*virtutem ipsam*, 16.21.1). At the same time, a philosophic death does not necessarily mean a grimly serious death. Socrates ends his life with an enigmatic statement about owing a cock to Asclepius. Seneca himself recounts with admiration the bon mot of Julius Canus before being executed by Caligula (*Tranq.* 14.7).[43] As Tacitus notes, in his final moments Seneca himself quips that the bathwater that wets his servants is his libation to Jupiter the Liberator (*Ann.* 15.64.4).

The thematic interplay between tragedy and comedy, the contested nature of *gloria* and *constantia*, how to control the body and soul, and the self's relationship to imperial power form the crux of debates between Seneca and the *Satyricon* and within the Senecan corpus. This leads to the tempting speculation that Tacitus was familiar with the writings of both Seneca and Petronius and that by pairing them in his history he is highlighting key points of contact between their *oeuvres*, if not reflecting something of the nature of the actual relationship between them. Furthermore, Tacitus' narrative dramatically presents some of the paradoxes and contradictions inherent in the construction and revelation of the self during the early empire. We can see the multifaceted nature of self-shaping. Seneca cycles though various possibilities: bleeding like Cato, drinking hemlock like Socrates, and finally expiring in his private baths, joking about making a libation to Jupiter the Liberator.[44] Baths, jokes, and death bring to mind the world of the *Satyricon*. Indeed, Trimalchio has his own bathhouse. After presenting his own final image of his life by describing the construction of his funeral monument and epitaph, Trimalchio stops the lamentation that has filled the triclinium with this piece of advice: "Since we know we're going to die, why don't we live. So that I may see you all happy, why don't we throw ourselves into the bath" (*Sat.* 72.2–3). Although bathing after the dinner-funeral seems to conquer death for Trimalchio and his fellow freedmen—as Habinnas says, it "makes two days out of one"—Trimalchio's proposal has the opposite effect on Encolpius. He says to Ascyltus, "If I look at the bath, I'll expire immediately" (*Sat.* 72.4–6). While Seneca's final image is hybrid and even seems to stray into the world of the *Satyricon*, Petronius is able to present himself exactly as he wishes. His manner of death follows logically upon his manner of living. He remains fully in control of his body as well as the model and target of his parody. Yet as I have suggested, these facts also place Petronius in Seneca's world: his life mirrors his art.

Death is the final, most crucial moment of self-construction, as it leaves behind and crystallizes the final image of one's life. In the cases of both of our authors, this image is so powerful that it has influenced how we approach their texts and how we understand the "reality" of the cultural and political dynamics of Nero's court. As Tacitus also shows us, self-creation is joined with the final act of self-annihilation. Thus, self-creation is paradoxically linked with its apparent opposite, the destruction of the physical body. The key goal of philosophical training, of the techniques and care of the self, is the ability to die well.[45] The ultimate demonstration of self-creation and manifestation of virtues is the manner in which one dies.[46] The *Satyricon* likely plays with the finality of this connection and allows Trimalchio to continually reenact his final moments. Similarly, at the end of the surviving fragments we do not know whether Eumolpus has actually died or is only pretending. What is clear is that he wants his legatees to cut up and consume his body. According to the tenets of his will, only this act of bodily destruction will turn Eumolpus' heirs into wealthy men.

As Glenn Most demonstrates, linguistic and bodily destruction are defining characteristics of literature of the early empire.[47] In addition to focusing on fragmentation and destruction, Seneca and Petronius also consider the positive and productive aspects of language. In part 1 of this book I investigate the power of language to create and shape the self. Underlying these first three chapters is an investigation of how both Seneca and Petronius exploit the semantic and metaphorical possibilities of the Latin word *figura* and the related verb *fingere*, meaning "to shape," "to fashion," "to invent," or "to feign" (*Oxford Latin Dictionary* [*OLD*], defs. 1, 6, 9, 10). *Figura* refers both to the form of the physical body and, as a literary term, to "figures of speech" (*OLD*, defs. 1, 3, 11). According to rhetorical theory, these figures give life to the body of a text.[48] Seneca exploits this metaphorical connection with his use of self-apostrophe. As bodies within the text are torn apart or their integrity is threatened, the figure of apostrophe serves as a means to shape the self. Similarly, the verb *fingere* can refer to the shaping of the self (e.g., *finge te* in *Sat.* 141.7) but also to the creation of falsehoods, *ficta*. This semantic range calls into question the very nature of the self that has been created. Was it created by a confession of the truth or via a collection of lies and "fictions"? Finally, on another, related linguistic level, both Seneca and Petronius consider the fragile, fictile nature of the self as a vessel (*vas fictilis*) and the problems of what lies within.

Chapter 1 investigates the role of *imperium* in Senecan philosophy. It begins by considering how Seneca subordinates the traditional ideal of military and political power over others to the power to command the self (*sibi imperare*). Frequently, Seneca presents this reevaluation of the value of gaining *imperium* over others as a self-address. That is to say, he scripts a monologue outlining the true nature of power, command, and empire for his readers to listen to or repeat to themselves. Seneca's combination of self-address and *imperium* is significant for his theory of human psychology, as well as for his ideas of therapy and self-shaping. Building upon Stoic tradition, Seneca conceives of the soul as functioning imperatively. It issues commands to the agent. In addition, and perhaps departing from an orthodox Stoic position, Seneca argues that the passions command. Therapy follows from the theory of the grammatical nature of the soul and the passions. Self-address, specifically directing the imperious language of generals at the self, is a means to strengthen the command of the soul and defeat the command of the passions. In the final part of the chapter, I consider the role of monologues of self-directed commands in Seneca's philosophy, as well as in contemporary literature.

In chapter 2, I demonstrate how in Senecan tragedy the figure of self-address is used by Medea, Clytemnestra, and Atreus as a means for criminal self-control and fulfillment. I argue that Seneca's characters' repeated addresses to themselves, or most frequently to their souls, is a tragic investigation of the ideal of linguistic self-shaping. In fact, Seneca's tragic characters appear to have read Seneca on the therapeutic benefits of self-address. Their repeated addresses to their souls mimic Cato's heroic final monologue in *De providentia* (*On Providence*). By contrast, however, Seneca's characters address themselves in order to maintain their passions, rather than to quell them. In his dramas Seneca investigates how the Stoic ideal of consistency (*constantia*) and of always playing one role is used to achieve non-Stoic ends. I conclude the chapter by arguing that Senecan drama does not negate Stoic ideas but rather provides a crucial expansion of Seneca's philosophy on the nature of the passions and how Stoicism can contain and incorporate its antithesis.

In the third chapter, I investigate how Petronius' characters try to control their bodies, whether they are afflicted by impotence or indigestion or nauseated by the prospect of eating human flesh. I look at passages in which the *Satyricon* provides a comic investigation of the self-shaping potential of self-address, such as the passages describing Encolpius, in the days before modern pharmaceutical cures for erectile dysfunction, attempting to use self-dialogue and command to cure his affliction (132.9–11). His "Stoic" care of the self proves ineffectual, but Encolpius' self-address also causes him to stop and consider the propriety of his language. Encolpius worries about what speaking to a part of the body that "men of a more serious note" do not even think about reveals about him morally (132.12). I end the chapter with an investigation of how the *Satyricon* parodies the idea of *continentia*. In contrast to the Stoic notion of containing the passions, the *Satyricon* presents the self as a vessel for containing food. My focus in part 1 is on the monologues of self-address and command and the memorable outbursts that come from the depths of the soul that Seneca and Petronius script for their characters. By looking at Seneca's idealization of Nero and Cato in his philosophy, to the monologues of his dramatic characters, to Encolpius' impotence, this book aims to provide a more rounded portrait of the Roman care of the self.

In part 2, I investigate the role of self-revelation, one of the key problems of the early empire, which has famously been characterized as the period of dissimulation and of a crisis in the ability to trust words and appearances. Thus the role of language, the ideal of *talis oratio qualis vita*, and the role of the body as a reliable indicator of moral worth are subjected to continual questioning and scrutiny. While organizational necessity mandates that I treat the soul-shaping and soul-revealing qualities of speech in separate sections, in many passages from Seneca and Petronius both of these aspects of language are skillfully combined. For example, in *De clementia* Nero's opening monologue describes the merciful state of his soul, while at the same time attempting to shape his soul so that this disposition may be maintained. As I show in chapter 4, book 2 of *De clementia* also focuses on Nero's language, but Seneca offers a brief example of what Nero actually said as "proof" of the emperor's natural merciful tendency. Hence, an examination of both the soul-revealing and the soul-shaping speech of the emperor gives us a full picture of the importance of speech—both self-directed and outwardly directed—in the early empire. The fact that Seneca also held the unique position as Nero's speechwriter made him acutely aware of the connections between empire, self, and speech.

Chapter 5 follows a theoretical framework similar to that of chapter 3 and also presents the bodily manifestations of Senecan psychology. I examine how the soul is characterized in the *Apocolocyntosis* and the *Satyricon* as material and related to the body, death, and defecation. In the *Apocolocyntosis*, Seneca himself carnivalizes the idea of a material soul, as seen in his account of Claudius' famous last words and death, which graphically embody what the tyrant has done to the empire. As with self-command in the *Satyricon*, similarly grotesque manifestations of Senecan concepts of soul-revealing speech can be traced in this work. Specifically, Trimalchio's discussion in the *Satyricon* of deadly internal "vapors," or *anathymiasis*, parodies the orthodox Stoic concept of the material nature of the soul. These works show how Seneca's concept of soul-revealing language can again be related to the language of the body and deal with anxieties about the true nature of the self.

In the final chapter I consider the place of individual moral revelation in Seneca and Petronius. The first group of texts under analysis is Seneca's critiques of Maecenas in his *Epistles*, written after his retirement from politics. In these letters, Seneca again investigates the links between politics, language, and the soul, yet he moves beyond simply considering spoken utterances to show that written language can also reveal the *animus*. This is a significant shift, and I argue that it was motivated at least in part by the fact that at the end of his career Seneca had lost his place as Nero's speechwriter and the only public means of expression left to him was writing. No longer able to affect the political world through speech, Seneca focuses on the place of writing and looks back on his works from the beginning of Nero's reign and applies their political themes to describe "our soul."

From Seneca's judgment of the writings of the long-dead Maecenas, I move to arguing that both Seneca and Petronius attempt to move beyond the body as the privileged site for determining moral self-worth, and I examine the other methods they develop for displaying the soul and its virtues. Seneca's focus on the "first movements" of emotion calls into question the tradition of physiognomics, the idea that one's psyche and moral condition can be revealed by one's physical appearance and habits. The bodies of Petronius' freedmen, now destined to live out their lives in the hybrid position between slave and freeborn, would only be seen as sites of shame and degradation. The fact that Petronius' freedmen look to money as a means to display their social status has traditionally been interpreted as meaning that these characters are to be viewed as irredeemably base—as "plutocratic vulgarians," to adopt Roland Mayer's term for Trimalchio.[49] I demonstrate that money plays a much more complicated role for the freedmen. They claim that it displays their *virtus*, *fides*, and *frugalitas*. Furthermore, such claims about the relationship of money to virtue are not confined to the *Satyricon*. Seneca makes similar statements at the conclusion of *De vita beata*, when he argues that the Stoic *sapiens* will prefer wealth because it gives him greater opportunity to display his *animus* and its virtues. The discussion of the connections between money and the soul in the *Satyricon* and in *De vita beata* not only provide an unexplored link between Seneca and Petronius but also offers a way to understand Seneca's apparently anomalous stance toward the virtues of wealth in this treatise. While he was the princeps' favorite, Seneca may have been willing to consider money as a possible source of moral self-revelation. The final topic of investigation is Seneca's theory in *De beneficiis* (On benefits) of the social significance of the circulation of money and the exchange of favors. I conclude by contending that Petronius and Tacitus critique this theory, specifically Seneca's idealization of how these forms of exchange operate separately and with different social force.

This book demonstrates how Seneca and Petronius address the problems and possibilities of self-shaping and self-revelation in the new world of empire. Together they continually test a broad political and cultural spectrum ranging from emperor to slaves and from history to myth. The questions asked and the problems raised by these two authors demonstrate that Seneca did not hold the intellectual monopoly on investigations into the nature of the self. Indeed, reading these two "antithetical" authors in tandem suggests that the two literary luminaries did not simply cast scorn upon each other. Rather, we can see something of the admittedly not always decorous conversation that took place between Seneca and Petronius during this formative period in the development of the idea of the self and the concept of the individual.

Part I / Soul-Shaping Speech

CHAPTER ONE

Senecan Philosophy and the Psychology of Command

Two themes in Seneca's philosophy are *imperium*, conceived of as power, command, and empire, and self-address. Seneca frequently uses self-address in his reevaluation of political and military power.[1] Seneca's subordination of military and political *imperium* to personal *imperium* may be explicated by moving from the geographic space and history of the Roman Empire into the core of the Stoic self—the soul, or *animus*—and then out again to witness the performances of Seneca's philosophical exemplars. This journey reveals and addresses the tension between two forms of power, imperial command and self-command, which lies at the heart of Seneca's philosophical writings. He reevaluates the idea of *imperium* on several levels—political, personal, and linguistic.

Returning to the Senecan text that opens the introduction, Seneca's narration of a trip around the Bay of Naples, we find in letter 51, a letter perhaps most famous for its description of the revelers at the summer resort of Baiae (51.4), Seneca's specific condemnation of the *luxuria* of the place, which quickly becomes a general indictment of all vices (*vitia*) and an opportunity for Seneca to urge Lucilius to continually guard against all pleasures (*voluptates*, 51.13). His consideration of the present condition of Baiae takes him back two centuries to the Second Punic War. Hannibal may have ravaged Italy, but he was eventually defeated, not by Roman troops, but by the allurements of the region. Seneca offers the example of Hannibal's quick corruption and "weakening" during a winter in Campania as an example of how easily even the most austere warriors can be conquered by alluring vices (51.5).[2] Seneca urges Lucilius to play the soldier against the *voluptates*. This soldiering is more demanding than the conventional, however. There must be constant vigilance in this war, as Seneca warns: "We also must be soldiers, with a type of military service in which rest and retirement are never given: above all, the pleasures, which, as you see, are cruel and pillage and bring people's naturally strong character over to their side, must be beaten down" (51.6).[3] Daily personal struggles are more demanding than, and thus superior to, Hannibal's military campaign; yielding to the enemy vices brings more danger, and persevering against them brings more rewards. Seneca writes,

> If we were to do what Hannibal did, and pay attention to the care of the body during a break in the military campaign and forget about war, everyone would justly find fault with our untimely idleness, which puts victory in danger—especially for one who has not yet conquered. This is less permitted for us than for those who followed the Carthaginian standards: more danger remains for us if we yield, and there is also harder work if we press on. (*Ep.* 51.7)[4]

Seneca links his journey around Campania with the "softening" that affected Hannibal in the same region more than two centuries earlier. In this way, Seneca demonstrates how he must face the same difficulties as an empire-building and, from the Romans' point of view, potentially destroying general. Yet the philosopher has the intellectual skills necessary to defeat the allurements that conquered Hannibal. In this case, all that means is simply having the good sense to leave after one day (51.1). Yet Seneca also notes that Roman generals were wise enough to build their villas away from Baiae. Marius, Pompey, and Caesar enjoyed their leisure time away from the rigors of empire building by looking down on Baiae from the cliffs above (51.11).[5] According to Seneca, Cato never could have dwelled in the region (51.12). Thus, Seneca establishes an important link between the dangers of the geography of the Roman Empire, the fates of various generals, and his own philosophical travel and development.

While Seneca's "defeat" of Baiae came easily, he describes himself as nevertheless engaged in a continual struggle. He is locked in battle with Fortune, but he defiantly declares that he will not surrender and be forced to "carry out the orders" of this capricious general (51.8).⁶ Fortune is not Seneca's only adversary. The passions (*adfectus*) and pleasures (*voluptates*) threaten to tear Seneca apart as they battle for authority over him: "If I yield to pleasure, I must yield to pain, I must yield to hard labor, I must yield to poverty; ambition and anger will want to have the same right over me; among so many passions I will be pulled in different directions, or better, I will be torn asunder" (51.8).⁷

Philosophy, however, controls her own kingdom and issues her own commands (*exercet philosophia regnum suum*, 53.9).⁸ Indeed, Seneca imagines her as a warrior, easily deflecting weapons: "The ability of Philosophy to beat down all chance attacks is unbelievable. No weapon sticks in her body; she is well armored and solid; certain things she wears down and outmaneuvers with the folds of her toga as if they were light javelins, others she shakes away and sends back against those who threw them" (53.12).⁹ Seneca conceives of this journey around the Bay of Naples as a philosophical test in order to place himself more fully in the "kingdom of philosophy." For example, he explains that he tried to study above a noisy bathhouse during his travels because "I wished to test and exercise myself" (*experiri et exercere me volui*, 56.15).¹⁰ Here we can note an important linguistic connection. As Philosophy manages (*exercet*) her own kingdom, so Seneca tests (*exercere*) himself. Indeed, this sort of linguistic interplay between the political and the philosophical world is crucial for Seneca's project. Of particular importance for us is his use of *imperium* (power, command, empire) and the related verb *imperare* (to command). Seneca contrasts the external power and the ability to command others with the reflexive ability to command oneself (*sibi imperare*).

As the passages above demonstrate, Seneca argues that victory in war and empire building are no longer seen as the supreme accomplishments. Letter 113 is devoted to a technical discussion of Stoic theories on the corporeal nature of the soul. Yet, at the end of this letter, Seneca moves from a consideration of the *animus* to enumerate the failures of Alexander the Great. Seneca investigates and critiques the notion of command (*imperium*); he argues that Alexander and all those who desire only to subjugate others by means of arms are lacking true control. No matter how many lands and peoples they conquer, these empire builders do not have *imperium* over themselves, over their own emotions. Their belief in the traditional ideal of power is wrong; self-command is the greatest command:

> Alexander laid waste and put to flight the Persians, the Hyrcani and the Indians, and whatever people extend their territory eastward to the ocean. But he himself lay in darkness, now because of a friend who was killed, now because of one who was lost; at times he grieved because of his crime, at others because of his longing—the victor over so many kings and peoples succumbed to anger and sadness. He led his life in such a way that he would rather have had everything under his power except for his passions. Oh how humans are held by great error, desiring to be allowed the right of conquering across the seas and judging themselves to be most happy when they obtain many provinces by soldiering and add new ones to the old. They are ignorant of that great kingdom that is equal to the gods: self-command is the greatest empire. (*Ep.* 113.29–30)[11]

Similarly, in *De beneficiis* Seneca writes, "Who will you admire more than the man who commands himself, than one who has power over himself? It is easier to rule barbarian peoples who are unwilling to bear the authority of another than it is to control the soul and hand it over to itself" (5.7.5).[12] Elsewhere, Seneca contrasts the dissolution of the present age with the simplicity of the golden age. He states that during the early period of human history people were immune to contemporary vices because they "commanded themselves" (*qui sibi imperabant*, *Ep.* 95.18).

Seneca's theory of command engages with both Stoic ideas and traditional Roman ones. As Brad Inwood notes of the Stoic conception of the universe, "Right Reason or Nature issues for the agent a set of commands, one after the other. If he obeys these, he will adapt to the events of his life as they occur."[13] Command and obedience lie at the core of the Stoic universe. As Seneca notes in letter 107, god is at the top of the chain of command. The opportunity for military metaphor is not lost on him. We must behave like good soldiers and not grumble under the orders of the universal *imperator* (*malus miles est qui imperatorem gemens sequitur*, 107.9). In addition, Seneca's focus on *imperium* can be related to the contemporary social and political situation, specifically the problems of empire and autocracy. Matthew Roller argues convincingly that a major goal of Seneca's ethical system is to offer help and resolution to aristocrats in the face of new political and social conditions under the empire. One major problem and point of contention was "the unavailability of independent military commands for most aristocrats, along with the disappearance of concomitant military honors."[14] Throughout his philosophical writings, Seneca unites Stoic self-command with the traditional Roman ideal of military command. He describes the "battle within," the battle for self-mastery and consistency against the passions and mental fluctuation, in language based on the old Roman system of values. He uses language that is attractive, familiar, and persuasive to the aristocratic Roman reader. Yet Seneca takes this traditional language and value system and surprises his audience by placing a new category on top: self-command, power over one's self, takes precedence over military and political power.

Seneca's use of battle imagery and the equation of philosophy to the military life is, as one scholar has put it, "all pervasive."[15] This is not a simple one-to-one connection. As the brief examples above show, Seneca builds up his portrait of the exertion and demands of philosophy in the familiar and accepted terms of the Roman military value system only to declare that philosophical *exercitatio* is the most difficult, most rigorous, and thus most admirable way of life. Furthermore, Seneca does not simply present this refigured value system with a general declaration of the supreme difficulty of philosophy. He focuses specifically on the difficulty of achieving what he takes to be the ultimate goal of philosophy: self-command. As he says, it is easier to rule barbarians than it is to control one's own *animus*. Thus, Seneca appeals to the crucial aristocratic ideal that self-command justifies and legitimates rule over others.[16] Yet, Seneca writes, at least theoretically this ideal is within the power of all human beings, and it is necessary if one is to be fully human.[17] For Seneca, self-rule should be a daily practice, and not just a tool of political legitimacy for members of the elite.

Seneca's reformulation of the supreme goal of life effects a further reformulation of traditional terminology. For example, in letter 82, the Roman ideals of *gloria* and *virtus* become less a question of what one has done than of how one has done it. The new key for ascribing glory and virtue lies in the agent's psychological state at the time of action, not simply in the result. Thus, a glorious and virtuous deed is one performed in, and resulting from, a state of psychological command and consistency. It is not enough just to get the job done:

> Nothing happens properly except those things to which the entire soul has applied itself and for which it has been present, against which no part of it battles. But when one approaches an evil, either through fear of worse or in hope of goods of such value that in order to obtain them one evil must be swallowed and endured, the judgments of the agent quarrel among themselves. On the one side is the judgment that orders him to complete what he has started; on the other is

the judgment that drags him back and flees from the mistrusted and dangerous thing. Therefore he is torn in different directions. If this is the case, the glory is lost, for virtue completes its decisions with a harmonious soul. It does not fear what it does. (*Ep.* 82.18)[18]

Outward displays of prowess and success are no longer the sole means for demonstrating and displaying *gloria* and *virtus*. This shift is evident in the figures that Seneca sets forth as exemplary heroes of his new ideal. As Roller notes, Seneca's examples of virtue (*exempla virtutis*) are primarily those who show prowess in defeat, such as Cato (*Ep.* 24.9–10; *Prov.* 2.9–10, 3.14) and Metellus Scipio (*Ep.* 71.8–11, 104.29–30). According to Roller, Seneca argues that the traditional routes to glory and honor (e.g., military command and triumph) are useless; real *virtus* is an individual, internal good that replaces all others. Seneca focuses on the mental state of his heroes: "Seneca celebrates Cato's military defeats on the ground that his endurance of them proves his (Stoic) *virtus*"; he continually fought for the cause of *libertas* in full knowledge of its futility, "thus demonstrating the consistency of action and intention characteristic of the wise man."[19] For Seneca, consistency of action and desire, self-command and self-control, are more important achievements than military and political success.

A brief review of the portrayal of *imperium* in earlier texts will help us to more fully appreciate Seneca's reevaluation of traditional Roman ideals. First, let us consider the connections between *imperium*, individual virtue, and personal freedom contained in a fragment of a speech by the republican general Scipio Aemelianus, sacker of Carthage and Numantia: "From integrity is born esteem, from esteem, official office, from official office, the power to command, from the power to command, freedom" (*ex innocentia nascitur dignitas, ex dignitate honor, ex honore imperium, ex imperio libertas, Isid. Etym.* 2.21.4 = Malcovati, *ORF* 1.21.32). Scipio's series begins with internal, moral qualities, but the focus is squarely on the public, political, and military world. The community recognizes personal integrity, which leads to one's being considered worthy of rank and status (*dignitas*), high political office (*honor*), and the power to command others (*imperium*). Finally, this political power gives birth to freedom (*libertas*). As scholars have noted, despite the republican political context, Scipio is not referring to the *libertas* of the *populus Romanus*. The climactic reward of moral and political worth is the personal freedom that comes with holding *imperium*.[20] In this context, the supreme goals of *imperium* and freedom refer to the ability to command others. While this ability originates from an internal quality, personal integrity must be confirmed by public recognition and election to high office. Otherwise one cannot achieve power and freedom.

Although Scipio notes that only one primarily internal quality, *innocentia*, is necessary for *imperium*, by the end of the republic Cicero focuses on a wide range of moral qualities necessary for a leader to exercise his power throughout the empire. There is a terrible irony in that Cicero's support of the extension of unprecedented commands for Pompey may have precipitated the republic's end.[21] In his speech in support of the Manilian law, *Pro lege Manilia*, from 66 BCE, Cicero argues that the perfect general (*summo ac perfecto imperatore*, 36) must embody a full component of virtues; it is not enough that he simply display virtue in war (*bellandi virtus*, 36). Cicero then lists several other skills (*artes*), of which Scipio's *innocentia* is only the first: "integrity, self-control, trustworthiness, ability, natural talent, humanity" (*innocentia, temperantia, fides, facilitas, ingenium, humanitas*, 36). At first Cicero subordinates these abilities by calling them "aides and companions" to virtue in war (*eximiae huius administrae comitesque virtutis*, 36). In his discussion of these ancillary virtues, Cicero focuses on how self-control (*temperantia*) relates to a general's ability to assume command over others, specifically his ability to control his own avarice and keep his soldiers from pillaging the territories. Yet by doing so, Cicero inverts his earlier hierarchy of virtues, which set *bellandi virtus* at the top. In fact, self-control is a prerequisite for assuming command as a general. As Cicero sums it up, "A general cannot control his army if he cannot control himself" (*neque enim potest exercitum is continere imperator, qui se ipse non continet*, 38). As several scholars have noted, Cicero's praise of Pompey's self-control may be based more on Hellenistic treatises on kingship than on traditional Roman ideals of military virtue.[22] Whatever Cicero's sources may be, he quickly domesticates the ideal of self-control and states that Pompey's *continentia* and the subsequent behavior of his troops revive the ways of Roman generals of old: "Now at last people begin to believe that there were once Romans characterized by self-control, a trait that foreign nations were beginning to believe to be incredible and falsely handed down to memory. Now the glory of your empire begins to bring light to those races" (41).[23] And as Cicero notes repeatedly, this self-control enables Pompey to resist the allurements of empire as he travels through the luxurious East (40, 64–65, 67).

For all of Cicero's focus on Pompey's internal qualities, these are connected with the actual maintenance, defense, and expansion of the Roman Empire.

Some two decades later, after Pompey's defeat at the hands of Caesar, we can note an important shift in Cicero's praise of martial valor. In his speech in support of Caesar's allowing the return of the exiled Marcellus, *Pro Marcello*, Cicero also focuses on Caesar's geographic conquests but minimizes their ultimate significance. What really matters is Caesar's ability to conquer his *animus* and to behave mercifully in his position of absolute power. According to Cicero, this ability represents an entirely personal victory for Caesar. He must not share it with his troops or even with Fortune (7). Cicero continues,

> There is no power so great that it cannot be beaten down and broken by sword and strength. To conquer the soul, to inhibit one's anger to be mild to the defeated, not only to lift up one who lies low, who already excels in noble birth, talents, and virtue, but also to increase his former esteem: he who does these things I do not compare to the greatest men, but I judge him to be most similar to a god. (*Marcell*. 8)[24]

Thus, in Cicero's speeches we can already see the seeds for the ideal of self-*imperium* in Seneca.[25] There are also several important changes. For example, let us consider Seneca's method for giving advice to Nero in *De clementia*. In place of Cicero delivering a speech praising the self-control of a general or a general turned autocrat, Seneca imagines Nero giving this speech to himself. As with Cicero's *Pro Marcello*, the focus of *De clementia* is on mercy, but Seneca's opening move in this text is to demonstrate to Nero the "pleasures" of self-address.

Seneca begins by claiming that this treatise will not teach Nero anything new. It is just a "mirror" to display the emperor's virtuous self to himself. In reality *De clementia* is an attempt by Seneca to fashion and construct Nero as a benevolent and philanthropic emperor. While Shadi Bartsch notes that this treatise is more self-congratulatory than self-transformational, Seneca, like Cicero in *Pro Marcello*, must tread lightly when giving advice.[26] Both recognized that when addressing an autocrat, telling him how he already acted was the best way to get him to follow their advice.[27] Like all authors of advice to princes, Seneca knew that he could not simply tell Nero what to do; nor was it a simple matter of offering a logical argument and convincing Nero. Seneca was in a rhetorical and ethical bind: he had to get Nero to convince himself. Seneca's opening strategy for accomplishing this task of creating an ethical emperor is to show in his text Nero talking to himself, telling himself of his virtue.[28] Seneca puts words into Nero's mouth, words he envisions Nero saying to himself (*ita loqui secum*, 1.1.1). This monologue ends with Seneca having Nero declare:

> Severity is hidden away, but I have mercy at the ready; I thus watch over myself as if I were going to give an explanation to those laws that I have called from their place in the shadows into the light. By the young age of one person or by the old age of another I am moved to grant clemency; I have pardoned one because of his high standing; another because of his low standing; as many times as I have found no reason for mercy, I have spared people for my own sake. (*Clem.* 1.1.4)[29]

Except for perhaps the celebrated Quinquennium Neronis, Seneca failed in his efforts to create an emperor guided by *clementia* rather than by individual caprice. Yet the means by which Seneca tries to influence Nero at the opening of *De clementia* are significant for his overall philosophical project. Seneca's first move in this text is to have Nero talking to himself, telling himself how mercifully he has acted and will act in the future. Seneca subtly suggests to Nero that this sort of monologue is a way to evaluate past and present actions and, most important, to shape future ones. If Nero tells himself how wonderfully he acts, he perhaps will indeed act wonderfully. This connection between self-address, self-fashioning, and the shaping of imperial power is a central concept of Seneca's philosophy.[30]

We should not imagine that this is the historical Nero speaking. Here Seneca is most likely acting in his role as Nero's speechwriter.[31] Here we see Seneca using his position not simply to shape Nero's public proclamations but also to show Nero in a private moment, the young emperor in the very process of creating himself. Indeed, the opening of *De clementia* combines two philosophical techniques, moving from the metaphor of the mirror of philosophical self-speculation to self-address.[32] Seneca does not want Nero simply to look at himself; he wants him to talk to himself. The words Seneca puts into Nero's mouth perform several political functions. They display the "private" Nero to the public. As the emperor assures himself of his *clementia*, so he assures the public of it. In fact, Seneca moves from stating that Nero says these words to himself (*secum loqui*) to exhorting him to speak boldly out loud (1.1.5). Seneca encourages Nero to adopt this practice of linguistic self-inspection by claiming, perhaps contrary to his better Stoic sentiments, that it is a "pleasure" (*voluptas*, 1.1.1).[33]

If during the height of his political power Seneca uses Nero's self-address to shape the soul of the empire, in his later works he uses a similar tactic to shape the soul's relationship to empire. Seneca's travel experiences do not provide the only opportunity to consider the links between empire and philosophy. In letter 94 Seneca contrasts philosophical exercise with military exercise.[34] Toward the end of this long and important letter, Seneca notes that it is necessary to listen to the voice of someone of "good mind." This voice must be heard over the din and tumult of false people and the clamor of ambition, as it whispers healthy words (94.59). At first this voice recommends rejecting the trappings of high political office, which the *populus* believes make men great and happy. Instead, we should remove our vices so that we can "manage an empire that is useful to us and harmful to no one" (*si vis exercere tibi utile, nulli autem grave imperium, summove vitia*, Ep. 94.60). In order to manage this personal *imperium*, this voice launches into a lengthy description that begins by noting that one can find many people who have set fire to cities and sacked them. Then it turns to denigrating the famous empire builders from the past.[35] Seneca first attacks Alexander the Great, whose madness (*furor*) drove him to go beyond the boundaries of the sun and ocean and fight against nature itself (94.62–63). We meet Pompey, Caesar, and Marius again. Instead of praising them for building their villas at a distance from Baiae, as Seneca did in letter 51, here he condemns their personal ambition.

This "whispering" (*insusurret*, 94.59) philosophical voice explains that Pompey did not listen to virtue or reason. Rather his "insane love of false magnitude [and] boundless passion for growth" took him across the globe (94.64–65).[36] "Glory, ambition, and his limitless desire to stand above all others" sent Caesar to war (94.65).[37] Gaius Marius, seven-time consul, may have led his army, but ambition led Marius (*Marius exercitus, Marium ambitio ducebat*, 94.66). Seneca does not, however, only single out negative military examples. In fact, earlier in this letter he compliments Agrippa's own ability to use a method of philosophical exercise. According to Seneca, among those whom civil war had made famous and powerful (*claros potentesque*) only Agrippa remained happy (*felix*). This one fortunate general often said that he owed much to a passage from Sallust that reads, "Because of concord small things grow, because of discord great things collapse" (*nam concordia parvae res crescunt, discordia maximae dilabuntur*, Ep. 94.46 = Iug. 10.6). By means of this line, Agrippa would say, he became the best brother and friend. The following letter expands upon these themes and considers the results of the mad ambition of these generals.

In letter 95 Seneca attacks the gluttons of the present day. Whereas Pompey, Caesar, and Marius expanded the geography of the empire, now the fruits of their labors are stuffed into the bellies of the empire's inhabitants. It is the human body that now expands, as imperial foodies adopt the attitude of an autocrat, laying waste to land and sea to stuff the spoils down their gullets (95.19). Now, instead of soldiers, people manage armies of cooks and pastry chefs. "Good gods," exclaims Seneca, "how many men does one belly keep busy!" (*di boni, quantum hominum unus venter exercet!*, 95.25). With these two letters Seneca demonstrates a continuity between the republic and the empire. The crises of the last decades of the republic and the civil war continue, but they now manifest themselves in other aspects of human endeavor.[38] The crises have transformed into luxury and consumption.[39] These points might be taken to be no more than standard laments and moralizations if Seneca did not also link his version of Roman (moral) history so closely with his philosophical solutions and tenets.

Letter 94 focuses on therapeutic exercises, such as listening to the "healthy words" that reevaluate Roman history and repeating maxims from Roman literature, as in the case of the one *felix imperator*, Agrippa. Along with letter 95's satirical indictment of contemporary consumption, Seneca provides the theoretical knowledge necessary to buttress the work of philosophical exercises in order to manage one's own *imperium*. It is necessary to understand that our true commander is nature and our true home is the cosmos:

> Everything that you see, by which human and divine things are enclosed, is one; we are limbs of a great body. Nature has brought us forth related to each other; since she has produced the same things from the same things . . . by her command let us be prepared to offer helping hands. Let that verse be in our hearts and on our lips: "I am a human being, and I judge nothing of humanity to be foreign to me." (*Ep.* 95.52–53 = Ter., *Haut.* 77)[40]

Even if our final goal is to understand our place in the empire of nature, the path to this knowledge is through Roman history. Indeed, Seneca's cosmopolitanism doubles back upon itself and takes a decidedly Roman cast. In order to remain mindful of one's place in the cosmopolis, a line from the republican dramatist Terence should always be repeated, thus echoing the means by which Agrippa fashioned himself into "the best brother and friend," as Seneca notes in the previous letter. Furthermore, this vision of the cosmos is not the final point of the letter. One of the final images is that of Cato the Younger going fearlessly against the armies (*exercitus*) of Caesar and Pompey (95.69–71). We shall return to Seneca's obsession with portraying Cato below, but for now we shall consider a few more examples of Seneca's combination of Stoic self-address and reevaluation of *imperium*.

In the opening preface to what is now book 1 of the *Natural Questions*, likely written about the same time as the *Epistles*, Seneca imagines what the *animus* says to itself when, by studying the cosmos, it journeys into the inner bosom of nature:

> This is that pinpoint which is divided among so many nations by fire and sword? O how ridiculous are the boundaries of mortals! Let the Dacians not go out beyond the Ister, let the Thracians confine their empire by means of the Haemus; let the Euphrates block the Parthians; let the Danube divide the Sarmatians from the Romans; let the Rhine make a border with Germany; let the Pyrenees lift their ridge between the Gallic and Spanish provinces, let an uncultivated waste of sands lie between Egypt and Ethiopia. If someone were to give ants human intellect, would they not divide one small plot of ground into many provinces? When you lift yourself into the true greatness above, as many times as you see armies moving with banners unfurled, and, as if something great were happening, the cavalry now encircling the farthest points, now exploring points beyond, now massed on the flanks, it will be pleasing to say, "A black battle line moves across the plain." This battle line of yours is a movement of ants laboring in a narrow space. What difference is there between you and them except the size of a tiny body? (*Q Nat.* 1.pref.8–10 = *Aen.* 4.404)[41]

As in letter 95, Seneca encourages his readers to take a universal perspective. Similarly, the monologues in letter 94 and the *Natural Questions* appear to be the opposite of Nero's monologue that opened *De clementia*. There Seneca imagined the words the "soul of the empire" would speak to himself as he contemplated his position at the head of the *imperium Romanum*. In the *Natural Questions*, however, Seneca imagines the words the soul of the philosopher would speak to itself as it looked down on the world from its universal perspective.[42] This monologue may represent Seneca's rejection of the political world and the triumph of philosophical *otium* over the active political life.[43] Despite this contrast with Nero's monologue in *De clementia*, the same key themes remain constant: self-address, *animus*, and empire. And while Seneca imagines the soul of the philosopher ridiculing the size of the Roman Empire, this soul still gives detailed information about its natural and ethnic boundaries.

Like Seneca's *Moral Epistles*, the *Natural Questions* is dedicated to Lucilius and addresses his political position as procurator of Sicily. In letter 79, Seneca encourages Lucilius to explore the nature of the island and encourages him to investigate Mount Etna; in the *Natural Questions*, Seneca worries that Lucilius may have more elaborate political designs for the island.[44] In the *Epistles*, Seneca imagines the philosopher conquering the generals of the past; in the *Natural Questions*, Seneca is concerned that Lucilius' knowledge of history might lead to a dangerous self-satisfaction.[45] Seneca warns Lucilius not to turn his *procuratio* into an *imperium*. He imagines the dangers of Lucilius thinking to himself about how his current control over Sicily places him above the generals of the past.[46] Here again Seneca scripts a lengthy monologue of what he worries Lucilius must be thinking to himself:

> I have under my power this province, which has both sustained and broken the armies of the greatest states, when the great prize of war lay between Carthage and Rome. This province saw and nourished four Roman leaders, that is, the whole of the empire, as they contracted their forces into one place. This province lifted the fortunes of Pompey, wore out those of Caesar, transferred them to Lepidus, and held the fortunes of all. This province was present for that great spectacle by which it was made clear to mortals how swiftly the fall is from the highest to the lowest and how fortune destroys great power by different paths. For at the same time it saw Pompey and Lepidus cast down from the highest to the lowest point in different ways; while Pompey fled from his enemy's army, Lepidus fled from his own. (*Q Nat*. 4a.pref.21–22)[47]

Nevertheless, Seneca still implicates Lucilius in the expansionist imperial tradition.[48] Seneca turns Lucilius' attention from the dangerously fraught Sicily by asking him to consider why the Nile floods regularly (*Q Nat*. 4a.1.1). Yet by doing so, Seneca invites Lucilius to become an armchair traveler and learn about Nero's celebrated expedition to look for the source of the Nile.[49] In his investigation in book 6 of the causes of earthquakes, Seneca again returns to the mysteries of the Nile's flooding. He praises Nero for sending out an expedition and notes that he listened to the reports of the two centurions after they returned (*Q Nat*. 6.8.3–4). In fact, in the *Natural Questions* Seneca once again takes up his laudatory mantle from *De clementia* and praises Nero.[50] We can see how problematic the relationship is between Seneca's care of the self and the wider world of Rome.[51] While Seneca explicitly rejects the opinions of the crowd and praises contemplative communion with the universe and long-dead

philosophers, he also considers the place of the self within the Roman world.⁵²
On this topic his opinion seems to continually waver. We can surpass Hannibal, Caesar, and Pompey; yet such feelings of superiority risk making us just like the ambition-driven generals of the past. Throughout these passages, however, one point remains consistent: the cultivation of self-command and the evaluation of one's place in the empire is a linguistic process, whether it involves listening to the words of someone of "good mind" (*Ep.* 94) or words of self-address. To understand why Seneca links self-address with the reevaluation of empire, we must look at the importance of language in Stoic theories of impression and assent.

Command of the Soul

Seneca does not limit his discussion of self-*imperium* to the political and military sphere; nor is this demotion of martial prowess and success merely an easy salve to the egos of would-be aristocratic heroes, who under the new imperial regime find it increasingly difficult, if not impossible, to pursue the old paths to glory and power. Seneca wants self-command to be seen as the universal ideal. In *De vita beata* he outlines the specifics of psychological command, which he declares to be the "highest good" (*summum bonum*). The expansion and internalization that we saw critiqued in letters 94 and 95 is here portrayed as an individual psychological process that imitates the actions of the universal god.

> For god, the all-embracing universe and controller of everything, also extends out into external things; nevertheless he also returns from all directions into himself. Let our mind do the same thing: when it has followed its senses, through which it stretches itself out into externals, let it have power over them and over itself. In this way will one force and power that is concordant with itself be brought about; in addition, fixed reason will be produced that does not vary or hesitate in its opinions and decisions nor in its means of persuasion, reason that, when it has arranged itself and agreed with all its parts and, if I may so say, harmonizes, has achieved the highest good. For nothing crooked, nothing slippery remains, nothing on which it might butt up against or slip; it does everything by its own command, and nothing happens that it did not wish for, but whatever it does will turn out for the good, and it acts easily and preparedly and without the agent turning his back. For slowness and hesitation display an internal struggle and inconsistency. Therefore, one can confidently say that that the highest good

is concord of soul, for the virtues ought to be where there is agreement; the vices are at variance with one another. (*VB* 8.4–6)⁵³

In his definition of the highest good, Seneca employs several key ideas that themselves remain consistent throughout his philosophy. The *summum bonum* of concord of soul is understood as a direct union between opinion, desire, and action. Individual psychology and agency are inextricably linked in this idea of the good by the fact that the agent's opinions and thoughts remain unhesitatingly stable and thus each good action results without any difficulty or "backsliding" (8.5–6). This definition also contains *in nuce* the key idea that occupies this first section of this book. As I look at this psychological battle to gain self-mastery and self-*imperium*, I focus on Seneca's discussions of the continual struggle against hesitation and fluctuation, paying particular attention both to the innovative theoretical ideas he develops to describe and define the battle for self-command, which lie at the heart of his philosophy, and to the techniques and therapeutic advice he offers to his readers. I investigate literary and historical characters who battle to control their psychology and literally command themselves to act consistently and "without turning their backs."⁵⁴ The literary scenes do not, however, simply serve as an illustration of Seneca's philosophy. These modes of discourse will prove to be mutually dependent and illustrative. In fact, the above passage from *De vita beata* offers an important example of the means by which the soul functions.

In his description of the *summum bonum*, Seneca states that an essential component of the ideal of psychological consistency is the mind (*mens*) doing all things *by its own command* (*omnia faciet ex imperio suo nihilque inopinatum accidet*, 8.6). It is from this ideally powerful and consistent mental command that good and unhesitating actions originate. This statement is significant for two reasons. By saying that when the mind achieves the goal of the ultimate level of consistency, it will do all things *ex imperio suo*, Seneca continues the basic theme of *imperium*. On a deeper level, this statement explains the very core of self-command, while expanding it into a metaphor that describes the workings of the psyche. As Seneca explains, the mind functions by issuing its own commands, and these commands are the origin of actions. Thus, Seneca unites a general idea with a specific and technical one. Self-command (*sibi imperare*) is understood to be the result of consistent and powerful mental commands.

The idea of internal command as a hermeneutic device for understanding the initiation of action from a mental event has a long history. Inwood notes that Aristotle conceived of his theory of action in linguistic terms: the so-called practical syllogism. "He had used the syllogism as an analogue for the functioning of the desiderative and cognitive elements of action, suggesting that the action follows necessarily from these elements just as the conclusion of a syllogism follows from its premises. He occasionally likened the decisive moment in the generation of action to an imperative given to oneself."[55] For example, in *De motu animalium* Aristotle writes that desire (*epithumia*) says, "I must drink" (*poteon moi*, 701a32).[56] Inwood believes that the early Stoics refined Aristotle's theory and placed imperatival language at the basis of their theory of action. The Stoic self is the soul (*psyche, animus, mens*), or more specifically the *hegemonikon*, the "command center," located in the heart, which Seneca translates as *principale* (113.23).[57] This command center, it was theorized, functioned linguistically.[58] Chrysippus describes impulse as an imperative: "The impulse of a human is reason commanding him to act . . . repulsion is prohibitory reason." Inwood argues that "the description of impulse as the reason of man commanding him to act suggest[s] how the Stoics bridged the gap between practical knowledge and action. They did so . . . by construing impulse, which is the immediate cause of action, in grammatical terms on the model of a command to oneself which one obeys" (*SVF* 3.175).[59] From this sole fragment Inwood reconstructs an elaborate early Stoic theory of action. The Stoics' focus on the imperatival nature of the psychology of action may represent an important refinement and improvement on Aristotle.

Julia Annas, however, argues against Inwood's reconstruction. In fact, she cites Seneca on this point, who writes: "I will say what assent is. I ought to walk: I ultimately walk when I have said this to myself and approved of my opinion" (*Ep.* 113.18 = *SVF* 3.169).[60] She claims from this evidence that assent should be represented as "statements in the form 'I ought to F.' "[61] According to Annas, there is no reason to turn such a statement into an imperative. Nevertheless, Inwood's theory seems more fitting, despite the testimony from Seneca himself. Long and Sedley, for example, accept Inwood's hypothesis of the Stoic theory of command without reservation and in their commentary offer a helpful clarification of the difference between assent and impulse. We may assent to a proposition—a "should" or an "ought" statement—but that does not guarantee that we will act. There still must be the actual impulse to action, and this extra push is represented by the Stoics as a command. As Long and Sedley state: "In assenting, we approve the truth of a proposition—e.g. 'I should exercise.' On a Stoic analysis . . . the linguistic form that the impulse takes is to be imperatival, 'Exercise!'"[62] The impulse, rather, is directed toward the action itself, which is represented as a command to perform it. Furthermore, statements in the form "I ought to F" may be construed as true statements referring to one's desire. Desire and knowing what you "ought to do" may not always be enough to generate action.[63] There is need of something more. This problem is clearly stated in Aristotle's distinction between understanding and practical wisdom in the *Nicomachean Ethics*: "Understanding and practical wisdom are not the same thing. For practical wisdom is imperatival and understanding is only judgmental" (1143a4–8).[64] The difference between knowledge, a state of desire, the "ought to," and action is a command.[65]

Thus, Seneca's explanation of the highest good as the *mens* doing all things by its own command may be inherited from orthodox Stoic tradition. This is, then, a standard metaphorical means for describing how action results from a mental event. Whatever Seneca's debt to his predecessors, he uses the basic idea of psychological command with a new clarity and specificity; in fact, he takes the metaphor and runs with it. In letter 114, Seneca draws an extended portrait of the political commands issued by the soul:

> Our soul is now a king, now a tyrant. It is a king when it watches over virtuous things and cares for the health of the body that has been entrusted to it, and to that body it commands nothing base, nothing shameful; when indeed it is feeble and desirous and soft, it goes over into a detestable and abominable name and becomes a tyrant. Then the unbridled passions take it up and press upon it. (*Ep.* 114.24)[66]

In this passage, Seneca asks his reader to imagine the ideally strong *animus* as a king that commands only what is proper (*illi nihil imperat turpe, nihil sordidum*). Seneca also provides an important description of the inverse—the *animus* under the influence of the passions. Once the soul becomes weak (*inpotens, cupidus, delicatus*) and the passions (*adfectus*) take it over (*excipiunt et instant*), the *animus* turns from a beneficent king into a hateful tyrant, and presumably the commands it issues change accordingly. In this way, the two contrary states of the *animus* are based on the same theme. Seneca also suggests that the passions, like the *animus*, are imperatival. Inwood has demonstrated the importance of self-directed commands in Seneca's philosophy, concluding that they represent an event that can be approximated to an act of will.[67] These initial findings are important, and a major project of this chapter is to build upon his discussion. Indeed, Inwood's analysis can be extended. In the battle for self-command there are in fact three imperatival forces at work: the *animus*, the passions, and the self-directed commands of the agent.[68]

A detailed theoretical discussion of psychological *imperium* occurs in *De ira* (*On Anger*). In this treatise Seneca counters an important argument about human nature and humans' innate power to combat the passion of anger. Seneca presents the words of one (Aristotelian) who believes that the total extirpation of *ira* is impossible (2.12.3). This argument implies not only that *ira* is somehow naturally part of our psychological makeup but also that we are at times powerless to control it. In response to this claim, Seneca argues that we have the internal power to defeat this and the other passions. We need to work at it through constant mental exercise. "And so nothing is so difficult or arduous," he writes, "that the human mind cannot conquer it and continual practice [*meditatio*] cannot make it familiar; none of the passions are so wild and of their own power that they cannot be tamed by training" (2.12.3–4).[69] Thus, Seneca argues along standard Stoic lines that humans have the power to rid themselves of all passions and indeed must do so. He states that no passion (*adfectus*) is truly independent (*sui iuris*). We have ultimate power over them, but it takes training, *adsidua meditatio*, to conquer and tame thoroughly (*vincat, perdomentur*) every emotion. Seneca also shows us how this happens psychologically: "whatsoever the *animus* commands itself, it obtains" (*quodcumque sibi imperavit animus obtinuit*, 2.12.4). This is an important revelation. As in *De vita beata* and in letter 114, in *De ira* Seneca once again sets forth the theoretical premise of the command of the soul as the force that ideally controls our psychology and action. This idea accomplishes important theoretical and descriptive work for Seneca. It is perhaps the equivalent of the modern maxim, "You can do anything you set your mind to do," yet for Seneca, setting one's mind is a more specific event: the soul (*animus* or *mens*) commanding itself to act.[70]

In *De clementia*, Seneca combines the command of the *animus* with the metaphor of Nero as the "soul of the empire." Soon after Nero's monologue, Seneca explains to the young emperor,

> Just as the entire body serves the soul, and although this body is much greater and more attractive and the delicate soul remains concealed and where it hides is uncertain, nevertheless the hands, feet, and eyes perform its work, this skin protects it, by its command we lie down or run about restlessly; when it commands, if it is a greedy lord, we search the sea for the sake of gain, if it is ambitious, for a

long time now we have thrust our hands into the flames or willingly jumped into the earth. (*Clem.* 1.3.5)[71]

Seneca also uses the idea of the command of the soul in more mundane contexts. In letter 26 he describes the effects of old age. His *animus* has grown stronger, while his body has weakened (26.2–3). He describes his *animus* as flourishing, delighting, speaking, exulting, and even conducting a *controversia* with him about old age (26.2). It orders him to think about how to live in his advancing years (*ire in cogitationem iubet*, 26.3). In a later letter, also on the topic of old age, Seneca notes that one should not strive to live as long as possible; suicide is permitted. Yet there is an important concession: for the sake of family one may have to live, despite personal desires. The *animus* then would order itself to live, despite one's desire for death (*hoc quoque imperet sibi animus, Ep.* 104.3–4). This letter adds another facet to Seneca's theory of command of the soul. Here, psychological self-command is presented as a means to change desire and to fight against one's own personal wishes to die simply because of old age. If this desire is to the detriment of loved ones, it is simply selfish and unmanly (*Ep.* 104.3). Letter 104 sets up command as a means of self-correction; it is the means by which the *animus* defeats the "less noble" desires. The *animus* commands itself to do what is right. It can be the difference between life and death, acting rightly or wrongly. From these passages we can gain a picture of Seneca's concept of the command of the soul. It is the essence of the *summum bonum* of self-command (*De vita beata*). It can defeat the passions (*Ira* 2.12). It describes the initiation of contemplation (about old age in letter 26) and also the initiation of action (ordering oneself to live in letter 104). As Seneca notes in the *Natural Questions*, the *animus* is our "controller and master, by the command of which we are driven forward or called back."[72] Thus, command is the key idea that Seneca uses to describe the core workings of the soul; it is the mental event that is both the origin and the regulator of human thought and conduct.[73]

Command of the Passions

As we saw in letter 114, Seneca also suggests that the passions command the tyrannical soul. In *De ira* 3.13.2, he begins with a phenomenology of *ira*. This description of the physical effects of anger leads to a lengthy practical discussion on how to combat *ira*, which in turn leads to a theoretical explanation of how *ira* works. The moment that we begin to feel *ira* affect us physically, we must reverse its power over us, "let it be carried by us, not carry us away" (*feraturque, non ferat*). The way to achieve this is by reversing the outward signs of *ira*: "let us turn all the signs of anger into their opposites: let the face be relaxed, let the voice be softer, let the step be slower; gradually the interior of the self will be shaped along with the exterior" (*immo in contrarium omnia eius indicia flectamus: vultus remittatur, vox lenior sit, gradus lentior; paulatim cum exterioribus interiora formantur*). Seneca also suggests a change of environment. Those who handle their wine poorly are to order their friends to take them away from dinner parties. Those who are testy when sick are to forbid people to obey them (3.13). These techniques put the onus on others and do not necessarily prevent *ira* but rather lessen its effects on one's family and friends. This is essentially advice for mean drunks and cranky patients, to make the lives of those around them somewhat more pleasant. These techniques, especially the last two, do not affect *ira*. They are what Bernard Williams would call "tricks," not grounded in any philosophical theory of the passions.[74] Seneca himself admits that he has not yet given his best advice: what is best (*optimum est*) is to learn our faults through self-investigation and plan ahead to place barriers against them. Most important, we should shape our *animus* properly so that even the strongest and most unexpected blows will not affect it (3.13).

Seneca offers examples in order to prove that this high level of command is possible. Yet instead of giving a description of the purely internal workings of *ira* and our means to counter it, as we might expect, Seneca offers examples of the suppression of *ira* in the social world. Seneca writes that he will show us two things: how bad *ira* can be when it "uses all the power of the exceedingly powerful" and how much it is able to *command itself* when it is restrained by a greater fear (*quantum sibi imperare possit ubi metu maiore compressa est*, 3.13.7). In the examples that follow, this "greater fear" is fear of the excessive wrath of tyrants. Seneca offers a long series of vignettes of wicked rulers performing outrages against their subjects, who, instead of getting angry and retaliating, suppress their *ira*. These examples may appear to be contrary to Seneca's thesis that we ourselves are able to control our *ira*. Here the overwhelming fear of the king appears to accomplish these acts of self-control. Seneca sees only paradigms of slavishness and would rather these men confront their rulers (3.14). Despite the oddity of Seneca's examples, the language he uses to describe the workings of *ira* is consistent: *ira* commands itself. Seneca says that *ira* is able to command itself (and hence does not command us) when a greater fear checks it. While it is surprising that Seneca moves from the internal command of the soul and the passions to the external world of despots, this shift suggests that he is linking the two worlds. We may note a parallel between the workings of *ira* in the social world and in our own psychology. In these examples, anger is suppressed by fear of the absolute power of the ruler, specifically what he can in fact order to happen. Cambyses commands Praexaspes' son to be led into the dining hall to be shot (*filium procedere ultra limen iubet*, 3.14.2). The same is true for the nameless Persian who must flatter the king when his sons' heads are ordered to be brought to him as he eats their flesh (*adferri capita illorum iussit*, 3.15.1). Thus, the *ira* of these hapless fathers, its ability to command them to act when they are injured, is suppressed by fear of what the rulers are actually able to command. The metaphorical psychological command is suppressed by another, more powerful external and actual command. Good rulers, however, are not commanded by anger. Seneca notes that Augustus continually demonstrated in both word and deed that "*ira* did not command him" (*iram illi non imperasse*, 3.23.4).

The passion *dolor* also commands.[75] In his early consolation to his mother from Corsica, Seneca offers advice for dealing with her sorrow for her exiled son: "As often as the excessive power of *dolor* invades and orders you to follow, think of your father" (*quotiens te inmodica vis doloris invaserit et sequi se iubebit, patrem cogita*, Helv. 18.9). Interestingly, this advice on how to defeat the command of *dolor* is given as a command. Perhaps the imperative "think of your father" (*patrem cogita*) is intended as a brief self-address to be used by his mother whenever she feels herself being overcome by, or in Seneca's language, ordered to follow, *dolor*.[76] She can perhaps repeat these words to herself in order to fight the feeling of *dolor*'s emotional imperative.[77] Seneca suggests that a command repeated to oneself can be a weapon to fight against the command of the passions. But before we can begin the analysis of the Senecan self-address, it is necessary first to address an apparent problem in Seneca's philosophical theory. The idea of a command of the passions may seem to be a very "un-Stoic" idea, in that it seems to give the passions a life of their own and to deny the orthodox Stoic doctrine of a unified soul. This problem is particularly apparent in a passage from *De tranquillitate animi* (On tranquility of soul).

In the opening of this dialogue, Seneca defines the vice of inconsistency in terms as broad as possible. He runs through a long list of manifestations of this problem (2.6) and then defines one paradigm: "Then there are those for whom regret for what they have begun, as well as a fear of beginning, holds, and a shaking of the soul sneaks upon them that can find no end, because they are able neither to command their desires nor follow them" (2.8).[78] Here we see the problem of vacillation in an extreme form: inability to command the *cupiditates* or to submit to them fully (*obsequi*) and let the passions do the commanding. As we have seen, the command of the soul was a hermeneutic device used by Aristotle and the early Stoics to describe the initiation of action from a mental event. Yet Seneca speaks both of the command of the *animus* and of the command of the passions. The notion of command of the passions might seem to reveal the dualism Seneca has often been accused of.[79] Brad Inwood has written an extensive analysis of this question and concludes that Seneca's reference to an emotional imperative does not commit Seneca to the so-called Posidonian dualist school of Stoicism. In Inwood's view, we should not consider Seneca's psychological metaphor of the command of the passions to be an essential part of his philosophy.[80] According to him, it is simply literary ornament. Yet this metaphor is not to be written off as simply a figure of speech; it is central to Seneca's theory. Seneca is not trying to break with the orthodox Stoic theory of a unified, rational soul or to give the passions a life of their own. Rather, by describing the command of the passions along with the orthodox idea of the command of the soul, Seneca may be attempting to address and remedy criticisms that the Stoics perennially faced.

In Seneca's philosophy, there is not only an attempt to update and "Romanize" Stoic philosophy by making self-*imperium* the *maximum imperium*; there is also a move to correct two central failings of Stoicism. The Stoics were often attacked for their theory of the soul, in particular, their explanation of psychological conflict. In order to retain their doctrine of a unified soul, the orthodox Stoics could not posit two separate elements doing battle over what was right and how the agent should act. Their answer states that conflict per se does not exist; what occurs is a rapid succession of opinions within the soul. At no time is the soul actually divided, even in the throes of the most extreme passions and mental fluctuation. This answer may have preserved Stoic doctrine, but it most likely failed to convince or convert any new followers. The critics of the Stoics were quick to jump on this theory that so blatantly denies the qualitative feel of emotion. As Inwood writes: "The problem with this solution is that it is counter-intuitive. As Plutarch and Alexander pointed out, the feeling of psychological conflict is one which we all have."[81] Seneca's idea of the command of the passions grants some credence to the way the passions *feel*. Seneca quietly accepts the qualitative nature of the passions—they feel as if they have a life of their own and command us to act—without necessarily committing to define their true nature. Seneca never says that command of the passions is unbeatable or independent. His focus on the metaphor of command may be a response to the past Stoic overzealous adherence to doctrine. Thus, Seneca's repeated mention of the command of the passions is in part a rhetorical device for making his theory and therapy easily understood and convincing.

In general, Seneca may have believed that a more rhetorical version of Stoicism was needed because of the criticisms of the Stoics and their failure to write persuasive philosophy. As Catherine Atherton has pointed out, the early Stoics did not acknowledge rhetoric per se; they only considered it part of dialectic.[82] Even Cicero notes their lack of concern: "They do not pursue any flowery speech, nor do they expand their argument; but by means of the smallest little questions, little pinpricks, so to speak, they prove what they have set out as a proposition" (*Parad. Stoic.* 2).[83] Echoing another criticism of Cicero's, Atherton notes that the Stoics failed with their combination of dialectic and rhetoric because they did not engage the public.[84] The art of persuasion was not a Stoic goal. It was in fact systematically avoided. As Atherton writes, "Stoic appropriateness is appropriateness simply to the object in question, the *pragma*, no other factors are mentioned. The true nature and quality of the subject of discourse have to be straightforwardly communicated. An audience's assent cannot be secured by winning its pity or admiration, or by arousing its anger, or by playing on its snobbery or stupidity or vulgarity. Accordingly, the orator's language cannot be put to the service of any of these low purposes."[85] Seneca does not, however, use his rhetorical prowess to achieve any "low purposes." He specifically takes a stand against the Stoic reliance on syllogisms and claims that they are ineffectual for therapy.

Seneca addresses the failures of orthodox Stoicism and offers his own solution in letter 82. In this letter, Seneca not only disowns but ridicules outright the Stoics' use of syllogisms to aid in moral progress. Seneca categorically dismisses the "Greek method" as laughable. He specifically attacks Zeno and his means for ridding people of the fear of death, calling it useless sophistry (*cavillatio*). According to Seneca, Zeno's cure runs as follows: "No evil is glorious; death, however, is glorious; therefore death is not an evil" (82.9). This "cure" causes Seneca ironically to exclaim, "You have made progress! I have been freed of the fear of death; after this I will not hesitate to offer up my neck" (82.9). At the end of this letter he returns again to Zeno's syllogism. In order to show further that it is ineffective sophistry, Seneca imagines this syllogism being used in real-life situations. What if Leonidas had said this to his troops as they were preparing to meet certain death against the advancing Persian army at Thermopylae? The thought causes him to again exclaim in ridicule, "O effective harangue! Who after this would hesitate to carry himself to where the swords are the thickest and die with his boots on" (82.21). Seneca prefers what Leonidas actually said: "Eat your meal, fellow soldiers, as if you were going to dine among the dead below" (*"sic," inquit "conmilitones, prandete tamquam apud inferos cenaturi"*). Offering another example of the ideal way to defeat the fear of death, Seneca cites a certain Roman general who said to his troops before marching through a large enemy host, "We must go, my fellow soldiers, to that place from which there is no 'must' about returning" (82.22).[86] This letter is important because it not only demonstrates Seneca's explicit denunciation of the traditional Stoic valuing of abstract syllogisms over culturally engaged rhetoric but also shows the type of language Seneca considers most effective. Simple, "imperial" sentences and commands are the rhetorical means Seneca uses to convince his audience that death is not to be feared. The language of generals to their troops is to be directed at the self.

As R. J. Newman demonstrates, for Seneca "simple syllogisms do not have the same force as repeated, hard-hitting phrases, since syllogisms entertain the mind, but do not affect one's emotional reaction."[87] Indeed, in letter 94 Seneca is clear on how such phrases work. He argues that by constant repetition they become familiar and shape our animus (*familiariter in animum receptae formant eum*, 94.47). Thus, *sententiae*, precepts, and other short phrases or commands repeated to oneself are the necessary psychological exercises that Seneca continually prescribes. They are likened to a command but are specifically considered a type of "reminder" (94.44). Such short and simple *admonitiones* provide a way for us to perform right actions and to act in accordance with the philosophy we have learned (94.45). Furthermore, they are a way to fight against the emotions (94.47). For Seneca, pointed language is the most effective means for training and controlling the soul.

In Senecan philosophy, theory and practice are intricately linked and in fact mutually dependent. It is mainly because of this union that Richard Sorabji argues, convincingly, that Stoic philosophy can indeed be therapeutic. He gives the most credit to Stoicism's "arsenal of techniques" of therapy. As Sorabji puts it, "The Stoics do not just leave you there."[88] In other words, Stoic philosophy does not simply promise self-command and happiness, nor does it only urge one on without any clear explanation or theory of the process of self-mastery; it shows how to work toward this goal and offers an in-depth analysis of emotion, general psychology, and action. Indeed, Seneca's idea of *imperium* displays a particularly close connection between the overall goal of his philosophy, theory, and therapy. Sorabji's final summation of the successfully holistic nature of Stoic ethics can be applied to Seneca: "The desire to control emotion leads to acute observation which informs the analysis of what emotion is. The resulting analysis in turn is used in the fight to control emotion. The connection between practice and theory is seamless. This is how ethics should be done."[89] Seneca's theory and therapy skillfully combines Stoic philosophy and Roman mores. Seneca highlights the traditional Stoic theory of the imperatival language of the soul. He builds upon this by focusing on the traditional Roman ideal of military and political command, but he subordinates these to self-command, *sibi imperare*. I have also traced Seneca's ambiguous relationship to famous Roman leaders from the past. On the one hand, he condemns Marius, Pompey, and Caesar. Yet he also praises Agrippa's use of a maxim from Sallust. Similarly, Leonidas' and Calpurnius' utterances are worth repeating in order to alleviate the fear of death. In fact, Seneca declares that a maxim of the republican general Quintus Fabius Maximus is not simply applicable to the military world but is a universal human truth. He writes in *De ira*, "Fabius used to say that the most shameful excuse for a commander [*imperator*] was 'I did not think of it'; I think it is the most shameful excuse for a human being" (2.31.4).

Self-Directed Commands

Real progress is not to be gained simply by memorizing and repeating favorite tag lines and exhortations. One must adopt a fixed, daily regime of *meditatio*, setting aside a time each day for self-investigation and self-scrutiny. Although not a Stoic invention, the *meditatio* was placed at the center of the Stoics' therapeutic program. As Newman points out, "The Cyrenaics stressed the *praemeditatio futuri mali*, [but] the meditatio as the basic tool of ethical philosophy was an innovation of the Stoics."[90] The *meditatio* is an important means for ensuring that philosophical teachings are internalized and made ready to be put into action. As Seneca himself puts it, virtue is bipartite; one part consists of *disciplina*, the other of *exercitatio* (*Ep*. 94.47).

After the theoretical discussions of the command of the *animus* in book 2 of *De ira* and of the passions in book 3, Seneca gives a lengthy example of the *meditatio* as the primary way to strengthen the soul and prepare it to fight against future attacks of *ira* and the other emotions. He describes a thoroughly linguistic process; the emotions (*omnes sensus*) are brought under control as the *animus* is called on daily to "explain itself" (3.36.1).[91] Seneca then offers the example of Sextius' method, in which he asks the following questions of his *animus*: "What evil have you healed today? What vices have you resisted? In what part are you better?" (3.36.1). Seneca knows from experience that this end-of-the-day interrogation is successful; once the *animus* has been praised or admonished, a most peaceful sleep follows (3.36.2). The goal is to transfer the tranquility that follows immediately after self-scrutiny and self-admonition to the daylight hours and preserve this psychological stability for one's actions. The example that Seneca then gives of his own daily practice of *meditatio* differs considerably, however, in form and content from that of Sextius' brief and simple questions.[92] Seneca's *meditatio* is a long series of commands to himself not to react in anger (3.36–37). Short, pointed commands make up its core. He begins with an opening prohibition, "See to it that you do not do this anymore; this time I forgive you," and then gives a series of vignettes in which he reacts in anger. After each, he commands himself to act correctly. Seneca imagines a situation in which he was too argumentative in a disagreement—"In that argument you spoke too combatively, from now on, do not congregate with the ignorant" (3.36.3–4)—and corrects himself for admonishing others too harshly by ordering himself, "In the future see to it not only that you are speaking the truth but that the man to whom you are speaking can handle the truth" (3.36.4). He advises himself against foolishly getting angry for the sake of a friend with another command: "Walk far away and laugh!" (*recede longius et ride!*, 3.37.2). Seneca ends with a blanket exhortation to prepare his *animus* for any possible future difficulty: "Anticipate with your soul that you must endure many things" (3.37.3).[93] We see that a nightly dose of self-directed commands is the way to fight the passions and work toward gaining self-mastery; or to use Seneca's own terminology, *adsidua meditatio* (*Ira* 2.12.3, 3.41.1; *Ep.* 82.8) helps one fight against *adsidua iactatio* (*Ep.* 120.20). Seneca does not only concern himself with the formalized practice of the *meditatio*, however. Throughout his writings he also focuses on specific instances of self-command.

In letter 65 Seneca writes of an afternoon when he was convalescing after being ill the entire morning. As he started to feel the sickness leave him, he first made a trial of his *animus* (*itaque lectione primum temptavi animum*, 65.1); then once he realized that he truly was recovering, he ordered it to get back to work (*plus illi imperare ausus sum*). Seneca started writing "more intently than usual," until he was interrupted by some friends who forced him to stop out of worry for his health. Indeed, in another letter self-directed command enables Seneca to have the power of life and death over himself. As a complement to letter 104.3–4, where Seneca says that the *animus* can order itself to live for the sake of others, in letter 78 he notes that he too was once so sick that he had decided to die, but that the thought of the effect this would have on his father caused him to change his mind. He thus commanded himself to live (*itaque imperavi mihi ut viverem*, 78.2). Self-command, Seneca's order to himself, is presented as the means he uses to change his motivation; it enables him to act against his desire and decision to die.[94] Conversely, we can also order ourselves to die. For Seneca, this is an especially admirable act. Seneca admires those who find remarkable ways of dying in particularly difficult situations: "He is a great man who not only commands himself to die but also finds a way" (70.25). Seneca assures us that this is something we can all do if necessary. He gives examples of humble people (*sordidis exemplis uti*, 70.22) so that that we can see that "ordering death" is in our power. Thus, the examples of Cato and Socrates are not "beyond imitation" (70.22).

One of Seneca's examples is of a barbarian slave destined to die fighting in a sea battle staged in the arena. He stands waiting with a lance in his hand, a lance that normally would be used to defend himself and kill others. Instead, this barbarian "plunged the whole thing into his throat" (*totam iugulo suo mersit*, 70.26). This would seem to be a remarkable example of "ordering death," but Seneca goes on to illustrate this ideal. Seneca does not portray this barbarian as silently ending his own life. Before he dies, the barbarian gives a short speech rebuking himself for accepting his situation and not acting: "Why, why, have I not already escaped from all torment, from all insult. Why, armed as I am, do I wait for death?" (70.26). We can imagine the barbarian then dying as an example for all. The barbarian's supreme moment of "ordering death" is represented by an act of self-address. His words mark the transition between knowing what he ought to do and actually doing it. Thus, the barbarian questions the appropriateness of the situation, rebukes himself for accepting it, and then takes action to change it. The rhetoric the unnamed barbarian uses on himself convinces him that he does not have to play the role of spectacle, or at least that he can choose what sort of spectacle he will be.

For Seneca, even the lowliest of characters have a moment of rhetorical flourish in which they command themselves to act.

Rather than focusing on the goal and ideal state of consistency itself, Seneca is concerned with showing the means by which one is able to achieve it. As Marcus Wilson points out, "Seneca's language suggests that while he is striving to create the idea of a soul immune to disturbance . . . its attraction lies not so much in the freedom from perturbation as in the act of self-assertion involved in preserving it. Applied to the passions, to the extent that the Stoics advocate extirpation of the destructive passions, Seneca is more interested in the act of extirpation than in the ideal state of serenity to which it should lead. Seneca locates value in the heroism of the battle, not in enjoying the rewards of victory."[95] The practice of self-assertion and mastery of fortune can be portrayed as a full-blown declamatory moment, and thus the grammar of Senecan psychology takes on a specific rhetorical form. In letter 70, Seneca shows his readers the "sordid" example of the self-rebuking, suicidal barbarian in order to prove that the noble example of Cato's intrepid death is not an unattainable ideal. In *De providentia* Seneca portrays the final scene of Cato at Utica. This is the paradigmatic image of the rhetoric of self-command.

Seneca imagines Cato, sword in hand, acknowledging in a brief monologue the total victory of Caesar and declaring that he will now make his exit: "Cato has a way out: with this one hand he will make wide the way to liberty" (*Prov.* 2.10). Before he performs this final act, which will complete his image as the champion of freedom and Stoic autonomy, Cato apostrophizes his *animus* and twice commands it to act: "Undertake, my soul, this long planned deed; rip yourself from human affairs" (2.10).[96] With this apostrophe Cato demands consistency from himself. He orders his *animus* not to waver and to remain firm in his long-thought-out plan and course of action. By the performance of this final act, Cato ensures that he will continually remain the champion of liberty. Cato fashions himself and perfects his exemplary final image; he will be remembered and praised as the Stoic model for generations to come. Of course, as he does with Nero in *De clementia*, Seneca is putting words into Cato's mouth. The historical Cato's final words were not recorded.[97] Instead, Seneca invents a monologue in order to illustrate his own ideas of the links between language, psychology, and action.

Seneca continues to play with history and moves Cato's monologue into the realm of theater. Cato is performing on the world stage, and the gods are his approving audience. Seneca attributes Cato's unsuccessful first suicide attempt to divine intervention. He does not state that the gods wished to preserve Cato so that he could continue to fight for liberty; rather, according to Seneca, the gods so enjoyed watching Cato's performance of self-exhorting monologue and suicide that they called him back for an encore. The gods want to see Cato display his *virtus* in a more difficult role. They desire to witness his "famous and memorable *exitus*" again (2.12). For Seneca, Cato cannot simply commit suicide; he must give a speech urging himself on.[98] In particular, the apostrophe and commands to his *animus* display Cato's voluntary commitment to his plan of accomplishing this final and supreme act of self-fashioning. Cato's actual suicide is minimized by Seneca, reduced to subordinate *dum* clauses (2.11). Instead, Seneca focuses on Cato's (ahistorical) performance of a presuicide monologue that serves as a verbal externalization of Cato's desire to act consistently. The death scene as presented in *De providentia* leads us to believe that this monologue of self-command, perhaps even more than the act of suicide itself, so enthralls the gods that they make Cato perform his "more difficult" encore. In fact, in Seneca's view it was a "great joy" for the gods to watch all of Cato's final moments (2.11). There is no suggestion that they enjoyed watching any of Caesar's victorious performance.

Seneca's Cato does not seem to come from history, but rather straight from the declamation hall. The words Seneca puts into his mouth are generally considered representative of Seneca's penchant for rhetorical excess. At best, they are seen as a "protreptic device."[99] Not to be outdone by his critics, both ancient and modern, Seneca himself is aware of how dangerously close his philosophy often is to rhetoric, or even worse, to declamation. In letter 24, he imagines the anger Lucilius will feel because of his not providing any true philosophical help or comfort to ease his worries about the outcome of a court case. Seneca only offers old declamations. He imagines Lucilius accusing, "These stories of yours have been repeated in every school." All Seneca does is "narrate Cato" (24.6). Cato's speech in *De providentia*, as well as the one Seneca offers to Lucilius despite his protests in letter 24, may seem to be a product of the overblown rhetorical mind-set of the early empire. Seneca is developing a declamatory set piece. Cato's self-apostrophe and command to his soul are ultimately based on passages from Greek epic and tragedy. Hence, we cannot gain any deeper philosophical insight from Cato's monologue. As we have seen, however, in the larger context of Seneca's philosophy Cato's speech illustrates the ideal of self-command. Seneca uses self-apostrophe for philosophical purposes, not simply for stylistic ones.

Self-Apostrophe in Contemporary Rhetoric and Epic

Traditionally, the general state of Roman rhetoric in Seneca's time is lamented as being ruined by the excessive influence of declamation. For example, Stanley Bonner repeats the ancient criticisms that declamation has no practical value in the courts and that it ruined rhetorical practice in general.[100] He investigates to discover whether the laws in the various declamations are real or fictitious, and he is an assiduous cataloger of the influence of declamation on literature, notably the writings of Seneca, which he lists without much comment.[101] The analyses that he does provide are only stylistic. The influence of declamation can make one's style "pointed" or "neat," but there is always the risk of running over into "rant and bombast, false effect and artificial expression."[102] Even more recent studies conclude that too often any moral problem that may be at the core of the declamation is sacrificed to the overpowering demands of style and *sententiae*.[103] Yet the Romans themselves were aware of the problematic status of declamation. We have already seen Lucilius' imagined critique in letter 24. Declamation was recognized as being at once a central part of Roman education, culture, and society and detrimental to them. Indeed, we can find this recognition within declamations themselves. Seneca's father tells a story of the hard fate of Albucius Silus, who did not know to curb his declamatory excesses and fondness for figures of speech in the open air of the forum (*Controv.* 7.pref.8). Even in his collection of the great moments in declamation, Seneca the Elder admits that the real world of Roman political affairs often seemed like another planet to the declaimers (*Controv.* 3.pref.13).[104]

The surviving text of the *Satyricon* opens with Encolpius giving a declamation against declamation. Similarly to Seneca the Elder, Encolpius argues that the teachers of rhetoric can only speak of overblown subject matter and make empty noises with their *sententiae* (*et rerum tumore et sententiarum vanissimo strepitu*, 1.2). Indeed, students neither see nor hear anything useful in the schools. According to the fashion of the day, they must declaim little scenes of "pirates standing on the shore holding chains, tyrants ordering sons to kill their fathers, or oracles demanding the sacrifice of three or more virgins to cure a plague" (1.3). The result is that neither students nor their teachers can function in the forum. The traditional aim of their education has been lost.

Reminiscent of Seneca the Elder's critique, Encolpius states that when orators come into the sphere of public, forensic rhetoric, their school training proves to be useless, and they think they have stepped into another world (1.2).

In his interpretation of the *Satyricon*, Gian-Biago Conte argues that the crux of this work, the goal of the "hidden author" Petronius, is to demonstrate the baneful effects of declamation through the actions of Encolpius, Giton, and others. Conte claims that Petronius blames declamation in large part for the "degradation of sublime literature." For him, declamation "cheapens the noble tradition of forensic oratory and produces only empty academic inventions. There is a converging process that blends literature and rhetoric and contaminates one with the other, 'corrupta eloquentia' overflows more and more into literature and, conversely, literature draws more and more on the apparatus of *loci communes*."[105] According to Conte, Petronius so corrupts his characters, especially the "mythomaniac narrator" Encolpius, because of their madness for declamation that for them the banal, everyday world ceases to exist. They make the world declamatory and interpret it according to the rules of high literature. It is our job as readers to discover this indictment of scholastic culture run wild and laugh along with Petronius at his characters' folly and their inability to function in the real world.[106] Yet while Conte argues that Petronius himself is out to show the destructive effect of declamation on Roman culture, Encolpius and Agamemnon also are aware of this ruin and voice similar concern and disgust. The declamations of Encolpius and Agamemnon address precisely the same problems that Conte raises. Thus, the very faults that Encolpius finds with the practice, such as declamation's overreliance on topoi, themselves become topoi, and the indictment of the material that makes up declamation itself becomes material for a declamation. As Jas Elsner notes, the "standard" image of the early empire as degraded by declamation and theatricality is suspect because this portrait "has its origins as an ironic *self*-image playfully propagated by the writers of the very period which we dismiss with a version of their own words."[107] It is precisely this problem that Seneca addresses in the complaints of Lucilius in letter 24. Lucilius accuses Seneca of not doing philosophy but just narrating hackneyed set pieces. Nevertheless, Seneca implicitly sees the value of scripting such speeches as he launches into yet another version of Cato's last words (*Ep.* 24.7).

A closer look at declamation and oratorical theory gives us an insight into the significance of the self-apostrophe and self-command that Seneca puts in the mouth of the declaiming Cato in *De providentia*. From evidence provided to us by Quintilian, we can develop an ethics of apostrophe. As Brian Vickers points out, rhetoric should not be dismissed as an "interminable enumeration of stylistic devices," and these stylistic figures should not be designated as simply "ornament."[108] We must, rather, begin to consider seriously what function these figures play. Indeed, in his definition of apostrophe Quintilian delineates the formal characteristics of the figure, and he also notes its general effect on the audience:

> Speech that turns away from the judge, which is called "apostrophe," is exceedingly moving, whether we attack our enemies: "What was your sword doing on the field of Pharsalus, Tubero?"; or we turn to invoking something: "I call on you again, O Alban hills and groves"; or [employ it] as an invidious means to call for help: "O Porcian and Sempronian laws!" (*Inst.* 9.2.38)[109]

Apostrophe is formally a turning of language from one addressee to another. In Quintilian's examples, apostrophe moves from the judge to the adversary or is used to invoke something absent (the Alban groves and hills) or something abstract (the Porcian and Sempronian laws). Quintilian defines the specific function of this sudden change of addressee as a means of attack (*invadimus*), invocation (*ad invocationem aliquam convertimur*), or entreaty aimed at bringing ill will on one's opponent (*ad invidiosam inplorationem*). Thus, apostrophe is an important psychological and persuasive element of a speech. It is, as Quintilian puts it, "exceedingly moving" (*mire movet*). This is a helpful definition, and we only need to amend Quintilian's placing its usage exclusively in the courtroom. The specific form of Cato's apostrophe is not a "turning from the judge" to any variety of new addressees but rather a turning to the self, to the *animus*.

Given Quintilian's definition, it seems almost impossible to write self-apostrophe off as "mere rhetoric" or a declamatory gesture, as if this figure were simply without meaning. Rather, we must consider self-apostrophe as part of the larger cultural system, and we must assume that it has a deeper significance both for the authors who used this figure and for their audiences. Seneca's portrayals of "the dying words of Cato" do seem to be taken directly from a declamation, and it is from contemporary declamations that we gain important information about the significance of self-apostrophe for the Roman audience. Declamation provides an ethics of apostrophe and explains this figure's significance for both the speaker and the audience. In fact, rhetorical sources prove more illuminating than literary sources. We need not look so far from Seneca's home, to examples of similar figures from Greek epic and tragedy, when investigating Seneca on self-apostrophe and self-command; we can look in his home.

Seneca's father preserves several declamations concerning a rapist who accuses his father of madness because he will not immediately forgive his son, even though the victim's father has done so. If he does not receive his father's pardon, he will be killed (*Controv.* 2.3). The declamation of Junius Gallio presents a long speech by the boy's father in which he justifies himself for not pardoning his son immediately. The father opens his speech by claiming to his son that he will take the full thirty days to deliberate with friends and family members on the problem: "I will deliberate with my friends, I will deliberate with my relatives, I will deliberate with your mother" (2.3.6). His speech then shifts to himself with an apostrophe and command, "Be strong, my soul, be strong; yesterday you were braver" (<*dura*>, *anime, dura; here fortior eras*). After this brief interruption, the speech returns to its original course.

Writing a few decades after the elder Seneca, Quintilian also appreciates this declamation, especially the father's apostrophe to his *animus*. It is from Quintilian's comments on this passage that we gain further knowledge of the broader cultural implications of self-apostrophe. Quintilian includes this in the discussion of *figurae* in book 9. On figures in general, he remarks that they have a wonderfully moving effect on the audience; he claims that they are subtle in their working. He then comes to figures that involve innuendo to be understood by the audience. According to Quintilian, such figures are especially effective for declamation because they keep the often convoluted topics afloat. He gives an example showing such a figure to be necessary in the case of the *raptor* in particular: if the father pardons his son, there is no need for a hearing. Similarly, if the father categorically refuses to do so, then he is obviously crazy and there is no declamation. The trick for the declaimer is to come up with a means to avoid these two extremes while also avoiding the suspicion of collusion. Quintilian notes with approval how "Pater Gallio" manages to express the father's emotional state and cites his self-apostrophe and self-command (*dura, anime, dura, here fortior fuisti*, 9.2.91). For Quintilian, these are the words upon which the entire declamation hangs. The father briefly swerves away from his interlocutor and addresses himself. This swerve creates an ethical moment in which the father reveals his true psychology. He is having difficulty with the situation and has some desire to pardon his son immediately. His plan, however, is to deliberate the problem over the course of the allotted time. He commands himself to keep to this plan. Indeed, as crazy as this self-address may seem to us, it appears that for the Roman audience this was a means for proving the speaker's sanity. As for Seneca's Cato in *De providentia*, self-command is what makes the father keep to his plan of action.[110]

To return to examples from Seneca's family, his nephew Lucan provides another important instance in his epic account of the civil war, *De bello civili*. Seneca was not alone in scripting a monologue of self-address and self-command for a defeated republican general. In addition, Lucan's Pompey provides a striking pendant to Cicero's praise of him as the "consummate and perfect general" who is able to control himself and his troops as he wars throughout the empire. We can see how Lucan shrinks Pompey's sphere of command from the vast territory of the Roman Empire to the internal landscape of the self. After fleeing the battle of Pharsalus, Pompey eventually decides to go to Egypt and seek help from Ptolemy. The Egyptian court, however, realizes that Caesar is now master of Rome and decides to have Pompey murdered immediately. Those charged with murdering him go in a small boat to meet Pompey's fleet in Pharos. Pompey is called by the Egyptians to come onto their boat alone. Lucan writes that once Pompey steps onto the boat, he loses all power over himself (*perdiderat iam iura sui*, 8.612). Even so, he remains in control of his mind and his reaction to his own death. He tries to maintain this last shred of self-control and not cry aloud. First he sees the drawn swords coming toward him. Then he covers his head, closes his eyes, and holds his breath to keep from weeping or crying out. Any sign of pain or emotion would ruin his *fama* (8.610–17). Pompey does not react to Achillas' first sword stroke. He does not moan, and he keeps his body still (8.618–20). He approves of how he is dying, but he knows that the Egyptians will not be so kind as to finish him off with one blow. Each will get a shot in, and they will continue to hack away at his body. Pompey thus encourages himself to continue dying well, to continue being silent despite his extreme pain. Lucan's Pompey "approves of himself as he dies and in his breast he turns over the following":

> The generations that will never be silent about Roman labors are at hand, and the age that follows is looking on from the entire world at the boat and the Pharian faith. For you the fates of a long life have streamed on prosperously: if you do not prove yourself in death, the people will not know whether you know how to

endure adversity. Do not yield to shame and be indignant at the author of your fate. By whatever hand you are struck, believe it to be the hand of your father-in-law. Let them scatter and rend me, I am nevertheless, o gods above, fortunate, and no divine power can take that away. Prosperity changes in life, death does not make one wretched. Cornelia and my son Pompey see this slaughter, so much the more patiently, I beg, *dolor,* close in your groans: my son and my wife, if they admire my death, love me. (8.622–35)[111]

The narrator sums up Pompey's internal monologue, noting that Pompey retains control over his *mens* and his *animus* (*talis custodia Magno / mentis erat, ius hoc animi morientis habebat,* 8.635–36). He does not react to Cornelia's long and impassioned lament (8.639–61). Despite her outcries for death and as the blows continue to rain down on his back and breast, Pompey is able to keep his dignity. He does not change his placid expression even when Septimius delivers the final *coup de grâce* and severs Pompey's head only after an "unskilled" and lengthy cutting through the veins, sinews, and bones. Pompey's small psychological victory of self-control despite his horrible death is attested by those who have seen his embalmed head (8.664–67).

For many readers today, Pompey's internal monologue ruins his death. John Bramble calls it a "literary failure."[112] According to Ralph Johnson, the narration of Pompey's death from his own perspective renders it ridiculous.[113] Lucan grants the reader access to Pompey's final thoughts in order to undermine him. Thus, the brief moment of interiority is a "deliberate cheapening of what could easily have been a brief yet authentic moment of Stoic grandeur."[114] Kirk Ormand shares this sentiment that Lucan gives the reader access to Pompey's psychology in order to undermine the general's desire to die decorously: "If we did not have Pompey's inner thoughts, we would see only what he projects: a silent, stoic death."[115] According to these critics, Lucan has once again let his love of excess get the better of him. By granting us access to Pompey's mind, he ruins the final image of Pompey, and we, the readers, are shown that Pompey died as he lived, greedy for public praise and renown and full of blustery, ineffectual rhetoric. His speech, then, is a joke, and a fitting coda to the failed language in his opening address to his troops in book 2.[116] Our investigation of Seneca suggests, however, that we should not be so quick to dismiss this speech. If we can agree with Ormand that Pompey at least *projects* a "stoic death," then we should not be so distraught when Lucan shows us the means by which Pompey is able to achieve this projection. The criticisms of Pompey's last thoughts show a marked misunderstanding of Stoicism and, most important, what it takes to act stoically. A quick dismissal of Pompey's final speech as a "literary failure" cannot be justified. The speech's combination of self-apostrophe and self-command as a means to achieve self-control is precisely what we have seen in Seneca.[117]

Both Lucan and Seneca portray their heroes' dying words of self-address and self-command at the moment when political autocracy and Caesarism are born at Rome. Remarkably, although neither lived to see it, the Julio-Claudian dynasty was imagined to end in a similar fashion. Nero's reign began with Seneca scripting a monologue that he hoped the emperor would say aloud for the world to hear. It ended in a pitiful fashion, with Nero left almost entirely alone. Although he had murdered Seneca years before, in the final moments of his life Nero still remembered his old tutor's precepts. Suetonius and Dio Cassius, our two sources for the fall of Nero in 68 CE, tell a similar story of the emperor's final moments. Even as the forces of Galba close in around him, Nero remains convinced of his artistic ability, declaring before his final act of suicide, "What an artist dies in me!"[118] The two give different accounts, however, of Nero's final words. Dio dramatically makes this declaration of irrevocable artistic loss Nero's ultimate utterance (63.29.3).[119] Suetonius, on the other hand, provides a more detailed portrait of a hesitating emperor who is at times equally fearful of either fate that awaits him—capture or suicide—and who constantly seeks help and encouragement from his secretaries, the only people who remain faithful. It is while he wavers between options, according to Suetonius, that Nero mutters this famous lament to himself over and over, "What an artist dies in me!" (*qualis artifex pereo!*, 49.1). Suetonius does not grant pride of place to this famous exclamation; he is aware of another tradition. After this memorable statement of his artistic glory, Suetonius' Nero is unable to bring himself to commit suicide. Hiding out with a few faithful companions against the onslaught of Galba's troops, Nero tries to convince himself that suicide is the right action. He asks his companions to tell him how terribly he will die otherwise, he continually tests the sharpness of the blades of two daggers he has with him, and he even asks one of his men to die first so that he can see from his example how to do it. He also curses himself for his delay: "I live shamefully, inelegantly" (*vivo turpiter, deformiter*, 49.3). Then he continues in Greek, "It does not become Nero, it does not become him—one must be resolute at such times—come rouse yourself" (49.3). With that, he hears the approaching troops, quotes a line from Homer, and plunges a dagger into his neck. Nero's hand apparently wavered as he went to strike the *coup de grâce*, and Suetonius tells us that Nero's secretary Epaphroditus had to help him drive the blade home. Nero still does not die immediately. The soldiers burst in, and his would-be captors, in a scene that seems almost to be a mockery of the discovery of the half-dead Cato at Utica, now pretend to be his saviors and feign an attempt to bandage their former leader's wounds. Their halfhearted efforts are in vain, and Nero expires with a final comment on the soldiers' false loyalty (49.4). Nero's self-apostrophe is not effective. He only thrusts the dagger into his throat once he hears the horses of the centurions approaching his hideout. Despite its failure, Nero's address to himself in between his begging and pleading with his companions for help is an important attempt to gain self-control and act under his own power. Nero briefly tries to cure his own delay (*mora*), trepidation, and fear of death; he tries to get himself to act on his desire for suicide, to do what he knows is right but hesitates to do.

For a contemporary Roman audience, self-apostrophe would have had a psychological quality and was an important and familiar element of declamation and other genres. It was not simply used to imitate and echo famous literary texts. From this context, Seneca develops a more specifically philosophical theory of self-apostrophe. He begins with his audience's familiarity with this figure as canonized in epic and tragedy and as given a new form and meaning in declamation. From this general resonance in contemporary society, Seneca takes self-apostrophe and self-command and "theorizes" it, turning this literary and declamatory figure of speech into a philosophical concept. It is this form that we shall investigate in the tragedies. Several of Seneca's characters use the same language that Cato uses in *De providentia* to order themselves to commit crimes. It may initially appear that the tragedies present a "negation" of Seneca's philosophy.[120] As I argue in chapter 2, however, the tragedies contain an expansion and an investigation of this theory of command. Thus far, we have only looked at instances of self-directed commands in which people order themselves to act in a morally proper manner. Even Suetonius' Nero tries to get himself to die with some honor. In one of his *Epistles*, however, Seneca presents an important exception to this idea.

Letter 99 suggests that it is not always the case that people order the passions to come under their control and demand from themselves that they act with Stoic consistency. It is possible to order oneself to succumb to the passions.

This letter to Lucilius contains a copy of a letter that Seneca had sent to Marullus after the death of his son. After spending the first third of the letter rebuking Marullus for his excessive grief, Seneca then changes his tone and assures Marullus that he is not forbidding him from reacting to his son's death; Marullus must simply keep his outward display of sorrow within certain bounds. Seneca explains to Marullus that people are capable of producing different types of tears. There are the proper ones, generated from the sadness that one naturally feels at the loss of a loved one; then there are those that we generate ourselves. Marullus must learn the difference between these types. Thus, Seneca is not forbidding Marullus from weeping for the death of his son.[121] Such a demand would be inhuman (99.15). Seneca says that some tears will come even if we want to forbid them (*puta autem me vetare: quaedam sunt sui iuris*, 99.15); such tears are impossible to stop, so we should allow them to fall. Other tears we order to fall. These tears, produced by our own command, are censurable, not crying per se (*permittamus illis cadere, non imperemus*, 99.16). The command to weep comes, not come from any natural and unavoidable feeling of sorrow, but from our own power and from a desire for ostentation (99.16). There is a limit to the time to be allowed for grieving, after which, Seneca claims, true *dolor* no longer affects people, while ostentation does (*plus ostentatio doloris exigit quam dolor*, 99.16). Seneca offers proof to back up this claim: people only grieve excessively when they are in public. When they have an audience, people stir up their *dolor*; the passion soon leaves when they are alone.

> They wail louder when they are heard; and they are tacit and quiet while alone; but when they see someone else, they are excited to weep anew; they beat their head with their hands (which they would have been able to do more freely if there were no one stopping them), then they call death down upon themselves, then they wrap themselves up in the funeral bed: without a spectator sadness stops. (*Ep.* 99.16)[122]

In this letter, Seneca repeats the key distinction between *allowing* oneself and *ordering* oneself to do something. Yet he concedes that individuals might not always choose to order themselves to act with Stoic self-control. People who do not—those who order tears to fall and stir up their *dolor*, as in this example—are playacting; this type of self-command is more akin to theater and is only done when there is an audience. Letter 99 makes a revealing point about the extent of the power of self-command: it is also capable of controlling the passions to act "on command." In fact, as Seneca states in the *Epistles*, a form of command lies at the core of all human action: "in short, whatever we do either of vice or of virtue, we do by command" (*denique quidquid facimus aut malitiae aut virtutis gerimus imperio*, *Ep.* 106.10). The idea of specifically commanding oneself to act "irrationally" and in accordance with the passions seems an innocuous and underdeveloped theme as presented in Seneca's philosophy. It is, however, the central concept of his tragedies.

CHAPTER TWO

Self-Address in Senecan Tragedy

The characters in Seneca's tragedies talk to themselves. While this trait is not unique to Seneca, Senecan characters address themselves, their souls, or their passions with a frequency that has often attracted the comments of scholars.[1] Analyses of Senecan tragic self-address, however, have been lacking. In this chapter, I investigate the language of self-address in Seneca's tragedies, focusing on *Agamemnon*, *Thyestes*, and *Medea*, in particular. I argue that the rhetorical language the characters in these plays direct at themselves has explicit connections to Seneca's philosophy. As they plot and carry out their revenge, Seneca's characters use the language of self-address to fashion themselves, battle against psychological fluctuation, and strive to achieve consistency of mind and action.

Seneca's tragedies provide an extended look at the language of the self and an important pendant to the ideas of human psychology, action, and self-command presented in his philosophy. These tragedies do not simply portray the passions; neither Clytemnestra, Aegisthus, Atreus, nor Medea passively describes or declaims the effects of the passions and their resulting psychological turmoil. Rather, in order to act, they all must command their souls and maintain their passions. The performance of their crimes of revenge is the result of a controlled and consistent process of self-monitoring and self-shaping. These tragedies function in terms of the Stoic dichotomy between the ideal good of consistency of action and mind (*constantia*) and the psychological fluctuation and inconsistency that afflicts humanity. Seneca's tragic characters battle for *constantia*. They work to gain this paradoxical and contradictory form of consistency and criminal self-fulfillment through the language, specifically the commands, they direct at themselves. I shall focus in this chapter on Seneca's characters' imperatival method for battling psychological fluctuation (*fluctuatio animi*). For Seneca, creation and maintenance of a consistent self are intensely rhetorical, based on the repetition of the figure of self-apostrophe and self-command.[2]

This linguistic mode of self-command and self-construction is found in Seneca's tragedies as well as in his philosophical works. The form and content of Seneca's tragic characters' self-address can be directly tied not only to his theory of personality shaping but also to his philosophical *exempla*. Seneca's Cato, the paragon of Stoic virtue, and Medea, Atreus, and his other passion-driven villains speak to themselves in the same way. In his philosophy, as discussed in the previous chapter, Seneca urges his readers to struggle for consistency of action and *animus* and "to play one role" (*Ep.* 120.22). In his tragedies, Seneca presents his characters as following this advice. Yet Seneca's portrayal of the passions and the explicit thematic connections this portrayal has to his philosophy seriously challenge Stoic ideas of the passions and the psychology of vice. Rather than working toward virtue and true Stoic consistency, Seneca's tragic characters work toward a consistently vicious and passion-driven self. According to the Stoic analysis, the passions represent the paradigm of inconsistency; they cause mental fluctuation and destroy self-control. In his tragedies, however, Seneca's characters take the Stoic ideal of *constantia* and self-command, which is one of the philosophy's key therapeutic means to battle the passions, and apply them toward their own un-Stoic goal of revenge. From this very application, Seneca's characters develop a contradictory ideal of a consistency of passions and vice.

It may seem that Seneca either has lost control of or is unconcerned with Stoic ideas in his tragedies or that his two bodies of work, philosophy and tragedy, contain essential contradictions that cannot be reconciled. Yet the tragedies are directly concerned with basic Stoic beliefs about the moral dichotomy between consistency and *fluctuatio animi*, self-command and the passions. Seneca's characters apply the Stoic system to their desire for revenge in a methodical, calculated, and self-conscious way that makes it clear that the structure of the system itself is under investigation. The characters' continual use and abuse of Seneca's theory suggest that reading his tragedies and philosophy in tandem reveals a holistic portrait of human psychology. We see the full nature of the passions, vice, inconsistency, virtue, control, and *constantia* and the hidden relationships between them. These apparent oppositions exist in a dialectical relationship, and through the figure of self-apostrophe Seneca mediates key Stoic dichotomies. Moreover, Seneca's tragedies offer a means to explain the anomaly of the passions, and instead of portraying the passions as foreign and inexplicable, he shows that the Stoic consistency of virtue can be linked to the inconsistency of the passions. These opposites exist together and mutually constitute each other.[3] Indeed, his villainous characters are formed through their repeated and deliberate application of Stoic ideas to their seemingly dissonant and fluctuating actions. This use of Stoicism to achieve un-Stoic goals places the tragic characters squarely within the Stoic paradigm. The success of their revenge is dependent on, and cannot escape, Stoicism.

This criminal application of Stoicism also reveals a horrifying danger that lies at the core of Seneca's theory of self-command. As the Stoics argue, the passions are intimately related to reason and intention, spring from the will (*voluntas*) and judgment, and thus can be quelled by the application of reason.[4] In his tragedies, Seneca isolates and reveals the rational and intentional element inherent in the passions; he shows that it is possible to create a consistently vicious character by manipulating and "misapplying" Stoic ideas. Self-control and consistency lie at the core of the performance of criminal acts. The control that the characters are able to exert over their passions brings out some of the darker, unspoken implications of the famous Stoic paradox of the relationship of the passions to reason and judgment.[5] Seneca's tragedies present the problem of an agent's wanting to maintain his *ira* once he feels it fading. Be it for any of a variety of reasons, such as self-image, self-creation, or an overriding desire for revenge, how would one deal with the fact that the passions are by their very nature changeable and short-lived?[6] Is a consistency of vice and passion possible, despite Stoic doctrine's claims to the contrary? The answer, Seneca's tragedies reveal, is yes. Ironically, the means to obtain this goal are contained within Stoicism itself. These tragedies reveal that the passions, the paradigm of inconsistency and fluctuation, are built upon and maintained by an element of rational and consistent control. The rhetoric of self-command and self-control that is involved with his characters' villainous actions reveals a link between the performance of vice and virtue, passion-driven action, and Stoic *constantia*. The oppositions of *constantia* and inconsistency, vice and virtue, are not as comfortably distant as we would like to believe. I examine here how the gulf between rational Stoic control and the inconstant fluctuation of the passions is mediated and elided by Seneca's characters.[7] I argue for a direct and ultimately dialogical relationship and engagement between Seneca's philosophy and his tragedy. In fact, the assumptions and ideals about character formation, psychology, and action in the two bodies of work challenge each other.[8]

In the Senecan corpus, the performance of virtue and the performance of vice are set in the same linguistic and imperatival terms. The exact figure of self-apostrophe and self-command that is employed by Cato in *De providentia* is repeated throughout Seneca's tragedies. In *Agamemnon*, *Thyestes*, and *Medea* the characters order themselves to plot and carry out criminal revenge. Through the use of this figure in his tragedies, Seneca explores the links between *constantia*, self-fashioning, control, and the "irrational" passions. He brings these opposites together to expand upon Stoic ideas. His tragedies reveal how the passions are ultimately related to and based upon ideas of control and rationality. Seneca's characters wish to commit the ultimate crime, to do away with the virtues and all forms of morality. From this angle, Seneca's characters seem to be set in drastic opposition to any Stoic ideal. Throughout the plays, the characters' own self-descriptions can reveal a lacerating psychological fluctuation and inconsistency that confirms standard Stoic ideas about the passions. Yet Seneca's characters are not simply antitypes; rather, they present a complicated and multilayered portrayal of the passions. Thus, while they appear to perform a transvaluation of Stoic values and embrace unspeakable crimes, vice, and the passions, this "transvaluation" is in fact set in Stoic terms. The means by which Clytemnestra, Atreus, and Medea achieve their goals are paradoxically based upon Stoic ideals of consistency and self-command. The implications of this fact are twofold. On the one hand, Seneca's characters remain parasitical upon Stoicism. Despite their declarations of "going beyond" all previous crimes, they cannot break free of the moral structures they wish to destroy. At the same time, however, the tragedies reveal that Stoic control and *constantia* contain the seeds of their opposites, the ideals of criminal self-control and consistency of vice.

Letter 120: Playing One Role

In order to clarify the connection between Seneca's philosophy and his tragedies, let us look again briefly at one of his letters. Letter 120 is particularly helpful for revealing Seneca's ideas of the relationships between self, psychology, performance, and language. In this letter Seneca advocates the orthodox Stoic goal of "living consistently," defining it as a consistency (*constantia*) and concord (*concordia*) of psychology and action.[9] Letter 120 describes the ideal state of the *sapiens* and concludes with an equally vivid analysis of how distant the rest of humanity is from this goal. Seneca begins letter 120 with a response to Lucilius' desire to learn "how the notion of the good and virtue has come to us" (*quomodo ad nos boni honestique notitia pervenerit*, 120.1). Seneca claims that nature does not grant us this knowledge; rather it is something that we ourselves have to learn by analogy (120.4). We gain knowledge about virtue by watching and observing people. Seneca places Lucilius in the role of spectator, scrutinizing those he sees, looking beneath the surface of their deeds to discover the origins of their actions and the state of their psychology.[10] Lucilius is instructed to look for psychological concord and consistency of action. Of course, Seneca does not suggest to Lucilius that he can readily go out and observe perfection of self-consistency. At the end of the letter, Seneca makes it clear that the ideal of "always being the same" (120.12) in action and *animus* characterizes the Stoic wise man (120.22). As Seneca soon reveals, humanity is plagued by psychological fluctuation (*mentis fluctuatio*) and a continual instability (*adsidua iactatio*, 120.20).[11] Near the start of this letter, Seneca urges Lucilius to play the spectator and consider his observations of people acting in all areas of life. In his closing description of the human condition, Seneca collapses the concepts of actor and spectator.

Seneca begins this transition from describing how humans developed the idea of the good to describing the imperfect, inconstant state of humanity by noting that "certain people" (*quidam*) continually change who they are. Such people constantly waver back and forth, following and emulating models at opposite ends of the moral spectrum ("certain people are at times Vatiniuses, at other times Catos"), or even try to outdo (*provocant*) their own exemplar: "And now Curius is not severe enough for them, Fabricius not poor enough, Tubero not sparing enough and content enough with cheap things; now they rival Licinus with wealth, Apicius with feasts, and Maecenas with pleasurable delights" (120.19).[12] At first Seneca takes a severely condemnatory tone, stating that this inconstancy is the "greatest indication of an evil mind" (*maximum indicium est malae mentis fluctuatio*, 120.20). After quoting a passage from Horace (*Sat.* 1.3.11–17), Seneca begins to expand his discussion and specify who exactly these constantly changing people are. According to Seneca, "many people" (*homines multi*) are "never the same, nor are they even similar to themselves; and so they wander off into something contrary" (*numquam eundem, ne similem quidem sibi; adeo in diversum aberrat*, 120.21). But Seneca soon corrects himself: he did not mean to attribute this condition just to "many people"; rather, it afflicts nearly all of humanity (120.21). Everybody, Seneca says, changes their plans and wishes daily. After this confession of the true state of affairs, Seneca goes through a long list describing the sea change that afflicts humanity, causing a continual shift from one extreme to another: "Now he wants to have a wife, now a girlfriend; now he wants to rule as a king, now he acts so that no slave is more dutiful than he" (120.21).[13] This pendulous shifting between lifestyle choices reveals the underlying state of the *animus* and betrays its true nature: "Thus the foolish soul is most clearly exposed: it shows itself first this way and then that, and what I judge to be most shameful, it is unequal to itself" (120.22).[14]

Nevertheless, it is the duty of the Stoic to work toward the ideal of *constantia* and equanimity of psyche and action. Seneca describes this goal using a theatrical metaphor. We are to play one role: "Consider it to be a big thing to play one human" (*magnam rem puta unum hominem agere*, 120.22).[15] While it is in the nature of the *animus* to remain equal and consistent with itself, only the Stoic sage is characterized by this psychological stability. The rest of us are inconstant and change our form: "Except for the wise man, no one plays one person; the rest of us are multiform" (*praeter sapientem autem nemo unum agit, ceteri multiformes sumus*, 120.22). Seneca expands on this metaphor and demonstrates the problem clearly and succinctly: "We continually change our masks and take up the one opposite from the one we just took off" (*mutamus subinde personam et contrariam ei sumimus quam exuimus*, 120.22).[16] Unlike typical stage actors, however, we should not aim to have a full and ever-changing repertoire. For Seneca, virtuosity is displayed not by the range of one's parts but rather by consistency in one role. It is, as he says, a big deal to play one person (120.22). Seneca concludes this letter with an exhortation to Lucilius to strive for self-consistency: "Therefore, demand this from yourself, that you continue to be the sort of person you decided to display yourself as up until the end; bring it about that you are able to be praised, or at least that you are able to be recognized" (120.22).[17] Not trying to play a consistent role, not trying at least to ensure that you are "recognizable" (*adgnosci*), risks an existential crisis. If you do not continually struggle to remain consistent, people will not even know who you are. As Seneca puts it in the coda to the letter, "With regard to that person you saw yesterday it might rightly be asked, 'Who is this guy?': there is so great a change" (120.22).[18]

In this letter Seneca acknowledges the infamous theatricality of the age of Nero.[19] While Seneca admits that all those around him are as changeable as stage actors taking up various roles, he sets this idea against itself. Seneca uses the "standard" image of Neronian society to make his own criticism of the age and generates a new idea from a familiar model.[20] Seneca takes the love of theater, props, and behind-the-scenes changes and turns it into a portrait of consistency. From his acknowledgment that people are actors, he creates a paradoxical category of *acting* consistently, always playing one role.[21] Seneca thus unifies acting, the paradigmatic example of mutability and falsehood, and the Stoic ideal of *constantia*. Throughout letter 120, Seneca creates links between actor and spectator, psychology and action. He tells Lucilius to observe the actions of those around him and consider the psychological condition and impetus that lie behind each act. At the same time that he is observing those around him and looking for examples of *virtus* lying behind their actions, Lucilius is to strive to give his own consistent performance. There is a continual movement between the internal and the external, as the goal of *constantia* is a unity of *animus* and action. At the end of letter 120 we can discern a series of oppositions that are united in Seneca's concept of the self. Human action and acting are linked; authenticity and the mask (*persona*) are elided; acting is transformed into the ideal of acting consistently and "playing one person." The quality of remaining consistent and being the same person is equated, not with essence, but with a choice to give a continual presentation up until the "exit."[22] After reading letter 120, the question still remains, how does one strive to achieve this level of consistency and play one role? Seneca only advises Lucilius to "demand it from yourself" (*a te exige, Ep.* 120.22). As we have seen, he means this literally. For Seneca, language creates a crucial link between psychology and action. A key therapeutic way to bring the external and internal into harmony is to tell oneself, or more frequently, command oneself, to do so. Living consistently, playing one role, can be a linguistic practice.

An examination of Senecan drama shows us that the problems, goals, and cures for his tragic heroes are the same as those found in his philosophy. Each character is afflicted by psychological wavering, conflict of commitment, and changes of plans and desires. By the end of the play, after a process of self-address and self-command, Seneca's avengers—Atreus and Medea in particular—have achieved their goal of consistency and have fashioned themselves into "recognizable" figures. The "revenge tragedies" (*Agamemnon*, *Thyestes*, and *Medea*) contain the clearest and most graphic examples of characters working to stay consistent and perform actions that they explicitly declare to be self-defining. This is not to say that letter 120, or Senecan philosophy in general, provides the "key" to Senecan drama. Seneca's philosophical texts do, however, provide us with a particularly important means for understanding the significance of a characteristic feature of Seneca's dramatic language. Similar to the advice Seneca gives to Lucilius, his characters demand consistency from themselves and order themselves to play one role. This demand takes the form of self-apostrophe and self-command, and it closely parallels the language of Cato in *De providentia*. This is not to argue, however, that Seneca's philosophy is to be given a hierarchical preference over his tragedies or that in his tragedies Seneca simply illustrates his theory of self-address and self-command in meter. Rather, the rhetorical connections between the two bodies of work demonstrate that Seneca's tragic language offers both a means for understanding and a critique of his philosophical language.

Self-Command in the Tragedies

Senecan characters fashion themselves through themselves, as Florence Dupont points out.[23] This process of self-fashioning follows a consistent pattern that is known to Seneca's characters themselves. The process and the difficulties of quelling psychological *fluctuatio* are outlined by the ghost of Thyestes at the start of *Agamemnon*. The play opens with Thyestes' horrifying realization that he has returned to his ancestral home. It was in these halls that his brother Atreus killed Thyestes' sons and served them to him in a cannibal feast.[24] Now Thyestes urges his son Aegisthus to continue the familial cycle and take vengeance on Atreus' son Agamemnon. At the end of this monologue, Thyestes addresses Aegisthus in order to assure him that playing the avenger is his proper role:

> The reason for your birth, Aegisthus, has come. Why does shame weigh down your face? Why does your trembling right hand waver with uncertainty? Why

do you take counsel with yourself, why do you torture yourself, why do you ask whether this befits you? Look to your father: it is fitting. (48–52)[25]

The play opens with a model describing the psychological difficulties the characters will have. Thyestes describes the onset of conflicting feelings manifesting themselves both physically and mentally. Shame is immediately seen in the face, and action wavers in the hand as the agent ponders various plans. Finally, this conflict leads to self-introspection and self-questioning. The solution to this problem of psychological fluctuation regarding what action is fitting and proper (*an deceat*) is to look to a familial exemplar, which Thyestes commands his son to follow. This apostrophe encapsulates the difficulties that Aegisthus and Clytemnestra will experience when they enter the play. Indeed, Thyestes' description and exhortation anticipate Aegisthus' own entrance monologue and the words he directs to himself to rebuke his psychological fluctuation and urge himself on to action. This speech could easily be placed in Aegisthus' own mouth.[26] Despite these ghostly assurances of propriety of action from beyond the grave, both Clytemnestra and Aegisthus go through this process before taking their revenge.

In her initial monologue, Clytemnestra tries to persuade and command herself to continue with her plans for revenge. Her speech follows the pattern outlined by Thyestes. First, Clytemnestra recognizes her wavering resolve: "Why my sluggish soul, are you seeking safe plans? Why are you wavering?" (*quid, segnis anime, tuta consilia expetis? / quid fluctuaris?*, 108–9). She tells herself that the "better way" is closed to her; it is too late to play the chaste Penelope waiting at home. Nevertheless, as predicted by Thyestes, her thoughts turn to her sense of shame (*pudor*), as well as other concepts of virtue. "The better way is now closed off. Once you could have guarded your chaste bed and your widowed scepter with chaste fidelity; morals, law, honor, piety, and faith have perished, along with shame, which, once it dies, does not know how to return" (108–13).[27]

After this explanation that all virtue has died for her, Clytemnestra then repeatedly commands herself to carry out her revenge and offers a series of examples to follow:

> Loose the reins and, rushing forward, stir up all iniquity: through crime the way is always safe for crimes. Plan now with yourself feminine tricks—what any faithless wife out of control with blind love, what a stepmother's hands, what the

maiden burning with an unholy torch who fled the Phasian realm in that Thassalian boat dared: sword, poison—or secretly by boat flee the Mycenaean halls together with your companion. Why are you timidly talking about hiding, exile, and flight? Your sister did these things: a greater crime suits you. (114–24)[28]

The final two models for action in this series of exemplary deceit, the "stepmother's hands" (*novercales manus*) and the "maiden," refer to Phaedra and Medea respectively. But her first example of the "treacherous wife" (*coniunx perfida*) is harder to identify from the mythological tradition. In his commentary on the play, R. J. Tarrant notes the difficulty of making a positive identification. He remarks that Clytemnestra is the prototypical *coniunx perfida* and concludes that this passage seems to refer first to a generic *exemplum* and then ends with more specific ones.[29] Several Senecan characters call on themselves to live up to their own traditional reputation, however. For example, in the *Troades*, Ulixes rebukes himself for believing Andromache's story of Astyanax's death and commands his *animus* to become full of deception and turn into the "total Ulixes" (613–14). Seneca's Medea famously takes her mythical self as a model and declares at the start of the play that she will "become" Medea (*fiam*, 171). Given Senecan characters' penchant for mythical self-reference and fashioning, Clytemnestra may in fact be referring to herself here, ordering herself to get back into character and play her own role. Her opening monologue ends with echoes of Thyestes' opening psychological paradigm. She looks back to a familial model for guidance and tells herself that it suits her to outdo Helen; greater crime befits her (*te decet maius nefas*, 124). Clytemnestra concludes with the same declaration of the propriety of revenge as does the ghost of Thyestes (52, 124).

Clytemnestra's command to plunge herself headlong into vengeance (114) deserves specific attention. Clytemnestra orders herself to be consistent with her self-image and her desires, which is typically an act of rational self-control. Paradoxically, she uses this idea of consistency to give up control and act in accordance with her passions. The connection between more "Stoic" ideas of control and the paradoxical control needed for vengeance can be seen on a linguistic level throughout the exchange between Clytemnestra and the Nurse. Just as Clytemnestra orders herself to "loose the reins" (*da frena*, 114), so the Nurse commands her to "give herself time" (*da tempus ac spatium tibi*, 129). Echoing Clytemnestra's opening commands to let go of the reins (114), the Nurse's final monologue begins by repeatedly ordering Clytemestra to "rein herself in" (*regina, frena temet et siste impetus/ et quanta temptes cogita,* 203–4). The linguistic and formal parallels between these two exhortations are significant. The language of control, exemplified by the Nurse, and Clytemnestra's self-directed demands for "passion-driven" revenge are the same: both are imperatival.

In this scene, we have a complicated, two-layered portrait of the passions. In between her opening and closing monologues, Clytemnestra gives the Nurse an extended portrait of her psychological conflict at lines 131–44. She claims that her *pudor* is still "rebelling" inside her, that in order to continue with her plans for revenge she will go wherever *ira*, *dolor*, and *spes* carry her (142), and that she will "follow chance" (144). Here we have a standard, orthodox Stoic description of the passions as producing in the agent a volatile, inconstant state that takes over and renders one unable to control one's actions (see *Ira* 1.7 and 2.3–4). The fluctuation and short-lived intensity inherent in the nature of the passions are clear, especially from Clytemnestra's metaphor of clashing maritime forces (138–40). As Thyestes predicted in the prologue, the virtue of *pudor* still remains (138). Yet along with, in fact bracketing, this traditional description of the passions as taking over and forcing the agent to relinquish control (see lines 141 and 143), we have another, more complicated and problematic connection between the passions, rational self-monitoring, self-command, and the need to maintain consistency. As Clytemnestra's opening and closing monologues make clear, she has not simply surrendered to the passions and released all control from her hands (*omisi regimen e manibus meis*, 141); the process of the passions is not simply a matter of surrendering and abandoning restraint. In Seneca's tragedies the passions require self-command and consistency. Although at one point Clytemnestra describes her revenge as something irrational and out of control, she nevertheless requires a great deal of control and self-command to ensure that she carries it out. Clytemnestra must command herself to remain consistent, avenge her daughter, and kill Agamemnon. Clytemnestra must develop consistency in her passions and desire for crime. She achieves this goal by self-command. At the same time, the Nurse's language of reason and control reflects Clytemnestra's language. The Nurse commands Clytemnestra to command herself. The language for both virtue and vice is imperatival; the difference lies in which direction one orders oneself to act.

Seneca continues to investigate this process in *Agamemnon*. Aegisthus enters the play repeating his father's opening exhortation to battle against his psychological conflict and look to his family history for a model for action.

That time, which in my heart and soul I always feared, is truly at hand, the final moment for my affairs. Why do you turn your back, my soul? Why do you lay down your weapons before the first attack? Be assured that the cruel gods are preparing destruction and a dire fate: set your vile life against all punishments and meet sword and fire with your breast, Aegisthus; death is not a punishment for one so born. (226–33)[30]

Aegisthus' entrance monologue presents another crux concerning Seneca's tragic language.[31] Traditionally, scholars have interpreted Seneca's penchant for self-apostrophe as an unfortunate example of the excessively rhetorical nature of his plays, and more specifically, of how his tragedies have been corrupted by the influence of declamation. Indeed, Aegisthus' opening monologue is singled out as one of Seneca's literary low points. According to Bonner, Aegisthus' opening self-apostrophe descends *below* the level of declamation. Even the worst, most bombastic declaimer would never resort to saying, "Why do you turn your back, my soul?" (*quid terga vertis, anime?*).[32] Yet these apparent moments of bombastic self-address have crucial importance for the characters qua characters. As the characters enter the play "declaiming" their psychological conflict, they are simultaneously commanding themselves to be consistent and play their roles. These repeated instances of self-address and command provide important revelations of the psychology of Seneca's characters, which can in turn be directly related to Seneca's philosophical ideas of *constantia* and self-command. Through the repetition of the figure of self-apostrophe, Seneca investigates and expands these ideas in his tragedies. This "rhetorical" language is in fact the means by which Seneca portrays the relationship between action and the emotions.

Seneca's thinking about character formation and action remains consistent in both his philosophy and his tragedy. In letter 120 he takes images from the theater, links dramatic mutability with the Stoic ideal of *constantia*, and urges Lucilius to demand himself to play one role; similarly in his tragedies, Seneca joins his passion-afflicted and dissonant characters with self-command and consistency. Indeed, on a linguistic level, by the repetition of this rhetorical figure of self-apostrophe, Seneca draws his tragic characters together with the ultimate performance of Stoic virtue, Cato's suicide at Utica in *De providentia*. By these philosophical, thematic, and rhetorical connections, Seneca develops a portrayal of the passions and the psychology of vice that goes beyond basic Stoic theories of the passions as simply unstructured and inconstant: he develops a new image of the passions built around the Stoic ideal of *constantia*. Seneca's characters do fashion and guide themselves through their knowledge of the mythical and literary tradition, but they also seem to have read and learned from Seneca's philosophy. The language his characters direct at themselves displays an intimate knowledge of, and pathological delight in exploiting, one of Seneca's key philosophical ideas.

As noted in the previous chapter, Brad Inwood has demonstrated that in his philosophical works Seneca explores the difference between "allowing yourself to do something and commanding yourself to do it."[33] As Inwood has shown, self-directed commands in Senecan philosophy are what come closest to the modern notion of an "act of will." In Seneca, he argues, acts of will power are "portrayed as self-directed commands issued in the pursuit of moral self-control and character development."[34] According to Inwood, Senecan self-command isolates "a mental event that has an important, if not decisive bearing on action and ascriptions of responsibility."[35] In Seneca's philosophy, self-command is not simply a "mental event" but also a literal, self-directed imperative, which suggests that Seneca's own literary and declamatory tastes have influenced his theories of human psychology. As we have seen most clearly in Clytemnestra's descriptions of her psychology, it is precisely the key difference between weakly allowing oneself to follow a course of action and *commanding* oneself to follow it that Seneca investigates throughout his tragedies. Seneca's tragic characters do not issue their commands in order to strive after "moral self-control"; they do so in order to pursue their unique combination of *im*-morality and control. From these connections, we can gain an important insight into Seneca's conception of the relationship between the passions and action.[36] The passions as presented in the tragedies require a type of maintenance, monitoring, and self-command similar to the Stoic process of self-shaping and *constantia*. Clytemnestra begins and concludes her opening scene with repeated commands to herself not to abandon her plans for revenge (108–24, 192–202). She may be afflicted by intense psychological conflict, yet she knows how to battle against it and cure her mental fluctuation.

Tarrant points out in his commentary on *Agamemnon* that Clytemnestra's and Aegisthus' opening speeches are representative of a phenomenon that is evident throughout Seneca's plays.[37] As Tarrant argues, Senecan "*irati* find that their passion fails them before the critical moment."[38] They are afflicted by the psychological fluctuation and *displicentia sui* (cf. *Tranq.* 2.10) that is the "mark of a disordered personality."[39] Nevertheless, psychological instability and loss of resolve are not only the marks of *irati*, or those wholly in the grip of passion. The actions, attitudes, and psychology that define Seneca's characters are not mysterious and inaccessible. As letter 120 makes clear, psychological instability and *fluctuatio* affect the entire spectrum of humanity. Although Seneca's characters do indeed waver and are beset by fear, *pudor*, and conflicting feelings, they all have the means to fight these psychological problems. They all dramatize Seneca's advice to Lucilius and demand consistency from themselves.

It is fitting that Thyestes in *Agamemnon* should know about the difficult psychological processes that lie behind the act of revenge. In his eponymous play, Thyestes falls victim to his brother's revenge, and the ultimate success of Atreus is predicated on his ability to master himself. *Thyestes* focuses both on the power and the problems of mental command and self-transformation. At the conclusion of the play, we observe with Atreus the festal Thyestes as he unwittingly gnaws on his children's bones and drinks their blood. Atreus remarks that his brother is "unable fully to command his mind" (*nec satis menti imperat*, 919). Nevertheless, Thyestes does try. The song that Atreus listens to his brother sing contains a lengthy series of commands in which Thyestes exhorts himself to transform and send away the "old Thyestes" (*veterem ex animo mitte Thyesten*, 937).[40] In the end, Thyestes realizes why he is unable to make himself become the new and consistently happy Thyestes: Atreus has trumped him, and Thyestes acknowledges the success of Atreus' controlled transformation. As Atreus gradually reveals the full extent of his revenge, his true self is revealed and recognized by Thyestes (*agnosco fratrem*, 1006).[41] In order to reach this goal, Atreus commands himself in a fashion similar to that of the younger generation of his family in *Agamemnon*.

In a recent analysis of *Thyestes*, Alessandro Schiesaro notes that Atreus is firmly in control of the play. He argues that Atreus overpowers his brother Thyestes on several levels: Atreus is a master of language and has a cunning knowledge of the literary tradition, as well as a "deep understanding of human psychology."[42] We have already seen Atreus' ability to observe and analyze the mental weakness that lies behind Thyestes' actions.[43] For Schiesaro, Atreus' psychological understanding is best displayed by his ability to fathom Thyestes' true motives.[44] Atreus knows that his brother will willingly come back to his ancestral lands, because he wants them for himself. Thyestes' real desire is to rule and enjoy regal wealth and power; all of his claims to prefer a life of exile are false. Yet Atreus' knowledge of human psychology extends deeper to include the workings of his own mind. Atreus' literary and linguistic knowledge encompasses Seneca's philosophy and tragedies. As it is for his dramatic counterparts, the use of self-directed commands is the primary means by which Atreus is able to achieve his revenge. His knowledge of his own psychology and his ability to use language to shape and control it determine Atreus' final success and recognition.[45]

Atreus' opening monologue is a study in the process of self-transformation via self-directed commands. Throughout act 2, both in his opening monologue and in his discussion with the Satelles, Atreus repeatedly commands himself to act in conformity with his desire for revenge.[46] He enters the play describing his current state in terms of both his action, or rather inaction (*inulte*, 178), and his psychology. He rebukes himself for being "without spirit, idle, and weak" (*ignave, iners, enervis*, 176), and merely an "angry Atreus" (*iratus Atreus*, 180). Although he is a self-described *iratus*, the simple presence of the passion *ira* itself is not enough to make Atreus do what he ought to do (*debebat*, 181) and what is fitting for him (*decuit*, 183). *Ira* itself is not enough; Atreus requires a means to control his passion and transform it so that he can consistently move toward his goal of revenge. Atreus effects this transition from a state of *ira* and a desire for revenge by the continual commands to action (*age, anime, fac*, 192), which he directs at himself.[47] "Come, my soul, do something that the succeeding generations will not approve but will never keep silent about. Some unspeakable act must be dared, fierce, cruel, the type that my brother would prefer to be his—you will not avenge crimes unless you outdo them" (192–96).[48] Rather than being simply another example of Seneca's over-the-top rhetorical bombast, self-apostrophe and command reflect important psychological insights. As Atreus demonstrates, *ira* and a desire for revenge are not sufficient means for action. Atreus must command himself; these self-directed commands allow Atreus to affect his own motivation and begin the transition from desire to action.[49] By these commands, Atreus begins to become who he wants to be: no longer the *inultus*, simply angry Atreus, whose desires and actions are not consistent with each other, but rather an avenged Atreus.[50]

Medea provides the most complicated and extended investigation of self-command. Unlike Atreus', Clytemnestra's, and Aegisthus', Medea's construction of herself as criminal avenger is a continual process of self-monitoring and self-exhortation that lasts through the entire play. In this play, we also witness Medea using self-directed commands in two opposed ways. Medea commands herself to maintain the vigor of her passions. Yet unlike the other characters we have investigated, who only construct themselves through crime and strive to play a consistent role as avengers, Medea also commands her passions to subside and to "act better." Thus, Medea appears, if only briefly, to command herself in a traditional "Stoic" manner, and not in accordance with her passions. The conflict that lies at the heart of *Medea* can be traced in the opposing ways in which Medea commands herself to act. Medea's final triumph of "becoming Medea" is a hard-won process that is ultimately both determined and jeopardized by the imperative language she directs at herself.

One of the most enduring and familiar statements about Seneca's Medea is Wilamowitz's claim that she has read Euripides' *Medea*.[51] Seneca's Medea indeed seems to be aware of her own mythical and literary history; she takes strength from and models herself on her own image. Yet it is not enough that Medea promises that she will "become Medea" (171) or that she draws on the simple power of her name (166–67, 567, 910). As with Seneca's other characters, Medea's real power comes from her psychological self-knowledge. She follows a fixed and specific process of self-monitoring and self-command to ensure her successful transformation into "Medea," and, more important, to ensure that she acts like and remains Medea. Well before she declares to her Nurse what she will become, Medea begins her path of self-shaping. Like Atreus, Clytemnestra, and Aegisthus, Medea apostrophizes and commands her *animus* in her opening monologue. After calling on the gods to aid her in revenge, Medea turns from invoking divine help and directs her language at herself. She concludes with an extended series of imperatives and orders her *animus* to regain its old power: "Through the very guts seek a path for punishment, if you still live, my soul, if anything of your old power remains; drive off feminine fears and cloak your mind with the inhospitable Caucasus" (40–43).[52] Medea concludes this opening scene by urging herself to act with rage and madness: "Gird yourself with *ira* and prepare yourself with total *furor* for destruction" (51–52). Like her counterparts, Medea also declares that carrying out her criminal revenge is fitting and proper: "Greater crimes suit me now that I have given birth" (50; see also *Ag.* 52, 124, and *Thy.* 183).

The ethical implications of Senecan self-apostrophe and command can be seen by comparing the nature of Medea's imperatives in the opening monologue with those of her second speech. After hearing the opening chorus celebrate the wedding of Jason and condemn Medea to the "quiet shadows" (114), Medea begins another lengthy monologue of self-exhortation. She directs her still-developing plans for vengeance specifically against Jason's new bride (125–26). As she continues, Medea considers Jason's actions more fully, and she begins to debate with herself the level of his responsibility for this new marriage. At first Medea absolves Jason of all guilt and notes that he was powerless to act otherwise: "What could Jason have done, since he was under the authority of a foreign judge and law?" (137–38). But she immediately changes her opinion: Jason could have acted differently, and he should have killed himself rather than submit to this new marriage (138–39). Before she can finish, Medea cuts herself off and does what none of Seneca's other avengers do. She commands her passions, her *dolor*, to subside and to "speak better" (*melius, a melius dolor / furiose, loquere*, 139–40).[53] For the moment, Medea claims that the fault is entirely Creon's, and thus the full force of her vengeance will be directed at him (143, 146). Of course Medea will not remain lenient for long, and the intensity of her psychological conflict can be documented in the commands she issues to herself. In addition, Medea's self-directed commands reveal the paradoxical nature of self-command and psychological control in the tragedies. Medea uses the same imperatival language to shape and direct her actions, *animus*, and passions in two contradictory directions. Medea either orders her *dolor* to subside, as she does here, or commands herself to stir up her passions and keep herself consistently on the path of "becoming Medea." We can follow this conflict and the opposing nature of her self-directed commands throughout the play.

In her analysis of *Medea*, Helen Fyfe draws particular attention to the power of Medea's language. The other characters fear her speech and wish for her to be silent. Their fear is well justified. Fyfe points out that Medea demonstrates the objective power of her language through her magical incantation.[54] Through her magic spells, Medea is able to control the natural world and indeed the entire cosmos. Medea herself is aware of this power and draws specific attention to the imperatival force of her words, e.g., "I have sent away the shadows by the command of my voice" (*amisit umbras vocis imperio meae*, 767).[55] Medea must use her language not only to control the cosmos but also to control herself.

Medea builds to her self-declaration by first recognizing her psychological instability. The initial success of her revenge causes her to react in shock. She is able to do away with any lingering traces of remorse and love for Jason (897), however, by a continual barrage of self-commands—*sequere* (895), *quaere* (898), *para* (899), *incumbe, excita* (902), *hoc age!* (905)—culminating in her declaration "Now I am Medea" (910). Despite this apparent expression of self-fulfillment and self-completion, the specific nature of what it means to "be Medea" is not yet defined. The immediate difficulties inherent in defining herself and completing her revenge are revealed in Medea's commands to her *dolor*.[56] With the apostrophes that Medea directs to her *dolor*, we see most clearly the dual nature of control and self-command that is developed in the tragedies. Medea first commands her *dolor* to develop and perfect her revenge, to continue being Medea the infanticide: "Seek out the plan, *dolor*: to every crime you will not bring an unskilled hand" (*quaere materiam, dolor: / ad omne facinus non rudem dextram afferes*, 914–15). Once she develops her plan to kill her children, she reacts with horror. She realizes that her *ira* has left, and in place of an avenging wife, Medea the mother has fully returned.[57] "Horror has struck my heart, my limbs grow sluggish with cold, and my breast trembles. Anger has left its place, and the mother has returned entirely since the wife has been driven out" (926–28).[58]

Even though she initially declares the murder of her children to be "justly pleasing" and prepares her *animus* to get ready to perform the "ultimate crime" (922–25), Medea now denies that she could perform such an act. After she defines her psychological conflict (926–28), Medea apostrophizes her *furor* to act better: "Could *I* really pour forth the blood of my children and progeny? Better, ah better, mad *furor*" (929–30). Medea debates these two positions, whether she should complete her revenge with the "ultimate crime," as her soul continues to waver (*quid, anime, titubas?*, 937). Her passions (*ira, dolor*) and her *pietas* successively put each other to flight (943–44). Finally, she appears to secure her position as *mater* by commanding her *dolor* to subside and yield to her *pietas* (944). As she did in her second monologue and at the beginning of this debate over possible "Medeas" and courses of action, Medea again commands herself to act better (to *dolor*, 139–40; to *furor*, 930). With this command to her *dolor* (944), Medea attempts to fashion herself into someone who cannot kill her children, but rather acts "better" and in accordance with *pietas*, despite her anger and desire for revenge.[59]

With these apostrophes, it is possible for Medea to construct herself into two diametrically opposed figures. She is either one who commits the *ultimum scelus* (923) or one who yields to her motherly duty and spares her children (929–30). The methods she uses to fight her psychological impasse and bring about one of these two opposing ideas of "Medea" are consistent. In both cases, she uses identical imperatival language. Thus, at the conclusion of the play we see that the process of "becoming Medea" (*Medea fiam*, 171), "being Medea" (910), and then finally acting like Medea are all based on the same linguistic process. Indeed, as we have seen from Medea's internal debate, after her triumphant declaration of selfhood in line 910, what it specifically means to be Medea is in no way fully defined. Seneca does not let this simple statement be the end of Medea's psychological fluctuation and continuing need to control herself and her passions. Seneca does not stop focusing on and dramatizing the difficulties of Medea's self-definition. It is not enough simply to declare "Now I am Medea." In fact, as we have seen, it remains unclear even to Medea what exactly it means to "be herself." She must continually work to achieve psychological *constantia*, a unity of her psychology, her desires, and her actions. Seneca continues to couch this struggle for a consistent self in imperatival language. Here, Seneca displays the full complexity of the struggle for selfhood and reveals the paradoxically dual nature of self-command and self-control. Medea attempts to follow what she admits to be the better course by the same means with which she devises and continues with her plans for revenge. Medea commands herself to act in *both* directions. Both types of action, criminal revenge and acts of *pietas*, require and are preceded by the linguistic act of self-directed command.[60]

Medea's controlled self, guided by *pietas*, lasts only briefly. As she calls her children to her and desires to kiss and hug them (945–51), Medea is unable (or unwilling) to control her *dolor*, her *odium*, and the onset of the Furies (951–53). Instead of continuing to control her passions and ordering them to "yield to *pietas*," Medea apostrophizes her anger (*ira, qua ducis, sequor*, 953). With this declaration she becomes set on infanticide and wishes that she had borne "twice seven" (955) children, upon whom she could exact her punishment. From her description of herself as "following *ira*" and the ensuing visions of the Furies and the ghost of her murdered brother (958–66), it seems that Medea has surrendered to hallucinatory madness. Her actions are no longer her own, and she is fully in the grip of her passions and underworld powers. After her surrender to *ira* and to visions of the ghost of her brother and the Furies, however, there is a shift in Medea's language. Despite this apparent "surrender" to madness, Medea must continue to monitor and command herself to ensure that she perfects her revenge. Medea moves from commanding her brother and the Furies to control her (965–66) to commanding her brother to drive off the Furies and leave her to herself (967–69). She orders her brother to "use her hand" as she draws her sword and kills the first child as an appeasement to his soul (969–71). From these lines it would appear that Medea has relinquished all agency.[61] Left alone in a state of hallucinatory madness, she imagines that her infanticide is a way to assuage the guilt she feels for killing her brother.[62] Once Medea hears the sounds of the approaching Corinthians, however, her language shifts, and she directs her commands to herself.

> What does this sudden sound announce? Weapons are being prepared, and they seek me out for destruction. I shall climb the high rooftop of our house while the slaughter is still unfinished. You come with me as a companion. I myself shall also drag your corpse with me from here. Now do it, my soul: your virtue must not be wasted in hiding; prove to the people the deeds of your hand. (971–77)[63]

This inward shift of her language and return to a series of self-directed commands ensures that Medea will not simply complete her revenge but perform it publicly. Her language urges her to "stay in character"—her final lines reveal that she is acting as she always does (*soleo*, 1022)—and display her *virtus* before the Corinthians (*populo*, 977). While, at the end of her final monologue, Medea's language shifts back to herself, at the same time it urges her out into the public sphere. Medea commands herself to display, demonstrate, and perform her psychological control and her self-perfecting act of infanticide.

As she prepares to display her so-called *virtus* in her final performance, Medea is still plagued by intense psychological difficulties. She first appears atop the palace before her audience and claims to have achieved the ultimate level of *constantia*. She declares that she has fashioned herself *back* into her original state as the virginal Colchian princess. By regaining her former self, she has never changed (982–86).[64] This regression and return to her original self appears to be enough. Medea tells herself to go, now that her crime is complete (986), but she immediately catches herself and realizes that her revenge is not yet fulfilled. Instead of appearing briefly and quickly making her exit, Medea tells herself to continue on and perfect her vengeance as the crowd assembles: "Go, your crime is complete, but your revenge is not: continue on while your hands are at it" (987). Just as Medea has not yet perfected her revenge, so she has not yet achieved psychological consistency. Her soul immediately begins to waver, and her *ira* begins to subside. She asks herself, "Why do you now delay, my soul? Why do you hesitate? Has your powerful *ira* already fallen off?" (988–89). This time in full public view, Medea must once again control her *animus* and passions in order to act as she desires. In this final instance of psychological wavering and hesitation, Medea does not, however, command herself to continue on. Instead of the usual self-directed command, Medea reminds herself of the performance she is giving and must continue to give if her actions are to have any value. Jason must observe her: "This one thing was lacking, that man as a spectator. I think nothing of the deed as yet: whatsoever crime we have done without him is wasted" (992-24).

In the final scene of the play, Medea's self-display before Jason and the Corinthians links together two levels of performance; Medea's criminal act of infanticide is immediately preceded by her public performance of psychological control. As Medea taunts Jason before she kills their surviving child, she apostrophizes her *dolor* (1016).[65] This brief apostrophe both incorporates and inverts her earlier commands to this passion. Only seventy-two lines earlier Medea commanded her *dolor* to yield to her *pietas*, to act virtuously: (*cede pietati, dolor*, 944). Here Medea checks her *dolor* so that she does not rush to act and enjoys a controlled performance of her crime: "Fully and slowly enjoy the crime; do not hasten on *dolor*" (*perfruere lento scelere, ne propera, dolor*, 1016). With this final, paradoxical act of self-control, Medea has successfully fashioned herself into the avenging character she promised to become at the start of the play. She quickly rebukes Jason's demand that she kill him instead (1018) and stabs her child in final appeasement of her *dolor* (1019–20).

With this public performance of (passion) control and revenge, Medea surpasses even Atreus. Despite the praise he heaps on himself at the end of *Thyestes*, Atreus laments that he did not perform his revenge publicly before the victims. Unlike Medea, who ends by commanding herself not to complete her act too hastily, Atreus regrets that he rushed along; he was not fully in control of his passions and thus cheated them: "From the very wound, I ought to have poured the hot blood into your mouth, so that you might drink the blood of the living—my *ira* was deceived while I hastened on" (1054–57; see also *Med*. 1016: *ne propera, dolor*).[66] Although she must command herself, often in conflicting directions throughout the play, in the end Medea gives a superior performance of psychological control and revenge. As Medea prepares to exit, she demands that Jason observe and recognize her: "Lift up your swollen eyes, ungrateful Jason. Do you recognize your wife?" (1020–21). Her question is reminiscent of Thyestes' terrible realization and reply to Atreus' revelation of the remainder of his children's bodies: "I recognize my brother" (*agnosco fratrem*, 1006). *Thyestes* and *Medea* end with the avenging characters being recognized by their victim; for both Medea and Atreus, this final recognition is the result of their successful ability to demand consistency of psyche and action from themselves.

In *Agamemnon*, *Thyestes*, and *Medea*, a series of oppositions are juxtaposed and ultimately united: soul and action, psychological control and the irrational passions, *constantia* and crime, allowing action versus commanding it. This paradoxical unity is based on the "rhetorical" language of self-apostrophe and self-command. Through the continual repetition of apostrophe, Seneca provides a sustained investigation of the springs of his characters' self-creation, self-monitoring, and action. The process of striving for consistency through self-address and self-command is based on Seneca's ideas of how humans act and how they come into being. Thus, Seneca brings together his final dichotomy: philosophy and tragedy. *Agamemnon*, *Thyestes*, and *Medea* give a holistic view of Seneca's philosophical ideas of psychology, consistency, and selfhood. In these tragedies, the psychology of vice is dissected and shown to be no different from "rational" psychology and action. *Furor, ira, dolor*, madness, and the passions are not simply irrational, out of control, mysteriously inexplicable forces. Each of Seneca's characters must maintain his or her passions, and this maintenance follows a specific process of self-monitoring and linguistic performance. The language of virtue and vice, control of the passions and "rational" Stoic self-control and *constantia*, does not vary between Seneca's philosophy and his tragedy; both are based on self-address and self-command.[67] In his tragedies, Seneca is neither negating, inverting, nor denying his philosophical ideals; rather, he is expanding them.[68] He renders vice and *nefas* part of his known and mapped psychological territory. Despite their claims of outdoing all former crimes and their desire to surpass all others in evil, Seneca's characters can only become who they are and act in accordance with their desires by following a fixed and defined process of psychological self-monitoring and self-command.[69] They cannot step outside of this linguistic system of Stoic self-creation as they struggle for criminal perfection and psychological consistency of vice. As they urge themselves on to vengeance, Medea, Atreus, Clytemnestra, and Aegisthus all use the same rhetorical self-apostrophe and imperatival language as Cato, Seneca's ultimate Stoic exemplar. Seneca's characters depend on Stoicism to achieve their goals, but, through their repetition of Stoic forms and language, they also create a deadly new category that links vice with *constantia*. It is at these moments, when his characters seem to be at their most bombastic and theatrical, that Seneca performs a probing analysis of the possibilities of Stoicism and human psychology.

CHAPTER THREE

Self-Address in the *Satyricon*

As noted in the introduction, there is a striking interplay of narrative themes as Seneca and Encolpius relate their travels. Just as Seneca writes of himself as the "seasick Ulysses," so Encolpius bills himself as Polyaenus, hounded by the divine wrath of Priapus. When Seneca has his lodging above a bathhouse, he hears the bothersome shouts of the ball counter. As Trimalchio exercises in the baths, he employs his ball counters in a new and "revolutionary" way. As Seneca travels by Vatia's villa near Cumae, he describes it as the underworld home of the living dead. Encolpius is trapped in the hellish labyrinth of Trimalchio's home, which like Hades is easy to enter but difficult to leave.[1] I shall resist the temptation to write about a postmodern meeting of Seneca with Trimalchio and Encolpius in Campania. My point in drawing these connections is to show how both Seneca and Petronius construct their narratives around similar themes and topoi. If we can step back from viewing Seneca as the stern Stoic moralist and appreciate him in his unfamiliar role as fool, self-satirist, and travel writer, then it does not seem out of place to de-familiarize Petronius and read him for the philosophical undertones of Encolpius' narrative of his travels around southern Italy. Here, I focus on four main passages from the

Satyricon that, I argue, take the Stoic *meditatio* and bring it down to the lower stratum of the body. Instead of focusing on shaping souls, these passages focus on the genitals and eros and on the stomach and digestion. They problematize the nature of the *meditatio* as a form of self-shaping and question whether this process is a confession of the truth or a means of self-deception.

By reading Seneca and Petronius in tandem, I am not attempting to revive the old view of "Petronius the Moralist."[2] I realize that by analyzing Petronius' fools under a Stoic lens I run the risk of using them as Seneca uses his wife's fool, Harpaste, in letter 50, that is, as ready-made tools for moralization. My main task is to illustrate and elucidate a level of the text of the *Satyricon* that is too often ignored or declared to be simply a "philosophical parody." Just as Seneca is able to confess that he does not have to look far if he wants to be entertained by a fool, for he can laugh at himself (*Ep.* 50.2), so I look at Petronius' fools and investigate what they have to say about the self. As Gareth Schmeling notes, the fragments of the *Satyricon* bear witness to the fact that the larger whole may have been written as a "confession" by Encolpius as he looked back on his life.[3] We will never know whether Encolpius, like Lucius in the *Metamorphoses* or Augustine in his *Confessions*, gained any knowledge or enlightenment, let alone transformation or religious conversion. Rather than entertaining hypotheses about the larger structure of the narrative, I focus on specific instances of self-confession and address within the surviving fragments in order to demonstrate the interplay between self-creation and narrative creation.

While Encolpius' narrative purports to relate the candid truth about what people do, and Seneca's *Epistles* give the appearance of a real series of letters written while abroad from Rome, we must always bear in mind how both these texts create this representation of reality.[4] The two authors construct this representation similarly in terms of both form and content. Both Seneca and Petronius construct their texts by interrupting the prose narrative with poetic composition and quotation. Each author creates his works from a bricolage of rhetorical, philosophical, and literary topoi to fashion something new and greater. Seneca describes his process of composition in terms of an economic metaphor of testamentary exchange. He views the discoveries of past ages as a great inheritance that he must manage like a good paterfamilias. He must work to make this intellectual patrimony greater and then pass it on to posterity.[5] Closer to the *Satyricon*'s focus on the consumption and expulsion of food and literature, Seneca also describes his creative process in alimentary terms

(*Ep.* 84.5–6). Although Encolpius defends his work to the Stoic Catos as a simple narration of reality (*quodque facit populus*, 132.15.4), this stance is itself a topos.[6] As several critics have demonstrated, the characters in the *Satyricon* view their lives in terms of the great moments of literature. They are declamatory time bombs ready to react to the mundane and sordid events of their lives with a gesture and a flourish that apes and degrades the classics. Petronius' characters' manipulation of literary topoi is not simply the act of unknowing fools whose minds have been warped and corrupted by declamation and the entire "Silver Latin" literary milieu.[7] Rather, the characters' misuse of literature and philosophy is frequently a self-conscious act that locates the process of self-construction in the netherworld between truth and fiction.[8]

Self-Address and Eros I: Encolpius to Himself

Both Seneca and Encolpius vividly relate the travails of their travels. After his letter written from above the bathhouse, Seneca writes about his trip from Baiae back to Naples. This is the last letter in the first group of letters, which recount his travels around Campania (*Ep.* 49–57). Since he had such an unpleasant journey by sea (*Ep.* 53), he travels by land and takes the shortcut through the Crypta Neapolitana (*Ep.* 57).[9] This choice only leads to new forms of inconvenience. First he is covered with mud as he travels along the open road. Then he is surrounded by dust and darkness as he passes through the tunnel. In the middle of this dark, foul, and "new" type of journey, Seneca directs his attention to his soul. He feels that it has received a blow, but this change has occurred "without fear" (57.3). This must be something similar to what the wise man experiences, he surmises. The wise man, Seneca confesses, will still change color, and his hair will stand on end when, for example, he looks out over a vast chasm. These reactions do not signify fear but rather are "natural" reactions and cannot be defeated by reason.[10] Once Seneca returns to the light, he begins to speak to himself about the fear of death, specifically about the fear of dying by being crushed by a mountain (57.6). Buried underneath the mountain, Seneca experiences the lot of the soul trapped in the dark prison of the body.[11] This experience leads to self-dialogue as Seneca, ever the watchful and self-monitoring Stoic, considers his own emotional reactions and then the nature of the soul itself.

Likewise, Encolpius' journey by sea out of the Bay of Naples leads him to investigate his emotions. Soon after his reunion with Giton, Encolpius learns that he has another rival for the boy's affections: his new companion, the poetaster and sham philosopher Eumolpus. The two fight angrily over Giton. Once Encolpius and Eumolpus are reconciled, the three, along with Eumolpus' servant, set off for the harbor to leave Campania by ship. After a break, the text resumes with Encolpius considering his new love triangle. Buried inside the ship, he turns to self-dialogue. Unlike Seneca, however, Encolpius does not discuss fear of death and the nature of the soul. Rather, he tries to convince himself not to be bothered by Eumolpus' sexual interest in Giton.

> "It's bothersome that the boy is pleasing to the stranger. What then? Are not the best things those that nature made held in common? The sun shines for everybody. The moon, accompanied by countless stars, also leads the wild beasts to food. What can be called more beautiful than water? Nevertheless, it flows as public property. So only love will be a theft rather than a right? Yes indeed, I do not wish to have goods except those that make people envious. He is one person, and an old man, it won't be difficult; even when he wants to take something, he'll betray his act by his panting." I put forward these things less than confidently, and I deceived my dissenting soul. I buried my head in my tunic and began to pretend I was asleep. (*Sat.* 100.1–2)[12]

As J. P. Sullivan points out, Encolpius' platitudes on the communal goods of nature parodies similar points Seneca makes in the *Epistles*.[13] For Sullivan, the erotic context deflates Encolpius' initial moralizing. In addition to these connections, it is possible to look for deeper links between Encolpius' self-address and Seneca's prescriptions for the practice. In fact, Encolpius' *meditatio* about Giton comments directly on Seneca's description of his own nightly self-investigation in *De ira* 3.36. Encolpius' self-address, in which he considers why he refuses to share Giton's love, comes after a day of anger. Prior to their reconciliation, the *ira* of Encolpius was the dominant theme. As soon as Encolpius realizes that Eumolpus is interested in Giton, he regrets that he no longer has his sword (which was taken by a "soldier," 82.4). Otherwise, he would busy his soul (*animus*) in the blood of Eumolpus (94.3). His anger (*ira*, 94.4) is briefly allayed when Giton leaves. Nevertheless, he soon confesses that he is easily prone to anger (94.5), and he threatens Eumolpus, "Imagine that I am raving mad, yield to insanity, that is to say, leave quickly" (94.6).[14] After they reconcile, Encolpius offers Eumolpus some reflections on *ira* and its relationship to the soul. He asks Eumolpus to remove the irritation (*scabitudinem*) from his soul and heal it so that it does not show a scar (*sine cicatrice*), as is fitting for a "master of all good arts" (99.2).[15] This ability would surpass even that of the Stoic *sapiens*. In *De ira*, Seneca notes that according to Zeno, even after the soul of the wise man has been healed, the scar of the passions will remain (*cicatrix manet*, 1.16.7 = *SVF* 1.215). In addition, Encolpius describes the place of anger in people's minds (*mentes*) by making use of a geographic metaphor: "Just as snow clings longer to uncultivated and harsh regions and leaves quickly from plowed lands, so anger sits in people's breasts. It takes possession of untamed minds, but it falls out of the educated" (99.3). In *De ira* Seneca also relates the passions to the landscape of the soul. Seneca counters his interlocutor's argument that the fierce native characteristics of the Germans and the Scythians prove that *ira* is a noble trait by noting that these nations are naturally prone to anger and hence need to be softened and tamed (2.15.1). He notes that empire is usually in the hands of those who live in a milder climate: "Those who turn toward the cold and the north have 'untamed characters,' as the poet says, 'most similar to their own climate'" (2.15.5).[16]

Furthermore, the tenets of Seneca's *meditatio* in *De ira* are inverted by Encolpius. Both Seneca and Encolpius engage in nocturnal self-investigation and dialogue. Whereas Seneca declares that this practice of investigating the soul results in a deep, free, and tranquil sleep, Encolpius can only pretend to be sleeping.[17] Seneca conceives of the *meditatio* as a court of the self, in which he daily pleads his case to himself (3.36.3). As such, Seneca's *meditatio* is a confession of the truth, he scrutinizes his entire day, he hides nothing from himself, and he passes over nothing (3.36.3). For Encolpius, on the other hand, the *meditatio* is said without any confidence (*fiducia*) and serves as a means to deceive his still wavering soul (100.2). As if to show how useless this act is, Encolpius says that when the familiar voices of his enemies Lichas and Tryphaena strikes his "palpitating soul," his *constantia* is immediately destroyed (100.3–4). The aspect of Encolpius' *meditatio* that would most likely give Seneca palpitations, however, is the purpose for which he uses it. Encolpius is trying to relieve his concerns about Eumolpus as a rival for his boy lover. Seneca, however, places his *meditatio* squarely in a conjugal context. He states that he begins his self-investigation once his wife has fallen asleep (3.36.3). Thus, we see a debate not only on the value of the *meditatio*—is it a helpful act of self-confession or is it a worthless act of self-deception?—but also on the role *eros* plays in the care of the self.

One of the main critiques of the Foucauldian picture of the care of the self is that it only involves philosophical and medical texts, so-called normative discourses. Foucault's picture of calm reflection and valorization of conjugal love is immediately revealed as one-sided at best when literary texts are brought under consideration. As Simon Goldhill has shown, the relationship between care of the self and erotic desire changes radically when the Greek novels from the Second Sophistic are brought into play.[18] Daniel McGlathery has also demonstrated Foucault's unjustly brusque treatment of the Roman novels. Foucault laments the "lack of 'seriousness'" in the works of Petronius and Apuleius. As McGlathery shows, Foucault's comments about the Roman novels demonstrate that "he subscribes to a limited view of parody as a derivative exercise, a petty or pejorative imitation of an original rather than a creative and fertile artistic exercise."[19] Along similar lines, Paul Allen Miller has argued forcefully that the "lyric consciousness" of Catullus' poems does not fit the portrait of the calm *meditatio* portrayed in the pages of Seneca and heralded by Foucault as demonstrating a new and important moment in the development of the self. Significantly for our purposes, Miller focuses on Catullus' poems of self-address, or "interior monologues." For Miller, poems such as 8, 70, 72, and 76 are characterized by self-division. While Catullus is clearly trying to care for himself, the subjectivity presented in them cannot be seen as a calm and rational *meditatio*.[20]

Poems 8 and 76, where Catullus tries first to harden himself and then to cure himself of the "disease" of his love, are built around self-address and command.

> Wretched Catullus, stop playing the fool, and consider what you see to have perished to be destroyed. (8.1–2)

> Now she no longer wants you: you also, although powerless, don't want her, and don't continue to pursue her as she flees, nor live like a wretch any longer, but endure through it all with a resolute mind, be firm. (8.9–11)

In the middle of poem 76, Catullus also employs self-address and self-commands to harden his *animus*.[21]

> Why don't you harden your soul and take yourself away from here and stop being wretched, since even the gods do not want you to be? It is difficult to suddenly place aside a long love; it is difficult, but you must do this by any means necessary: this is your one safety, this must be conquered by you, this you must do, whether or not it is possible. (76.11–16)

As Miller rightly points out, the lyric and amatory tradition of self-address must be taken into account when constructing a portrait of the ancient care of the self. Indeed, the lover's lamenting self-address can be traced back at least to Theocritus' Cyclops (11.72–79).[22] This connection would seem to be a problem for Seneca *philosophus*, and as Miller has well argued, it provides an important challenge to the normative presentation of self-address in his philosophy. As we saw in the previous chapter, however, the calm, cool, collected presentation of the *meditatio* is exploded by Seneca himself in his tragedies. Clytemnesta, Aegisthus, Atreus, and Medea all command themselves to commit acts of revenge because the bonds of conjugal love have been broken. Martha Nussbaum has argued powerfully that *Medea* questions many of the Stoic strictures on erotic passion and demonstrates the triumph of love.[23] Medea herself notes that her past crimes are not the result of anger, but of love (*saevit infelix amor*, 136). *Hercules* opens with Juno's monologue lamenting how she can only be properly called Jupiter's sister. Her place as wife has been given to a series of "mistresses" (*paelices*, 1–5). After fainting in the presence of Hippolytus, Phaedra commands her soul to confess her love (592–99). Thus, Senecan drama is deeply concerned with the potentially lacerating effects of eros on the self.

By contrast, Seneca's philosophy focuses on the conjugal relationship and puts forth as the model the wise man who avoids the dangers of passions by loving his wife "deliberately" (*De matrimonio*).[24] Even in his prose works, however, Seneca is aware of the other side of the mirror, so to speak. In the *Natural Questions*, Seneca also tells the story of the debauched Hostius Quadra. Although he begins his story noting that Hostius met his proper end—he was murdered by his slaves, and the crime was not even avenged by Augustus (*Q Nat.* 1.16.1)—Seneca concludes by granting Hostius a brief monologue in which he explains the method and rationale behind his sexual practices (1.16.7–9). Like his tragic characters, Seneca's Hostius outlines his intentions and the reasons for his "deviant" actions. In addition, Hostius' monologue problematizes philosophical ideals. As several scholars note, Hostius' use of distorting mirrors so that he can fully appreciate his acts and can knowingly deceive himself into believing that the sizes of things reflected are real debases the philosophic project of self-knowledge.[25] As Seneca has Hostius declare, he uses these mirrors so that no one will think that he does not know what he is doing (*Q Nat.* 1.16.7). Hostius' libidinous monologue exists at the pole opposite Seneca's normative portrait of his own practice of self-knowledge at *De ira* 3.36. Similarly, Encolpius also deconstructs the normative aspects of the *meditatio*. Unlike Seneca's Hostius or the characters investigated in chapter 2, Encolpius does not voice his desire to commit crimes that surpass the limits of nature.

Encolpius' *meditatio*, however, cannot cure his psychological anxiety. Indeed, as the text progresses, Encolpius soon moves from taking the stance of the aggressive Catullan poet to taking that of the impotent Ovidian elegiac lover. Yet throughout his difficulties with Giton, Eumolpus, and eventually Circe, Encolpius continues to talk to himself to try to cure his problems.

Self-Address and Eros II: Encolpius to Himself, Again

"Believe me, brother, I do not perceive myself to be a man; I don't feel it. That part of my body with which I once was Achilles is dead," Encolpius admits to Giton (129.1). This confession comes after his failed attempts with Circe and Giton, who states that Encolpius loved him with "Socratic faith" and that Alcibiades did not remain as untouched when he lay with Socrates (128.7). Encolpius imagines himself as the Ovidian *miles amator*. The impotent condition of his body, however, forces him to play the role of the "chaste" philosopher. I argue that Encolpius' amatory pursuit of Circe combines the heroic and erotic world of elegy with the philosophical care of the self. The irony of this combination is twofold. First, except for his brief night of happiness with Giton after leaving Trimalchio's, we never see Encolpius live up to the reputation he claims for himself. Second, Encolpius appropriates the care of the self in order to solve physical rather than psychological problems. Indeed, his philosophical self-dialogue does not appear to work. In the final sections, which deal with his amatory plight at Croton, Encolpius abandons it and turns again to magic. We never learn the source of the cure for his impotence, although in a brief and apparently disconnected fragment Encolpius himself attributes it to Mercury the psychopomp, who leads souls to the other world and brings them back (140.12).[26] As we have seen, Encolpius' *meditatio* on board Lichas' ship not only inverts the tenets of *De ira* 3.36 but also proves to be worthless in granting any sort of confidence (*fiducia*) or *constantia*. Encolpius himself admits that he is only using it to deceive his soul, and instead of the deep calm that Seneca promises, he can only feign sleep (*mentiri*). Nevertheless, while in Croton, Encolpius frequently turns to self-dialogue.

After escaping from Trimalchio's feast, the civil strife aboard Lichas' ship, the storm, the shipwreck, and the death of the ship's captain, Encolpius, Giton, Eumolpus, and Corax set off from the seashore. After climbing a mountain, they find themselves gazing upon a nearby town set on a high peak. A passing manager of one of the area's country estates (*vilicus*) informs them that the town is Croton, "a most ancient city and once the first of Italy" (116.3). When they ask what type of business would be most lucrative now that the inhabitants' wealth has been worn down by frequent wars, the *vilicus* warns them to look for another area if they are businessmen. The city they are considering entering does not value the standard forms of commerce, nor the arts of literature and rhetoric, nor traditional morality. Although the city's wealth has been destroyed by wars, a civil war continues within it over the exchange of personal wealth and the granting of legacies (116.6). The *vilicus* ends his famous description of Croton by saying, "You will enter a town that is just like plague-ridden fields, in which there is nothing except corpses torn apart or crows that tear them" (116.9). Eumolpus is intrigued by the "newness" of this social situation. Although he wishes he had more elaborate theatrical elements, he nevertheless begins to form his plan to compose a "mime" of the shipwrecked and childless sick old man (117.1–10).[27]

Encolpius admits that Eumolpus' performance of their "play" is a big hit in Croton and that each day he fattens his body more and more with the ever-flowing goods that the *captatores* shower upon him (125.1–2). Eumolpus is "full of happiness" (*felicitate plenus*) and begins to think that fortune is no longer concerned with him. Despite this apparent good luck, Encolpius admits that he thinks about his situation more often than he is accustomed to doing. With his own version of the philosophical *praemeditatio futuri mali*, Encolpius wonders about the future evils that he might face:

> What if a clever legacy hunter sends a spy into Africa and discovers our lie? What if even Eumolpus' hireling, tired of the present happiness, discloses the truth to his friends and uncovers the entire lie by means of an envious betrayal? Surely we'll have to flee again, and our poverty, which had finally been fought off by this new form of mendacity, will be called back. Gods and Goddesses, how terrible it is for those living outside the law: whatever they deserve they always expect. (125.3–4)[28]

This speech moves from considering the possible results of the discovery of the lies that are being perpetrated on the inhabitants of Croton to Encolpius' own confession of the truth. He admits that he is living "outside the law."

Nevertheless, Encolpius' performance as Eumolpus' slave is credible. He takes the Odyssean name Polyaenus and catches the eye of the wealthy woman Circe.[29] These scenes are based on a paradoxical union of false identities and confessions of the truth. When Encolpius first sees Circe, he addresses Jupiter in a brief poem of elegiac couplets and wonders why he has thrown away his weapons and become a silent fable in heaven. Now would be the time for him to "dissimulate" by turning himself into a bull or a swan, because the "real" Danae is present (126.18). Indeed, Encolpius soon grants himself the Iliadic role of Zeus making love to Hera atop Mount Ida (14.346–51), but once these characters try to move to the "robust pleasure," it becomes time to confess the truth to each other.[30] Despite a lacuna, it is clear that Encolpius is unable to perform. The text picks up again with Circe asking, "Do my kisses offend you? Do I have bad breath? Do my armpits stink? If it's not these things, are you afraid of Giton?" (128.2). Encolpius can only blush and answer that he has been harmed by poisoning (128.2). After another break, Circe turns to her slave to discover the truth about what she did wrong (128.4). She does not wait for an answer, however, but turns to self-speculation. She picks up a mirror, makes "all the faces that usually create a simile among lovers," and then sets out for the temple of Venus (128.4).[31] By contrast, Polyaenus/Encolpius begins to question his *animus* about whether he was cheated out of true pleasure (128.5).[32]

More "confessions of the truth" come; this time they take the form of an exchange of letters. While the amatory letter would already have been familiar from Ovid's *Heroides*, it is here that for the first time in Latin we see this theme written in prose.[33] Circe's letter cites the authority of doctors (*medici*, 129.5) and offers a remedy to Encolpius: he should sleep apart from Giton for three nights (129.8). She concludes by noting that her mirror does not lie; it has granted her a true vision of herself (129.9). After Encolpius reads this letter, Chrysis suggests that a letter from Encolpius, written with sincere kindness (*candida humanitate*), can restore the soul of Circe (129.11). She also must confess the truth to Encolpius; since her rejection, Circe has not been herself (129.11). Encolpius then begins his letter outlining the truth about himself and his transgressions. He writes, "I confess, mistress, that I have often done wrong; for I am a human and still young. . . . You have a confessing criminal; whatever you order, I deserve. I've committed treason, I've killed a man, I've violated a temple" (130.1–2).[34] He then adopts the theme of the soldier-lover to explain his impotence (130.4).[35] This pose soon turns into a confession of ignorance concerning the underlying cause of his impotence. Nevertheless, Encolpius offers two possibilities that suggest that his *animus* or his desires were not in harmony with his body (130.5). After this letter's confessions, Encolpius sets out to care for his "guilty body" (130.7).

Encolpius gives a detailed account of the care he takes to ensure that when he visits Circe the next day he has suffered no injury to mind or body (131.1). As part of his evening regimen of mental and physical preparation, Encolpius decides to skip his usual bath and has only a light rubdown. He eats strength-giving foods, onions and snail heads without sauce. He drinks only a small amount of wine with his meal. He composes himself for bed by taking a leisurely stroll before turning in. Finally, he makes the ultimate sacrifice during this brief program of self-care: he goes to bed without Giton (130.8). The next morning it is unclear, however, to what extent Encolpius' care of the self has helped him. Apparently not trusting in Polyaenus/Encolpius' abilities to cure himself, Circe sends a "little old lady" (131.2) along with Chrysis. Before they bring him to Circe, the old lady immediately goes to work on Encolpius by performing a Priapic magic spell. She then tests the strength of Encolpius' loins, which immediately "obey the command" (*dicto citius nervi paruerunt imperio*, 131.6). Thus, we are unsure of the source of this bodily obedience. Was the care Encolpius took the night before a necessary part of the cure? Or should it all be attributed to magic? After Encolpius' second failed attempt with Circe, perhaps the answer is that neither have any efficacy. This time Circe has no sympathy; she orders Encolpius to be punished by her slaves and spinning maidens. Along with Chrysis and the old lady, whose charm was obviously only temporarily effectual, he is thrown out the door while being beaten and spat upon (132.2–5).

Encolpius' next attempts at a cure do not involve the careful austerity of the night before. Blurring the lines between self-fashioning and self-destruction, Encolpius turns "all the fire of his anger against that part which had been the cause of all evils" (132.7). Three times Encolpius takes up the terrible two-bladed axe; three times he is unable to achieve his goal. Encolpius' Vergilian attempts at self-castration have been widely chronicled by scholars. As many note, Encolpius' three failed efforts (132.8.1–2) are reminiscent of Aeneas' attempts to embrace the ghosts of Creusa (2.792) and Anchises (6.700).[36] As the rest of the poem makes clear, Encolpius' lack of success is due to the conflict between his desire and his ultimate physical inability to carry out the deed. Rather than the typical wavering of the hand or *animus*, which can be found frequently in Seneca's tragedies, here the effects of Encolpius' conflict render him physically unable to carry out his punishment. The "victim" has shrunk so far back into Encolpius' loins that no matter how strong his desire, performing the act of castration would now be impossible (132.8.4–6). Encolpius continues to try to remedy himself. He turns to words, which he claims are able to hurt more (132.8).

Sitting up in his bed, he castigates (*contumacem*, 132.9) the defiant member with an oration, which he pours forth in his anger (*haec ut iratus effudi*, 132.11):

> "What do you have to say," I asked, "you shame of all the gods and men? For it is not even proper to name you among serious things. Did I deserve this from you, that after I was placed in heaven you drag me down to hell? Or that you should betray my years that flourish with the first strength of youth and place upon me the lassitude of extreme old age? I ask you, give me a clear and lengthy proof outlining your case." (*Sat.* 132.9–11)[37]

The languidly silent "response" is narrated in a quotation of three Vergilian lines that brilliantly fuse Dido's disdain for Aeneas when they meet in the underworld (*Aen.* 6.469–70) with a combination of two half-lines from *Eclogue* 5.16 and *Aeneid* 9.436 describing pliant plants (132.11).[38] Critics frequently place Encolpius' speech within the tradition of impotence poems, often citing Ovid's *Amores* 3.7 as the main source.[39] Others have focused on how the Vergil cento demonstrates that Encolpius once again tries to see himself in epic terms, only to reveal to the reader the distance between the heroic world and his own mundane impotence.[40] While Encolpius' quotations of Vergil in the context of self-castration and impotence may seem to be the nadir of his abuse of high literature, at the same time he is also concerned about the propriety of his words.[41] Furthermore, for all his literary posturing throughout the *Satyricon*, the role of the impotent Ovidian lover in *Amores* 3.7 is the one role that Encolpius refuses to take on. Thus, by means of this process of self-address and self-command, Encolpius thinks about not only the propriety of his language but also the relationship between language, the passions, and self-construction.[42]

Like Seneca's philosophical exemplars and tragic characters, Encolpius commands himself. Yet here the idea of "rousing oneself to action" takes on a new, erotic meaning. Seneca writes of the need to harden the soul by means of continual *meditatio*, saying, for example, in *De ira* that "all the senses must be led to firmness" (3.36.1).[43] For Encolpius, self-command is quite literally a means of self-arousal. He uses this technique to achieve bodily hardness.[44] Encolpius' engagement with Seneca goes deeper than sexualizing the role of self-command. He does not simply command his body to "rouse itself." Rather, he envisions a self-dialogue and a juridical confession of the truth. Encolpius begins his invective with a series of accusations and then demands that a justification for his member's (non)action be returned. This demand contains specific and technical oratorical language. Encolpius wants more than an answer: he wants an *apodixis*. This Greek grammatical term, rarely used in Latin, is defined by Quintilian as a "clear proof" (*evidens probatio*, 5.10.7).[45] This idea of a forensic court of the self also bears a strong resemblance to Seneca's description of his own self-investigation in *De ira* 3.36. As he notes, anger must be brought before a judge (*ad iudicem esse veniendum*, 3.36.2). Each day Seneca conducts a trial with himself (*cotidie apud me causam dico*, 3.36.3). He notes that the soul must be called to give an account of itself. Encolpius, in turn, asks for the same from his body (*ad rationem reddendam vocandus est*, 3.36.1; *apodixin... redde*, 132.10). In addition, Encolpius adopts the language of morality. He asks for a response from his offending member, calling it "the shame of all gods and men," and notes that it "is not lawful to be named in serious affairs" (132.9).

After his travesty of Vergil, Encolpius admits that he regrets speaking so shamefully. He blushes over the fact that he spoke with a part of the body that "more serious men" do not even think about (132.12). For all his ridiculous posturing throughout the text of the *Satyricon*, this is the first time that Encolpius reveals any concern for the "appropriateness" of his language. The only literary gestures that bother him are self-address and self-command. He does, however, start to think about his use of language. After he rubs his brow for some time (132.13), an action that looks proleptically to the Catos with their furrowed brows, the result of Encolpius' considerations is yet another self-address. This time he offers his own metapoetic theory of the practice.

> "But what evil have I done," I ask, "if I lighten my pain and sadness with a natural invective? Or what is there in the human body that makes us curse our stomachs or our throats when they are in pain more often than usual? What? Did not even Ulysses litigate with his heart, and do not certain tragic characters castigate their eyes as if they could hear? People with gout curse their feet, people with arthritis their hands, those with eye ailments their eyes, and those whose toes often hurt them bring whatever sadness and pain they have down upon their feet." (132.13–14)[46]

In this short speech Encolpius comments on both self-address and the practice of literary appropriation and "gesturing" that he and his compatriots perform throughout the *Satyricon*. He suggests that the two are intimately related. Encolpius justifies his address by first noting that there is something in human nature that makes us speak to our bodies when they are in pain. He then turns to examples from epic and tragedy, but he immediately offers a series of other examples from everyday life: people with gout, arthritis, eye ailments, and even those who stub their toes.[47] This juxtaposition and instant collapse of literature into the mundane provides *in nuce* the *Satyricon*'s process of literary appropriation.

Encolpius defines self-apostrophe and self-command as a natural form of discourse (*naturali convicio*, 132.13). He declares it to be a means to "lighten the load" (*exoneravi*) of physical and mental *dolor*. This form of self-invective, Encolpius suggests, is a natural human response, a linguistic event that seems to be a hard-wired reaction for remedying bodily pain. When our belly or throat or head hurts, we regale against it with the implicit hope that it might make the pain go away.[48] Or in Senecan terms, we address our *animus* when we are acting inappropriately and want to change. Petronius shows that Seneca's therapeutic language of psychological command is ultimately related to the everyday language of the body and also demonstrates how Seneca takes a literary topos and turns it into the basis of his theory of therapy. While this literary figure has its ultimate origins in Odysseus' "litigating with" (or to be more accurate to the text of the *Odyssey*, commanding) his heart to endure, Encolpius is quick to demonstrate that self-apostrophe is not simply a literary phenomenon. True, certain tragic characters castigate their eyes, but so do people in general who have any sort of eye affliction (*lippi*).[49] Thus, Encolpius suggests that the construction of the body and the construction of the *animus* can be couched in the same form of language and that this language is at once literary and "natural." The lines between rhetoric and "real life" are blurred yet again, as Encolpius states that self-apostrophe is a rhetorical figure that can be found in literature and oratory, while it can also be an informal facet of everyday language. This figure is, as Brian Vickers claims is true for all *figurae*, part of the "natural language of the passions."[50]

Moreover, Encolpius considers the dual nature of language, how it can both shape and reveal the self. For a brief moment, Encolpius worries that what he says to himself may reveal something about him morally, or as Seneca puts it in letter 114, he worries that his use of language is an indication of his moral life (*talis hominibus fuit oratio qualis vita*, 114.1). Encolpius immediately rejects this idea, however, in his poem addressed to the Stoic Catos. As Encolpius concludes about the "naturalness" of self-address, so he declares that his opus reports candidly, simply, and with pure speech what people do (132.15.1–4).

There has been considerable debate among scholars concerning who is speaking here. Some take this poem to be the words of Petronius himself, defending his newfangled work against the traditional moralists.[51] Others do not take this poem to be an aside to the reader but believe that Encolpius is still speaking.[52] While the next line preserved in the fragments continues to attack false morality (132.16), when Encolpius unambiguously speaks again in the next section, he states that he has just finished making a declamation (133.1). Unless this section is misplaced, or a large portion of the text is missing that reintroduces Encolpius as narrator, it appears that his concerns with morality and feigned severity were simply a declamation.[53] In this declamation Encolpius is not concerned with the ideal of a one-to-one relationship between language and morality. Instead, he cycles through the different methods of the construction and presentation of the self. He demonstrates that this can be achieved by a variety of methods—through the lens of literature (Odysseus and the *tragici*), natural language (*naturali convicio*, 132.13; *novae simplicitatis opus*, 132.15.2), traditional Roman and Stoic morality (*Catones* 132.15.1), or trivializing and opportunistic Epicureanism (*telos* = *amare*, 132.15.5–8)—or it can be simply an invented pose (*ficta severitate*, 132.16).

Self-Address and Consumption I: How to Be a Cannibal

The text as we now have it opens with Encolpius and Agamemnon decrying the contemporary state of education and how parents sacrifice their children to their own ambition (4.1–2). The fragments conclude with the sacrifice of Philomela's children to the *praeceptor* Eumolpus' lust (140.1–3) and finally with the apparent sacrifice of Eumolpus to the consuming greed of the *captatores* (141).[54] In this final section, the *meditatio* as a means for self-fashioning again comes into play. Eumolpus instructs his legatees to cut up and consume his body, and Gorgias tells the *captatores* how to do it. Thus, we move to another region of Bakhtin's "grotesque body." Petronius' carnivalization of Stoic self-fashioning moves from the genitals and *eros* to the belly, consumption, and digestion.[55]

Both Seneca and Petronius are concerned with the reading and writing of wills. In letter 64 Seneca offers a programmatic description of the interplay between literary creation and monetary and intellectual inheritance. In letter 50 he tells a brief anecdote about how everybody laughs at his wife's fool, Harpaste. She suddenly went blind, but did not realize it. Instead, she asked to be moved, saying that the house was dark (*Ep.* 50.2). It may come as a surprise that Seneca's household has a court jester, but Seneca is quick to explain how his household came to possess Harpaste. He calls her a "burden of an inheritance" (*hereditatrium onus, Ep.* 50.2), which implies that she was left to his wife as part of a larger estate she inherited, as opposed to a specific legacy left to her.[56] Whatever burden Harpaste may be, it should come as no surprise, that Seneca is able to gain philosophical currency from this inheritance and turn it into a topic for one of his *Moral Epistles*. Indeed, after narrating the anecdote about Harpaste, Seneca turns from physical to moral blindness, to the shaping of the soul.[57] The role of wills and inheritance in the closing fragments of the *Satyricon* provides a stark contrast. Here the sham poet, philosopher, and rich old man Eumolpus has composed a will that imposes a considerably greater burden upon his legatees. Nevertheless, this testamentary bequest also presents the opportunity to teach several lessons.

It has been well noted that the society of Croton is based on a series of inversions.[58] What is the deeper significance of the carnivalesque "world turned upside down"? Croton brings to life several Roman nightmares. It continues the factionalism and destruction of the civil war. The peacetime ideals of honest business and the bonds created by family, commercial exchange, and the bequeathing of patrimony are destroyed by legacy hunters (*captatores*). On the one hand, it is tempting to look for a level of social reality in this city dominated by them. As Keith Hopkins notes, the very fact of a special name for legacy hunting (*captatio*) suggests how well established it may have been.[59] The practice can be seen as a symptom of the double bind of imperial society. It was socially based on openhandedness and ostentation but economically built upon a limited income base.[60]

Petronius is not the only writer to deal with the topic. *Captatio* is a theme that stretches across literary genres and history, from Plautus' happily childless bachelor in *Miles Gloriosus*, to Ovid's *Ars Amatoria* (2.271–72, 329–32), to Horace's *Epistles* (1.1.77–79) and his placing of the phenomenon in the Homeric past (*Sat.* 2.5), to the satires of Juvenal and Martial. In addition, the philosophy of Cicero, Seneca, and Epictetus, the historical works of Tacitus, the natural history of Pliny the Elder, and the letters of Pliny the Younger also bear witness to the fears associated with this practice. Several Greek writers also make note of the topic.[61] As Edward Champlin cautions, while the subject may be widespread in a variety of sources, we have no real evidence of how legacy hunting actually worked or how successful the *captatores* were. Even if we do not have any real evidence that it was a social problem, it clearly was seen as a moral problem by the Romans. During the imperial period in particular, *captatio* became another example of the contemporary decline of morality.[62] Seneca himself notes that the hope of receiving a bequest can be potentially injurious to society (*Ben.* 4.20.3, 6.38.4). He also gives valuable evidence that it was hard to judge whether someone was in fact a *captator*. The act of sitting at a sick friend's bedside can either be shameful or honorable. One has to judge the underlying disposition, the how and the why that motivate the act in order to decide whether one sitting by the bed of a sick friend is performing the duties of *amicitia* or simply anticipating a legacy (*Ep.* 95.43). Seneca's treatment of *captatio* comes in the middle of one of his lengthiest letters, and the example of it serves to buttress his argument concerning the necessity of *doctrina* for the performance of right actions. Yet even in the midst of this philosophizing about the need for principles to shape social duties, Seneca and Petronius seem to speak in tandem. Petronius' *vilicus* describes the inhabitants of Croton as divided between cadavers and crows. Seneca keeps the corpse but changes the carrion bird: "but he who sits beside a sickbed for the sake of inheritance is a vulture that waits upon a cadaver" (95.43).[63]

The final section of the *Satyricon* (141) is so fragmentary that we do not know the precise nature of the circumstances surrounding the reading of Eumolpus' will. Has he died, or is he only pretending to have died, or is he, like Trimalchio, reading his will in public?[64] Although we do not know who the speakers are in this final section, we do know that the *captatores* are becoming stingy with their liberality, since the ships, money, and slaves that Eumolpus promised have not arrived from Africa (141.1). While Seneca and Petronius may describe legacy hunting with similar language, in the *Satyricon* the problems of judging the motives behind the act, which are central to Seneca's discussion, fade away in Petronius' Croton. Social and familial duties count for nothing, as the *vilicus* has pointed out.[65] In fact, the difficulties inherent in judging the difference between a true friend and a legacy hunter, which Seneca describes in letter 95, pose no problem for Eumolpus. He knows the *captatores'* souls. He knows that his "friends" curse each breath he takes: "I call on my friends not to refuse what I order, but with the same souls (*animis*) with which they cursed my breath (*spiritum*) they should consume my body" (141.4).[66]

Why does Eumolpus require that his heirs consume his body in public? Several reasons present themselves.[67] Turning the inhabitants of Croton into cannibals reverses the city's reputation as the traditional home of Pythagoras and his vegetarian followers. This topic had been taken up recently by Ovid. Pythagoras's speech on vegetarianism and metampsychosis to Numa and his assembled initiates takes up nearly half of the concluding book of Ovid's *Metamorphoses*.[68] The speech is indebted to the literary tradition of cannibalism. As Pythagoras warns, since the souls of human beings can be transferred to the bodies of beasts, all forms of meat eating run the risk of cannibalism and repeat the Cyclopean and Thyestean feasts (Ov., *Met.* 15.93, 462). Eumolpus' will is also part of the literary tradition of the Thyestean feast.[69] In fact, Eumolpus' testament fulfills one of Atreus' wishes for his brother's cannibal feast in Seneca's play. After revealing to Thyestes the contents of his feast, Atreus laments that he has been deprived of inflicting the full horror of his vengeance since Thyestes did not knowingly eat his children.[70] In contrast, Eumolpus wishes for his heirs self-consciously to become cannibals.[71]

Eumolpus' ability to rewrite the tradition of Croton as a vegetarian haven and to go beyond the literary tradition of Thyestes' feast reveals the paradoxical power of *testamenta* in general. They are able to enforce the will of someone who no longer has one. Looking disapprovingly at the Romans' fascination with the practice, Augustine notes that *testamenta* enable a person's words to survive and have power even though he is dead and buried.[72] Those more sympathetic to the practice also recognized the power of testamentary words. They served as a mirror of one's mores and provided a means for revealing one's emotions.[73] In *De beneficiis*, Seneca comments on the power of *testamenta* to affect people's emotions as they consider and write up their bequests. In language that may seem strange coming from a Stoic, Seneca twice refers to the pleasure involved in the act.[74] Seneca notes that great *voluptas* comes over a person as he thinks to himself, "I shall make this man richer, and with this increased wealth, I shall add something of splendor to his status" (4.11.5).

Eumolpus's testamentary pleasure, on the other hand, appears to go beyond thoughts about making people rich. Indeed, his will demonstrates the power of his words to fulfill his desire on several levels. We have already seen how his requirements for inheritance surpass the famous mythological cannibal feast of Thyestes. Furthermore, his will has the power to make metaphors real. Typically described as carrion birds, the *captatores* are now turned into real eaters of human flesh. As John Bramble notes, they will turn the notion of "consuming one's wealth" (*comedere divitias*) into a gruesome reality.[75] The combination of money, eating, death, and disgust with which the surviving fragments of the *Satyricon* close is a central theme of the *Cena*. It is succinctly summed up by

Phileros' description of the recently deceased Chrysanthus: "He grew from a penny and was prepared to take less than that with his mouth from a pile of manure" (43.1).[76] Most significantly for our purposes, Eumolpus' will turns the Stoic ideal of self-control into a graphic reality. *Continentia*, which can refer to the restraint of the emotions in Seneca (e.g., *Ira* 3.16.2), refers to the control of the stomach in the *Satyricon*.[77] This word is reduced to its core idea of containment, or *continere* (*OLD*, def. 9), as the stomach is forced to hold in human flesh.

Just as Seneca's tragic characters use the *meditatio* to achieve their version of *constantia*, so the *Satyricon* turns Stoic *continentia* into a digestive process, which literally involves the containment of food.[78] Indeed, the final fragment reads like a *meditatio* on how to be a cannibal. It remains unclear who is speaking in these final lines. The first few sentences appear to be part of Eumolpus' will, laying down the cannibalistic prescriptions for inheritance and then offering examples of the practice, either as part of the written testament itself or as a spoken commentary (141.2–4). There is mention of a certain Gorgias, who is ready to follow through with the tenets (141.5). Given the rhetorical lineage of his name, it may be appropriate to imagine that in the final lines of the text he is offering his advice on cannibalism (141.6–11).

The command of the stomach (141.6) is linked to a rhetorical mastery of the cultural geography of the world, both beyond the borders of the empire, as well as knowledge of the "history" of Rome's empire building. The first defense of cannibalism offers a culturally relativistic explanation of the practice claiming that certain people still eat their dead relatives and get angry at the sick ones for spoiling their flesh (141.3). This statement most likely refers to Herodotus' ethnographies of peoples living on the borders of the known world. Herodotus writes of three instances of endocannibalism, the eating of relatives. He claims that it occurs among the Massagetae, specifically mentioning that they will not eat the elderly who die of disease (1.216). He also mentions the Padaeenas, who live east of the Indians (3.38, 3.99), as well as the Issedones, who like the Massagetae live beyond the Scythians (4.26).[79] From the borders of the known world, Eumolpus' testament moves inside the borders of the human body and draws a parallel between the souls of the *captatores*, Eumolpus' breath of life, and his own cut-up and digested body (*animis, spiritum, corpus consumant*, 141.4; *corpus meum in partes conciderint*, 141.2). The next fragment of narration continues this focus on the dark regions of the body, noting that the promise of money was blinding the eyes and souls of the wretched legacy hunters (141.5).

Although we do not know who is speaking in the final fragment, it is likely that Gorgias continues this journey into the depths of the individual. His discussion offers several techniques for fulfilling the tenets of Eumolpus' will. At first a system of self-control via delayed gratification is outlined. An hour of disgust will produce a great payout (141.6). From this rational view of economic exchange and quick return on an "investment," we move to blindness and imaginative, metaphorical exchange. Gorgias advises the *captatores* to close their eyes and imagine themselves eating a million sesterces (*centies sestertium*) rather than human viscera (141.6–7). Gorgias does not fully trust these techniques of imagination and of economic self-bargaining. He will also use more direct means to make Eumolpus' flesh palatable and find some appetizing condiments to change its taste (141.8). By a combination of these processes, the stomach will submit to the command of Eumolpus' testament (*iubeo*, 141.4) and to the *captatores*' desires for money (*sequetur imperium*, 141.6).

In his treatise *De beneficiis*, Seneca states that testamentary bequests are an important example of disinterested giving. He also claims that in writing wills, great pleasure arises from imagining and telling oneself how the economic and social condition of a friend will be improved through one's posthumous favor (*Ben.* 4.11.6). Eumolpus' will inverts these tenets. The will is self-interested in that it is likely trying to save Encolpius, his companions, and possibly Eumolpus himself from the *captatores*. It will not increase the recipients' *dignitas*, as Seneca claims bequests do, but will rather degrade them to the level of cannibalistic beasts. Of course, there is in fact no money to be given. In place of pleasure, the final fragments of the *Satyricon* focus on disgust.

My analysis of Senecan philosophy has shown the importance of self-address and of imperatival language for psychological therapy. In this closing fragment of the *Satyricon* the stomach is described in grammatical terms. The stomach can express its objection (*recusatione*, 141.6), but Gorgias' techniques will make it "following the command" (*sequetur imperium*, 141.6). In this *meditatio*, the means for enforcing command over the belly is an act of imagination (*finge te*) and metaphoric transfer (human viscera = money). Whereas in Seneca self-directed commands or a "confession of the truth" is used as a means to fashion the self, here we see blindness (*operi modo oculos*) and self-deception presented as means to control the emotion of disgust and the physical nausea that accompanies it.[80]

As the surviving text concludes, Gorgias suggests that getting the belly to follow the command and to contain human flesh is easy. In *De ira* Seneca outlines how comparatively easy it is to perform various feats of physical containment: "Some people have never laughed, some have forbidden wine, others Venus, others all liquids from their bodies . . . others have learned to submerge themselves to great depths in the sea without breathing" (2.12.4–5). If, as Seneca argues, these trifling corporeal feats are examples of the soul's ability to command itself (*quodcumque sibi imperavit animus, obtinuit*, 2.12.4), then it will be so much more worthwhile to gain the "great reward of the unmoved tranquility" of the blessed person who has expelled *ira* from his soul (2.12.6). On one hand, Seneca and Gorgias focus on the opposite ends of the spectrum of bodily control. Gorgias talks about ingestion; the majority of Seneca's examples are about people closing up their bodies, such as people who do not laugh or drink or who can hold their breath under water for lengthy periods of time. Nevertheless, their construction of the self is similarly imperatival and economic. Seneca says that the soul obtains whatever it commands itself to obtain and that the mind can conquer anything by means of continually practicing the *meditatio* (2.12.3). He then offers some examples and declares that the extirpation of anger will be so much easier because there is a great reward for achieving it (*tantum praemium*, 2.12.6). Similarly, Gorgias says that he knows that the stomach will follow the command if it is promised the compensation of a great reward (*multorum bonorum pensationem*, 141.6). He then offers a series of examples of cannibals who did so without the promise of gaining an inheritance (141.9–11).

In the concluding sentences of the *Satyricon*, Gorgias' speech moves from subduing the stomach out into the world of Roman imperial history.[81] The explanation of cannibalism began with a culturally relativistic description of the customs of those living outside of the empire. It ends by looking at the fates of inhabitants of Saguntum, Petelia, and Numantia, three cities that were central to the growth of the Roman Empire. Throughout these final fragments there is a complicated interplay between geographic expansion and individual consumption. As boundaries on the map are tested, so the boundaries of the self are violated. This violation takes place on a metaphorical level, as money, a marker of social exchange, is imagined as taken out of circulation and stuffed into the duped belly, as well as on a "historical" level, as the mothers at Numantia are forced to eat their children.[82] Empire building has the power to force others to consume their family members and countrymen. The cultural boundaries are elided as the people of Saguntum, Petelia, and Numania must adopt the customs of barbarian peoples. In the *Satyricon*'s world of commerce and exchange after the empire has been built and after the civil war, the same problem of consumption remains. It is no longer to be forced through military power, but rather through economic power and the triumph of the rhetoric of self-control. People have eaten human flesh before, so the argument runs, and they did not have the promise of an inheritance (141.9). They could not imagine that they were eating money, because all they were trying to do was keep from starving. Thus, Eumolpus' (imagined) economic power is aligned with the might of Hannibal and Scipio Aemilianus. All three have the power to force the consumption of humans. Of course, this is all a rhetorical farce. These apparent horrors of cannibalism and the growth of empire are not based on historical fact. As Courtney points out, these examples of besieged cities resorting to cannibalism are likely taken straight from Valerius Maximus.[83] Be that as it may, this concluding passage makes an important connection between empire, wealth, the power of rhetoric, and viewing the self as a vessel for consumption and containment. Since the text ends here, we cannot discover the fate of Eumolpus and his testamentary ability to enforce the containment of human flesh upon others. We can only speculate on the inverse of this process of consumption and containment—release. The *Cena*, on the other hand, is relentlessly concerned with both processes, and the self-appointed master is Trimalchio.

Self-Address and Consumption II: The Dangers of *Continentia*

In the final surviving fragment of the *Satyricon* we see how imperial power is equated with the power to force people to consume. Throughout his dinner party, Trimalchio, the tyrant of the *Cena* (41.9), revels not only in filling his guests with dubious dishes but also in stuffing food inside of food. After being declared wiser than Hipparchus and Aratus in his knowledge of the zodiac, Trimalchio has a large boar brought in, out of which fly thrushes (40.1–5). Later, out of a pig that all the guests think has not been gutted spill blood sausages.[84] At the start of the feast, Encolpius almost throws away one of the dishes out of disgust. He thinks he has been given a soft-boiled egg with a chick already in it. Following the lead of one of the older, more experienced guests, he discovers that the "egg" is made out of bread, and within he finds a fat figpecker covered with egg yolk and pepper (33.5–8). Trimalchio's ability to control the consumption of his guests, as well as the insides of the very food they eat, is dependent upon the geographic expansion of his estates. He hopes to buy Sicily so that he can travel to Africa without ever having to leave his property (48.3). Setting his sights to the north, he claims that he will have lived long enough if only he can join the region of Apulia to his land (77.3). He gets rams from Tarentum and honey from Attica (38.2–3). He sends out to India for mushroom spores (38.4). Trimalchio passes this expansionism off as necessary for achieving the dream of autarchic self-sufficiency. His doorway proudly bears the inscription that he only eats out twice a year (30.3). He boasts that thanks to the benefit of the gods, he has not purchased the wine they are drinking. It is from his estate that borders on Tarracina and Tarentum, some 150 miles apart (48.2). In his own private bathhouse, Trimalchio brags that nothing is better than bathing without a crowd (73.2).

This geographic expansion and alimentary self-sufficiency have a paradoxical effect on humans. While Trimalchio may expand his estates and his wealth, human beings are physically constricted and limited. Trimalchio's private bath is a cramped space, similar to a cold-water cistern (73.2). Toward the end of the feast, Encolpius realizes that he is trapped in a new kind of labyrinth (73.1). Perhaps Encolpius should have known how difficult it would be to sneak out. The first inscription he reads on Trimalchio's doorpost warns that any slave who exits without the master's order will receive one hundred lashes (28.7).[85] While the desire and potential for territorial and economic growth is unlimited, the human body is different. On the one hand, Trimalchio views people as mere receptacles for food. His claim that slaves are human beings is put in alimentary terms. He notes that slaves have drunk the same milk as the rest of us. He will free them in his will so that they can taste "free water" (71.1). Yet just before this claim, Trimalchio notes the limitations of the human vessel to expand; "so may I grow in patrimony, not in body," he wishes (70.1). Here we see the paradox. The human body cannot keep expanding as it consumes the fruits of its ever-growing monetary and geographic acquisitions. Eventually it will reach a breaking point, and then what we have enclosed within us must come spilling out.[86]

Viewing the human body as a vessel or container is of course a common enough metaphor. In what is likely his earliest surviving dialogue, the *Consolatio ad Marciam* (Consolation to Marcia), however, Seneca claims that this realization is the goal of self-knowledge. Seneca writes that the Delphic command to "know thyself" means finding the answer to the question, "what is a human being?" (11.3). Seneca answers by stating that a human being is "a vessel that is easily destroyed by any shaking or tossing. A great disturbance is not necessary for you to be shattered: wherever you strike, you will be broken apart" (11.3).[87] Seneca presents a fairly standard interpretation of the Delphic maxim as an injunction to know one's limits, to know that one is mortal.[88] Yet his claim that Apollo's injunction admonishes one to know that a human being is defined by the limits of the body rather than by the soul's divine potential is striking, especially considering that for both Plato and Cicero knowing one's self is equivalent to knowing one's soul.[89] Indeed, the passage from Cicero's *Tusculan Disputations* is worth quoting. "When therefore he says, 'know yourself,' he says this: know your soul. For indeed the body is just like a vessel or some little container of the soul" (1.52). For Cicero, that the human body is a *vas*, a poor little receptacle for the soul, is hardly a revelation. He presents this concept as a given; the true intellectual work lies in discovering the nature of the soul, not of the body.[90] Seneca, on the other hand, focuses his interpretation of this central maxim of philosophy on how weak and fragile the human body is (11.3–4).[91] If Seneca's interpretation of the Delphic maxim to "know thyself" (*nosce te*) in the *Consolatio ad Marciam* seems foreign to the world of philosophy, it finds a home in the world of the *Satyricon*. Indeed, this metaphor for the fragility of the human body, the self as vessel, and vessels in general are central to the imagery of the *Cena*.

Just after his confession that one can never be too rich or too thin, Trimalchio has to pass judgment on two slaves who have apparently gotten into a fight as they returned from a well with amphorae of water. Seemingly unhappy with his decision, one slave breaks the vessel of the other. At first the guests are stunned by the insolence of these apparently drunken slaves. Yet they quickly realize it is another one of Trimalchio's tricks. Oysters and scallops come pouring out of the belly of the jar (70.6). Trimalchio famously says that he has seen the aged and shrunken Cumean Sibyl hanging in a jar (*in ampulla pendere*, 48.8).[92] His supposedly one-hundred-year-old wine is brought out in glass amphorae that are thoroughly sealed with gypsum (34.6). On his tomb Trimalchio wants his guest the stonemason Habinnas to carve amphorae that are again thoroughly sealed with gypsum so that the nonexistent wine will not flow out (71.11).[93] Why this concern with sealing in wine? Perhaps because, following Trimalchio's logic, wine is life (*vinum vita est*, 34.7). In addition, Trimalchio wants Habinnas to sculpt a broken jar with a boy crying over it (71.11). A tender acceptance of the fragility of the human vessel! Nevertheless, even in death Trimalchio will attempt to control what goes into and what comes out of those around him. In his will he has appointed one of his freedmen to keep watch over his monument so that passing travelers do not defecate on it (71.8). He will also place a clock in the center so that whenever someone wishes to know the time, they will read his name, whether they like it or not (*velit nolit*, 71.11).

Trimalchio also views drinking vessels as a sign of status. To the cook who brought out the sausage-filled "Trojan pig," Trimalchio drinks a toast and gives a silver crown and a cup on a tray of Corinthian bronze (50.1). Later he brags about the size, weight, and decorative craftsmanship of his various types of drinking vessels (52.1–3). In between his ridiculously false claims that Corinthian bronze was first discovered when Hannibal sacked Troy and that his goblets have wrought images of Cassandra killing her children and Daedalus shutting Niobe into the Trojan Horse, Trimalchio admits that he prefers glass vessels, because they do not interfere with the aroma of their contents.[94] In fact, if glass did not break, confesses Trimalchio, he would prefer it to gold (50.7). These reflections on the relative value of glass and gold lead Trimalchio to tell a story about a craftsman who was able to make an unbreakable glass bowl.[95] The craftsman presents his invention to Caesar, demonstrates its properties, and then thinks he has attained Jove's throne after Caesar asks him if anyone else knows this method of glassmaking. When the craftsman reveals that he alone possesses this unique knowledge, Caesar orders his execution. Otherwise the entire value system would be destroyed, and gold would be worth mud, Trimalchio explains (51.6). This story anticipates the closing fragments of the text, where first the power of empire and then the power of money and testaments forces humans to consume others. In Trimalchio's story the same themes are brought together: imperial power, economic value, and human life. Whereas Eumolpus' will orders his body to be dismembered and exchanges human flesh for money, here Caesar orders the craftsman's head to be cut off because gold cannot be exchanged for glass. We can also think again of the passage from the *Consolatio ad Marciam* where Seneca says that the goal of self-knowledge is to understand the fragility of the human vessel. In Trimalchio's story, however, the craftsman's life is literally dependent upon an unbreakable glass bowl.

Trimalchio is not alone in equating humans and human worth to vessels. Among the many insults that Hermeros throws at Ascyltus for laughing at the freedmen, "earthenware vessel" (*vasus fictilis*, 57.8) may not stand out as the most damaging, yet it aptly illustrates the value system of the *Cena*.[96] Moreover, this designation has ties to other, more famous earthenware vessels. At the end of letter 95, Seneca recounts the public feast that Q. Tubero once offered in honor of Scipio. Instead of the expected regal accouterments, Tubero set out wooden couches, goatskins, and, before the shrine of Jupiter himself, earthenware vessels (*vasa fictilia*, 95.72). This one act, according to Seneca, places Tubero among the Catos, because he did not give a feast, but rather a moral censorship. The gold and silver that the other Romans displayed has been melted down thousands of times over, Seneca declares, but the earthenware of Tubero will last for all time (*fictilia*, 95.73). Here again we see Seneca and Petronius employing the same images as metaphors for human beings and, by further extension, for the morals and values of society.[97] The two authors approach this metaphor from opposite directions. For Petronius' Hermeros, earthenware vessels are a term of insult; they are as worthless in his eyes as is Ascyltus. For Seneca, earthenware vessels are priceless. Their display on the Capitol caused the Romans to marvel at them and catapulted Tubero into the pantheon of republican heroes. Incidentally, Seneca's love of paradox may have caused him to distort the Romans' reaction. As Cicero notes, the public did not approve of such Stoic austerity on display, or as Cicero calls it, Tubero's "perverse wisdom" (*perversa sapientia*). Tubero subsequently lost his bid to be elected praetor (*Mur.* 75).[98] Thus, although Cicero may not approve of Hermeros' grammatical forms (*vasus* for *vas*), Hermeros' valuation of earthenware vessels is closer to that of Cicero and his take on the "standard" Roman view of their value.

Just as they can stand for the fragility of our mortal condition or hold food and drink, so vessels can house excreta, the results of feasting. Contrary to a standard philosophical view that sees the body as a container for the pure and immortal soul, in the *Cena* only the most vile objects reside within the human vessel.[99] As if to drive this point home, immediately after Encolpius first catches sight of his host exercising in the bathhouse, Trimalchio snaps his fingers and one of his eunuchs places a silver chamber pot (*matella*) under his master so that he can relieve the weight of his bladder while continuing to play ball (27.5–6).[100] Here we see that no matter how beautiful, vessels may contain excrement within. In addition, the necessities of nature, as well as the fact that the human body must continually contain and release, become grossly apparent. The closing fragment on cannibalistic *continentia* only tells half of the story. The *Cena* is concerned with the results of ingestion, as well as the problems of indigestion.

Although the *Cena* begins with Trimalchio easily emptying his bladder, throughout the narrative there is a focus on satiety and on being overly full. By the time Encolpius and his companions arrive at the door of Trimalchio's villa, they are already "full of admiration" from having watched him take his exercise, bathe, and set off for home with a quasi-triumphal procession (28.6). Before even entering the triclinium, they are "full of pleasure" after marveling at the inscriptions and decorations on the doorposts (30.5). Metaphorically stuffed full to begin with, Encolpius is soon disgusted by what he is served. He nearly throws away the "egg" that starts the feast (33.8). By the time Carpus arrives to serve the first main course, Encolpius is not able to taste anything more (37.1). Thus, he almost breaks the "law" of the feast, which is simply to eat, as Trimalchio makes clear in his pun on *ius* ("law" and "sauce," 35.7). As we have seen, it is the fate of animals to be killed, gutted, and then stuffed with more food. The same fate awaits living animals as well. Trimalchio's *deliciae* Croesus stuffs his "indecently fat" puppy Margarita full of half-eaten bread. The puppy refuses it by vomiting (64.6).[101] Margarita's sickness soon becomes that of Encolpius, who narrates that Trimalchio's mock funeral brings the affair to the "height of nausea" (78.5).[102]

While we as readers may be disgusted by this grotesque focus on the cracks in the "leaky vessel of human life," according to Trimalchio, there is no need for anyone to feel any shame (47.4).[103] In fact, this concern with bodily processes involves a necessary, even life-saving "confession of the truth." Along with his love for drinking vessels, jars of wine, and filling food with more food, Trimalchio is fascinated with and tormented by what is inside him. He uses various methods to gain access. Toward the end of the meal, he praises the abilities of the soothsayer Serapa, claiming that "he knew my intestines." Serapa's apparently stunning abilities to witness Trimalchio's digestive processes are quickly undercut, however. Trimalchio admits that the one thing Serapa did not know was what he had eaten the day before (76.11). Indeed, Trimalchio's previous meals still weigh heavy upon him, and for relief he has turned to doctors. Here again specialized knowledge has failed him: "The doctors have no idea what they are doing," he complains.[104] Nevertheless, a mixture of pomegranate rind, pine pitch, and vinegar has helped him (47.2). Although Trimalchio wishes to be remembered in perpetuity for never having listened to a philosopher, he also seeks relief in the form of a therapeutic self-dialogue. Trimalchio's discussion of the stomach provides a crucial supplement not only to Seneca's ideal of psychological self-knowledge and control but also to Gorgias' closing discussion of ingestion.

Mirroring the body's metabolic functions of containment and release, the Stoic self is constructed around two ideas of control. On the one hand, the emotions must be contained within and not be allowed to escape (*continentia*; see *Ira* 3.16.2). At the same time, the passions must also be driven out, extirpated from the soul, lest they create psychological fluctuation and instability (*ex animo tolli*, *Ira* 2.12.3). For example, Seneca advises Polybius that if he is able, he should cast out all his sadness, but if not, he should hide it and contain it (*Polyb.* 5.5).[105] Gorgias' *meditatio* on cannibalism only focuses on one aspect, containment. When Trimalchio returns from the restroom, he offers his own account of the difficulties of "extirpation" and the limits of *continentia*.

No one is born solid, Trimalchio declares (47.4). Unless the body's insides are regulated and emitted, one risks vapors (*anathymiasis*) creating fluctuation throughout the entire body. As Trimalchio makes clear, excessive *continentia* is the greatest form of torture. Jove cannot command it. Even the doctors are wise enough to forbid it (47.4–5). Many have died in this way, according to Trimalchio, because they did not wish to confess the truth to themselves (*multos scio sic periisse, dum nolunt sibi verum dicere*, 47.6). Indeed, Trimalchio conceives of his problems in terms of a breakdown of self-dialogue. His stomach has not responded to him in several days. While he hopes that it will regain its old sense of shame, as of late his stomach bellows like a bull.

As Courtney has suggested, Trimalchio's claim about the necessity of confessing the truth likely echoes Serenus' statement at the start of Seneca's *De tranquillitate animi* that many people do not wish to engage in a therapeutic and truthful self-dialogue. Serenus states, "I think many people would have been able to come to wisdom if they had not thought they had already arrived at it, if they had not dissimulated certain things in themselves and passed over certain things with their eyes closed. There is no reason for you to believe that we are ruined by another's adulation more than by our own. Who has dared to tell the truth to himself" (*Tranq.* 1.16).[106] Admittedly, it is difficult to think of Trimalchio as an enlightened Stoic. Yet what are we to make of Trimalchio's concerns with self-confession and regulation of internal fluctuation? We can see these connections as a simple, carnivalizing parody. Petronius brings Senecan "command psychology" down to the body. Stoic *continentia* is turned into the body's ability to contain food, and Stoic extirpation becomes the necessary evacuation of food. Petronius' characters remind us that the care of the self is not to be directed to the *animus* to the exclusion of the body. We have not, however, exhausted the possibilities for analyzing this passage's engagement with Stoic ideas. Specifically, Trimalchio's discussion of the dangers of internal vapors, or *anathymiasis*, speaks to concerns about self-revelation and the material nature of the soul. We will return to this passage again in part 2.

In a manner similar to Seneca's tragedies, the *Satyricon* investigates the problems and limits of self-address and self-fashioning. Encolpius focuses on eros, while Trimalchio and Gorgias focus on consumption. On several levels, Gorgias moves closest to the world of Senecan tragedy. He develops a method of self-fashioning (*finge te*) that commands the stomach to commit an act that is not only philosophically repugnant (especially for the philosopher founders of Croton, the Pythagoreans) but tantamount to breaking the very boundaries that separate gods from men, and men from beasts.[107] Petronius' Gorgias offers the means to persuade and command the stomach in order to achieve a criminal form of self-control. The *captatores* would go beyond the feast in *Thyestes* by becoming self-conscious cannibals. In addition, Seneca's Medea and Atreus continually address their souls and order them to carry out their acts of infanticide. The theme of infanticide is also present in the closing fragments of the *Satyricon*. Philomela, whose namesake is famous for butchering and serving Itys to his father, entrusts her children to the "care" of Eumolpus (140). The final sentence of the final fragment describes mothers holding the half-eaten bodies of their children at Numantia (141.11). Furthermore, in all the texts we have investigated, exemplarity is an important technique of self-fashioning. The *captatores* can fulfill the tenets of Eumolpus' will, or Seneca's Medea can become Medea, or the Stoic *proficiens* can make progress by looking to past examples for inspiration. It is not enough simply to call to mind models for action. Seneca's characters also fashion themselves by self-address and self-exhortation. Petronius' Gorgias states that the stomach will obey the command if you close your eyes and imagine that you are not eating human flesh but rather a million sesterces. While Seneca advises a philosophical confession of the truth to the self, metaphorical transference is also a part of Stoic therapeutic techniques. Seneca frequently advises his readers to change the way they look at the world by using different terms to describe things. Thus, exile becomes "a change of location" (*Helv.* 6.1), and money becomes "a burden" (*Ep.* 22.12).[108]

Finally, we can note how the semantic range of the verb *fingere* is treated by Seneca and Petronius. Gorgias' exhortation "imagine yourself" (*finge te*) cuts to the core of the idea of self-fashioning and of Roman heroism and the development of *imperium*. Gorgias' words recall a passage from the *Aeneid*. After visiting the future site of Rome and hearing the story of Hercules' defeat of Cacus, Evander exhorts Aeneas: "Dare, my guest-friend, to scorn wealth and to fashion yourself worthy of the god" (*aude, hospes, contemnere opes et te quoque dignum / finge deo*, 8.364–65). Seneca quotes this passage twice in the *Epistles*. In letter 18 he encourages Lucilius to devote certain days to frugal living and "fashion himself worthy of the god" (18.10).[109] He concludes letter 31 by stating that a good soul can descend into anyone regardless of social station. "One may leap to heaven from a slum. Only rise up and 'fashion yourself worthy of the god.' You will not fashion yourself out of gold or silver; an image similar to the god cannot be pressed out from this material; think that those gods, when they were propitious to men, were made of earthenware" (31.11).[110] The ideal of Roman self-creation from Vergil's epic is taken down two different paths by Seneca and Petronius. For Gorgias the exhortation *finge te* is an act of self-imagination or fiction that is driven by greed and creates a cannibalistic beast. By contrast, for Seneca it represents both the acceptance of the humble and fictile nature of humanity and the divine aspiration of Stoic self-shaping.

Part II / Soul-Revealing Speech

CHAPTER FOUR

Political Speech in *De clementia*

In the history of social and political thought, it is doubtful that there are two more opposed texts than the American Declaration of Independence and Seneca's *De clementia*. Based on Enlightenment thought, the Declaration was written and signed by earnest citizen-soldiers in order to cast off despotism and establish a sovereign republic in the New World. *De clementia*, on the other hand, is full of rhetorical tropes and technical discussions of Stoic theory. Written by the "imperial voice" for the young emperor of Rome, this text's forerunners are the (largely lost) Hellenistic kingship treatises, or "mirrors for princes."[1] It praises that most unrepublican of virtues, mercy.[2] Seneca does not base Nero's authority to rule on any constitutional powers or senatorial or popular mandate (1.19.1). Rather, he is the gods' choice, as Seneca has Nero declare to himself (1.1.2). He equates the principate with kingship (1.3.3, 1.4.3).[3] Seneca dispels any possibility of return to republicanism by stating that autocracy did not begin with Augustus but was already a political reality under Julius Caesar (1.4.3). Despite these vast differences between the two texts, two important points of contact can be noted. First, both seek to differentiate a king from a tyrant.[4] The Declaration sets out to prove that this dreaded transition has already occurred in the case of King George III. Seneca is trying to keep it from happening to Nero. Second, as evidence of the shift from kingship to tyranny, both texts focus on the ruler's relationship to the courts of law.[5] In addition, the populace, when it perceives the ruler's abuses of the judicial system, will be driven to violent rebellion against the tyrant. However intriguing the influence of monarchical thought on republican ideas may be, my reason for briefly bringing the Declaration of Independence and *De clementia* together is to highlight the crucial role of judgment of both kings and subjects in determining the specific nature of autocracy.[6]

The primary goal of *De clementia* is the fashioning of a merciful autocrat, one who willingly submits to virtue and reason and from this "noble servitude" (1.8.1) gains "freedom of judgment" (2.7.3). This treatise does not simply focus on Nero, however. Another important aspect is the shaping of the populace's capacity for critical judgment of Nero in order to determine whether he is a king or a tyrant. Seneca frequently makes use of the body-soul metaphor to define the relationship between Nero and his subjects (e.g., 1.5.1).[7] A major problem that Seneca tackles is how to get Nero, who is the soul of the state, to reveal his soul and have it properly interpreted and obeyed by the body politic. Mirroring the constitution of a human being on a macrolevel, the political body and the imperial soul are intertwined and interdependent. This interdependence can have both positive and negative consequences. As Seneca notes in book 2, ideally Nero's merciful soul will diffuse itself and shape the body of the state (2.2.1). On the other hand, if Nero is tyrannical, if he does not care for his soul, then the entirety will collapse, or the body will rebel against the soul. Thus, Seneca endeavors to shape not only the soul of the empire but also the body of the empire so that the two can work harmoniously. In order to do so, Seneca attempts in *De clementia* to make both the emperor and his subjects experts in rendering judgments and interpreting appearances.[8] The need to render proper judgments exists on several levels. Seneca must make sure that Nero is able to render merciful judgments in the courtroom and discern the irredeemably corrupt and criminal from those worthy of clemency. In addition, Nero must learn how to differentiate between virtue and vice and between a king and a tyrant. The populace must also be able to judge Nero correctly. If he is perceived to be a tyrant, then the people will revolt. Thus, *De clementia* must not only fashion a merciful princeps who acts with full understanding of this virtue but also enable Nero to reveal himself properly to the wider public so that they are not deceived by the appearances of his actions.

This project is complicated by the fact that, as Seneca points out, kings and tyrants, as well as virtue and vice, can appear to be the same.

Martha Nussbaum has argued that Senecan tragedy encourages critical spectatorship from its audience. They are to judge Seneca's characters and look beneath the surface to see the condition of their souls.[9] A similar process is at work in *De clementia*. While, as Shadi Bartsch reminds us, the so-called theatricality of Nero's reign is more likely the reflection of our sources' desire to embellish the history of the "actor-emperor" than a reflection of reality, the number of dramatic elements already present in *De clementia* is striking. Images from the theater have an important place in this treatise. Seneca describes the population of the city of Rome as being so large that it requires three theaters to hold it (1.6.1). In an act that combines political theater with courtroom drama, Seneca directs Nero's judgmental gaze outward to his subjects. Seneca asks Nero to imagine the desolation that would be wrought on the city if only those people whom a stern judge would acquit were allowed to remain (1.6.1).[10] With this reference to the theaters of Rome, it appears that Seneca is imagining Nero performing his role of the merciful princeps simultaneously in the theaters of Balbus, Marcellus, and Pompey. If so, the performance the Romans will watch will be Nero playing Nero. After Nero's opening monologue declaring his mercy, Seneca states that Nero does not need any other imperial exemplar to follow besides himself.[11] His goodness is genuine and not covered by a false mask (*nemo enim potest personam diu ferre*, 1.1.6).[12] Not only does Seneca imagine Nero mercifully judging his audience but he encourages Nero to allow himself to be watched: "You are fixed in your pediment . . . a great light is facing you, the eyes of all have been turned toward it. You think you are setting out in the morning? You are rising" (1.8.3–4).[13]

Nero must be not only seen but also heard. Thus, Seneca scripts for him a dramatic monologue at the start of *De clementia*, and opens book 2 with Nero's magnanimous utterance, which he hopes the entire world can hear. Indeed, Seneca assures Nero that his words will be heard by nations everywhere (1.8.5). Everything that Nero says and does is seized upon by rumor. Thus, according to Seneca, he must speak in a specific and majestic way. Kings must neither shout nor use intemperate words. In short, they do not have freedom of speech (1.7.4–1.8.1). While Seneca notes that Nero's performance is genuine, he paradoxically creates a script for Nero that reveals his relationship to the laws and the mercy of his soul. Rather than focusing on Nero's appearance, Seneca turns to language's ability to reveal the emperor's soul and how "spirited utterances" can make manifest the difference between merciful kings and cruel tyrants. The hope is that if Nero follows Seneca's script, not only will he render merciful judgments properly but he himself will be judged correctly by his subjects.

The King Bee

According to Seneca, nature itself has provided an example of the true, merciful ideal of kingship, the so-called king bee. Seneca has already prepared his readers' minds for the metaphorical connections between bees, the workings of the human body, and empire. In his description of Nero as the controlling force of the empire, Seneca quotes a passage from the fourth book of Vergil's *Georgics* in which he describes the importance of the king bee's safety for the survival of the hive: "That man is the chain by which the republic is held together, that man is the vital spirit that so many thousands breathe in, who would be nothing on their own except a burden and prey if the mind of the empire were taken away: 'While the king is safe, the mind is the same for all; when he is lost they break their alliance'" (1.4.1 = G. 4.212–13).[14] Later in *De clementia*, Seneca follows a long, biologically mistaken tradition of using the society of the beehive under the rule of the "king bee" as a political metaphor (1.19.2–4).[15] Seneca first focuses on how physical appearance differentiates the king: "The appearance of the king is distinguished, and he is different from the others in both size and splendor" (1.19.2).[16] Yet it is not simply the king bee's more impressive appearance, nor the fact that the other bees are entirely obedient and devoted to the safety of their monarch.

According to Seneca, the greatest difference between the king bee and the others is that while bees in general, despite their small size, are highly irascible and pugnacious and leave their stingers behind after they attack, the king bee does not even have a stinger (1.19.3). According to Seneca, nature does not want the king to be cruel. Realizing that if the king bee were to act on its anger and exact punishment, the cost would be its life, nature took away its stinger (1.19.3).[17] Seneca laments that the same principle does not apply to human beings: if only humans, like bees, could act on their anger once and at the cost of their lives (1.19.4). By extension, the security of the ruler would be assured if only his inability to harm, like the king bee's, could be displayed for all to see (1.19.5–6). Here Seneca runs into the problem of differentiation. The perfect physical example of kingship exists only in the world of nature. The king bee is more impressive in appearance, directs the work of all the others, and lives in the largest and safest part of the hive. The king bee's major defining physical characteristic, the lack of a stinger, provides the most potent physical manifestation of its kingship, and perhaps in Seneca's mind the ultimate justification for the other bees' devotion and obedience. Because the king bee is physically unable to punish or take revenge, he is merciful by default. He is not to be feared; hence his safety is assured. Human rulers do not have this luxury and are not in so fortunate a position as the king bee, whose lack of a stinger provides a physical manifestation of its gentleness. In fact, the appearances of rulers can be deceptive.

The Dangers of Relying on Appearances

In his description of the civilly minded and merciful princeps, Seneca notes that his primary characteristics include affability of speech, ease of access, and being "friendly in face." Seneca claims that this final trait "most easily gains the affection of the people" (1.13.4). Despite this claim, Seneca devotes little attention in *De clementia* to Nero's physical appearance.[18] In fact, earlier in the text Seneca suggests that the body is dangerously deceptive. Seneca's opening body-soul analogy is used to demonstrate the people's dedication to Nero. In his description of this relationship, however, Seneca problematizes the role of each. Seneca assures Nero that all will obey his commands, just as the body obeys the soul, but he also notes that the body is "much larger and more attractive." The soul, however, "remains delicate and hidden, and it is uncertain in which location it hides" (1.3.5).[19] Nero may be the soul of the empire, but the actual condition of his own soul is hard to discover. There is no general guarantee of the soul's beneficence or purity. As Seneca admits, the *animus* itself can be a "greedy lord" (*avarus dominus*, 1.3.5). And as we shall see, the commands, actions, or appearance of the ruler are of less importance than the intention, the moral character, and specifically the merciful or cruel state of the ruler's soul. Seneca needs to be sure that Nero's soul is not greedy and domineering and that it is not perceived as such by his subjects. Although the body is at the service of the soul, Seneca confesses that the body is more impressive and more attractive (*speciosius*).[20] Thus, Seneca subtly introduces the crucial problem of the deceptiveness of external appearances (*species*). In fact, kings and tyrants may not differ in appearance; the real difference between the two resides in their souls.

The question how to tell a king from a tyrant was likely asked by many members of the Roman elite during the early empire.[21] For Seneca, the answer is easy (1.11.4, 1.12.3). He need not appeal to any constitutional limits or ideals of public consent.[22] The difference between the king and the tyrant is mercy. As might be expected from a Stoic, in this treatise Seneca focuses less on the deeds of a ruler as the true means for displaying *clementia*; it is, rather, the ruler's psychological disposition underlying the act that effects the political divide between kingship and tyranny. Thus, Seneca develops a means to display the psychological disposition of the autocrat. As Seneca makes clear, the political and juridical ideal of *clementia* initially arises from the *animus*.[23] He defines *clementia* as a condition of the soul. It is "a temperance of soul in its power in avenging, or the leniency of a superior toward an inferior in handing out punishment . . . an inclination of the soul toward leniency in carrying out punishment" (2.3.1).[24] One must not assume, however, that *clementia* automatically means forgiveness and that in an empire guided by a merciful emperor, harsh, even capital punishments will be unnecessary. Both kings and tyrants can act cruelly (*saeviunt*). The difference is that tyrants are cruel for their pleasure, and kings act so in accordance with reason and out of necessity (1.11.4). Kings will execute their subjects, but "only when the public good dictates it. A tyrant's savagery comes from the heart" (1.12.1). Seneca makes it clear that capital punishment will continue under Nero. Book 2 opens by recounting an incident in which Nero, albeit reluctantly and after much delay, signs the death warrant for two robbers. Further problematizing the use of external appearances for judgment, Seneca notes that both kings and tyrants have the same appearance of good fortune and power (*species enim ipsa fortunae ac licentia par est*, 1.11.4). Indeed, kings and tyrants may even have the same foreboding surroundings; as Seneca admits, "each may be fenced in with arms as much as the other" (1.12.3). Thus, a person judging solely on the basis of action and appearance runs the risk of error. One must look beyond them to understand the true nature of the autocrat. The psychological disposition of the ruler must be made clear: the good ruler must reveal "his reluctance to apply harsh remedies" (1.13.4), a point that clearly foreshadows the opening of book 2. What Seneca's readers need to learn, then, is the ability to differentiate between virtue and vice, in other words, the specific conditions of the ruler's soul.[25]

We have already seen how Seneca's quaint metaphor of the "merciful" king bee reveals the physical differences between humans and the world of nature. The "mercy" of the king bee only exists by default, as the bee is physically unable to punish. The de facto clemency of the king bee also reveals two crucial differentiations that, for the Stoics, separate the animal world from the human.[26] Adult human beings possess the critical judgment of the rational soul, which enables them to interpret appearances properly. In addition, only human beings possess articulate speech. In *De clementia*, both of these defining characteristics are stressed. Not only does the king bee lack a stinger but, more important, it lacks judgment, specifically the ability to get beyond appearances and distinguish virtue from vice. Animals only have impression and impulse; they lack the rational ability to judge appearances and decide on a proper course of action.[27] Thus, after praising Nero's impossible wish for illiteracy while signing death warrants (*vellem litteras nescirem!*, 2.1.2, discussed below), Seneca writes that he will focus on Nero's good deeds and sayings so that the emperor's nature and impetus will become a matter of fixed judgment (2.2.2).[28] Similarly, at the start of the treatise, Seneca writes that it is the reason and discernment of Nero's soul that keep the body politic of the empire from breaking apart (1.3.5).[29] Seneca stresses that mercy is the most appropriate of virtues for human beings, because it is the most humane (1.3.2). Therefore, humans' ability to discriminate and judge is of paramount importance. As Julia Annas notes, the Stoics put a great deal of stress "on our developing good habits in the way we deal with appearances."[30] Seneca's focus on defining "inclinations of the soul" and correcting false classifications of virtues and vices in *De clementia* is not simply an exercise in abstract Stoic ethics. Seneca's goal is to make his readers critical and expert judges of appearances in the social world. The emperor's ability to judge virtue and vice without being deceived by appearances must be enacted in the courtroom so that the citizens can judge whether they are ruled by a king or a tyrant. Indeed, these two acts of judgment depend on each other. The manner in which the ruler judges will reveal his clemency or his cruelty and hence will determine whether his subjects consider him a king or a tyrant and whether they consider themselves to be guilty or innocent. Thus, Seneca sets Nero's predecessor Claudius' behavior up as the prototypical example of how not to render judgment and mete out punishment.[31]

According to Seneca, in five years Claudius undid centuries of social philosophy and legal practice by his frequent, gruesome, and public punishment of parricides:

> With the greatest foresight the most profound men and the men most experienced in the ways of the world preferred to pass over this crime as if it were

inconceivable and beyond human daring rather than show that it could happen when they punished it. And so parricides came into being with the law, and the crime was shown to them by its punishment. Indeed, familial duty was at its lowest point when we saw the sack more often than the cross. In the state where people are punished rarely, there is a consensus of innocence, and it is indulged just like a public benefit. (*Clem.* 1.23.1–2)[32]

We can note the centrality of vision in this passage. The spectacle of Claudius' punishments shows people the way to further crime (*ostendere*). Seneca implies that the sight (*vidimus*) of slaves and others of low status punished on the cross may be a necessary social deterrent to keep those orders in line. Paradoxically, the sight of parricides being sewn into the sack destroys familial bonds and duty (*pietas*), as children, presumably primarily members of the upper orders, turn to murder to rid themselves of oppressive parents. Punishment should not be applied too frequently, for its stigma (*nota*) will be less serious because it is lost in a crowd of the condemned (1.22.2). By removing the public spectacle of frequent and indiscriminate punishment, Nero will shape the public's self-image and eventually turn that image into a reality. Seneca writes, "Let the citizens think they are innocent; they will be" (1.23.2).

Of course, Nero should not pardon indiscriminately. He must learn to discriminate and judge properly. As Seneca declares at the start of the treatise, "For when the distinction is taken away between the good and the bad, confusion and an eruption of vices follow; and so use must be made of moderation, which knows how to distinguish between characters that can be healed and those that are beyond hope" (1.2.2).[33] Yet this crucial need for discernment is complicated by the fact that certain vices can imitate virtues. Thus, Seneca promises to mark each one with a distinguishing sign (*nam cum sint vitia quaedam virtutes imitantia, non possunt secerni, nisi signa quibus dinoscantur impresseris*, 1.3.1).[34]

Seneca fulfills this promise in book 2. The process of differentiating between vices and virtues is not a simple task and is hindered by appearances.[35] Indeed, even the "beautiful name of mercy" (*speciosum clementiae nomen*, 2.3.1) can be deceptive. Some have claimed that severity is the opposite of mercy. According to Seneca, however, *severitas* is a virtue and thus cannot be in conflict with another virtue. The true opposite of *clementia* is cruelty. Like mercy, it is defined as an inclination of the soul. Unlike mercy, however, *crudelitas* inflicts severe punishments (2.4.3). It is savagery and lack of self-control in punishing

(2.4.1–2). Mercy must be further differentiated from the vice of pity (*misericordia*). Unlike mercy, pity is a characteristic of a weak soul that is irrationally moved by appearances (*speciem*).³⁶ Pity looks at one's bad fortune instead of its cause; mercy assents to reason (*misericordia non causam, sed fortunam spectat; clementia rationi accedit*, 2.5.1). Indeed, Seneca connects the irrationally sympathetic vice of pity to those who have weak eyes and cry simply when they see others crying (2.6.4).³⁷ The wise man, on the other hand, guided by reason and mercy, will cast down neither his face nor his *animus* when seeing someone's crippled leg or ragged poverty or an old person leaning on a walking cane (*vultum quidem non deiciet nec animum ob crus alicuius aridum aut pannosam maciem et innixam baculo senectutem*, 2.6.3). Nero's ability to judge and discern must be shaped in two interdependent ways. On an abstract level, he must be able to differentiate virtue and vice, which Seneca promises to "mark with a distinguishing sign." On a practical level, Nero must learn how to render merciful judgments in court so that the "stigma" or "brand" (*nota*) of punishment is not used indiscriminately. These points are crucial for developing a healthy, sympathetic body-soul relationship between the emperor and his subjects. Even more essential for understanding and judging the nature of the autocrat is the language the emperor uses, specifically the way in which he declares his relationship to the laws. The voice of the emperor has the power to reveal the true nature and judgments of his soul.

Judging the Voices of Autocrats

Seneca's reliance on the moral psychology underlying the ruler's actions placed him in the difficult position of finding a way to reveal the soul of Nero.³⁸ In order to do so, Seneca turns to language. Both surviving books of *De clementia* open with a focus on what Nero says and then discuss the state of the emperor's soul and its relationship to the body politic. As we have seen, the treatise begins with Nero's private, self-shaping *meditatio* on his position as a merciful emperor. Here Seneca writes a script for Nero in which he declares his relationship to the laws: "I thus watch over myself as if I were going to give an account to the laws, which I have called forth from their neglect and darkness into the light" (*sic me custodio tamquam legibus quas ex situ ac tenebris in lucem evocavi rationem redditurus sim*, 1.1.4). Nero will be ready should he be called before the divine court (1.1.4).³⁹ The relationship of Nero's imagined self-address to juridical concepts recalls the manner in which Seneca frames his own *meditatio* in *De ira*.⁴⁰ Just as Nero should give an account of himself before the courts of Rome and of the gods, so Seneca calls on his readers to bring the passions before the court of the self (*ad rationem reddendam vocandus est*, 3.36.1; *ad iudicem esse veniendum*, 3.36.2; *cotidie apud me causam dico*, 3.36.3). Thus, Seneca's care of the self is similar for both the emperor and his subjects. While *De ira* describes the *meditatio* as private practice of psychological self-observation, self-exploration, and self-censorship (3.36.2), the judicial metaphor of *De ira* is moved to the actual courts of law and judgments pronounced by the emperor in *De clementia*.⁴¹ Nero's words, however, have the power to shape not only Nero himself but the entire empire. Seneca imagines Nero describing the power of his own language as follows: "What fortune wishes given to each mortal is announced from my mouth; from my reply peoples and cities receive reasons for happiness" (*meo ore pronuntiat; ex nostro responso*, 1.1.2).⁴² In addition, Nero has a unique position with respect to the laws, a fact that Seneca advises the young emperor to always keep in mind.

> For what is more memorable than the man against whose anger nothing stands in the way, whose more severe sentences even those punished must agree to, whom no one is going to obstruct or even plead with if he grows vehemently angry, who takes hold of himself and uses his power for better and more peaceful things and thinks to himself: "everyone can kill contrary to the law, no one except me can save a life"? (*Clem.* 1.5.4)⁴³

Book 2 opens with Nero's exclamation before signing a death warrant that he wished he had never learned to write (2.1.2). Not only was this revelation of Nero's natural clemency the main reason that Seneca decided to write this treatise but Seneca also declares that it should be heard by those who inhabit the empire and those who threaten along its borders (2.1.3). In addition, this remark has given Seneca cause to hope that a happy and pure age is dawning, as the mildness of Nero's soul will gradually spread throughout the entire body of the empire, and all will be shaped into Nero's likeness (2.1.4–2.2.1).⁴⁴ Why are Nero's words, both those that Seneca has scripted for him and those that the emperor actually said, treated in such detail in *De clementia*? In order to understand more fully the significance of Seneca's focus on Nero's speech, let us consider the role of imperial speech in Roman culture more generally.

According to Tacitus, Nero's funeral oration for his adopted father, Claudius, which was his first public act as *princeps*, was written by Seneca and elicited several responses, ranging from seriousness to laughter to a comment on the unique position of Nero as an emperor needing to borrow the eloquence of another. Tacitus puts this final comment in the mouths of the "older" members of the audience, whose age gives them the leisure to compare past with present (13.3.2). Natural eloquence and imperial power (*qui rerum potiti essent*) are believed to be so closely linked that Tacitus offers a succinct analysis of the rhetorical abilities of the Julio-Claudian dynasty beginning with Julius Caesar.

> For Julius Caesar was the rival of the greatest orators; and Augustus had ready and easy-flowing eloquence, as was fitting for a princeps. Tiberius also was skilled in the art of weighing his words carefully and so was either forceful in his meaning or purposely ambiguous. Even the disturbed mind of Gaius Caesar did not corrupt his power of speech. And you would not look for elegance in Claudius on any occasion that he spoke on things he had thought over beforehand. Straightaway from his youth Nero directed his lively soul to other things: sculpting, painting, singing, or practicing chariot driving; and sometimes in the composing of poems he showed that the elements of learning were in him. (*Ann.* 13.3.2–3)[45]

This brief rhetorical history performs several complex tasks. It begins by implying that eloquence justifies Caesar's political power.[46] Just as he possessed the highest power as dictator, so he was the rival of the greatest orators. Augustus' ready and easy-flowing eloquence befits his position as princeps. Tacitus' *Annales* famously memorialize Tiberius as the master of dissimulation. The tenor of his reign is summed up by his skilled use of words.[47] This analysis also considers the links between the emperor's psychology and his oratory. Caligula may have had a "disturbed mind" (*turbata mens*), but that did not impair his linguistic abilities. Whenever Claudius prepared beforehand (*meditata*), his speech would be elegant.[48] Nero's *animus* goes in another direction, however. For Tacitus, this rhetorical history at the start of Nero's reign presages the end of the Julio-Claudian dynasty, as Nero breaks the crucial link between *oratio*, psychology, and imperial power.[49] The mad Caligula and even Claudius, whom Seneca condemns for his incomprehensible voice in the *Apocolocyntosis*, had their own rhetorical power and elegance.

For modern readers who generally accept without comment, moral or otherwise, the fact that political figures rely upon the "eloquence of others," this brief passage in Tacitus may merit little comment. Yet it demonstrates a key aspect of ancient political thought: the emperor's language was a topic to be investigated and judged. Nero's "borrowed eloquence" breaks a decades-long tradition. Moreover, it suggests the urgency with which Seneca, precisely because of his new role as imperial speechwriter, must attempt to make clear the links between Nero's language, his *animus*, and his power in *De clementia*.[50] Thus, he opens both books of this treatise by focusing on what Nero says and how this language both shapes and reveals the emperor's soul. As we shall see in chapter 5, the inverse is performed on Claudius in the *Apocolocyntosis*. The dead emperor's attempts to describe himself in epic terms are misunderstood or thwarted. The only expression of Claudius that is allowed to define him and his reign is his final soul-revealing utterance.

While we should be wary of accepting the veracity of the words that our literary and historical texts preserve, this skepticism should not blind us to the fact that several ancient authors use them to explain a ruler's actions.[51] Whether the ruler actually said them matters less when we consider the important tradition of thinking through autocracy and explaining an autocrat's actions by reporting his speech. Particularly in the biographical tradition, the formal oratorical speeches of autocrats rarely come under investigation. Rather, Suetonius and Plutarch focus on short, ad hoc utterances. In fact, the origins of autocracy at Rome were encapsulated by a pithy quotation spoken by Julius Caesar before he crossed the Rubicon. According to two of our sources, the civil war between Julius Caesar and Pompey Magnus that precipitated the end of the Roman Republic and eventually established the Julio-Claudian line began with a hackneyed phrase, yet one that is remembered today even by those who have never studied Latin.[52] Caesar himself makes no mention of this famous crossing in his *Commentarii de bello civili*. In one sentence, Caesar is waiting in Ravenna, north of the Rubicon; in the next, the army is taking Ariminum, south of the river (*B. Civ.* 1.7–8). For the details of the crossing, as well as the famous phrase about the die being cast, we must turn to Suetonius and Plutarch. Yet their presentations and interpretations of Caesar's famous words differ considerably. Suetonius' version preserves the more familiar words that Caesar reportedly uttered before crossing the Rubicon, *iacta alea est*. His version focuses on the divine portents that preceded and justified Caesar's crossing.

> As he delayed, this portent occurred. A person of great size and beauty suddenly appeared, sitting close by and playing music on a reed. When many shepherds, along with some soldiers who had left their posts (some of the trumpeters were

among them), ran together in order to hear him, he grabbed one of the trumpets, sounded the call to arms with a mighty blast, and crossed to the other bank of the river. Then said Caesar, "Let us go where the portent of the gods and the inequity of our enemies call us. The die is cast." (*Iul.* 32)[53]

In this version, Caesar's famous phrase is an acknowledgment of the divine authority for his action.

Plutarch presents a different narrative of events. In his biography, Caesar is worried about the civil strife he knows will be the result of his crossing. He carefully considers his course of action with his friends. Plutarch notes that rational calculation only leads to aporia, and Caesar abandons himself and his plans to passion and chance.

> Finally, with a sort of passion, as if abandoning calculation and casting himself upon the future, and adding that exordium commonly used by those who enter upon difficult and daring fortunes, "Let the die be cast," he rushed to cross the river. (*Caes.* 32.8)

For both authors, this famous phrase encapsulates and reveals Caesar's line of thinking before crossing into Italy and beginning the civil war. Yet in the two biographies it is used to represent radically different states of mind. In Suetonius, the use of the perfect passive, *iacta alea est*, after Caesar's interpretation of the portent indicates that the die of fate and chance have already fallen in Caesar's favor. The imperative used in Plutarch, "Let the die be cast," suggests something entirely different.[54] According to Plutarch, Caesar uses a famous, perhaps even clichéd phrase to express his inability to decide rationally and his willingness to give himself over to chance. In his life of Pompey, Plutarch makes this point again. In this version Caesar does not deliberate with his companions before crossing the Rubicon, but only with himself. He quickly casts off reason, submits himself to chance and fortune, and exclaims in Greek to all those around him, "Let the die be cast" (*Pomp.* 60.2).[55]

This trend of using quotations to explain autocracy is not confined to the imperial period; it is already present in Cicero's *De officiis* (*On Duties*). Toward the end of the work, Cicero addresses the topic of whether evil actions can ever be justified by the reward (3.79). Under this rubric, he turns his attention to the recently assassinated Julius Caesar.[56] As proof that Caesar valued absolute power over justice and pious duty, Cicero states that he always quoted two lines of Eteocles from Euripides' *Phoenissae*: "If the law is to be violated, it must be violated in order to rule; in all other affairs you should respect your sacred duty."[57] Centuries later, in his biography of Julius Caesar, Suetonius references this passage from Cicero and offers his translation of Euripides as the culmination of his list of possible reasons why Caesar crossed the Rubicon and initiated the civil war. According to Suetonius, *dominatio* had been Caesar's desire from earliest youth (*Iul.* 30). He cites as proof the fact that Caesar always had on his lips (*semper in ore habuisse*) the verses from Euripides. It is admittedly very difficult to accept the historical veracity of this claim. The image of Julius Caesar traipsing around Rome quoting Euripides on the extralegal, hence justified status of the pursuit of absolute power borders on the ridiculous.[58] The truth of Cicero's and Suetonius' claims is less at issue here; what matters more is that both of these writers demonstrate the Romans' thinking about autocracy through speech, be it literary quotations, excited utterances, or formal orations. Indeed, we have seen how contested the interpretations of several imperial utterances could be. Did Caesar claim to be following an already decided fate when he crossed the Rubicon, as Suetonius suggested; or did he in a fit of passion commit himself to the whims of chance, as Plutarch's biography states? The fact that Caesar himself makes no mention of this famous incident only renders it more fertile ground for various, even conflicting fictionalizations and interpretations.[59] For Cicero, Caesar's quoting of Euripides' *Phoenissae* proves that he was not the dutiful father of his country but rather a mad (*amens*) murderer of his fatherland (*Off.* 3.82–83). Suetonius, on the other hand, includes Cicero's evidence as only one possibility among many attempts to explain the origins of the civil war (*Iul.* 30).[60] Seneca follows Cicero in *De officiis* in using language as a crucial means for revealing the political ideals and morality of the autocrat. Unlike Cicero, who uses the quotation from Euripides to condemn all forms of autocracy, Seneca must use language to differentiate its positive and negative forms.

The Language of True Greatness of Soul

As we have seen, Seneca makes it clear that the actions of kings and tyrants, as well as their outward appearance, can be the same.[61] Their language will not be, however.[62] Let us look again more closely at the opening of book 2 of *De clementia*, where Seneca steps away from his role of providing Nero with eloquence and offers a brief example of something Nero himself said.

That I might write on *clementia*, Nero Caesar, one utterance of yours especially compelled me, for which I remember that I was not without admiration both when I heard it, when it was said, and then when I reported it to others; a noble utterance, of great soul, of great gentleness, which, neither composed nor given for others' ears, suddenly burst forth and made public your goodness fighting with your fortune. Burrus, your praetorian prefect, an exceptional man, born for you as princeps, was going to execute two robbers and was demanding from you that you write whom you wished to be executed and the reason you wished them to be. This was often delayed, and he was insisting that it happen at last. When Burrus unwillingly had brought out and handed over the paper to you, who were also unwilling, you exclaimed: "I wish I had never learned to write!" O worthy utterance, which all people who dwell in the Roman Empire and those who lie nearby with insecure freedom and who raise themselves against it with their strength and animosity should hear! O utterance that must be sent into the assembly of all mortals, upon which words princes and kings should swear! O utterance worthy of the common guiltlessness of the human race, to which that ancient age might have been returned! Now indeed, it would be proper to decree that equity and good (once all desire has been driven out, from which every evil of the soul arises) and that duty and integrity with good faith and restraint rise again and that vices, long misusing their reign, give place at last to a happy and pure age. (*Clem.* 2.1.1–4)[63]

De clementia begins with Seneca's version of Nero's self-address and *meditatio*. In this case, Seneca continues in his role as Nero's speechwriter but reveals the "private" Nero to the public. To begin the second book, Seneca describes a brief and impromptu exclamation made by Nero while conducting judicial business. Although Seneca demurs that this expression was not intended for the ears of others—proof of its genuine power to reveal Nero's soul—Seneca makes sure that it is made public.[64] Seneca first repeats the story to others; then he publishes it, claiming that it served as the inspiration and impetus for *De clementia*. That Seneca's goal was in part accomplished is attested by the fact that Suetonius also recalls this same exclamation several years later (*Ner.* 10.2).[65] Indeed, Seneca wishes that this expression could go beyond the confines of his book's audience to reach all mortals and become an oath for all rulers. Seneca continues with his hyperbolic claims, stating that this brief expression provides proof that the golden age is returning and that Nero's *animus* is naturally mild and will thus shape the citizens as it diffuses itself through the body politic (2.2.1).

From the standpoint of modern political philosophy, we may be justified in dismissing Seneca's claims of psychophysical sympathy between ruler and ruled.[66] Seneca does, however, go on to offer further explanation of the importance of Nero's exclamation. After his exclamatory praises of Nero's impossible wish that he had never learned to write, Seneca gives his reasons for being so moved by Nero's words:

> Allow me to dwell on this a little longer, not in order that I may flatter your ears (nor indeed is this my custom: I would have preferred to offend them with the truth than to please them with fawning). Why then? Besides the fact that I desire you to be as familiar as possible with your good deeds and words, in order that what now is nature and impulse become judgment, I think to myself about how many great but hateful utterances have made their way into human life, famous ones which are commonly spoken, as that "let them hate, provided that they fear," and that Greek verse similar to it in which one orders earth to be mixed with fire after he is dead, and others of this type. And somehow or other, characters that are savage and odious have expressed fierce and excited thoughts through more favorable material; until now, I have not heard any spirited utterance from a good and gentle person. (*Clem.* 2.2–3)[67]

Seneca's explanation is twofold. Directly concerning Nero's development, he states that the emperor's apparently simple and unscripted utterances need philosophical explication so that what Nero does naturally may become an act of conscious judgment (*ut quod nunc natura et impetus est fiat iudicium*). In addition, Seneca states that the emperor has solved the problem of people's only remembering and quoting detestable and tyrannical lines.[68] Before Nero's exclamation, Seneca had not yet heard a spirited expression from a good and gentle person (*nullam adhuc vocem audii ex bono lenique animosam*, 2.2.3).[69] In fact, Nero's "spirited utterance" solves a problem of political and psychological revelation that Seneca has been investigating both earlier in *De clementia* and in the dialogue *De ira*.

According to Seneca, despite the republican constitution under which Sulla lived, he is properly classified as a tyrant. In order to prove this point, Seneca does not simply bring his murderous proscriptions to bear as witness; he also includes what Sulla said to the Senate to explain his orders.[70]

> What tyrant ever drank human blood as avidly as that man who ordered seven thousand Roman citizens to be butchered? And when he heard so many thou-

sands shouting when they came under the sword as he sat next door in the temple of Bellona, he said to the terrified Senate, "Let's get to work, conscript fathers; only a few traitors are being executed by my order." (*Clem.* 1.12.2)[71]

"He wasn't lying," concludes Seneca. "To Sulla it seemed to be a few."[72] It is not simply that Sulla ordered the executions, or even the number of them, that reveals his tyrannical nature. As Seneca makes clear in *De ira*, reason can do similar work if necessary. *Ratio* can destroy entire households that are pestilences to the state, including women and children, and raze entire buildings (1.19.2).[73] Sulla's statement in *De clementia* makes manifest his deranged sense of what constituted a "few executions" and demonstrates the delight he took in terrifying those who were not at present his victims. Language is thus a crucial means for identifying the tyrant. After telling this story, Seneca first mentions the famous tag line from the republican poet Accius, "Let them hate, provided that they fear" (*oderint dum metuant*, 1.12.4), and notes that tyrants can use it to easily sum up their method of political command.[74] Using language to manifest the merciful soul of the good king is a considerably more difficult task, however, as Seneca's hyperbolic praise of Nero's wish makes clear. According to Seneca, for some unknown reason it is much easier to express forceful thoughts with inhuman language. This is not the first time Seneca has puzzled over this problem. In fact, the falsely attractive language of tyrants receives a lengthy treatment at the end of book 1 of *De ira*. In order to understand better Seneca's praise of Nero's "great-souled" utterance, we must turn to his investigation of the concept in *De ira*, as well as to another philosophical discussion of greatness of soul.

The debate on the contradictory meanings of the term greatness of soul (in Greek, *megalopsychia*; in Latin, *magnitudo animi*) is outlined by Aristotle in the *Posterior Analytics*. Aristotle does not fully discuss the ethical implications of each meaning. He simply brings up the term in a discussion of the difficulties that can arise in providing a single definition for one word, and for Aristotle, greatness of soul is the textbook example of an equivocal term. He flatly concludes that there must be two types of greatness of soul.[75] The examples that Aristotle uses to illustrate the dual meaning of this term suggest a conflict between a heroic ideal and a philosophical ideal. First, Aristotle considers those traditionally seen as possessing greatness of soul and suggests Alcibiades, Achilles, and Ajax as examples. The characteristic that unites the three is an unwillingness to put up with insult or dishonor. Aristotle also notes that

Lysander and Socrates can also be considered to possess greatness of soul. Their lives are characterized by the opposite quality; they accepted insult and thereby demonstrated their imperviousness to the whims of fortune (97b15–26).[76] While Aristotle may be happy simply to present and accept the ambiguity of this term, conceding that there must be "two types" of greatness of soul, Seneca will not allow the two concepts to be equally acceptable.[77] Like Aristotle, Seneca admits that there are two rival ideals, but for him the heroic, angry, and spirited concept of greatness is decidedly wrong.

Seneca begins his discussion in *De ira* by countering the argument that anger contributes to *magnitudo animi* (1.20.1).[78] In order to discredit the idea that greatness of soul equals a refusal to put up with insult, Seneca himself employs all levels of insult.[79] Yet Seneca is not simply differentiating character types, such as Aristotle's heroic and philosophical types; rather, he is describing different conditions of the *animus*. The truly great soul is lofty, sublime (*sublime*, 1.20.2, 1.20.3) and at the same time unshaken, solid within, and equally firm from bottom to top (1.20.6). By contrast, the falsely great soul is described as an excessive, sickly growth, a *tumor* (1.20.1). It is mad. There is no base to support its growth. It is windy and empty (1.20.2).[80] Without a foundation, this soul comes crashing down upon itself (1.20.2). Falsely admired "greatness" is in fact characteristic of a sickly and miserable soul that is conscious of its own weakness (1.20.3). Anger contributes nothing to it, since it is an especially womanly and childish vice (1.20.3).

Despite Seneca's degradation of the manliness of those who think *ira* contributes to greatness of soul, his interlocutor is not yet convinced. Perhaps referencing some now-lost index of "great sayings," Novatus asks, "What then? Are there not some utterances let out by those in anger that may seem to be sent forth from a great soul?" (*quid ergo? non aliquae voces ab iratis emittuntur quae magno emissae videantur animo?*, 1.20.4).[81] With Novatus' question, Seneca starts to focus on language's ability to reveal the soul. Such angry expressions are said by those ignorant of true *magnitudo animi* (1.20.4). Seneca cites as his prime example of falsely great expressions that "terrible and abominable 'Let them hate, provided that they fear,'" and he connects the expression with Roman politics: "You might know that it was written during the time of Sulla" (1.20.4). Although Seneca likely gets the original date of composition of this line incorrect—Accius is traditionally considered to have died about 90 BCE, before the true "age of Sulla" in the 80s and 70s—it is clear that Seneca is claiming that an utterance can reveal the political spirit of the age.[82] This belief of Seneca's is further buttressed by the fact that when he quotes this line again in *De clementia* (1.12.4), he does so immediately after arguing that Sulla is properly considered a tyrant not simply because of his actions but also by virtue of his exhortation to the Senate during his proscriptions (1.12.2).

Cicero also quotes this line from Accius in *De officiis*, and it is instructive to compare his discussion of it with Seneca's political and psychological interpretation.[83] In book 1, Cicero discusses the links between decorum and virtue.[84] Cicero first illustrates this topic by considering how playwrights make sure that their characters are represented on stage with appropriate speech and action. He claims that if a playwright went against tradition and put evil expressions in the mouths of noble characters, the audience would find it inappropriate.

> If Aeacus or Minos were to say, "Let them hate provided that they fear" or "The father himself is a tomb for his children," it would seem inappropriate, because we approve of them as having been just. But when Atreus says it, applause breaks out, for the speech is worthy of the character. (*Off.* 1.97 = Accius, frag. 190 Loeb = 203 Ribbeck)[85]

Cicero will not, however, extend this type of speech beyond the stage. Expressions such as *oderint dum metuant* are only for poets who handle a wide variety of purely literary and mythical characters. Actual human beings, Cicero continues, would never see such language as fittingly representative of their character (1.97–98). Even in the twilight of the republic, the horrors of Atreus' tyrannical anger and revenge remain safely on the stage. Because of their distance from reality, they are worthy of the audience's applause in appreciation of the poet's ability to have language appropriately express Atreus' savage character. For Seneca, who was long experienced in the realities of imperial rule, however, this expression is not representative of a character on stage, but rather indicative of the despotic times during which he believes it to have been written. Whereas Cicero praises Accius for his artistic choice of representation, to Seneca it appears that Accius could not have written otherwise. The *Zeitgeist*, for Seneca quite literally the "spirit of the times," structures artistic and political language. In fact, as Seneca was likely aware, centuries after this play was first performed Atreus would indeed walk off the stage and be embodied in the tyrannical Caligula, who, according to Suetonius, repeatedly vaunted that tragic line: "Let them hate, provided that they fear" (*Cal.* 30.1).

Caligula is not far from Seneca's mind when he discusses falsely great utterances.[86] After quoting this line from Accius in *De ira*, Seneca tells of a time when thunderbolts disturbed Caligula as he was watching comic actors. The emperor called Jupiter down to a fight to the death, exclaiming in Greek a line from Homer: "Either lift me or I you" (1.20.8).[87] After this story, there is no need for philosophical explication; Seneca only exclaims, "What great madness that was!" (*quanta dementia fuit!*, 1.20.9). This incident leads Seneca to consider the role of violent political action under the principate. This look at tyrannicide runs counter to the main political points of *De ira*. Throughout, Seneca considers a historically wide-ranging series of vignettes between courtier and king, many of which must have been old favorites, such as the stories of the Persian kings found already in Herodotus.[88] Indeed, much of the political advice Seneca gives is gloomy. His advice for living under a tyrant is to learn to say "thank-you" when one is wronged (2.33.2). His advice to one punished unjustly by a king is to "accept your fate" (2.30.1). If the situation is ever too much to handle, all violent impulses are to be directed at the self. The path to freedom is achieved, paradoxically, through self-annihilation. The natural world can offer the freedom that the political world cannot. A barren tree or a precipice offers *libertas*. Likewise, the path to freedom is contained in our own bodies. "You wish to find the road to freedom?" asks Seneca. "Take any vein you like" (3.15.3–4).[89]

At points, however, Seneca struggles with his Stoic ideals concerning the extirpation of anger and vehemently criticizes obsequiousness to tyrants as slavery (3.14.3).[90] It is only in the case of Caligula, however, that Seneca describes actual political revolt. In fact, Seneca surmises that Caligula's quoting of Homer provided a crucial impetus, "I think that this utterance of his was not of small importance for rousing the minds of the conspirators; it seemed to be the limit of endurance to put up with a man who could not put up with Jupiter" (1.20.9). In this passage, Caligula's language works on two levels. It reveals his tyrannical madness, and for his subjects it serves as a mental impetus to effect political change.[91] Popular revolt against the tyrant is a real danger that lurks below the placid surface of *De clementia*. Indeed, Seneca attributes the overthrow of tyrants to that "accursed verse, 'Let them hate, provided that they fear.'" According to him, this line has sent many to their ruin. Tyrants invoke it in ignorance of the madness that arises when hatred grows beyond its proper limit. Seneca admits that a moderate amount of fear is necessary to restrain the souls of the populace. But when it is continual and extreme, fear rouses even the lazy to boldness and urges them to use any means to overthrow the tyrant (1.12.4). Indeed, the appeal to Nero's fear of assassination or political insurrection may be the strongest part of Seneca's argument for being merciful (1.11.4).

Even Augustus, before he adopted a policy of mercy, was continually hounded by assassins.[92] Life in such a state of political unrest is so unbearable that Seneca imagines Augustus himself taking the advice from *De ira* and contemplating suicide. Here again, the emperor is presented as talking to himself.

> After being silent for some time, and now more angry at himself than with Cinna, he spoke, this time in a much louder voice: "Why do you live, if it is important to so many that you die? What end will there be of punishment? What end will there be of bloodshed? I am the one against whose exposed head the noble youth sharpen their swords; my life is of no value if, in order that I may not die, so many things must be destroyed." (*Clem.* 1.9.5)[93]

Seneca's presentation of Augustus parallels his presentation of Nero, but the contrast is noteworthy. Both emperors are given a monologue of self-address and then declare their clemency aloud. Augustus' monologue, however, is full of suicidal despair. When he finally adopts a course of clemency, he does not do so following his nature or his judgment. It is a policy adopted later in life, and only because his cruelty has been exhausted (1.11.1–2).[94] In addition, Augustus cannot encapsulate the virtue of *clementia* as cogently and succinctly or as memorably as Nero. Seneca starts to recount what Augustus says when he forgives the would-be assassin Cinna, but he stops short, realizing that Augustus' speech would take up a large part of his book . According to Seneca, Augustus spoke for two hours, but the length of the speech was Cinna's punishment (1.9.11). Nero's expression, however, has memorably revealed his natural clemency for all to hear, not just Cinna.

Such, at least, was the hopeful vision at the start of Nero's reign.[95] After his retirement, if we can believe Suetonius and Tacitus, Seneca's condemnation of falsely magnanimous utterances would go unheeded. We have very little evidence of Nero's actual words.[96] Seneca's position as Nero's ghost writer, once a means for displaying his own talents, eventually required Seneca to use his oratorical *ingenium* to cover up Agrippina's murder. Less than five years after ignoring the death of Nero's rival Britannicus and calling the emperor "bloodless" in *De clementia,* Seneca likely helped to provide the official story to cover up Nero's murder of his mother.⁹⁷ According to Tacitus, although Rome and Campania were outwardly providing supplications to the gods in thanksgiving for the safety of the princeps, and although Agrippina's birthday was officially included among the "unspeakable days" (*dies nefasti*), the truth of Nero's matricide was clear to all. And since all also knew who provided Nero with eloquence, Seneca also became the subject of damning rumors because in Nero's speech he "inscribed a confession," to quote Tacitus' famous phrase (14.11.3). That this speech was indeed circulated and published is confirmed by Quintilian, who preserves a phrase from the speech as an example of a poor *sententia*: "Simple doubling makes certain *sententiae*, as in that writing of Seneca that Nero sent to the Senate after his mother had been killed because he wished it to appear that he had been in danger: 'That I am safe as yet I neither believe nor rejoice'" (*Inst.* 8.5.18).⁹⁸

Presenting an incident that occurred after Nero's "graduation" from the school of Senecan rhetoric in 62 CE, Tacitus explicitly claims to preserve the actual words of the princeps (*ipsa principis verba referam*, 14.59.3). In an effort to bind Nero closer to him through crime, the new praetorian prefect, Tigellinus, plays upon Nero's fears of assassination and insurrection. Pretending to be devoted entirely to Nero's safety, in contrast to the "divided loyalties of Burrus," Tigellinus worries about the noble lineage of Plautus and Sulla and their proximity to the armies in the East and in Germany, respectively. His worries are heeded. In six days, Sulla is killed while reclining for dinner. When the head is brought back to Nero, he is shown to be like the tyrant Caligula, making his violent actions even worse by what he says (Suet., *Calig.* 29.1). According to Tacitus, he mocked Sulla's head as being deformed by premature greyness.⁹⁹ In this instance, Nero's insult is only reported indirectly; Tacitus does not give us Nero's exact words of mockery (14.57.6).

When the head of Plautus is brought in, Nero also remarks upon its appearance, and Tacitus makes the extremely rare claim that he will record Nero's actual words. By an unfortunate accident of manuscript transmission, a lacuna exists in the text, so that we only know the first two of Nero's words. Tacitus writes, "The head of Sulla was brought in; at the sight of which (I shall repeat the very words of the princeps), 'Why,' he said, "Nero..." (*caput interfecti relatum; cuius aspectu (ipsa principis verba referam)* "*cur*", inquit, "*Nero...*", 14.59.4).¹⁰⁰ The conjecture, "Why, Nero, did you fear a man with a big nose?" has been supplied on the basis of the text of Dio Cassius, which does retain Nero's words (62.14). Adding his own comment, Dio ironically surmises that Nero would have spared Plautus had he known about his nose beforehand.

Lest Seneca seem overly careful in his creation of a script for Nero that both shapes and reveals him to be a good prince, we must consider the unfortunate consequences of the second example Seneca cites of an inhuman and hateful utterance: "Let earth and fire be mixed after I am dead" (2.2.3). According to Suetonius, the great fire of Rome in 64 CE came about when someone quoted this line to Nero in the course of general conversation. Nero corrected this proverb, saying in Latin, "Rather," then adding in Greek, "while I'm alive" (*Ner.* 38.1). Of course, it is unlikely that this is how the great fire actually started.[101] This quotation demonstrates, however, the important place that proverbs and brief quotations spoken by emperors held in the Roman imagination. They served as a means both to represent his morality and to provide an impetus and justification for action. Suetonius' anecdote supports Seneca's belief that such imperial utterances, no matter how brief or apparently impromptu, could have a great effect on shaping and representing the emperor. Although figured by Seneca simply as the body to Nero's soul, the populace did not lack the capacity to remember, record, and pass judgment on the words of autocrats, even if it meant, as Seneca himself did, inventing them.

In part 1 we witnessed the transformation of philosophy into tragedy and comedy as we traced how Stoic self-address is turned into tragic monologues of self-fashioning in Seneca's plays and then into grotesque comedy in the *Satyricon*. We can see a similar dialectic at work here. The Stoic script that Seneca writes to fashion and display the soul of the merciful princeps eventually went unheeded. Tacitus and Suetonius present Nero adopting language that Seneca specifically told him to avoid, thus creating a tragedy of the murderous and destructive tyrant.[102] In this case, however, Seneca himself wrote the comic double. In the *Apocolocyntosis*, Seneca uses the death of Claudius to transform the "spirited utterances" and psychological revelations of the autocrat into graphic reality. Beneath this comedy, however, lurk anxieties about what lies within the human vessel, the true nature of the soul, and the soul's relationship to the body both on a macro- and microcosmic scale. These anxieties are addressed by the petty tyrant Trimalchio, and they also work their way out of the confines of Seneca's satire and into his philosophy.

CHAPTER FIVE

Soul, Speech, and Politics in the *Apocolocyntosis* and the *Satyricon*

The following quotation from Jonathan Swift's *Gulliver's Travels* highlights the parameters of this chapter:

> The good Woman with much Difficulty at last perceived what I would be at: and taking me up again in her Hand, walked into the Garden where she set me down. I went on one Side about two Hundred Yards; and beckoning to her not to look or to follow me, I hid my self between two Leaves of Sorrel, and there discharged the Necessities of Nature.
>
> I hope, the gentle Reader will excuse me for dwelling on these and the like Particulars; which however insignificant they may appear to grovelling vulgar Minds, yet will certainly help a Philosopher to enlarge his Thoughts and Imagination, and apply them to the Benefit of publick as well as private Life; which was my sole Design in presenting this and other Accounts of my Travels to the World wherein I have been chiefly studious of Truth, without affecting any Ornaments of Learning, or of Style.[1]

Swift's startling combination of excessively detailed satire on the "Necessities of Nature" with the elevated concerns of the philosopher demonstrates the trajectory I will draw from Seneca's political and philosophical thoughts on empire, soul, and language to the satire of the *Apocolocyntosis* and the *Satyricon*.[2] At first glance, the *Apocolocyntosis* would appear to be at once the Senecan text closest to Petronius and the anomalous orphan of the philosopher's corpus.[3] Thus, my goal in this chapter is twofold: to draw Seneca's satire even closer to the *Satyricon* and to show that it serves as the comic double to the roughly contemporary *De clementia*.[4] My analysis reveals that despite the work's "unofficial" and mocking content, it is right to consider the *Apocolocyntosis* as a relevant commentary on political judgment, as well as on the use of language as a means to reveal the emperor's soul. These connections not only provide the necessary lens through which to view the various utterances of the emperor Claudius and their relation to Nero's, but also offer a means for understanding Seneca's ideas about the nature of the soul and its relationship to bodily materialism in general. Seneca's account of Claudius' death, which represents what the tyrant has done to the empire, is linked with Trimalchio's warning to his dinner guests in the *Satyricon* concerning the deadly, internal "vapor," or *anathymiasis*. I argue that this word can be interpreted in the context of Stoic psychology. I also contend that this focus on death-dealing, noxious "air" in the *Apocolocyntosis* and the *Satyricon* can be linked to works from late in Seneca's career, the *Epistles* and the *Natural Questions*. The *Apocolocyntosis*' famous portrait of the dying fool Claudius struggling to breathe and gasping out his life's breath provides a strangely prophetic precursor to Seneca's later portrait of himself as the sickly, valetudinary old man afflicted by asthma and catarrh.[5] When Seneca investigates inside the bowels of the earth, he discovers the same phenomenon: lethally foul and uncontrolled air and wind.

On one level, reading the *Apocolocyntosis* together with *De clementia* and the *Satyricon* reveals a dichotomy between the praise of kings in the genre of political theory and the ridicule of tyrants with the bodily materialism of satire. Yet the links between the *Apocolocyntosis*, the *Satyricon*, and Seneca's serious works of political, moral, and natural philosophy demonstrate satire's dangerously infectious instability. The image of the world and of the self presented in satire spreads out and contaminates other "serious" texts.[6]

Claudius' "Spirited Utterance"

Twitching uncontrollably, limping, stammering—roughly two thousand years after his "apotheosis," Claudius' physical and linguistic disabilities continue to be remembered thanks to Robert Graves' historical novel *I, Claudius*, as well as Derek Jacobi's memorable performance in the BBC adaptation of the novel. For all the humanity of Graves' and Jacobi's Claudius, in Seneca's text he is a monster of archetypal proportions. He breaks boundaries and unifies oppositions.[7] Like Oedipus, he is the lame king, a liminal figure who is at once regally exalted and physically and socially debased. Also like Oedipus, Claudius was joined in an incestuous marriage that led to his destruction.[8] He is a foreigner, "a genuine Gaul" (*Gallus Germanus*) who is also at the center of power in Rome (*Apocol.* 6.1). He is the *Saturnalicius princeps*, and the man who made good on the proverb that one should be born either a fool or a king, as Seneca states (1.1). Claudius' "stupidity" also goes to the heart of the Roman tradition of the founding of the republic. According to legend, Rome's first consul, the man who established freedom by driving the Etruscan kings from the city, Lucius Junius Brutus, feigned stupidity in order to remain safe under the tyrannical Tarquins.[9] According to Suetonius, Claudius formally addressed his reputation for stupidity in several speeches. He declared that he had feigned it under Caligula in order to appear harmless and avoid the emperor's familial purges (*Claud.* 38.3). Despite his efforts, Claudius failed to persuade anyone. In fact, an anonymous book was circulated bearing the Greek title *Môrôn epanastasis* (The rise of fools). The book rebutted Claudius' speeches, arguing that no one would feign stupidity (*Claud.* 38.3). It is tempting to think that with the *Apocolocyntosis* Seneca was following precedent, albeit adopting a much safer course and writing after the emperor's demise. If in fact the earlier text mocked Claudius' official explanation of his elevation (*epanastasis*) to the principate, it would provide fitting closure to circulate a satire on his final "apotheosis." Indeed, Seneca mercilessly dubs Claudius an idiot or fool throughout the text, occasionally using the Greek *môros* in standard expressions where *theos* (god) would be expected.[10] As a further paradox, Claudius, the fool king, the Saturnalian "lord of misrule," arrogates the judicial system to himself and unifies carnivalesque license with the rule of law.[11] As the threat of assassination and political insurrection lurk beneath the hyperbolic praise of Nero in *De clementia*, more troubling concerns lie beneath the humor and ridicule of the *Apocolocyntosis*.

Given the nefarious circumstances surrounding his death, the historical Claudius left no "famous last words."[12] To remedy this situation, however, Seneca is more than happy to take up his role as voice of the princeps and posthumously lend Claudius his eloquence.[13] He scripts for the dead emperor a suitably memorable and "spirited utterance":

> And he did indeed bubble out his life, and from then on he ceased to seem to live. Moreover, he expired while listening to comic actors, so you may know that not without reason I fear them. His last words heard among humans were these— after he had let out a greater sound from that part by which he used to speak more easily: "Dear me, I think I've shit myself." I suspect that he did; he certainly shat on everything else. (*Apocol.* 4.2–3)[14]

In the *Apocolocyntosis*, the tyrant Claudius can easily "externalize" himself. Unlike Nero, who must seek the right expressions to reveal his internal state and the merciful condition of his soul, Claudius with his last words easily reveals his essential nature: flatulent wind and excreta. His death also realizes the ideal of sympathy between the ruler's insides and the larger world of politics. Claudius' final words and deeds provide a fitting end to his political career, as the excrement with which he covered the empire now covers the emperor. This scene provides the comic double to the political ideals that are central to *De clementia*.[15] Seneca parodies his role as the voice of the emperor; with specific parallels to book 2 of *De clementia*, he scripts for Claudius a soul-revealing utterance. Yet where *De clementia* is allusive and metaphorical, the *Apocolocyntosis* is graphic and literal. In the opening of *De clementia*, Seneca states that Nero is the "soul of the empire," but he admits that very little is known about the nature of the soul itself. That it is delicate (*tenuis*) and hidden is the only clarification Seneca will offer (1.3.5). Discussion of the *animus* remains on the level of metaphor, such as the body-soul relationship between king and subjects, and the citation of *Georgics* 4.212–13 concerning the devotion of bees to their king. Instead of directly discussing the soul, Seneca focuses, in the *meditatio* that opens book 1 and with Nero's great-souled utterance at the start of book 2, on the power of language to reveal or shape it. In the *Apocolocyntosis*, however, there is no need for metaphorical and indirect revelations of Claudius' soul. It is a noxious wind that comes bubbling out along with excreta. His end provides graphic proof of what he has done to the empire. In *De ira* and *De clementia*, Seneca debates the true meaning of a "spirited utterance" (*vox animosa, Clem.* 2.2.3); in the *Apocolocyntosis* Seneca focuses on the "windy" nature of Claudius' soul. Before we move to such esoteric questions as the material nature of Claudius' soul and that of the soul in general, it seems appropriate to ask a more basic question here. How could a

Stoic philosopher and political adviser write a work characterized by obscene humor? How does Senecan satire relate, if at all, to the discussion of politics and selfhood found in his serious works?

Obscenity, Laughter, and Saturnalia

Claudius' death scene is not the only passage in the Senecan corpus to combine impolite bodily noises with a would-be apotheosis.[16] In the *Thyestes*, Atreus looks in on the conclusion of his brother's unwitting cannibalistic feast and describes the setting: "He lies down lazily on purple and gold, resting his head, now heavy with wine, on his left hand. He burps. O I am the highest of the gods and the king of kings! I have surpassed my desires" (*Thy.* 909–12). Both of these texts show the transgression of Roman moralizing ideals about the decorum and bodily control necessary for the elite male. As Catharine Edwards comments on Cicero's political attacks on Mark Antony, by vividly describing how the triumvir vomited in public after an evening of debauchery, "We catch a glimpse here of the self-presentation expected of Rome's political leaders, who should feel ashamed even to belch in front of others."[17] Thus, Atreus may briefly feel that he is the highest god and the greatest king because his brother's eructation demonstrates a "fatal loss of self-control," as Gottfried Mader suggests.[18] The self-described tyrant Atreus, on the other hand, is able to command and control himself in order to carry out his revenge.[19] In the *Apocolocyntosis*, Seneca demonstrates that Claudius is unfit to rule and control others because he cannot control the basic functioning of his own body.[20] Indeed, in his philosophical works, Seneca sternly condemns the bodily eructations and effusions of those addicted to food and drink. For example, in letter 95 Seneca attributes some of the stomach ailments suffered by gourmands to the fact that they insist on eating food that is too hot for their insides to handle:

> Do you think that that corrupt pus which is carried from the very flames of the stove into the mouth is extinguished in the stomach and intestines without causing any harm? How disgusting and deadly are their belches, how disgusted with themselves are they as they breathe out their hangover! You know that what has been taken in is rotting, not being digested. (*Ep.* 95.25)[21]

Similarly, in *De vita beata* Seneca inveighs against the Epicureans because they attempt to link virtue with pleasure. He paints an ironic portrait of a "virtuous" reveler: "That man pours himself forth into pleasures and is always belching and drunk; because he knows he lives with pleasure, he believes he lives with virtue (for he hears that pleasure cannot be separated from virtue); then he ascribes his vices to wisdom and parades what must be hidden" (12.3).[22] Yet the potential laughter generated by the obscene humor in the *Apocolocyntosis* appears to be counterproductive to the points Seneca is making about political control and self-control. Why does Seneca go to such graphic extremes and encourage his audience to laugh, an act that might risk disturbing individual and civic harmony?

As Simon Goldhill demonstrates, laughter has a problematic and hence tightly regulated place: "There is ... within the Greek intellectual tradition that stretches from Plato to Plutarch (and deeply influences Latin writing) a particular worry not merely about the threatening violence of laughter ... but also about the propriety of humor, its balance of *aischrologia* and *huponoia*, 'obscenity', and 'suggestiveness', and how such humor can challenge the self-control of the individual and the group."[23] Furthermore, one's sense of humor is an indication not only of one's sense of decorum but also of one's social status. In the *Nicomachean Ethics*, Aristotle notes that the type of things that a man allows himself to say and hear in jest marks the difference between a free, virtuous, and educated man and a slavish and uneducated one (1128a).[24] In *De officiis* Cicero notes that, as with all passions, by succumbing to laughter one risks losing self-control (1.102).[25] He advises that nature has not created us simply for play and jokes, but rather for sternness and more serious and important pursuits. Laughter, like sleep, is only permitted once one has worked long enough on weighty and serious affairs (1.103). This does not mean that all types of joking are allowed, however. Cicero differentiates two species of joking, and like Aristotle he notes that each type marks the difference between a free and a servile man.[26]

> The type of joking itself ought not to be excessive or immodest, but upright and witty. As we do not give children license to all types of games, but only allow those that are not devoid of good actions, so in jokes themselves some light of good wit must show through. To be sure, there are two types of joking: one is servile, wanton, disgraceful, obscene; the other is elegant, urbane, talented, witty.... Therefore it is easy to make a distinction between jokes worthy of a freeman and those worthy of a slave. The one is worthy of a most serious man, if the time is right, as, for example, when taking a break from mental labors; the

other is not even worthy of a freeborn man if it contains foul subject matter and obscene words. (*Off.* 1.103–4)[27]

If, according to this line of thought, one's laughter and the jokes one makes can differentiate the free and noble from the base and servile, then Seneca's portrayal of Claudius' death may link him with that paragon of the ignoble, the uneducated former slave Trimalchio. Seneca's joking about the loosening of Claudius' bowels seems dangerously close to Trimalchio's discourse concerning his own digestive problems (*Sat.* 47.1–7). Trimalchio is gravely concerned about the fact that "his stomach has not responded to him for many days" and about excessive bodily restraint in general. Nevertheless, the ridiculousness of Trimalchio's speech is signaled in the text. He is laughed at by his wife as he is speaking (47.5). His guests ironically thank him for his liberality and advice, but they restrain their laughter by taking frequent drinks from their cups (47.7).[28] Furthermore, there may be historical reasons for Seneca's description of Claudius' death. Tacitus writes that the poison first administered to Claudius by his wife, Agrippina, was rendered ineffectual by an evacuation of his bowels (*Ann.* 12.67.1). According to Suetonius, in an example of imperial micromanaging of subjects that baffles the imagination, Claudius, after learning of someone who was imperiled by excessive *pudor* and *continentia*, is said to have contemplated an edict in which he granted freedom and forgiveness to the regulation of the belly at the dinner table (*Claud.* 32).[29]

Cicero informs us that the Stoics did not censure obscene language if its use was necessary, nor did they subscribe to traditional ideals of bodily decorum. In response to Paetus' use of *mentula* in a previous letter, Cicero responds with a lengthy letter containing his thoughts on obscenity. He concludes by contrasting the modesty of the Academy with the straight-talking Stoics:[30]

> What about the fact that the thing itself is sometimes respectable, sometimes shameful? He breaks wind softly; it is a disgraceful act. If he's naked in the baths, you won't censure him.
>
> You have my Stoic lecture: "the wise man will speak in a straightforward manner" (= *SVF* 1.22). How much from one word of yours! You are welcome to dare all things in front of me; I am keeping and will keep (for thus I am accustomed) Plato's modesty. And so I have written with veiled language those things which the Stoics do with the most uncovered. But they also say that one ought to break wind and belch equally freely. Let me respect the Kalends of March.
>
> Love me and be well. (*Fam.* 9.22.4)[31]

In his philosophical works, however, Seneca adheres to a more traditional sense of shame than Cicero attributes to the typical Stoic. In *De ira* he admits that obscene language can cause us to blush uncontrollably (2.2.1). In *De beneficiis* he apologizes for using the word *matella*, "chamber pot" (3.26.2).[32] This is a word used without comment by Encolpius when he describes the silver chamber pots Trimalchio has at the ready during his game of ball (*Sat.* 27.3) and then uses to empty his bladder (27.5–6).[33] While Seneca does not encourage obscene language or indecorous bodily outbursts, he also does not discourage laughter, nor does he mark it as dangerous to society or self. In contrast to the frequent philosophical warnings that laughter may destroy one's decorum and self-control, Seneca in fact prescribes laughter as part of the care of the self.[34]

As part his lengthy enumeration of techniques for avoiding and curing anger in *De ira*, Seneca advises not to be overly curious. Nevertheless, spiteful gossip can simply be laughed away (3.11.1). Indeed, anger can be averted by turning things into a joke and a jest (3.11.2). In the *meditatio* that closes the dialogue, Seneca critiques himself for getting mad at a slave who was blocking his friend's entrance to some advocate's or rich man's door. In the future, he orders himself, instead of becoming angry, he must simply walk away and laugh (*recede longius et ride!*, 3.37.2). In *De ira* and *De tranquillitate animi* Seneca presents what may be the earliest attested pairings of Heraclitus and Democritus as the weeping and laughing philosophers.[35] Heraclitus pitied the lost souls around him and those who were falsely happy; Democritus, on the other hand was never in public without laughing. Thus, Seneca concludes, there is no place for anger; everything in the world must either be laughed at or wept at (*Ira* 2.10.5). In *De tranquillitate animi* Seneca sides with Democritus' reaction, saying that "it is more characteristic of a human to laugh down life than to bewail it" (15.2).

Even one of the most physically and psychologically damaging experiences imaginable, submission to torture by means of "fire, the rack, hot irons, or that device that reopens the still swollen wounds and drives their imprint even deeper" (*Ep.* 78.19), is an occasion for laughter and derision. Seneca claims that laughter can be a means to separate the soul from the body and not give in to physical pain, even under increasingly excruciating torture. Seneca praises the man "who does not stop laughing, although his very laughter caused the torturers to grow angry and try all the instruments of their cruelty. How can pain not be conquered by reason if it is conquered by laughter? . . . 'Not enough,' says the torturer; still he does not ask him to stop; 'not enough'; he does not answer. 'Not enough'; he laughs, and does so from his soul. After this example, will you be willing to laugh down pain?" (*Ep.* 78.18–19).

Yet the goal of Stoicism is not necessarily to be able laugh one's torturers to scorn while on the rack, although the Stoics would claim that this would be one of the perks of following their sect. Nor is the extirpation of the emotions an absolute goal. In contrast to the four "bad emotions"—pleasure, desire, pain, and fear—which should be eliminated, the Stoics claim that there are three "good emotions," or *eupatheiai*—joy, volition, and caution—which are felt by the wise man.[36] As the Stoic must work to rid the passions from the soul, the *eupatheiai* are the result of training as well. Seneca writes in letter 23: "Do this before all else, my Lucilius, learn how to feel joy . . . the other forms of merriment do not fill the breast; they relax the brow, they are light, unless by chance you judge that he who laughs feels joy: the soul ought to be lively and faithful and elevated above everything. Believe me, true joy is a serious thing" (23.3–4). In *De constantia sapientis* (On the constancy of the wise man), Seneca notes that the Stoic sage considers injury worthy of laughter (10.4) and insult the occasion for jokes (12.3). He encourages his readers to adopt a similar attitude (14.1, 17.1) and concludes that no one can be ridiculed if he is ready to laugh at himself first (17.2). In his letters, Seneca is unafraid to declare his independence from what he takes to be overly subtle, which is to say overly Greek, philosophical problems. His main strategy for dismissing such problems is derisive laughter.[37] Although in the *Apocolocyntosis* Seneca condemns the fool Claudius, later in life he admits that he too plays that role: "If ever I wish to be entertained by a fool, I don't have to look far: I laugh at myself" (*Ep.* 50.2).[38] Despite this focus on Stoic joy and laughter, in *De clementia* Seneca acknowledges that because of their reputation for excessively grim and unfeeling severity, Stoics are unpopular and considered to be unsuitable for giving advice to rulers (2.5.2). Seneca counters that the "uninformed" who view them this way are mistaken: no group is in fact more loving of the human race and more concerned for the common good (2.5.2).

If Seneca saw laughter as a means for self-correction, it is likely that he also would use it for social correction.[39] We have already considered Tacitus' description of the audience's reaction to Nero's funeral oration for Claudius. Now let us consider Tacitus' portrayal of the audience's reactions during the speech. According to the historian, Seneca's eloquence elicited public and derisive laughter at Claudius' expense. At the end of book 12 of the *Annales*, Tacitus notes that heavenly honors were decreed for Claudius and that the solemn rite of his funeral was celebrated in the manner of that of the Divine Augustus, with Agrippina rivaling the magnificence of her great-grandmother Livia (12.69). In the next book, Tacitus notes that the Senate decreed to Agrippina two lictors, a priesthood devoted to Claudius, as well as a state funeral and then a divinization for the emperor (13.2.3).[40] Tacitus then describes the eulogy that Nero gave on the day of the funeral (13.3). Written by Seneca, the *laudatio* is described as very refined, as would be expected from a man with such pleasing literary talents. It is tailored to the current tastes of the audience (13.3.1). This careful construction elicits two contradictory reactions from the audience. At first, both speaker and audience are earnest, as Claudius' lineage, accomplishments, and learning are enumerated. Yet as the speech turns to his foresight and wisdom, no one is able to restrain his laughter (13.3.1). Tacitus seems to believe that this laughter was an unintended consequence that destroyed the opening solemnity and occurred in spite of Seneca's careful composition. Nevertheless, the praise of Claudius' wisdom may have been intentionally ironic.[41] Seneca may have hoped to bring about the laughter from the audience as a means to test their view of Claudius and exclude him from the new imperial "in group" and also as a harbinger for his satirical portrayal of the "real" apotheosis of Claudius in the *Apocolocyntosis*.[42]

In addition, it appears that Seneca partially succeeded in changing the stereotypical view of the Stoics as grim, unbending, and humorless, at least with respect to his own public image. In republican times, the stereotype of the harsh, asocial Stoic could be used to win a jury trial, as Cicero humorously attacks Cato the Younger's misguided adherence to the Stoic paradoxes in *Pro Murena* (esp. secs. 60–67).[43] During the empire, however, accusations of adopting the "arrogance of the Stoic sect" could be grounds for political execution. According to Tacitus, Tigellinus brought this charge against Plautus (*Ann.* 14.57.3). Capito Cossutianus equated the enmity between the Stoic Thrasea Paetus and Nero to that of Cato and Julius Caesar and decried how Stoicism had always produced people "unwelcome to the state" (16.22.4). When Seneca comes under attack by Nero's toadies, they do not describe him as a stereotypical Stoic with a grim expression who refuses to take part in public affairs. Rather, Seneca's mocking wit is one of the charges brought against him.[44] According to these anonymous "baser people" (*deteriores*) toward whom Nero inclined after the death of Burrus in 62 CE, Seneca was openly (*palam*) hostile to Nero's pastimes.[45] He disparages his chariot-driving abilities and mocks (*inludere*) the emperor's voice every time he sings (14.52). We have already seen that one of Seneca's first official acts as speechwriter for the new princeps may have been to elicit derisive laughter at Claudius' expense; likewise, at the end of his period of power and influence over Nero, Seneca will not allow Nero to have a voice of his own. Rather, whenever Nero sings, Seneca provides his own ridiculing commentary. While we may be hesitant to believe Tacitus' claims that Seneca ironically mocked Claudius at the beginning of his regency and then openly made sport of Nero toward the end of his period of influence, laughter undeniably plays an important role in his philosophical works.

The worries that some authors express about the potentially disruptive forces of laughter only tell part of the story. The juxtaposition of solemnity and laughter lies at the core of ancient literature and culture. Fifth-century Athenian tragedy was followed by a satyr play, and Roman tragedy was followed by *exodia*, usually Atellan farces.[46] In his famous analysis of the development of novelistic discourse, Mikhail Bakhtin argues that all seriously elevated classical discourse had its "own parodying and travestying double, its own comic-ironic *contre-partie*."[47] Indeed, in Bakhtin's view, the Roman tradition of parody and of "Roman laughter" should be seen as Rome's great gift to the world, "as profoundly productive and deathless a creation ... as Roman law."[48] While the work of Bakhtin has proven invaluable for the study of satirical play and parody in the ancient world, we should be wary of seeing these elements as diametrically opposed to official discourse. As Terry Eagleton notes in his critique of Bakhtin's socially liberating view of laughter and carnival, it must be remembered that carnivalesque play is officially sanctioned and licensed play, and therefore we should be wary of any revolutionary potential it may have.[49] This connection between official political power and "Roman laughter" becomes painfully clear in the case of the *Apocolocyntosis*.

Much of the *Apocolocyntosis* is concerned with defining the official and legitimate forms of play and Saturnalia. While Claudius may be the fool king, the *Saturnalicius princeps*, his foolish appearance should not lead anyone to believe that he is harmless. He is in fact a savage and capricious tyrant, made worse by his stupidity, as Augustus warns the divine Senate (10.2). Claudius' monopoly of the court system also reveals the faulty relationship his reign established between Saturnalia and political power and between license and law. Saturnalia in the *Apocolocyntosis* is not simply an apolitical loosening of social hierarchy; it is a dangerous social weapon that was misused and manipulated by Claudius and those who benefitted financially from the emperor's monopoly on the legal system.[50] Under Claudius, the wrong people enjoyed an overextended period of power, and Seneca singles out the venal lawyers, or *causidici* (*causidici, venale genus*, 12.3.42).[51] Only for these few is the death of the fool king a legitimate cause for weeping. During Claudius' celebratory funeral one of the formerly respected interpreters of law, the *iurisconsulti*, steps out from the shadows and reminds the lamenting *causidici*, "I used to tell you: it won't be Saturnalia forever" (12.2).[52] Nevertheless, Claudius' funeral is presented as a Saturnalia in its own right. As Seneca characterizes it, "All were happy, merry: the Roman people were walking about as if free" (12.2). The Saturnalia of the *Apocolocyntosis* is not a period of social liberation and inversion. Rather than inverting the social order, the celebration of Claudius' death reaffirms and reestablishes the proper functioning of society. In the *Apocolocyntosis*, two types of Saturnalia, serving as metaphors for contrasting political regimes, are contested.[53] The false Saturnalia of Claudius is brought to an end by the true, socially solidifying Saturnalia that begins the reign of Nero.[54]

In the *Satyricon*, Petronius frequently portrays Saturnalia as a tool for reaffirming status and order, even among provincial politicians and ex-slaves. During the *Cena*, the freedman Ganymede begins his long harangue against the current political and alimentary situation by alleging that the aediles and the bakers are colluding on the supply of bread: "And so the little guy suffers," he laments, "for those big jaws always are celebrating Saturnalia" (44.3). Similarly, when the "slave" Giton laughs at the freedman Hermeros' attack on Ascyltus' own derisive laughter, Hermeros turns to him and asks: "Now you . . . you also are laughing, curly headed onion? Io Saturnalia, I ask, is it the month of December? When did you pay your liberation tax?" (58.2).[55] With Hermeros' indignant questions to Giton, Saturnalia becomes a tool for reestablishing social hierarchies and mores. Rather than as a celebration of unity, Hermeros mockingly uses the ritual cry of Saturnalia to put Giton back in his place. There is no solidarity between slave and ex-slave, as Hermeros references the everyday world of the slave marketplace and the monetary valuation of human beings. We can see something of the pride that Hermeros takes in his social position as a freedman. He has worked his way up from servile status, he has paid his liberation tax, and he is not going to let those below him easily and prematurely break any social boundaries and return to the golden age of Saturn.[56]

Claudius' Voice and Judgments

When Claudius first arrives at Olympus, a messenger gives a description of him to Jupiter that focuses on his physical appearance. It first begins with the matter-of-fact note that he is of good stature with very grey hair. The description quickly turns to Claudius' physical ailments: he continually shakes his head and drags his right foot (*Apocol.* 5.2). Yet it is not so much his appearance that causes any real consternation among the Olympians as it is his voice, or rather the fact that Claudius' speech is entirely incomprehensible. When the messenger asks Claudius' nationality, the emperor replies with a wild noise and indistinct words (*perturbato sono et voce confusa*, 5.2). The messenger could not understand him, as Claudius appeared to be speaking neither Greek nor Latin, nor any known language (5.2).[57] When the well-traveled Hercules is sent to figure out who this new arrival is, the god is immediately frightened by Claudius' monstrous appearance. Claudius' voice, however, is so disturbing that it puts the emperor out of the realm of all terrestrial dwelling creatures. It is like that of sea monsters, "hoarse and inarticulate" (*raucam et implicatum*, 5.3).[58] Upon closer inspection, Hercules realizes that he is confronted with something like a human being (*quasi homo*, 5.4), so he asks Claudius' lineage, quoting an easy line from Homer: "Who of men are you, and from where? What kind are your city and your parents?" (5.4).[59] Claudius immediately understands the quotation and cites a Homeric line in return to indicate that he is a Trojan Caesar: "The wind bore me from Ilium and brought me to the land of the Cicones" (5.4 = *Od.* 9.39). At this point the narrator interrupts; he will not let Claudius choose his means of epic self-presentation. In an aside, he notes that Claudius should properly be defined by the next verse, which is "truer, and equally Homeric: 'and there I sacked a city and destroyed the people'" (5.4 = *Od.* 9.40).

In fact, Claudius' use of Homer to claim Trojan ancestry is doubly attacked. The goddess Fever, who alone has accompanied Claudius on his ascent, sets the record straight. She claims that Claudius' true origins are not by the banks of the river Xanthus but rather on the Rhone. He is not heir to the line of Caesars but rather a true Gaul. Picking up on the narrator's preference that Claudius use Homer not to describe his origins but to describe the destruction he brought to Rome, the goddess Fever claims that Claudius lived up to his Gallic birth. Referring to the famous sack of Rome in 390 BCE, Fever states that Claudius acted as a Gaul should and captured the city (6.1).[60] This statement so incenses Claudius that he orders her execution. Here again Claudius' inarticulate voice fails him; no one has any idea what he is saying (6.2).

Since he cannot describe himself in Homeric terms, Claudius turns to his forensic abilities. When he is allowed to give an extended speech, he focuses on his role as the master of the Roman courts. Unfortunately, only the opening of what may have been a lengthy and persuasive speech to Hercules survives.

> I was the one who, before your temple, used to pronounce judgments every day during July and August. You know how much misery I bore there when I listened to lawyers day and night. If this happened to you, although you yourself seem to be very strong, you would have preferred to clean the sewers of Augeas: I drained off much more manure. But since I wish . . . (*Apocol.* 7.4–5)[61]

For a brief moment, Claudius is granted a modicum of self-definition and eloquence.[62] Yet even this opening passage focuses on Claudius' transgressions. While he was alive, there was no end to the courtroom drama. He did not respect temporal boundaries, and his Saturnalia paradoxically turned into a never-ending court docket.[63] Indeed, it appears that with Hercules as his champion, Claudius is nearly able to live among the Olympians and have his apotheosis added to the end of Ovid's *Metamorphoses* (9.5). Only Augustus, who speaks for the first time since joining the divine Senate, prevents Claudius from duping the other Olympians.[64] Augustus' argument focuses on the capital judgments Claudius rendered against the imperial family. Augustus' description of the murder of Messalina, his great-great niece and Claudius' third wife, merits particular attention. "You killed Messalina, whose great uncle I was as much as yours. 'I don't know,' you say? May the gods curse you: it is so much more shameful that you did not know than that you killed." (11.1).[65] Seneca's Augustus treats Claudius the way Seneca himself treats Nero: he puts words into his mouth. The "I don't know" (*nescio*) that Augustus attributes to Claudius not only demonstrates that he is an ignorant judge but also suggests that Claudius acts only on impulse and lacks the basic self-knowledge and ability to form rational judgments that, according to the Stoics, would qualify him as a human being. At the end of his oration, Augustus gives Claudius a chance to speak for himself, but he knows the emperor will simply stammer away.[66] If Claudius suddenly gained the ability to speak clearly, the lines between emperor and slave would be redrawn. Augustus confidently wagers, "You want to make this man a god? Look at his body, made while the gods were angry. In short, let him say three words quickly and he can lead me off as his slave" (11.3).

When Claudius arrives in Hades, his words again mark him as an ignorant judge. Here, at least, he is allowed to speak for himself. Upon entering, he is met by a battle line of his victims (13.5). Claudius, who in fact only realized he was dead as he passed his funeral on earth, mistakes this procession for the welcoming wagon. He claims in Greek, "Everything is full of friends!" but then asks, "How did you all come here?" (13.6). One of his victims, a certain Pedo Pompeius, cannot believe Claudius' ignorance: "What are you saying, most cruel man? You're asking how? Who sent us here other than you, murderer of all your friends?" He then takes Claudius to the tribunal of Aeacus (13.6). Thus, Claudius is twice marked as a murderous tyrant by the manner in which he renders judgments, or better, by his confessions—one put into his mouth by Augustus, the other given in his own words—that he has no knowledge of what he did. As Augustus himself says, Claudius should be cursed not simply because he killed but because he did not know he killed (11.1). In *De clementia*, by contrast, Nero's words before signing a death warrant demonstrate his inherent beneficence and self-awareness. Even in the case of two common thieves, Nero delays and struggles with the sometimes grim demands of his imperial position. In full knowledge of his decision, Nero exclaims that he should never have learned how to write (*vellem litteras nescirem!*, 2.1.2).

Judging Rulers in This World and the Next

Claudius' voice and judgment are not the only topics of ridicule. At the start of the text, Seneca quotes Vergil and states that his eyewitness authority claims to have seen Claudius making the journey to heaven "with uneven steps" (*non passibus aequis*, *Apocol.* 1.2). This passage from the *Aeneid* (2.724) describes the child Iulus' attempts to keep pace with his father's steps as they flee Troy. Again, the only epic citation that truly fits Claudius concerns the destruction of a city. While he is equated with Aeneas' son, the comparison is infantilizing and stresses the physical traits that prohibit Claudius from being properly considered a *pater patriae*. Though Claudius attempts to define himself by displaying his philological knowledge and quoting Homer, the only literary quotations that accurately characterize him are those chosen by others.

As Claudius' ascent to heaven mimics the halting steps of the young Iulus, so when the god Mercury urges the Fates to hasten the emperor's death, he does so with a quote from Vergil. Here the line is not from epic but from the didactic and metaphorical political world of book 4 of the *Georgics*. Claudius' initial death throes are described as follows:

> Claudius began to gasp for his life and was not able to find a way out.
>
> Then Mercury, who had always been delighted with his talent, took one of the three Parcae aside and said: "Why, most cruel woman, do you allow this poor man to be tortured? . . . Do what must be done: 'give him over to death; let the better one rule in an empty hall.'" (*Apocol.* 3.1–2 = *G.* 4.90)[67]

With its concluding quotation of *Georgics* 4.90, Mercury's speech persuades the Fates to act, and the thread of Claudius' life is cut. This Vergilian citation is not to be seen simply as a clever use of poetic authority; nor is it to be understood simply as another humorous travesty of the Vergilian corpus. The larger context of this passage also must be considered. Vergil describes what to do when two king bees are competing for the loyalty of one hive (4.67–102). After the battle is concluded, Vergil orders the beekeeper to kill the king who seems to be the worse (*deterior qui visus*, 4.89) and allow the better to rule in the royal hall (4.90). As Richard Thomas notes in his commentary, these lines have traditionally been interpreted as pure allegory for the post-Actium political situation: Mark Antony is the worse king; Octavian, the better.[68] Thomas is right to caution the modern reader against pushing Vergil's text in this direction. Seneca, however, does not shy away from the metaphorical potential of this passage. The political parallels between Vergil's two king bees and Nero and Claudius are clear.

The lines following this excerpt, which likely would have been triggered in the mind of Seneca's audience, describe how physical differences will allow one to differentiate between the good and the bad king.

> One will be bright with spots coated with gold—for there are two types: the better one is conspicuous in appearance and bright with golden scales; that other one is bristling from laziness and ingloriously drags its wide belly. As there are two appearances for the kings, so there are two bodies for the people. (*G.* 4.91–95)[69]

The physical differences between kings are central to the *Apocolocyntosis*. Claudius limps his way to heaven. His grotesque, half-human appearance disgusts and frightens the gods, causing Hercules to think that his thirteenth labor had arrived. Like Vergil's "better king," Nero is appropriately handsome. In Apollo's poem, sung as the Fates spin Nero's endless golden thread, the god describes the new emperor as similar to him in looks and appearance (4.1). He is like the dawn or the evening star rising. The concluding lines of the poem celebrate Nero's radiant countenance. On the one hand, these elements appear to be standard fare for satire. A line from a classic text is placed in a ridiculous context. The focus of the political theory is squarely on bodily appearance.[70] The good king, both human and apian, is attractive; the bad king is ugly. The satire of the *Apocolocyntosis* goes deeper. As we have already seen with Claudius' speech and judgments, much of the material in the *Apocolocyntosis* serves as a comic precursor to the political and psychological themes developed in *De clementia*.

The quotation from *Georgics* book 4 can be related to *De clementia* in several ways. As demonstrated in the previous chapter, in this treatise Seneca twice uses the king bee to define the ideal king. In both the *Apocolocyntosis* and *De clementia* (1.19) he focuses on the king bee's appearance. In *De clementia* Seneca takes the fact that the king is without a stinger to be proof that nature intended the human king to be mild. This physical appearance of the king bee should metaphorically structure the inner reality of the human king. In the opening of this treatise, Seneca also quotes from *Georgics* book 4 to describe the sympathetic psychological relationship between the king and his subjects, in order to stress that while the king, the soul of the empire, is safe, all act with one mind. But when the king has left, the state breaks apart (*rege incolumi mens omnibus una / amisso rupere fidem, Clem.* 1.4.1 = G. 4.212–13). Thus, in both of his texts from the start of Nero's reign, Seneca uses Vergil to define and differentiate the good king from the bad in terms of *animus*, body, and political life. Vergil's bees provide the basis for several complex metaphors that range from contrasting the appearance of Nero and Claudius in the *Apocolocyntosis* to elucidating the psychology of kingship in *De clementia*. In addition, as we have seen, *De clementia* also stresses the unreliability of appearances. The king bee's merciful appearance does not translate into the political world of humans. Similarly, as frightful as Claudius' appearance is, he still almost manages to deceive the Olympians and join their pantheon. It is only when Augustus demonstrates his inability to speak and his rendering of death sentences in ignorance that the vote is cast to banish Claudius.

There are related problems with sentencing Claudius in Hades. In a fitting piece of poetic justice, the judge who is celebrated as "deciding cases after only hearing one side, and sometimes neither" (12.3.20–22) is condemned and sentenced by Aeacus before his advocate, P. Petronius, is able to answer the charges. Yet Aeacus' quotation of the Hesiodic law of retaliation ends with a bathetic thud (14.2 = Hes., frag. 286 Merkelbach and West). Claudius, the inveterate dice player, is sentenced to gamble eternally with a bottomless dice cup. Once again, an emperor is necessary to assign Claudius to his proper place. Caligula suddenly appears and produces witnesses who testify that they saw him repeatedly beating his old uncle Claudius. He is given as a slave to Caligula, who in turn gives him to his freedman Menander to be his legal secretary (15.2). Thus, Claudius will still endlessly toil away in the courts, but now without any influence. As Claudius was accused of being under the thumb of his freedmen in life, now in Hades he is a slave to one. In addition, Claudius' appearance before Aeacus may also have a deeper significance that problematizes the Platonic tradition of the judgment of the souls of kings in Hades.

At the end of the *Gorgias*, Socrates tells a story that he thinks his listeners might consider a myth (*mythos*) but that he himself considers to be a rational account (*logos*, 523a). According to Socrates' tale, during the time of Cronus and early in the reign of Zeus final judgments for mortals were rendered while they were still alive. People stood fully clothed before their judges. Because the judges were deceived by people's outward appearance, judgments were rendered poorly, and Tartarus and the Isles of the Blessed were filled with undeserving people (523a3–c2). Zeus rectified the situation by having people judged after they died and by appointing three of his sons as judges—Minos and Rhadamanthys for people from Asia, Aeacus for those from Europe. He also ordered people's souls to be judged rather than their bodies (523c2–524a9). Socrates offers his reasoning for this practice and the result in the underworld.

> Well then, I think that the same thing that concerns the body also concerns the soul, Callicles. Everything is clearly manifest in the soul, when it is stripped from the body, both the things that are there naturally and the experiences that a person has in the soul through the pursuit of each of his affairs. So when they come to the judges, those from Asia to Rhadamanthys, he stops them and looks at the soul of each. He does not know whose it is, but often when he has taken hold of the Great King or some other king or dynast, he sees that there is nothing

healthy in the soul but that it is severely whipped and full of scars from false oaths and wrongdoing, which each deed has imprinted on the soul. And he sees that everything is crooked from lies and falsehood and nothing is straight, because the soul grew up without the truth; and because of power and luxuriousness and hybris and lack of self-control in its actions, he sees that the soul is full of disproportion and deformity. After seeing this soul, he sends it away ignominiously straight toward the prison, and once it arrives there, it will endure the punishments that are fitting. (*Grg.* 524d4–525a)

The Romans knew this passage and applied it to their own political situation. Tacitus approvingly cites Plato when describing the psychological torments of Tiberius:

The opening of Caesar's letter seems to be revealing, for he began with these words: "What I should write, senators, or how I should write, or what I should not write at this time, may the gods and goddesses destroy me worse than I already feel myself to be perishing, if I know." To such an extent were his crimes and his disgraceful acts themselves turning into punishment. And that man most outstanding in wisdom did not vainly assert that if the minds of tyrants were uncovered, the lacerations and the blows would be seen, for just as bodies are torn apart by beatings, so the soul is torn apart by cruelty and passion and evil plans. Indeed, neither his position nor his seclusion was protecting Tiberius, but he himself confessed the torments of his breast and his punishment. (*Ann.* 6.6)[71]

Thus, Seneca parodies Plato's myth of judgment in the underworld and the marks on the tyrant's soul.[72] There are no distinguishing marks on Claudius' revealing him to be a tyrant. Similarly, his body does not reveal traces of the servile abuse he suffered. Just as he was almost able to deceive the Olympians, so in Hades Claudius is almost able to deceive Aeacus. It is only when Caligula calls witnesses to attest to the beatings he inflicted upon his uncle that Claudius is sentenced to suffer a harsher and more fitting punishment. Two emperors, representing the positive and negative poles of the concept, keep Claudius from slipping through the cracks of the justice system of the afterlife.

While Seneca mocks the abilities of the divine senators and judges, the problematic marking on Claudius' body and soul speaks to a theme that I have traced in *De clementia*. The idea of marking virtue and vice in order to enable Nero to render proper judgment is a metaphor that structures *De clementia*: "Since some vices imitate virtues, they are not able to be differentiated, unless you brand them with a mark by which they can be distinguished" (*nam cum sint vitia quaedam virtutes imitantia, non possunt secerni, nisi signa quibus dinoscantur impresseris*, 1.3.1).[73] When laying down rules for punishment, Seneca tells Nero that he must not only address the health of the body politic but also care for the scar that is left behind (*sed etiam honestae cicatricis*, 1.17.1–2).[74] As we have seen, Petronius also refers to curing the psychological scars of anger. When they end their fight over Giton, Encolpius urges Eumolpus to heal his soul and leave it "without a scar" (*sine cicatrice*, 99.2).[75] We have already looked at Encolpius' self-address while aboard Lichas' ship and seen how his psychological *constantia* is destroyed once he hears the voices of his enemies. Let us return to this passage and consider their various plans for escape. From the metaphor of scars on the soul, this section of the *Satyricon* quickly moves to considering the role of scars on the body, both real and artificial.

After the suggestion and rejection of several stratagems to avoid discovery, Encolpius suggests that Eumolpus cover them with his black ink (*atramentum*) so that he and Giton can pretend to be Aethopian slaves (102.13). Giton debunks this plan, noting that the ink will simply stain their bodies, not change them (102.15). Before reaching this conclusion, he runs through a list of distinctive bodily markings employed by non-Romans throughout the empire.[76] "Why don't you circumcise us to look like Jews," Giton asks ironically, "and pierce our ears to imitate Arabs, and whiten our faces so that even the Gauls think we're fellow countrymen?" (102.14). Returning to the original plan to be disguised as Aethopian slaves, Giton adds, "Are we able to cut our foreheads with scars? Are we able to bend our legs into a circle? And are we able to bring our ankles down to the ground?" (102.15). Eumolpus, however, combines the ideas of Encolpius and Giton and turns the tradition of scarring and marking on its head. Instead of being a permanent mark of recognition, scars are drawn by Eumolpus' artistic hand on the faces of Encolpius and Giton as a temporary means of disguise. They go up on deck, where Eumolpus' servant shaves their heads and eyebrows. Then Eumolpus cleverly marks their foreheads to make Encolpius and Giton appear to be runaway slaves who have been branded (103.2).[77]

Their plan is quickly foiled. A seasick passenger notices our heroes having their heads shaven and reports the bad omen to Lichas.[78] Eumolpus explains that he cut their hair even though there was no storm so that the marks of the letters on their brows could more easily be read (105.2). In order to expiate the gods, Lichas orders the "slaves" to receive forty lashes. Encolpius is able to endure three with Spartan bravery, but Giton shouts so loudly after the first blow that Tryphaena recognizes his voice. After Giton is revealed, Lichas confirms Encolpius' identity by grabbing his loins. This act leads Encolpius in his guise as narrator to once again connect himself to Ulysses, this time commenting on the original scar-recognition scene: "Now let someone marvel that after twenty years Ulysses' nurse discovered his scar as an indicator of the truth, when that most shrewd man so cleverly went straight to the single thing that identified the runaway even though all the lineaments of the body were confused" (105.10).[79] Encolpius and Giton are marked with faux scars in an effort to avoid being captured and likely tortured; nevertheless, they are captured and tortured. Thus, Petronius inverts the tradition of scars as marks of recognition with Eumolpus' scripted scars and then references the ur-scene after Encolpius and Giton are beaten. The real whip marks on their backs lead to recognition of their true identity. Similarly, before the infernal judge, Claudius lacks all the distinguishing scars he received during his life as marks of his tyranny and servility. Only Claudius' last words on earth fully reveal his true essence.

What Lies Within?

Do our insides house the soul? Or are they home to other, seemingly more elemental necessities of life, such as air, blood, and food in various states of digestion? Is the soul mixed with these elements, or does it remain pure and separate? What is the proper relationship between the internal and the external? While these may seem to be questions that apply to the fields of medicine, philosophy, or even theology, they are also central to the *Satyricon*. Our heroes' entrapment within the body of Lichas' ship and their subsequent struggles to escape serve as a larger metaphor for their own bodily experiences in this scene. After Encolpius and Giton hear the voices of Lichas and Tryphaena, they "lose their blood" in fear (100.5).[80] Giton struggles to catch his breath and remain conscious (101.1). He only calls back his spirit when sweat pours out over both him and Encolpius (101.2). When they go up on deck to carry out their plan, they are seen by a seasick passenger who is leaning over the side vomiting (103.5). Giton suggests that in order to avoid being discovered, they get the ship to turn around because one of them is dying of seasickness (101.8). One of Eumolpus' rejected plans is to hide Encolpius and Giton with his clothing in two leather sacks, which will be left slightly open, of course, so that they can get air and food (102.8). Encolpius quickly quashes this suggestion, pointing out further "necessities of nature." What goes in must come out; human beings are not solid inside (102.10). This is a comically basic statement about simple bodily truths, to be sure, but we have also heard such words of wisdom from that master of what lies within, Trimalchio.[81]

After returning from the restroom, Trimalchio allows all of his guests to avoid excessive internal *continentia*, stating, "No one of us is born solid" (*nemo nostrum solide natus est*, 47.4). We looked at this passage briefly in chapter 3. Now let us look at it in more depth, first to focus on a particular word used by Trimalchio, *anathymiasis*, and then to consider further what lies within Trimalchio, Claudius, and then Seneca himself.[82] Trimalchio concludes his speech by saying,

> "Believe me, *anathymiasis* goes into your brain and makes a disturbance (*fluctum*) in your entire body. I know that many have died in this way, since they do not wish to tell the truth to themselves." We thanked him for his kindness and his understanding, and straight away we restrained our laughter with frequent sips from our drinks. (*Sat.* 47.2–7)[83]

As we have seen, Trimalchio's language can be related directly to Seneca's language in *De tranquillitate animi*.[84] As Edward Courtney notes, Trimalchio's claim that many people have died from *continentia* because they were unwilling to tell themselves the truth (*nolunt sibi verum dicere*, 47.6) echoes Serenus' opening statement that many people do not make moral progress because of self-deception and unwillingness to tell themselves the truth (*quis sibi verum dicere?*, *Tranq.* 1.16).[85] Trimalchio's words can be linked even more closely to the passage in which Serenus asks Seneca to give him a cure for "movements of his soul" (*motus animi*) and his "fluctuation" (*fluctuationem*, 1.17). Similarly, Trimalchio describes the dangers in terms of vapor (*anathymiasis*) that can travel to the brain (*cerebrum*) and create a flux (*fluctum*) throughout the entire body. For each author, bodily and psychic problems are described in the same terms of fluctuation and flux.

According to Trimalchio, the dangers of internal, physical flux come from *anathymiasis* that is not properly regulated and is contained too long within the body. Where did Trimalchio learn the word *anathymiasis*? It only appears here in Latin, and the *Oxford Latin Dictionary* translates it as "vapors" but uses quotes, presumably for decorum. It is a rare word in Greek as well, appearing primarily in philosophical and medical texts. It is so rare in fact that Liddell and Scott's *Greek-English Lexicon* (9th edition) has to stoop to citing Petronius alongside Heraclitus, Aristotle, and Galen. So, again, where did Trimalchio learn this word? In the past, scholars have focused exclusively on the medical context of *anathymiasis*. In his commentary on the *Cena*, M. S. Smith cites Galen, who "speaks of an exhalation (*anathymiasis*) from the humors being drawn up toward the head."[86] More recently, Peter Toohey has written two lengthy analyses on the topic of Trimalchio's constipation. In his latest analysis, a chapter titled "Time's Passing" in his 2004 book *Melancholy, Love, and Time*, Toohey argues that Trimalchio's bodily difficulties are a corporeal registering of the irrevocable linearity of the passage of time. Toohey follows Smith's commentary and singles out Galen and the Latin medical writer Celsus, who is more likely to have influenced Petronius, to explain *anathymiasis*, stating that it "must inevitably point to a humoral context."[87] While Trimalchio's use of the word *anathymiasis* should be seen within the context of medicine in the ancient world, further investigation of this curious word is necessary. In fact, *anathymiasis* brings together the discourses of Stoicism and medicine.[88]

The concept of the soul as consisting of or being nourished by *anathymiasis*, a specific kind of air or vapor, has a long history, stretching back to Heraclitus.[89] In *De anima*'s opening run-through of various concepts of the nature of the soul, Aristotle writes that Heraclitus constructed all things from the soul's emanation (*anathymiasin*, 405a25). The Stoics adopted this Heraclitean concept of the soul. In fact, what many scholars take to be the only authentic, verbatim quotation of Heraclitus' famous "river fragment" is preserved by Arius Didymus, quoting Zeno and Cleanthes on the nature of the soul.

> Concerning the soul, Cleanthes, setting out the doctrines of Zeno for comparison with the other natural philosophers, says that Zeno says that the soul is a perceptive vapor (*aisthêtikên anathymiasin*), just as Heraclitus does. For wanting to show that souls are always becoming intelligent by exhalation (*anathymiômenai*), he likened them to rivers, saying that "upon those who step into the same rivers different and different waters flow" and "souls are exhaled (*anathymiôntai*) from moist things." So, like Heraclitus, Zeno says that the soul is a vapor (*anathymiasin*). (*SVF* 1.141)

In addition, Galen writes,

> Everyone who supposes that the soul is breath (*pneuma*) says that it is preserved by exhalation (*ek te tes anathymiaseos*) both of the blood and of the <air>

drawn into the body by inhalation through the windpipe. (*SVF* 2.782 = Long and Sedley 1987, 53E)[90]

In their commentary on this passage, Long and Sedley write that the terms *anathymiasis* and *pneuma* establish "the Stoic provenance of Galen's generalized statement."[91]

This is not to claim that a Stoic reading is to be privileged over a strictly medical one. Trimalchio's two references to doctors (*medici*) make a medical context abundantly clear.[92] We should remain aware, however, of the important Stoic context of the word *anathymiasis*. More specifically, this word and Trimalchio's discussion of *continentia* fit directly into a Senecan context. Petronius' engagement with Seneca in this passage exists on two levels. First, Trimalchio stresses the importance of self-address and self-evaluation, "confessing the truth to yourself," as well as the dangers of internal fluctuation, advice that can be found throughout Seneca's writings but that also points specifically to the opening of *De tranquillitate animi*.[93] In Trimalchio's formulation, Stoic *anathymiasis* also necessitates language, but rather than being an ethical indication of one's internal state, Stoic "confession of the truth" becomes a confession of the condition of one's bowels. Rather than being "a perceptive vapor," *anathymiasis* becomes, in the *Satyricon*, deadly gaseous exhalations that challenge the ideal of Stoic *continentia* and produce bodily flux and death. Second, Trimalchio's connections between noxious internal vapors, defecation, and death highlight key aspects of the death of Claudius in the *Apocolocyntosis*. Let us now consider Claudius' death again, focusing on the theme of the emperor's death as a struggle with the breath of life that finally results in his release of excreta and noxious winds.[94]

As we have seen, in *De ira* and *De clementia* Seneca debates the true meaning of a spirited utterance (*vox animosa*, *Clem*. 2.2.3). In the *Apocolocyntosis* he focuses on the "windy" nature of Claudius' soul and turns a "spirited utterance" into a graphic reality. Claudius "bubbles out his life" (*et ille quidem animam ebulliit*, 4.2). The Latin word *anima* functions on two main levels: on the physical level, the word can mean "breath," or the natural element air or wind; on the more abstract level, it can mean "life" and hence "soul" or "spirit" (*OLD*, defs. 7, 8, 9). In fact, Seneca continues to focus on the exhalations and the air involved in Claudius' death. He notes that Claudius "expired" while listening to some comic actors (*expiravit autem dum comoedos audit*). Similar to *anima*, the verb *expirare* contains both the literal idea of "exhale," for example, vapors, and, with or without the complementary *animam*, the transferred sense of "to breathe one's last" or simply "expire," "die." Finally, we have Claudius' penultimate "utterance" and release of wind: the "greater sound" that he emitted "from that part out of which he spoke more easily" (4.3).

Claudius' death starts off as a fatal loss of *anima* and then progresses to a literal loss of everything that is inside him: air, the breath of life, flatulent wind, and finally excreta. Thus, Seneca's two political works focus on the extremes of high and low, the good king and the base tyrant. Seneca attempts to differentiate the two in terms of a strict political dichotomy.[95] In the *Apocolocyntosis* Seneca has no trouble developing Claudius' death and final words to reveal his internal state and to display on a graphic level what the emperor had metaphorically done to everything around him. This scene would appear to be typical fare for satire and comedy. Seneca's relentless descriptions of the emperor's inability to control his body, and his body's orifices in particular, turn the Saturnalian princeps into the grotesque and carnivalesque body par excellence. The classical body remains firmly under control. From the standpoint of traditional Roman mores, a political leader should display a closed, "classical" body in public.[96]

The *Apocolocyntosis* and *De clementia* do not simply portray the gulf between Claudius and Nero as unbridgeable. There are political and psychological anxieties present in these works. In the *Apocolocyntosis*, Claudius can easily "externalize" himself, but in *De clementia* Seneca worries about how Nero can reveal the merciful state of his soul through actions and declarations. Both texts suggest that dichotomies are in danger of breaking down. As Seneca notes in *De clementia*, since some vices can imitate virtues, he will brand each one with a distinguishing mark. Yet the judgments of the divine Senate and of Aeacus concerning Claudius question this ideal. In the *Apocolocyntosis*, both the Olympian Augustus and the infernal Caligula are necessary to interpret Claudius properly and ensure that he is judged correctly. By bringing these positive and negative imperial exemplars together to perform the same task, Seneca also reveals the ambiguities of the principate. Furthermore, the problematic political dichotomy of *De clementia* and the *Apocolocyntosis* also structures a problematic psychological dichotomy and opposing views about the core makeup the self. Claudius' windy death and soul-revealing utterance speak to philosophical concerns and questions about the material nature of the soul. *De clementia* describes the soul as delicate and refined, *tenuis*. It is impossible to locate or perceive it directly (1.3.5). In the *Apocolocyntosis*, as in the *Satyricon*, however, the vile body of the tyrant only contains even more vile bodies, in addition to deadly, polluting air.[97]

The idea that the soul is air, wind, or the breath of life has a long history in Greek and Roman thought.[98] An investigation of the origin of the word *psyche* plays a brief role in the etymological games in Plato's *Cratylus*. Socrates suggests that the originator of the word noticed that the life force was related to the power to breathe and to revive and hence called this power *psyche* (399d–e). He immediately notes that this off-the-cuff history is liable to ridicule, so he quickly offers another possibility. Yet even on his dying day, as depicted in the *Phaedo*, Socrates again jokes about this relationship. As Socrates makes the transition from proving that the soul exists before birth to the more difficult proof that it survives death, he plays with the anxieties of his interlocutors, Cebes and Simmias. Socrates notes that they seem "to fear childishly that when the soul leaves the body, the wind will actually blow it apart and scatter it, especially if someone happens to die not in windless weather but in some great windstorm" (77d–e). While this claim draws some nervous laughter from Cebes, similar anxieties persisted into the Roman era.

The Stoics argued that the corporeal soul was a piece of the fiery air (*pneuma*) that permeates and gives life to the universe.[99] All objects, from rocks and logs to humans, have a share of this *pneuma*. The different levels of being are determined by the various degrees of tension at which this *pneuma* exists, the degree to which it is rarified. Thus, the levels of tension transform and build the universal *pneuma* from *hexis*, the simple binding structure that characterizes nonsentient objects such as rocks, logs, or bones; to *physis*, or growth, which defines the level of plants; to *psyche*, which resides at the core of animals; to the rational soul that defines humanity for the Stoics.[100] According to the traditional Stoic view, at their essential core human beings are "intelligent warm breaths," as Anthony Long puts it succinctly.[101] This materialism led to concerns, much like those in Plato's *Phaedo*, about what happened to the airy, material soul after death. This question was especially pressing for the Stoics, who, while being materialists like the Epicureans, were unwilling to admit with them that the soul simply dispersed after death.[102] Cicero takes up the problem in book 1 of the *Tusculan Disputations*. He discusses the Stoic notion that the soul is warm air and assures his readers that despite its material nature, the soul can survive any form of death. Since the Stoic soul is part of the firey *pneuma* that permeates the universe, it is able to survive the damp, thick, and murky lower regions of the air and hold together as it rises up through the atmosphere to its kindred fiery and rarified upper regions (1.42–43).

Seneca also writes, in letter 57, about the soul's ability to endure and escape any form of death, even being crushed by a mountain. Seneca addresses anxieties about the soul being trapped after he himself is buried deep within the earth on his difficult journey through the Crypta Neapolitana from Baiae to Naples. Seneca concludes this letter,

> Now you think I am speaking of the Stoics, who think that the human soul when crushed by a great weight is not able to remain intact but is scattered immediately, because there will not be a free passage for it? But I am not doing this: those who say this seem to me to be wrong. Just as a flame is not able to be crushed (for it escapes around what oppresses it), just as air is not harmed by beatings or blows, nor is it cut, but it flows back around the places it has left, thus the soul, which consists of the most subtle matter, is not able to be caught within a body that has been crushed, but by virtue of its fineness it breaks through the very things by which it is crushed. Just as lightning, though it strikes and flashes far and wide, can return through the smallest hole, so the soul, which is still finer than fire, escapes through every body. (*Ep.* 57.6–9)[103]

Seneca's journey through mud, dust, and foul air (*Ep.* 57.2) inside the mountain pass leads him to consider the nature of the soul and its ability to escape the disgusting foulness of the earth and the body. Seneca's experience of being trapped inside the dank, dark earth serves as a metaphor for the soul's imprisonment in the body.[104] Indeed, this letter, in which Seneca concludes his first Campanian travel narrative, encapsulates Seneca's problems with air, breath, and soul.

During his travels, Seneca notes that his lifelong struggles with his ailing body have become particularly troublesome. Although Seneca claims to have lived such a sickly life that "no disease is unknown to him," he writes that difficulty breathing occasioned by chronic asthma seems to be the particular ailment assigned to him (54.1). With this claim, the elderly Seneca of the *Epistles* describes himself in much the same way that he described Claudius in the *Apocolocyntosis*.[105] Just as Seneca has been attended by asthma throughout his life, so the goddess Fever, who lived with the emperor for all of his years, follows Claudius to heaven (6.1). Both are afflicted with breathing problems. Claudius has struggled with the breath of life for sixty-four years (3.1). As the emperor begins to die, he first struggles to breathe and cannot find a way out

(2.4). Similarly, Seneca describes the onset of asthma as a process of breathing one's last (*Ep.* 54.1–2).[106] He describes this sickness as a casting out of the breath of life (*hoc animam egerere, Ep.* 54.2). Even after the attack subsides, Seneca still struggles to breathe normally (*Ep.* 54.6).[107] After this statement, Seneca makes an important distinction between his difficulty breathing, the affliction inside his lungs, and the condition of his soul. He writes that he remains unconcerned about his problems breathing so long as he does not breathe an asthmatic sigh from his soul (*quomodo volet, dummodo non ex animo suspirem, Ep.* 54.6). Here we can see a crucial difference between Seneca and the dead emperor. Although both are sickly and gasp for life (*animam*), Claudius is never described as having a soul (*animus*). What comes out of him when he dies, as well as what lies trapped inside of Trimalchio, is only noxious flatulence and excreta. This suggests that what lies inside of the two revelers is not a rational soul capable of judgment but something lesser, capable only of ingestion, digestion, and excretion. In fact, as Julia Annas points out, according to Stoic theory, the soul was not in charge of metabolic functions.[108]

Yet this dichotomy that Seneca sets up between his chronic difficulty breathing (*suspirium, spiritus, anima*) and his healthy soul (*animus*) inside his body is continually under attack.[109] In letter 78 he again describes his respiratory problems and sympathizes with Lucilius, who is also afflicted with a respiratory infection (catarrh) and fevers.[110]

> You write that you are afflicted by frequent attacks of catarrh and by the brief fevers that follow when it has become a chronic affliction. This is all the more troubling for me to learn because I have experienced this sort of sickness, which at first I did not think much of—my youth was still able to bear injuries and conduct itself defiantly against illnesses—then I succumbed to it, and I was led to such a state that all I did was drip with catarrh, and I was reduced to skeletal thinness. (*Ep.* 78.1)[111]

When considering the recent earthquake in Campania in the *Natural Questions*, which was written at roughly the same time as the *Epistles*, Seneca thinks of his own respiratory ailments: "Why should I, whom a thick catarrh chokes, fear earthquakes?" (*et ego timeam terras trementis, quem crassior saliva suffocat?, Q Nat.* 6.2.5).[112] Within a treatise on natural philosophy, Seneca's statement about his chronic respiratory infection may seem gratuitous.[113] Nevertheless, there is an important connection between the deadly breath that suffocates Seneca and earthquakes.

Throughout book 6 of the *Natural Questions,* Seneca argues that earthquakes are caused by air beneath the earth's surface.¹¹⁴ Thus, the bodies of the emperor, Trimalchio, and Seneca and the body of the earth itself are all endangered by deadly "winds" (6.23.4–6.24.3). This air trapped in the earth is doubly deadly: not only does it cause earthquakes but it can also cause plagues.¹¹⁵ Thus, Seneca explains why flocks of sheep were killed by the recent Campanian earthquake. It was not simply because sheep are timid creatures.

> We say that after large earthquakes plagues frequently happen. It is no wonder. Many death-bearing things lie beneath the surface of the earth: the air itself, which, either through fault of the earth or through sluggishness and the eternal night growing thick . . . or corrupted by the fault of the flames under the earth, is too heavy to breathe. When sent out after lying inert, it stains and pollutes this pure and liquid air and brings new types of diseases to those who breathe this unfamiliar air. (*Q Nat.* 6.27.2)¹¹⁶

Indeed, throughout the *Natural Questions* Seneca notes that what lies within the "bowels of the earth" is foul and deadly. He tells a story about people who died from eating fish that lived beneath the earth's surface:

> Accept my proof that there is a great amount of water hidden in subterranean places, full of fish that are inedible because of their inactivity. If ever this water breaks out, it carries with it a great number of animals that are horrible to see and foul and deadly to the taste. Certainly in Caria near the city of Idymus, such a river came out and killed whoever ate the fish, which were unknown before that day when the new banks of a river brought them forth. (*Q Nat.* 3.19.1–2)¹¹⁷

Of course, the bowels of the earth hide more ruinous dangers.¹¹⁸ Not only is the greed caused by gold, silver, and other gems and metals responsible for the moral corruption of the human race but it degrades their "upright spirit" (*recto spiritu*).¹¹⁹ Seneca inveighs against digging into and exploring the depths of the earth:

> Before Phillip the king of Macedon, there were men who pursued money down into the deepest hiding places, and despite their free and upright spirit, they sent themselves down into those caves where there is no difference between night and day. What hope was so great as to make them leave the light behind them? What necessity is so great as to curve and befoul a human being who is erect to look up at the stars and then sink him in the depth of the earth so that he might

dig up gold, which is sought with no less danger than that with which it is possessed? (*Q Nat.* 5.15.3)[120]

This rejection of digging into the earth stands in sharp contrast to Seneca's continual injunctions to recede, flee, and even dig into the self, to call the soul away from externals and back into itself.[121] Thus, in Seneca there is an unresolved tension between the macrocosm of the physical and earthly empire and the microcosm of the self. How, then, do self-investigation, fleeing, and receding into the self avoid the dangers of digging into the earth? According to Seneca, the human body houses the soul, which is made up of celestial matter and is cognate with the stars.[122] Paradoxically, "digging" into the self is not akin to digging into the earth. For Seneca, the act of self-investigation is not simply an inward or downward glance. Rather, the study of the depths of the self is equivalent to looking up to study of the cosmos.[123] For the ancients, the ability to look upward, to raise one's face to the sky, differentiates humans from all other animals and enables them to commune with the heavens and with the gods.[124] Yet in book 7 of the *Natural Questions*, which moves from the terrestrial world to consider the heavens, Seneca admits that people do not contemplate their celestial home with any regularity; they only look up when something out of the ordinary is present (7.1.1–2).

Despite the soul's supposed celestial origins, Seneca suggests that what lies within the earth is no different than what lies within the self. Claudius' and Trimalchio's Saturnalian bodies contain what we might expect to find: excrement and deadly, noxious air. Yet Seneca's self-analysis in the *Epistles*, coupled with his investigations of the natural world, suggests that a strict differentiation between the foul insides of these tyrants and the purity of soul of the philosopher and of the good king may be difficult to maintain. What lies within the earth can be as foul and lethal as what lies within the body. The air we breathe, even the very breath of life, can be diseased and bring with it death. Seneca's focus in his later writings on his respiratory ailments and the dangerous foulness of air and wind suggest that the corruption that characterized the reign of Claudius returned under Nero. As Seneca notes in *De clementia*, Nero is "the vital spirit that so many thousands breathe in" (*ille spiritus vitalis quem haec tot milia trahunt*, 1.4.1).[125] Nero's once sustaining breath of life has become like Claudius'. Seneca himself suffers, and the empire is shaken by deadly earthquakes. Indeed, the spirit of Claudius' excessive Saturnalia does not stay put in Hades. Seneca opens one of his letters as follows:

The month is December, although the city is in a great sweat. Law has been given to public excess; everything resounds with great preparations, as if there were some difference between Saturnalia and regular business days; so true is it that there is no difference between the two that I think the man was not wrong who said that December used to be a month, now it is a year. (*Ep.* 18.1)[126]

Seneca may be slyly quoting himself here. In the *Apocolocyntosis*, one of the gods condemns Claudius for celebrating "Saturn's month throughout the entire year" (*si mehercules a Saturno petisset hoc beneficium, cuius mensem toto anno celebravit Saturnalicius princeps, non tulisset*, 8.2). Seneca's hoped-for return to the golden age, guided by the soul of the merciful princeps in *De clementia*, gives way in the *Epistles* to the eternal return of imperial dystopia. Seneca's plight can be likened to Encolpius' fate during the *Cena*: both are trapped in the foul and boundary-destroying Saturnalia of tyrants.[127]

CHAPTER SIX

Writing, Body, and Money

The funeral inscription on Trimalchio's planned tomb, so vividly described in the closing sections of the *Cena*, reads as follows:

> Gaius Pompeius Trimalchio Maecenantius rests here. He was elected to the sevirate in absentia. Although he could have been in all the guilds at Rome, he did not wish to, nevertheless. Dutiful, strong, faithful, he grew from little. He left behind thirty million sesterces, and he never listened to a philosopher. Farewell: and you, too. (*Sat.* 71.12)[1]

Trimalchio's surprising usurpation of the name of Maecenas, Augustus' adviser and fabulously wealthy supporter of the arts, is considered by some scholars to have been influenced by Seneca's own condemnatory description of the man in letter 114.[2] Indeed, Seneca's portrayal of the dissolute Maecenas may be echoed in Petronius' description of Trimalchio. Seneca claims that Maecenas was accompanied by two eunuchs (*spadones duo, Ep.* 114.6); when we first meet Trimalchio he is playing ball in the baths, attended by two of the same (*duo spadones, Sat.* 27.3). Trimalchio appears at the banquet wearing a purple Greek cloak that reveals his shaved head (*pallio enim coccineo adrasum excluserat caput*, 32.2). Seneca's Maecenas also wears a cloak, from which both ears stick out (*sic adparuit ut pallio velaretur caput exclusis utrimque auribus, Ep.* 114.6).[3] Trimalchio's attempts at poetry have also been linked to two of the surviving fragments of Maecenas' *oeuvre*.[4] Trimalchio's "quotation" of a poem by Publilius inveighing against luxury may be an appropriation of some lines written by Maecenas.[5] Furthermore, the conclusion of Trimalchio's three-line poem in which he encourages his guests to live well while they are still able (*ergo vivavmus, dum licet esse bene*, 34.10) is similar to part of a poem by Maecenas quoted by Seneca (*vita dum superest, benest, Ep.* 101.11).

Scholars have interpreted these links between Seneca's condemnation of Maecenas in the *Epistles* and Petronius' characterization of Trimalchio as an example of the adversarial relationship that might have existed between the two courtiers. Thus, Shannon Byrne surmises, "Petronius took pleasure in endowing his decadent freedman with the very qualities that Seneca meant to be demeaning."[6] Byrne also argues that Seneca's vehement denunciation of Maecenas in letter 114 is not inspired by his dislike of Augustus' adviser but rather is a veiled lament for his own fall from imperial favor and a critique of Petronius himself, Nero's new favorite "judge of good taste."[7] Such parallels are significant for establishing further links between the two authors. Rather than looking solely for examples of a possible "literary feud" between Seneca and Petronius, I shall treat Seneca's evaluation of Maecenas not simply as a jibe at Petronius but as a project of literary analysis that he returns to throughout the *Epistles*. Letter 114 is particularly significant. Seneca's critique of Maecenas' writing and politics reevaluates ideas from Seneca's earlier political works. In addition, this letter's focus on the theme of *talis oratio qualis vita* is masterfully problematized by the *Satyricon*. This is accomplished in several ways. Petronius never reveals himself or provides any personal guidance to our interpretations of his text. Nevertheless, Tacitus' portrayal of the life and death of the courtier Petronius seems to mirror the world of the *Satyricon*. The narrator Encolpius, a debased rogue scholar, writes learned and elegant Latin prose and poetry rich in literary allusions. Paradoxically, Encolpius denies using any artifice and states that he simply reports what people do. We get a taste of Encolpius' attempts at realism, as well as his prejudices, in his efforts to capture something of the dialect of Trimalchio and his fellow freedmen. As scholars have noted, the freedmen's Latin deteriorates when they deal with high learning and education.[8] Because the freedmen lack the traditional means to display their status and virtues, namely, literary education and the inviolate body of a freeborn citizen, economics is their primary means of self-presentation.

These two themes, moving beyond the body and privileging economic activity, also have an important place in Seneca's thought. In fact, not only does Trimalchio's unauthorized cognomen on his funeral inscription point us in the direction of Seneca's treatment of Maecenas, but the enumeration of his personal virtues, along with his wealth and his ability to create himself virtually *ex nihilo* demonstrates his own version of self-fashioning and self-presentation.[9] Trimalchio's boast that he could live a full life without philosophical training may speak to a general Roman mistrust of philosophy.[10] It also highlights what Victoria Rimell has identified as the *Satyricon*'s ambiguous relationship with learning and intellectualism. As she notes, the experience of reading this text is "more sensual than intellectual, more ludic than learned." At the same time, however, "the *Satyricon* is also incredibly demanding, immersed in and descriptive of dense, high-pressure systems of education, and a text which imagines a symbiosis of corporeal and intellectual knowledge."[11] The portrayal of Trimalchio as Maecenas does more than simply suggest a feud between Seneca and Petronius. His and his fellow freedmen's self-presentation presents an avenue for exploring the intellectual engagement between the two authors on problems of the self's relationship to politics, literature, and economics.

Reading Maecenas

As Pierre Hadot has demonstrated, the ancient spiritual practice of the *meditatio* needs "nourishment" on which to feed itself. This psychological "food" consists of "the intellectual exercises . . . : reading, listening, research and investigation."[12] Indeed, Hadot concludes that the seemingly simple process of reading can be turned into "one of the most difficult" forms of spiritual exercise.[13] Along these lines, Michel Foucault has shown that during the Hellenistic and Roman periods writing also developed into a "technique of the self."[14] Seneca's *Epistles* are deeply engaged with the spiritual practice of philosophical reading and writing. Though he wrote them late in his life, and perhaps during a time of political isolation and seclusion, Seneca continues to work through several ideas that, as we have seen in the previous two chapters, are central to *De clementia* and the *Apocolocyntosis*. Both political texts are concerned with manifesting the ruler's soul by means of magnanimous and spirited utterances. At the end of letter 108, a fascinating letter in which Seneca compares the ways in which a philosopher, a grammarian, and a philologist would read the same passages from the *Aeneid* and Cicero's *De republica* (*On the Commonwealth*), he succinctly sums up his program for philosophical study. "I advise this," he writes, "that the philosophers' practice of listening and reading must be ascribed to the purpose of the happy life, not so that we may seek out archaic or invented words and improper metaphors and figures of speech, but so that we may seek out precepts that will benefit us and great and spirited utterances that will soon be transformed into deeds" (*Ep.* 108.35).[15] One should not spend all one's time simply reading and memorizing the maxims of great philosophers. Seneca exhorts his readers to produce their own memorable imperatival statements: "One should say these things, not hold on to them . . . command and say something that can be handed over to memory. . . . let there be some difference between you and a book" (*dicat ista, non teneat . . . impera et dic quod memoriae tradatur. . . . aliquid inter te intersit et librum, Ep.* 33.7–9).

As part of this program of philosophical *askesis*, the works of Maecenas serve as an important example of how to read and how not to write.[16] Seneca's first citation of Maecenas is initially employed to encourage Lucilius to retire from public life:

> Does it matter if you should wish to retire? Your fortunate position does not allow it. What if you permit it to grow? It will achieve equal amounts of success and fear. At this point I wish to quote a statement from Maecenas, which he spoke truly while on the very rack: "The highest height is thunderstruck." If you want to know in which book he wrote it, it is in his *Prometheus*. He wanted to say this, "the greatest is thunderstruck." (*Ep.* 19.8–9 = Maecen., frag. 10 Lunderstedt)[17]

While Seneca may agree with the substance of what Maecenas "wanted to say" (*hoc voluit dicere*), he immediately condemns the style and the author. Seneca suggests, perhaps half jokingly, that if Lucilius remains in politics, a similar literary and personal fate awaits him:

> Is any power worth so much if it will result in your language being so drunken? He was a talented man, and he could have given a great example of Roman eloquence if his good fortune had not weakened, or rather castrated, him. This end awaits you unless you draw in your sails, unless you choose the land—a thing that Maecenas desired too late. (*Ep.* 19.9)[18]

From this brief analysis of a single fragment, presented with no indication of context aside from the title of the work, it should be clear that Seneca believes that the value of a piece of writing is determined by the life of its author. At first Seneca appears to approve of what Maecenas wrote and to consider it a worthy token of wisdom to offer Lucilius. As he performs an exegesis of the passage, however, his consideration of the author's writing style, life, and habits determines whether it can serve as a precept and a guide to life.[19] Taken in the abstract, Maecenas' passage may have influenced Lucilius' decision about his political life. Nevertheless, according to Seneca, Maecenas' own life renders his work a debased currency of philosophical exchange. Seneca turns to Epicurus to settle this letter's philosophical debt with Lucilius: "I was going to use this passage from Maecenas to balance the accounts, but you will object, if I know you well, and you will not accept what I owe unless it is paid out in fresh and good coin. As affairs now stand, a loan must be made from Epicurus" (*Ep.* 19.10).[20]

The next two analyses of Maecenas are closely related. Seneca interprets them to refer to Maecenas' opinions on the value of the body vis-à-vis death, disfigurement, and mutilation. In addition, Maecenas' writings are read in tandem with lines from the *Aeneid*. At the conclusion of letter 92, Seneca quotes Vergil (*Aen.* 9.485) to illustrate the prototypical horrors that can be inflicted on the body after death. Then he cites a line from Maecenas to demonstrate the proper attitude toward these "horrors." After presenting what the soul properly says about the fear of death, Seneca writes, "Maecenas said eloquently, 'I do not care for a tomb: nature buries the remains'" (*diserte Maecenas ait: "nec tumulum curo: sepelit natura relictos"*, *Ep.* 92.34–35 = Maecen., frag. 6 Lunderstedt). Here again Seneca almost approves of a passage from Maecenas, and once again he stops short of endorsing it because of Maecenas' inability to handle his political good fortune: "You would think he said this with his toga belted high up; indeed, he would have had both a great and manly intellect if his prosperous life had not unbelted it" (*alte cinctum putes dixisse; habuit enim ingenium et grande et virile, nisi illud secunda discinxissent*, *Ep.* 92.35).[21]

Letter 101 contains the lengthiest citation from Maecenas. For Seneca, this passage demonstrates that Maecenas' apparent disregard for his body, as discussed in *Epistle* 92.35, was in fact improperly motivated. Maecenas is willing to endure debilitation and crucifixion so long as he can continue to live a bit longer. The life Maecenas is willing to live is no life, according to Seneca:

Make my hand paralyzed,
Paralyze my foot with lameness,
Swell my back into a hunch,
Shake my teeth loose;
As long as life remains, all is well;
Sustain this life for me even if
I should sit on the piercing cross. (*Ep.* 101.10 = Maecen., frag. 1 Lunderstedt)

After critiquing Maecenas' poem, Seneca cites a line from the *Aeneid* (12.646). In this case, however, he quotes Vergil as proof that Maecenas did not learn from the poet: "You would think that Vergil never recited the line to him: 'Is it that wretched to die?'" (*Ep.* 101.13).[22] In his final analysis of Maecenas, Seneca moves from considering his writings on the body to evaluating his soul.

In letter 114 Seneca explicates at length what he claims to be a common expression that has even become a proverb among the Greeks: "the character of people's language reveals the character of their lives" (*talis hominibus fuit oratio qualis vita*, 114.1).[23] Cicero lends credence to the Greek origins of this idea, as he attributes it to the princeps of philosophy, Socrates (*Tusc.* 5.47). At the start of letter 114, Seneca states that he will answer Lucilius' question about how different styles of *oratio* are favored at different times. This letter is not simply a history of the development of style; rather, Seneca uses it to relate *oratio* to society, as well as to the *animus*. After he quotes from the "Greek proverb," Seneca provides a sociology of styles of speech (114.2).[24] From the start of this letter, Seneca makes it clear that he is not focusing simply on the individual and literature in isolation from the larger social patterns. He thus prepares the reader for the important connections he will draw between the individual soul, writing, and politics at the conclusion of this letter.[25] Seneca quickly progresses from society and *oratio* to the *animus* and "innate (literary) talent," or *ingenium* (114.3).[26] Style of speech and writing are key indices of the state of the *animus*. In fact, according to Seneca, the study of literary *ingenium* is a more powerful means for revealing the soul than the study of the body (114.3).

Seneca's next move is to put his theory to the test. Seneca claims that even if one did not know of his notoriously dissolute, luxurious, and uxorious lifestyle, one could discover it from a few lines of his writing. He begins his series of quotations asking, "What is more shameful than 'a stream and a bank with hairy forests'?" (*quid turpius "amne silvisque ripa comantibus"?*, 114.5). He rapidly lists six more examples of Maecenas' unprecedented word choices and careless syntactical arrangements, or rather, as Seneca puts it, Maecenas' desire not to be understood (114.4; see also 114.7).

> Look at, for example, "They plow the riverbed with skiffs and, having turned from the shallows, they leave behind gardens." What? If someone "curls his hair with the look of a woman and makes a noise like a dove with his lips and starts sighing, just as the tyrants of the forest grove act in a frenzy with downbent neck." "A deadly group searches at feasts and attacks houses with wine cups and exacts death with hope." "A guardian spirit that could hardly be witness to its own feast." "Or threads of thin wax candles and crackling meal." "The mother or the wife clothes the hearth." (*Ep.* 114.5 = Maecen., frag. 11 Lunderstedt)[27]

From reading his writing, Seneca concludes that one can imagine Maecenas always walking around the city with an unbelted tunic, dressing outrageously, and being excessively devoted to his wife.[28] Recent analyses of this letter have proven helpful for understanding the problematic relationship Seneca draws between the written word and Roman ideals of manliness, as well as his characterization of the historical figure of Maecenas.[29] These studies do not, however, fully treat the conclusion of Seneca's letter, where he returns to Maecenas and expands his theory of the links between the *animus* and *oratio*. Furthermore, Seneca's analysis highlights how the political aspects of Maecenas' life can be extrapolated from his writing. The political point of Seneca's literary critique is also further developed in the letter's conclusion and hence warrants further investigation.

As we saw in *De clementia*, Seneca developed his position as Nero's speechwriter in order to stress how the new emperor's language could both shape and reveal the mildness of his soul. Now in political retirement and no longer able to affect political speech, Seneca considers the role of Augustus' right-hand man, Maecenas. Seneca does not consider Maecenas as he is typically viewed today, as Augustus' so-called minister of culture; rather, he looks at his position as vice-regent and his performance of the public duties of Augustus. As in *De clementia*, so in letter 114 Seneca is concerned with the *oratio* of a potentate and how this language externalizes the soul inside. In this letter, Seneca provides a crucial supplement to *De clementia*'s focus on spoken language. He shifts his analysis from what a ruler says to what he writes. Seneca's point in looking at Maecenas is to argue that his literary style reveals that his manner of living was incongruent with the imperial power he was granted. Maecenas went through the city with an unbelted tunic even when he was performing the duties of Caesar Augustus. Seneca then recalls that when acting in his official capacity from the tribunal or speaking from the rostra, Maecenas would wear a headdress that made him look like a runaway slave from a pantomime. He was no better during times of strife. In the middle of the civil war, while the city was under arms, Maecenas would go about in public accompanied by two eunuchs who, according to Seneca, were more masculine than he was (114.6).

Despite his unmanly appearance, Seneca notes, Maecenas was praised for his political policy of mildness and mercy.[30] He spared the sword and kept from bloodshed, and he used his power only to provide freedom for his own licentiousness (114.7).[31] At this point we can begin to detect an important parallel to *De clementia*, in which years earlier Seneca tried to guide Nero to be sparing with the sword and bloodshed, to behave mercifully and humanely. If we believe Tacitus' claims, Seneca also let Nero indulge in Maecenas-like *licentia*, hoping that this this would keep him away from violent and tyrannical vices (*Ann.* 13.2.1). In this letter Seneca uses language to judge whether a potentate is truly merciful. In doing so, Seneca strips Maecenas of this virtue. In order to correct the traditional praise of Maecenas' mercy, Seneca must look beyond Maecenas' appearance and deportment, which seems to have wrongly influenced people's judgments about his political abilities. Thus, he turns to Maecenas' writing and then to the condition of this *animus*. Seneca states that after reading these few fragmentary passages, it becomes clear that Maecenas was not mild but simply soft and effeminate (*apparet enim mollem fuisse, non mitem*, 114.7). His style of writing has precluded any praise he might have deserved for his political acts. Basing his judgment on only a few lines, Seneca takes away the political virtue for which Maecenas is most praised, humane mildness (*mansuetudo*, 114.7) and turns Maecenus' real impetus for shunning violence into a softness unbecoming a real man.[32]

As we have seen, this moralizing and psychologizing reading from minor linguistic examples is a crucial facet of Seneca's philosophical thought.[33] Indeed, letter 114 performs one of the central tasks of *De clementia*. It uses language to judge the moral state of the ruler and to determine whether the ruler is properly mild. In this letter, however, Seneca moves from considering the spoken word to analyzing writing. Seneca needs only to read the writings of Maecenas to gain an accurate moral and political portrait of the man. Seneca's ethics of reading calls into question standard cultural poetics and physiognomy. By reading the words of the absent Maecenas, which are products of his soul (*hoc a magno animi malo oritur*, 114.22), both Maecenas' external appearance and his internal state are made present. Maecenas' appearance only seems to play a supplementary role, however. In fact, according to Seneca, his appearance is deceptive and does not reveal the psychological and hence the true political significance of his life. The people have been duped by his external appearance for decades, falsely believing Maecenas' dissoluteness to be a sign of mildness.

At the end of letter 114, Seneca clearly signals a return to his opening theme of the correlation between *oratio* and *vita* (*talis est oratio*, 114.21; *talis hominibus fuit oratio*, 114.1). He mentions Maecenas again, but he has finished his discussion of his "soft" style of *oratio* and political command. Seneca develops and expands the letter's opening connections between language, soul, and politics, from the specific case of Maecenas to the soul of each individual. With a powerful series of metaphors, Seneca states that an imperial microcosm structures our soul.

> Such is the character of language of Maecenas and of all others who do not go wrong by chance, but knowingly and willingly. This arises from a great evil of the soul: just as with wine the tongue does not stagger before the mind has submitted to being weighed down and is turned or even is betrayed, so that type of style, which is no different from drunkenness, is not troublesome to anyone unless the soul wavers. Therefore, let it be cared for: from it our emotions, from it our words come, from it our characters, our appearance, and our manner of walking. When it is healthy and strong, our language also is robust, strong, and manly; if it lies on the ground, everything else follows into ruin.
>
> While the king is safe the mind is one for all:
>
> Once he is gone they break their allegiance.
>
> Our king is the soul; while it is safe, all things remain at their tasks, they obey, they submit; when it wavers a little, at once everything else wavers. When it has indeed yielded to pleasure, its abilities and actions also droop, and it attempts everything with a soft and languid soul.
>
> Since we have used this comparison, I will continue. Our soul is now a king, now a tyrant. A king, when it watches over virtuous things and cares for the health of the body that has been entrusted to it, to that body it commands nothing base, nothing shameful; when indeed it is feeble and desirous and soft, it

goes over into a detestable and abominable name and becomes a tyrant. Then the unbridled passions take it up and press upon it. Indeed, at first the soul delights in this, as do the people when they are needlessly filled with a gift that will soon turn harmful, and they defile that which they cannot consume. (*Ep.* 114.21–24 = G. 4.212–13)[34]

This passage begins with a restatement and summation of the dependence of externally perceivable phenomena, both corporeal and spoken (*verba*), upon the hidden *animus*. In the next sentence, Seneca adds the dependence of *oratio* (*oratio quoque*). This specific inclusion after *verba* suggests that Seneca is referring to *oratio* as separate from speech and making clear his argument for including both writing and speech as being produced by, and in turn revealing, the *animus*. Seneca sums up this dependence with a line and a half from the book 4 of Vergil's *Georgics*. The significance of this quotation functions on several levels that relate to the politics of the soul with reference both to the wider context of the Vergilian corpus and to Seneca's own. In its original context, this quotation refers to Vergil's description of the beehive and the devotion that bees feel toward their king. Seneca uses the political metaphor that lies at the core of Vergil's poem: the society of bees stands for human society.[35]

Seneca also uses this metaphor to refer to the *animus*. Here again he is following Vergilian precedent. Traditionally, the bee also served as a metaphor for the disembodied and divine soul. Vergil in fact alludes to this connection in the succeeding lines of this poem (G. 4.219–21).[36] In the concluding discussion in letter 114, Seneca skillfully combines both metaphorical functions of the bee. When describing the nature of "our soul" (*animus noster*, 114.24), Seneca is thus able to speak on two levels at once, the psychological and the political. As we saw in chapter 4, Seneca uses this exact quotation from the *Georgics* (4.212–13) in *De clementia* (1.4.1) to describe the relationship between Nero and his subjects. In the *Apocolocyntosis*, Seneca quotes from *Georgics* book 4 to call for the death of the inferior and ugly "king bee" Claudius (3.2 = G. 4.90). The repeated citations from Vergil signals letter 114's strong connection to Seneca's early works of political theory and suggests how Seneca moves theoretically from the macrocosm of the Roman Empire to the microcosm of the empire of the self. Furthermore, the context in which Seneca quotes the *Georgics* in *De clementia* and in letter 114 shows how closely Seneca links the political with the personal. In *De clementia*, Seneca describes the dependence of the body politic upon the imperial soul: if the emperor is taken away, the state will crash into ruin (*si mens illa imperii subtrahatur . . . hic casus Romanae pacis exitium erit, hic tanti fortunam populi in ruinas aget*, 1.4.1–2). In letter 114, Seneca describes how each individual must care for the soul. The soul is the source of our bodily appearance and our *oratio*; if the soul is strong and manly, our *oratio* will be so as well. If the soul sinks into ruin, so will every other aspect of our being (*si ille procubuit, et cetera ruinam sequuntur*, 114.22).

In both the *Apocolocyntosis* and *De clementia*, Seneca maintains a strict divide between the soul of a king and that of a tyrant. Yet when he considers "our soul," he does not simply understand the *animus* as functioning solely as a beneficent king. Seneca develops his comparison (*similitudine*) and states that the condition of our soul is properly characterized by a political dichotomy. The *animus* functions like a *rex* when it remains safe, takes care of the body, and issues noble commands. Once the *animus* loses control of itself and becomes desirous and soft (*inpotens, cupidus, delicatus*), it takes on the hateful and detestable name tyrant (114.24). Within the soul of each person, in order to keep the soul in its proper state as a noble, caring king rather than a passion-controlled tyrant, there is a political struggle for empire. Seneca shows how difficult this conflict is and how easily the *animus* can vacillate between positive and negative forms of imperial command: "Our soul is now a king, now a tyrant" (*animus noster modo rex est, modo tyrannus*, 114.24). He continues to develop his political theme, adding another facet, the *populus*. At first the kingly soul feels joy as it is turned into a tyrant. This initial but ultimately destructive *gaudium* felt by the soul is compared to the pleasure the people feel when they are filled with some eventually harmful imperial gift (*largitione nocitura*, 114.24).[37] In letter 114, Seneca has reversed the sympathetic relationship between ruler and subjects. In *De clementia*, the state of the ruler's soul shaped that of his people. In letter 114 the people are metaphorically related to the passions; they determine whether the soul becomes a king or a tyrant.

It may seem that Seneca has strayed a great distance from his opening investigation of *oratio*. The very leaps that Seneca makes from evaluating Maecenas' style of writing and command to discussing the struggles between king and tyrant in the soul of each individual have their precedents in Seneca's political treatises. *De clementia* focuses on differentiating a king from a tyrant. In his later work from his political "retirement," Seneca moves that struggle into the souls of his readers. Thus, the key political question of the Roman Empire comes to be the key question each person must investigate and ask of him- or herself. The political macrocosm structures the microcosm of the individual. Of course, Seneca is not the first philosopher to link soul and state. This metaphor is an important and problematic crux in Plato's *Republic*.[38] Unlike Seneca, Plato acknowledges the presence of radically different types of people and government. In addition to the ideal of the philosopher king, Plato discusses aristocracy, timarchy, oligarchy, democracy, and tyranny.[39] He also offers a theory of how each person and government can be transformed.

Seneca stands in stark contrast. In place of the city-soul analogy, Seneca develops his comparison in imperial terms. As might be expected from a Stoic, when he looks at the soul, Seneca only sees monolithic forms of autocracy. As might not be expected, however, there is no stability, no self-controlled and self-controlling *hegemonikon* at our core. When he looks at "our soul" (*animus noster*), Seneca does not see immutability or constancy, but rather a ceaseless alternation between king and tyrant. At first he cannot offer a reason for why this change happens. The soul itself seems to shift capriciously from king to tyrant (*modo . . . modo*).[40] Seneca also adds a third element, the passions. In this letter, instead of using the metaphor of command to describe them, he relates the passions to the *populus* delighting in a public donative. Thus, the corrupt soul is not simply characterized as a tyrant; it is also related to the idle and sated people whom the ruler has created. The cry of "bread and circuses" has been internalized.[41]

Seneca remains close to Plato in one important respect, however. Jonathan Lear points out how the city-soul analogy in the *Republic* skillfully moves between considering the internal state of the psyche and considering the external world of politics and culture.[42] This same alternation is seen throughout Seneca's letter, and especially at its conclusion. Yet Seneca's vivid description is culturally specific and portrays the world of the Roman Empire. After considering how the passions turn the soul into a tyrant, Seneca notes the disastrous effects of this transformation on the body. The disease of the passions weakens the body to such a degree that it is unable to enjoy its own pleasures (*pro suis voluptatibus habet alienarum spectaculum, sumministrator libidinum testisque*, 114.25). Seneca states that the desires of the tyrannical soul exceed the individual's bodily capacity, and hence these inordinate desires destroy the body and spill out into the larger world. Those dominated by a tyrannical soul adopt the attitude of an autocrat and want the goods of the empire solely as a means to appease their insatiable desires, which break free from the narrow confines of the body. Seneca adopts the persona of a satirist and decries how these inordinate desires simply go to please one belly (*unum ventrem*). The desires of this one person overflow from the kitchen (*culinas nostras*) and destroy the physical world of the empire:

> Look at our wine cellars and our storehouses full of vintages of so many ages: do you think it seems right that for one belly the wines of so many consuls and regions are shut away? Look at how many places the earth is tilled and how many farmers plow it and dig it up: do you think it seems right that both Sicily and Africa are sown for one belly? (114.26)[43]

With this letter's skillful combination of literary criticism, political theory, psychology, and satire, Seneca forcefully shows the links between the internal and external worlds. He demonstrates that the real dangers to the world are not posed simply by the actual autocrat, but by each individual, who, by containing a microcosm of the empire within, risks destroying the empire without. The overthrow and ultimate weakness of the body is stressed as well. The soul will defeat the body whether it is motivated by vice, as at the end of letter 114, or by philosophical virtue and *askesis*.

Spiritual and Bodily Nourishment

Letter 114's opening analysis of Maecenas' writing and its closing vision of bodily consumption and overflow link literature with food and suggest that reading and writing follow a similar process of internalization and externalization. This in turn suggests a close relation to the *Satyricon*'s portrayal of literary production and consumption. As Victoria Rimell demonstrates, eating, drinking, and the bodily processes of digestion and emission form an important complex of literary metaphors in the *Satyricon*. Her analysis of this text shows how literature is frequently presented as food that is ingested and then comes flooding out of the consumer during performance.[44] The *Satyricon* as it has come down to us opens with Encolpius' declamation against declamation, in which he laments the overseasoned junk food on which the students of the day are nourished: "Little honeyed balls of words and all the words and deeds seem to be sprinkled with poppy and sesame seeds. Those who are nurtured among these things are no more able to become wise than those who live in a kitchen have a chance of smelling good" (1.3–2.1).[45] Agamemnon agrees with Encolpius, but he claims that teachers must use the right literary bait to attract students: "The teacher of eloquence is just like a fisherman. Unless he places food on the hook that he knows the fishies are going to go for, he will waste time on the rocks without any hope of a catch" (3.4).⁴⁶ In other words, the teachers will end up as Cicero says of the Stoics, "alone in their lecture halls" (*ut ait Cicero, "soli in scholis relinquentur"*, *Sat.* 3.2 = *Cael.* 41). The surviving text ends with the poet–sage–faux millionaire Eumolpus stipulating in his will that his legatees must eat his body (141.2). According to Eumolpus' own poetic theory, one must be "full of literature and tottering under the weight" (*plenus litteris, sub onere labetur*, 118.6). Similarly, Seneca writes, the light of philosophical wisdom will only begin to shine "if one does not simply flood himself in it, but stains himself with it" (*si illa se non perfuderit, sed infecerit, Ep.* 110.8). Nevertheless, Seneca, unlike Petronius, is careful to differentiate spiritual nutrition from bodily.

Letter 108 serves as a cover letter and instruction manual for Lucilius in advance of his receipt of the books Seneca is sending him, the now unfortunately lost *Libri moralis philosophiae* (Books of moral philosophy), which, according to Seneca, covered the entirety of the topic (*Ep.* 108.1).⁴⁷ He advises Lucilius not to take on too much of a burden; he should reign in his intellectual desires and only drink in as much as he can hold (*Ep.* 108.2).⁴⁸ The capacity of the soul, however, is not limited in the way that of the body is. If it is developed properly, Seneca assures Lucilius, he will be able to hold as much as he wishes. The "good soul" can expand to make room for as much as it receives (*Ep.* 108.2). Yet it is not enough just to read philosophy; taking it into the soul is only part of the process. In addition to literary consumption, one must also digest other people's works and produce one's own works. In letter 84, Seneca vividly describes the path of literary production in terms of the human body's nutritive processes. He also joins the human with the natural world and once again refers to one of his favorite metaphorical exemplars, the bee. As we have seen, for Seneca the humble bee has served as a model for the good king, the defeated tyrant, and the political condition of "our soul." In this letter, bees serve as a model for intellectual consumption and literary production.⁴⁹

At the start of this letter, apparently written during his second tour of Campania, Seneca notes the psychological and corporeal benefits of traveling. Seneca's love of literature causes him to neglect the body, so travel serves as his means of exercise. In addition, he is able to read without interruption during his journeys (*Ep.* 84.1). Reading allows Seneca to judge the discoveries of others and then decide what he himself should seek out. Furthermore, reading and writing should be practiced in succession so that the intellect can be nourished, rest, and develop properly (*Ep.* 84.1–2). If reading and writing are alternated, the two can be combined, and what has been collected from reading, the pen can turn into a body of work (*ut quidquid lectione collectum est stilus redigat in corpus*, *Ep.* 84.2). We must imitate the work of bees as they gather nectar and produce their honey (*Ep.* 84.3–4).[50] Seneca remains unsure exactly how bees make honey. Is the juice they gather already honey? Or do they mix and change the flowers' flavor by a property of their breath (*spiritus sui*)? Do they simply gather honey, which can be found like dew on flowers? Or do they store it away and let it naturally ferment like wine? Despite this confusion about the natural world, Seneca is nevertheless confident in his knowledge of how literary production works. First, we should bring together whatever we have gathered from our reading. Next, we should separate the distinct parts so that they can be preserved better. Then, by means of the care and ability of our *ingenium*, we should blend the flavors into a delicious compound that at once reveals its origins and is something entirely new (*Ep.* 84.5). As nature digests and changes the burden of food in the stomach so that it can be passed on to our sinews and blood, so the *ingenium* must be nourished. We must see to it that the reading we drink into our bodies is broken down so that it can become a part of us. We must digest it (*Ep.* 84.6–7).[51] After this description of the digestion of this spiritual nutrition, Seneca describes the process of literary creation: "Let our soul do this: let it hide away all the materials by which it has been aided; let it only reveal what it has created of them" (*hoc faciat animus noster: omnia quibus est adiutus abscondat, ipsum tantum ostendat quod effecit*, *Ep.* 84.7).

Elsewhere in the *Epistles*, however, bodily and literary digestion do not retain this positive connection. In letter 95 Seneca says that epicures who insist on having their food served scalding hot do not digest what they eat; it just rots (95.25). In this letter, Seneca also inveighs against a dish made by a fish market that was about to go out of business. All of the market's stock was put together, ready to be eaten at once. Seneca laments that people are ashamed to keep foods separate but rather blend all the flavors into one. As they sit at table, the work of their stomach has already been accomplished (*Ep.* 95.27).[52] Seneca concludes that vomited food could not be more mixed up (*non esset confusior vomentium cibus*, *Ep.* 95.28). Unlike with philosophical study, we should not be overly concerned about the type of food we put into our bodies; we are only going to lose it:

> We gather together all these precious things into our belly as if it could preserve the things it receives. It must be filled without fastidiousness. Why should it matter, if it is going to destroy whatever it receives? . . . But, by Hercules, all these things so carefully sought out and variously stored away, once they come down into the belly will all become one and the same mass of foulness. You wish to despise the pleasure of food? Look at the result. (*Ep.* 110.12–13)[53]

In contrast to the *animus*, which, if properly trained, can expand to hold all the "nourishment" put into it, the human belly is small.[54] It is not our eyes that are bigger than our stomachs, but rather our vices.

> Has nature given us so insatiable a belly, when she gave us such moderately sized bodies, so that we may conquer the greed of the largest and most voracious animals? Not at all; for how small an amount is given to nature. She is sent away with a little. It is not hunger that costs our bellies so much, but ambition. (*Ep.* 60.3)[55]

Trimalchio, of course, is the master of combining the physical with the literary. He interrupts his fellow freedmen's "sweet stories" to complain about his digestive problems, warn about the dangers of the deadly *anathymiasis*, and encourage all his guests to "tell the truth to themselves" about what is going on inside of them (47.1–7). Trimalchio's literary and bodily materialism is perhaps no more apparent than in the speech he gives after his Maecenan/Senecan/Publilian poem against luxury. He opens by declaring that "literature" is the most difficult profession. Moneychangers and doctors, who must perceive what lies beneath the surface of things, are tied for second (56.2–3). He grants this concession to doctors even though he hates them for continually placing him on a diet of duck. Moving from the work of humans to that of animals, Trimalchio claims that cows and sheep work the hardest. Cows allow us to eat bread. And sheep clothe us, so it is a great crime to eat them.[56] Then he treats one of Seneca's favorite topics, the bee. He declares bees to be "divine beasts" and reports that some claim they gather their honey from Jove. He also states that it could be their vomit (*apes enim ego divinas bestias puto, quae mel vomunt, etiam si dicuntur illud a Iove afferre*, 56.6). So much for Seneca's apian metaphor for nourishment of the soul, literary digestion, and production. Trimalchio may also trivialize Seneca's elaborate theory of the political significance of the fact that the "king bee" lacks a stinger (*Clem.* 1.19.3–4). Trimalchio concludes, "They also sting, however, because wherever there is something sweet, there you will also find the bitter" (*ideo autem pungunt, quia ubicumque dulce est, ibi et acidum invenies*, 56.6). Encolpius can only sum up this amalgam of philosophy, literary criticism, and natural history by stating ironically that Trimalchio is putting the philosophers out of business (*iam etiam philosophos de negotio deiciebat*, 56.7).[57]

Not only does Trimalchio mix food and literature but he continually mixes languages and genres. Trimalchio proves to Agamemnon that he does not hold literature in disdain (*studia fastiditum*) by pointing out that he has two libraries, one Greek and one Latin.[58] He then uses a fancy Greek technical term when asking Agamemnon to give the subject of that day's declamation (*peristasim*, 48.4).[59] Trimalchio follows up Hermeros' insulting of Ascyltus and his critique of the current higher-education system by bringing in his Homeristae.[60] The Homeristae speak the verses in Greek, while Trimalchio reads from a book in Latin in a singsong voice (59.3). In case his guests still do not understand the story, he "clarifies" it by giving his own garbled account of the Trojan War, at the end of which the "mad" Ajax enters to carve the food and serve it to the guests (59.6–7). After the *acta* of Trimalchio's mini-empire are read out, Trimalchio alone marvels at his acrobatic performers, calling theirs a "thankless profession" (*ingratum artificium esse*, 53.12). He again sets Greek against Latin, stating that he has purchased some actors of New Comedy, but he prefers them to perform Atellan farces; he has also ordered his flute player to sing in Latin (53.13). When not commenting on myth and literature (see also 48.7–8), or offering aetiological explanations (e.g., of Corinthian bronze, 50.1–52.3), Trimalchio encourages Niceros to tell about his encounter with a werewolf (61.1–62.14). He then tries to one-up Niceros by offering an account of his own encounter with the supernatural when he was a slave (63.1–10). Trimalchio calls on Plocamus to tell a story, but Plocamus can only lament that his singing and dancing days are over now that he has the gout (64.2–4). Plocamus does, however, whistle out something terrible, which afterwards he claims to be Greek (64.5). While in his private bathhouse, Trimalchio drunkenly enjoys the echoes of his own voice off the ceiling as he "mutilates the songs of Menecratis—or at least that is what those said who understood his language" (73.3).[61] Habinnas' slave Massa's performance of *Aeneid* book 5, a hybrid mixture of Vergil and Atellan farce, grates on Encolpius' ears and renders the great poet "offensive" (68.4–5).

Seneca tries extremely hard to differentiate between body and soul, between psychic and physical nourishment and digestion. The *Satyricon*, however, continually elides these boundaries and keeps literature and the self on the level of bodily materialism. Thus, we can comfortably separate the world of the philosopher from the world of the *Satyricon*. Alternatively, it could be claimed that Petronius, by demonstrating the embodied, physical reality of Stoic tropes and concepts such as *continentia* and *anathymiasis*, is ridiculing Seneca's philosophical denial of the body and his preoccupation with the *animus*. Indeed, Petronius may be philosophically justified for bringing everything back to the body. As stated in the previous chapter, the orthodox Stoics were psychological materialists. They considered the human soul to be "intelligent warm breath" and believed that it was made up of the fiery, divine *pneuma*, which they believed pervaded and ordered the universe.[62] The Stoics traditionally believed that the soul was not contained within the body but that the two were fully mixed together.[63] Several recent studies have highlighted the fact that since the Stoics were not body-soul dualists in the Platonic sense, their philosophy, along with Epicureanism, was one of "psycho-physical holism," to use Christopher Gill's terminology.[64] Seneca himself accepts the corporeal nature of the soul.[65] Yet, as Shadi Bartsch has suggested, Seneca's attitude toward the body-soul relationship moves away from traditional Stoic holism. According to Bartsch, Seneca adopts a Platonic "jettisoning of the body," and his philosophy is filled with "vivid renunciation[s] of the body-as-shell."[66] Seneca's focus on the freedom of the soul comes at the expense of stressing the permeability, penetrability, and ultimate expendability of the body.[67] For Bartsch, this is a move that is unprecedented in what she calls "Greek Stoicism," one that flies in the face of the inviolability that the Roman elite male citizenry traditionally attached to their bodies.[68]

Thus, while Seneca is not a body-soul dualist, he maintains an ambivalent and at times ridiculing stance toward orthodox Stoic psychological materialism.[69] For example, in letter 106 Seneca clearly states that the soul is corporeal, yet he writes that considering the deeper philosophical implications of this fact—that good, virtue, and the emotions must also be bodily—is a foolish game (*latrunculis ludimus*, 106.11).[70] In letter 113 he reluctantly continues his investigation of technical philosophical questions concerning the material nature of the soul and its attributes. Lucilius wishes to hear Seneca's opinion concerning the question often batted around the Stoic school concerning whether justice, courage, prudence, and the other virtues are living entities (113.1). While this may be an important and frequently debated Stoic question, Seneca immediately signals his independence from what he takes to be mainstream Stoicism and claims that the overly subtle topic of his letter does not befit a Roman; rather, such questions are more appropriate to one in Greek dress (*puto quaedam esse quae deceant phaecasiatum palliatumque*, 113.1).[71] As in letter 106, Seneca makes it clear that the topic of this letter is no more than merely an intellectual game. He accepts on logical and etymological grounds the *communis opinio* that the soul is a living being (*animal*), because it makes us so (113.2). As the letter progresses, however, Seneca soon leaves behind philosophical discussion of the "animate" nature of the soul and the virtues and declares his philosophical independence from such traditional Stoic questions. Instead of refutation, he resorts to derisive laughter as a means to counter the claim that the virtues are independent living beings (*derideat*, 113.23; *dissilio risu*, 113.26). As we have seen, Seneca prefers to describe the nature of the soul by means of metaphors, such as political command or the bee, and to focus on the ways in which it can be revealed by "great-souled" utterances, whether they are spoken or written.[72]

Critique of Physiognomics

In recent years there has been a growing emphasis on gesture, unspoken language, and nonverbal communication in the ancient world. Anthony Corbeill argues that gestures "can in fact be shown to belong to a self-consistent language, and to one no less complicated and subject to exploitation than the spoken language of Latin."[73] Corbeill begins his study by noting that Quintilian's *Institutio oratoria* (Education of the orator) not only focuses on teaching the verbal art of persuasion but also spends some fifty pages on the intricacies and nuances of the physical aspects of persuasion, how the various positions of the head and hands are to be learned and used.[74] Although he begins his study with examples from the imperial writer Quintilian justifying the central place of gesture, for Corbeill the consistent, readily identifiable cultural system of bodily gestures in fact ends with the rise of the emperors. His work thus concludes with an analysis of the inscrutable facial expressions of Tiberius as portrayed in the first six books of Tacitus' *Annales*.[75]

Seneca appears to work within both systems. The body can either signify the underlying psychological state or be merely a deceptive shell. Seneca is deeply concerned with the moral significance of gesture and bodily expression.[76] He opens *De ira* with a lengthy phenomenology of anger that focuses on the physical effects of anger on the body.[77]

So that you may know that those people are not sane whom anger has hold of, look at the very condition of their bodies. For as there are certain distinguishing marks of people who are raging mad, such as a bold and threatening face, a grim brow, a savage expression, a hastened step, waving hands, changed complexion, fast and very violent breaths, the same signs are also marks of those who are angry. The eyes flame and blaze, the entire face becomes hot and red with blood from the deepest depths of the body, the lips shake, the teeth are clenched, hairs bristle and rise up, breathing is forced and loud, the very joints of the body crack as they are twisted around themselves, there is bellowing and wailing and broken speech of words uttered without clarity, the hands are often pounded together and the ground struck by the feet, and the entire body is shaken as it makes the great threatening acts of anger; the face of people deforming and swelling themselves with anger is ugly and horrible to look upon—you would not know whether this was more of a hateful vice or a deformed one.

The other emotions are able to hide and grow in secret, while anger carries itself forth and goes out into the face; the greater it is, the more manifestly it boils over. (*Ira* 1.1.3–5)[78]

Senecan tragedy also describes the appearance of characters that are in the grips of emotion. The Nurse's description of Phaedra's lovesickness takes thirty-eight lines (*Pha.* 360–86). Similarly, in *Medea* the Nurse concludes her description of Medea's rushing across the stage like a possessed maenad with these words: "I know the marks of her old anger . . . I discern the face of Fury" (*irae novimus veteris notas . . . vultum Furoris cerno*, 394–96). While portraiture of the violent physical manifestations of emotion is present in both Seneca's tragedy and his philosophy, and while the Stoics in general were deeply concerned with the moral revelations to be gleaned from physiognomy, Seneca may break with the belief that bodily gesture and movements can be absolutely reliable indicators of underlying moral psychology.[79]

Seneca opens *De ira* with a horrifying description of what anger does to the human body, but in his technical discussion of the three stages of emotion, he claims that certain bodily movements are beyond the control of reason and hence morally insignificant. Such a claim would seem to stand in stark contrast to Diogenes Laertius' account of Cleanthes' physiognomic prowess. The philosopher was able to discern that a man was effeminate, despite his rough outward appearance, by the simple fact that he sneezed (7.137). Seneca, however, argues that certain bodily movements are simply reactions, rather than deeper indications of character. This differentiation occurs in *De ira*'s account of the "first movements" (*prima praeludentia*). Seneca outlines some of these involuntary preludes: "Shivering when cold water is sprinkled on you, refusal to touch certain things; hair standing on end from bad news, blushing when hearing obscene words, and the vertigo that comes upon some when they face a sheer drop-off" (2.2.1).[80] Indeed, Seneca removes several public acts from the realm of emotion and by extension, because they are involuntary bodily reactions, from the realm of moral significance. These uncontrollable responses include reacting to theatrical performances or the reading of historical events, laughing along with others, sorrowing with a group of mourners, or furrowing the brow at the sight of a shipwreck on stage (2.2.3–5). Seneca concludes that these are simply responses to chance events that strike the soul and are not to be considered emotions. The *animus* simply suffers them; it does not create them (2.3.1). After establishing this important category of involuntary bodily reactions, Seneca incorporates them into his theory of the origins of emotion.

> So that you may know how the emotions begin and grow and are carried away, there is a first movement that is involuntary, something like a preparation for emotion and a type of warning; the second is voluntary but not insistent, such as, for example, whether I ought to avenge myself when wounded or punish a man when he commits a crime. The third movement is already uncontrollable, and it is not a question of whether you ought to or wish to be avenged, but this movement overthrows reason and avenges, no matter what. (*Ira* 2.4.1)[81]

Lest we still remain unsure about the involuntary nature of the first movements, Seneca offers further explanation. They are a blow to the *animus* that cannot be avoided by reason; they are physical reactions that cannot be escaped. Perhaps they can be lessened by familiarity and constant attention (2.4.2).

Scholars debate the originality of Seneca's focus on the first movements, but as Richard Sorabji points out, with this analysis of the origins of emotion at the start of book 2 of *De ira* Seneca may provide an important defense of Stoic theory and also make a significant contribution to psychotherapy.[82] The early Greek Stoics only mention two stages of emotion, "impression" and mental "assent."[83] Cicero's *Tusculan Disputations*, however, contains a brief reference to the involuntary "bites" and "the slight contractions of soul" that may still be felt by the *animus* after grief (*aegritudo*) has been banished.[84] These reactions can be called natural but are not to be called "grief" or "sorrow" (3.83).[85] Whatever Seneca's ultimate sources are for this idea, what remains striking in his account of the first emotions is their effect on the body. Although the first movements can lead to emotion, at this preliminary stage the soul remains immune. Thus, for Seneca, bodily movements cannot provide an absolutely reliable system of moral significance.[86] Even the Stoic wise man cannot avoid having certain physical reactions, as Seneca makes clear in letter 57:

> But concerning that man against whom fortune has lost her right, his soul as well will be struck, his color will change. For there are certain things, my Lucilius, that no virtue is able to flee; nature warns us of our own mortality. And so he will contort his face at sad things and will shiver when something catches him by surprise, and he will feel dizzy if he looks into a vast abyss when standing at its edge: this is not fear but a natural condition that remains invulnerable to reason. (*Ep.* 57.3–4)[87]

In letter 11 Seneca argues that blushing, in particular, is beyond the power of wisdom to control. It is a natural bodily weakness that will remain even if one should become a wise man (11.1).[88] At one point, Seneca appears to admit that a blush can indicate something of deeper moral significance but says that the physical manifestation itself is extremely ambiguous and even contradictory. Seneca writes that when Sulla blushed, it indicated that he was at his most violent (*violentissimus*). Because his face was soft and gentle (*nihil erat mollius ore*), Pompey always blushed at a gathering, and especially at a public assembly (*utique in contionibus*, 11.4). Seneca himself remembers that Fabianus blushed when appearing as a witness before the Senate; according to Seneca, this manifestation of shame was greatly befitting (*et hic illum mire pudor decuit*, 11.4). Thus, even when Seneca appears to grant deeper meaning to a blush, it is not automatically certain what this meaning may be. A blush can be a sign of extreme anger, as in the case of Sulla, or softness of countenance, as with Pompey; or it can reveal one's sense of shame (*pudor*), as Fabianus' blush did. In fact, Seneca undermines any moral information that can be gleaned from this phenomenon.[89] He states that a blush shows that people have lost their sense of shame (*verecundia* for Sulla), but then he goes on to claim that a blush is a mark of it (*pudor* for Fabianus). This contradiction may be intentional, as it only strengthens Seneca's overall argument of the moral insignificance of many bodily actions.

Indeed, Seneca classifies proper bodily comportment, one of the crucial defining characteristics of the Roman elite identity during the republic, as merely an "indifferent"; he says that "some things are no more according to nature than contrary to nature, such as walking discretely or sitting properly" (*Ep.* 66.36).[90] In letter 95, Seneca admits that the philosophical and rhetorical tradition of "characterization" or "ethology" can be helpful in differentiating between virtue and vice. It is more useful, however, to know the marks of an excellent soul and then to transfer them to one's own soul (*quanto hoc utilius est excellentis animi notas nosse, quas ex alio in se transferre permittitur*, 95.67). In short, Seneca's ultimate goal is to flee from reliance on the eye and external appearances and have the soul judge other souls.[91] He writes at the start of *De vita beata*: "I call members of the vulgar crowd both those who wear the attire of a courtier as well as those who wear that of a slave, for I do not look at the color of the clothes in which bodies are enclosed. I do not believe the eyes concerning human beings; I have a better and more trustworthy light by which I can judge truth from falsehood. Let the soul find the good of the soul" (2.2).[92] And then: "Let us seek not something that is good in appearances but something solid and even more beautiful, since it comes from a more hidden place; let us dig this out" (*quaeramus aliquod non in speciem bonum, sed solidum et aequale et a secretiore parte formosius; hoc eruamus*, 3.1).

In the *Natural Questions*, Seneca states that earthquakes and unexpected disasters inspire us with fear because "we comprehend nature with our eyes and not with reason" (*quia naturam oculis non ratione comprehendimus*, 6.3.2).[93] Thus, reading, writing, and philosophical study are the means for probing the depths and revealing the secrets of nature, as well as those of the soul.[94] In letter 115, Seneca moves from a discussion of the proper, manly writing style to an ecstatic vision of the soul and its virtues. Retaining a metaphorical link between soul and body, he describes the soul as a beautiful and holy face shining with magnificent calm. Such a soul would be surrounded by the virtues of justice, bravery, moderation, wisdom, self-restraint (*frugalitas*), *continentia*, endurance, liberality, companionship, foresight, elegance, and, finally, magnanimity (115.3). Such a vision, according to Seneca, would be a religious experience. This vision of the soul of the good man would be akin to a divine vision; one would be inspired to bow down and worship it (115.4). Everyone would burn with love for this soul, if only we were allowed and our vision was not hindered (115.6). This vision of the soul cannot be perceived by the eyes. Instead, we must sharpen the sight of our soul (*aciem animi*), and then we will be able to see *virtus* even when it is hidden by the body, covered up with poverty, or blocked by low status or disgrace (115.6).[95]

According to Seneca, the philosopher does not rely on the eyes in order to judge a person's virtues. Thus, as we have seen, Seneca stresses the power of language, both spoken and written, to reveal the soul. He also notes that traditional status designations and bodily appearances are deceptive. These final two points are particularly important for considering the role of the freedmen in the *Satyricon*. In fact, Seneca notes that slaves and freedmen can be more free and noble than their freeborn "betters." As Elizabeth Asmis points out, Seneca's focus on the philosopher's striving for freedom can destabilize status distinctions and even valorize the position of the freedman.[96] Petronius' freedmen would seem to undermine this ideal and simply reinforce stereotypes of their inherent baseness. Nevertheless, Trimalchio and his counterparts also discuss their own self-transformation and how they made their fortunes by means of the traditional Roman ideals of *virtus*, *fides*, and *frugalitas*. Seneca also discusses the links between wealth and the display of virtue. This parallel treatment suggests that both authors are concerned with how economic power and domination are linked with the ideal of self-fashioning and self-command. In the new world of the empire, instead of being used to direct soldiers, the command of the soul and its virtues are directed outward toward economic activity and the world of business. We can see a practical benefit of philosophical training and self-development: self-discipline leads to economic discipline and successful functioning in the realms of commerce and exchange.[97]

Virtue and Economics

Trimalchio and his fellow freedmen's love of money have not received much sympathy from the critics.[98] Roland Mayer dubs Trimalchio a "plutocratic vulgarian."[99] Erich Auerbach says of the freedmen in the *Cena* that "they are nothing without money" but that their wealth does not grant them any substance.[100] According to Gian-Bagio Conte, Petronius' account of the world of the *Cena* signals the breakup of the traditional order. For him, new wealth is a symptom of a larger "cultural disintegration."[101] Yet the traditional order had broken apart long before Petronius, and the society of the early empire was in dire need of new cultural and moral bearings. John Bodel takes a more nuanced view of the role money could play in navigating this new world of empire. He writes that Trimalchio "shares with his fellow freedmen a conviction in the value of coin as a stable mooring—and thus a favored metaphorical and symbolic medium—in the fluctuating tide of economic and social change:

for one culturally at sea in the world of the Roman elite, the channels of respectable display were difficult to navigate, and no landmark could more securely mark the extent of his wealth than the semiotically crude but universally recognizable symbol of hard cash measured out in gold coin."[102] In fact, the relationship between virtue and money would have been familiar to members of Roman society on a general level because of the practice of imperial coinage, which frequently linked the emperor's portrait with a declaration of his virtues on the reverse.[103] Epictetus discusses the relationship between the imprint of one's moral character and the imperial images on coins: if a person bears a noble stamp, we accept him as we would a coin of the good emperor Trajan. The stamp of Nero is to be rejected (*Diss.* 4.5.16–17).[104] Throughout the *Cena*, money is used as a means for judging people. Indeed, the freedmen have their own unique adjectival forms based on monetary amounts in order to deprecate people, for example: "worth two cents" (*dupundiarius*, 58.5, 74.15); "worth a dollar" (*sestertiarius*, 45.8, 45.11).[105] As we saw earlier, despite his former status, Hermeros has no fellow feeling for the "slave" Giton. His method of invective involves attacking Giton in essential and monetary terms. He calls him a "curly-headed onion" (*cepa cirrata*, 58.2) and "a piece of meat on a cross, food for crows . . . a mouse, a mushroom" (*crucis offla, corvorum cibaria . . . mus, immo terrae tuber*, 58.2–4). Hermeros declares that Giton cannot claim monetary justification for acting above his status and asks him, "When did you pay your manumission tax?" (*quando vicesimam numerasti?*, 58.2).[106] Hermeros evaluates his enemies in terms of the lowest standards of monetary measure: Giton is "worth half a penny" (*besalis*), and his master is "worth two cents" (*dupunduarius*, 58.5). At the end of his attack, Hermeros claims that higher, rhetorical education does not produce anyone "worth two cents" (*dupondii*, 58.14).

Hermeros does not think simply in raw monetary terms, however. While he does view his adversaries as essentially worthless, both morally and monetarily, Hermeros claims that his *fides* is the quality that sets him apart from the freeborn scholars and enables him to function successfully in society. *Fides* can have financial connotations such as credit and a good name (*OLD*, def. 5), but it can also connote more general abstract virtues such as good faith, honesty, honor, and a sense of duty or loyalty (*OLD*, defs. 6, 8, 9).[107] Hermeros' *fides* works on both levels. After placing his bet and "proving" that money is wasted on rhetorical education (58.8), Hermeros displays his superiority more concretely: "Let us go into the forum and change money. You will see that the freedman's iron ring has good credit" (*eamus in forum et pecunias mutuemur:*

iam scies hoc ferrum fidem habere, 58.11).[108] Indeed, Hermeros' *fides* can be translated both figuratively and literally in the public forum as the trustworthiness and financial good credit that defines him and allows him to function in the world of monetary exchange. Yet for Hermeros, *fides* goes beyond his public and private financial success. It is a virtue that is ultimately beyond monetary value: "I would rather have my good faith than a treasure trove" (*ego fidem meam malo quam thesauros*, 57.9).

At the end of the *Cena*, Trimalchio narrates his personal history. He begins by declaring that his moral qualities have enabled him to accumulate his staggering wealth, transform his house into a palace, and even transform himself from a frog into a king.[109] Sounding strangely like a Stoic, Trimalchio declares that he has transformed himself and risen above those around him because of his *virtus* (*nam ego quoque tam fui quam vos estis, sed virtute mea ad hoc perveni*, 75.8).[110] His explanation then moves between the physical, financial, and moral realms. He defines virtue as one's "little heart" (*corcillum est quod homines facit*, 75.8), but he then sums up this quality in terms of the marketplace: "I buy well, I sell well" (*bene emo, bene vendo*, 75.9). This combination of the abstract *virtus*, his physical heart, and his monetary motto have led to Trimalchio's current state of *felicitas* (*felicitate dissilio*, 75.9). He begins by further clarifying the virtue that defines his worldly success: his *frugalitas* (*sed, ut coeperam dicere, ad hanc me fortunam frugalitas mea perduxit*, 75.10).[111] It was not simply this abstract quality that made Trimalchio a fortune, however. While his ability with money may have enabled him to work his way into the position of *dispensator* of his master's estates, it appears to have been his sexual attractiveness that enabled him to be named co-heir along with Caesar in his master's will (75.11–76.2).

Trimalchio himself perpetuates this combination of the virtue of *frugalitas*, finances, and sexual attractiveness now that he is master of his own household. At the end of this section, as the second feast begins, Trimalchio orders a new group of slaves to serve as attendants. This changing of the guard leads to an incident that first disturbs their good time (74.8). Among this new troupe of slaves is a "not unattractive boy" whom Trimalchio attacks and kisses for a very long time (*nam cum puer non inspeciosus inter novos intrasset ministros, invasit eum Trimalchio et osculari diutius coepit*, 74.8). Trimalchio's inability to control his sexual desire causes Fortunata to attack him with a barrage of insults. Trimalchio responds by throwing a cup in her face and recalling her former life as a flute girl, and he ends with the shocking "thunderbolt" (*fulmen*, 75.1): he orders the stonemason Habinnas not to include Fortunata's statue on his funeral monument. While they can suffer domestic violence and public humiliation, this final threat is too much for Habinnas and his wife to take. They begin to beg Trimalchio to relent, and soon Trimalchio cannot hold back his tears. He explains why he kissed the boy. It was not because of bodily beauty but because of the boy's *frugalitas*, as Trimalchio twice declares. Trimalchio enumerates how this quality has manifested itself: the boy is making strides with his mathematics, and he can read well. Thanks to his *frugalitas*, the boy has also procured for himself a little Thracian gladiator suit, a chair, and two wine ladles. It is for these reasons that he has caught Trimalchio's eye (75.4–6).

While we may find Trimalchio's claims that his attraction is based on the boy's *frugalitas* disingenuous, it must be noted that a similar connection between sexual desire and internal and external beauty is made in Platonic and early Stoic theory. For example, in the *Symposium*, which is generally accepted as one of the models for the *Cena*, there is a direct link between erotic experience and beauty of soul (210c; cf. *Phdr.* 250e–252c).[112] Trimalchio's account of his love for the slave boy denies Plato's claim that love is first based on physical beauty and then leads to love of soul (*Symp.* 210a–b). Like Niceros' claims about his love for Melissa (61.7), Trimalchio states that his attraction is not at all based on bodily beauty (*formam*) but rather entirely on the boy's virtue. The early Stoics made a direct connection between bodily appearance and underlying virtue; physiognomics was a key component of their theories of love and erotics. According to Diogenes Laertius, Zeno, Chrysippus, and Apollodorus all held the opinion that "the wise man will love young persons who by their appearance manifest a natural endowment for virtue" (7.129).[113] Trimalchio inverts this ideal and on the surface appears to be even more philosophical than the philosophers. He states that the boy only caught his eye because he so decorously manifests *frugalitas*, the very virtue that Trimalchio praises as leading to his own success. He claims to pay no attention to the boy's appearance. His lack of self-control and public assault on the boy, however, belie any true philosophical concern for the boy's education or moral development.[114]

On a basic level, Petronius' characters show the ease with which philosophical and moral ideals can be used to mask sexual desire and exploitation. Trimalchio's praise of *frugalitas* provides a flimsy excuse for his excessive luxury, his pathological need to display his wealth, and his lack of self-control around boy slaves. Thus, on this basic level we may be satisfied with the claim that by putting moral and philosophical maxims in Trimalchio's mouth, Petronius demonstrates their inherent instability and lack of authority. Platonic and Stoic erotics serve as a very thin veneer for Trimalchio's socially disruptive desire for the slave boy. On a deeper level, this close connection suggests that Petronius is not simply mocking philosophy but is engaged in a complex critique of several ideas and traditions.[115] Trimalchio inverts the ideal that eros is first directed at the body and then leads to the love of the soul and virtue. Indeed, at the start of the *Cena* Trimalchio's pet slave is specifically described as repulsive. He is bleary eyed, with extremely filthy teeth, even uglier than his master (*puer vetulus, lippus, domino Trimalchione deformior*, 28.4).[116] Trimalchio's underlying claim, however, that virtue can be displayed through the proper handling of money, echoes claims made by Seneca.

Seneca's hypocrisy for preaching Stoic austerity while being one of the richest men of his time has been a target for nearly two millennia. The criticism is perhaps best encapsulated by Publius Suillius, who, according to Tacitus, denounced Seneca's greed, stating, "By what wisdom, by which precepts of the philosophers, did he gain three hundred million sesterces within four years of royal friendship? At Rome, the wills of those without children were being caught, driven into his snare, so to speak, Italy and the provinces were being drained by his inordinate usury" (*Ann.* 13.42.4).[117] Recently, however, scholars have moved away from seeing Seneca's combination of Stoicism and wealth as contradictory.[118] As Paul Veyne points out, maintaining and growing wealth were acts that defined the ancient elite.[119] Catharine Edwards has demonstrated that we must understand the moralistic attacks on wealth, greed, and luxury to be part of a competitive practice to denounce rivals rather than a wholesale denunciation of these "vices."[120] In addition, James Ker has called on readers of Seneca to turn Suillius' objection on its head. Rather than seeing Seneca's Stoicism as negated by his economic activity, we should consider how economics shapes and informs his philosophical thought.[121]

An economic metaphor lies at the core of Seneca's care of the self. His language of self-investigation (*se excutere*) can be related to that of accounting (*rationes excutere*).[122] Seneca's *Moral Epistles* are deeply concerned with establishing the proper relationship with money. Rather than forbidding wealth, Seneca wishes to rid his readers of the fear of losing it.[123] Furthermore, throughout these letters, quantification and the language of economic exchange structure Seneca's relationship to his addressee, Lucilius. In the first sentence of his *Moral Epistles*, Seneca exhorts Lucilius not to waste his most valuable possession and commodity: himself and the time necessary to improve himself (*Ep.* 1.1). Anticipating Lucilius' question about how he is spending his time, Seneca boldly declares that his accounts are balanced (*ratio mihi constat inpensae, Ep.* 1.4). In the second letter, Seneca speaks out against what may be referred to as standard economic concerns, such as calculating how much money one has stored away in his strongbox, or how much grain is in his barn, or how much interest he is collecting on his loans (*Ep.* 2.6). Yet, Seneca does not avoid an economic metaphor of exchange to describe the debt he owes Lucilius.[124] This metaphor is particularly clear at the conclusion of several of the earlier letters, where Seneca typically closes with a "payment" of some words of wisdom that he has gleaned from his recent reading. For example, Seneca closes letter 6 with the following: "Because I still owe you a little payment, I'll tell you what delighted me today in my reading of Hecaton" (6.7).[125]

While the *Epistles* may be primarily concerned with alleviating the fear of losing wealth (e.g., *metu paupertatis, Ep.* 80.5), Seneca's dialogue *De vita beata*, likely written before his "retirement" from Nero's court, praises the possession of wealth as a means for displaying the soul and its virtues.[126] Rather than simply adopting the standard Stoic line that wealth is a "preferred indifferent" to be accepted over poverty, Seneca claims that wealth should not be rejected. Wealth is related to virtue, and one should hold on to riches because they supply greater material for exercising virtue (*maiorem virtuti suae materiam subministrari*, 21.4). Wealth is also connected positively to the *animus*: it allows the wise man greater means for displaying his soul. Seneca claims that poverty allows for the display of just one kind of virtue, endurance, whereas wealth allows for the display of several.[127]

> What doubt is there that there is greater material in wealth for a wise man for displaying his soul than in poverty? In poverty there is only one type of virtue: to be neither bent nor trampled down. In wealth self-control, generosity, diligence, order, and splendor are given an open field. (*VB* 22.1)[128]

The wise man will prefer wealth because it "adds something to the perpetual joy that is born from virtue" (*adiciunt tamen aliquid ad perpetuam laetitiam ex virtute nascentem*, 22.3). Wealth is "the gift of fortune and the fruit of virtue" (*munus fortunae fructumque virtutis*, 23.3). The wise man demonstrates that he has properly gained his wealth and lives with the proper attitude toward it by what he says to his fellow citizens. The *sapiens* displays his possessions openly and declares, "Whatever anyone recognizes as his own, let him take it" (23.2). Like Nero's great-spirited utterance, "I wish I had never learned to write," this expression also sends Seneca into exclamatory rapture: "O great man, o excellently wealthy, if after saying this, he still has the same amount!" (*o magnum virum,* <o> *optime divitem, si post hanc vocem tantundem habuerit!,* 23.2). The wise man's utterance concerning his wealth proves his greatness and demonstrates that his wealth is deserved, because it has been gained without guile or bloodshed. In this treatise, Seneca's two favorite exemplars of Stoic virtue appear in a radically different light. Rather than the typical focus on Cato's suicide or the equanimity with which he endured public humiliation, in *De vita beata* Seneca gives an exact reckoning of Cato's wealth: 4 million sesterces (21.3). Moreover, Elizabeth Asmis notes the unique way in which Socrates (25.4–28.1) is employed in this dialogue: "Seneca uses the example of Socrates in a way quite unlike the way anyone else ever did or he ever did elsewhere—to make an impassioned plea on behalf of those who combine the pursuit of virtue with the pursuit of wealth, and, in particular, of 'this' philosopher who lives so lavishly."[129]

Scholars have had difficulty explaining Seneca's philosophical stance regarding wealth in *De vita beata*. Despite Seneca's claims that he is not speaking in the first person, one standard view sees this treatise, and the conclusion in particular, as being a direct response to Suillius' attacks on Seneca's wealth described by Tacitus (*Ann.* 13.42).[130] Miriam Griffin gives both an autobiographical and a philosophical explanation.[131] According to Griffin, *De vita beata* shows Seneca attempting to justify his favored position under Nero. He bases his praise of wealth on the ideas of the more worldly and accommodating tenets of the Middle Stoa.[132] Asmis focuses less on biographical reasons or philosophical precedents and concludes that *De vita beata* is strongly indicative of the "individuality" of Seneca's thought.[133] Yet as we have seen, it appears that both Seneca and Petronius are wrestling with the problem of the relationship between money and individual *virtus*. Can money provide a reliable signification of moral self-worth? Are intellectuals always to be condemned to poverty, lest their message lose its value?[134] Are the proudly wealthy and acquisitive freedmen to be condemned simply because they are wealthy and acquisitive, or do their successes and self-transformations from slaves demonstrate their imperviousness to the blows of *fortuna,* as well as their *virtus, fides,* and *frugalitas*? In fact, there may be specific textual connections between *De vita beata* and the *Satyricon*. Toward the end of *De vita beata*, Seneca inverts the standard connection between philosophical authority and (lack of) money, commanding his critics to "stop forbidding philosophers from money: no one has condemned wisdom to poverty. The philosopher will have ample wealth" (*desine ergo philosophis pecunia interdicere: nemo sapientiam paupertate damnavit. habebit philosophus amplas opes*, 23.1). These words oddly mirror those of Petronius' impoverished poet-philosopher Eumolpus, who offers the hackneyed claims that love of intellectual pursuits and the right way of life always go hand in hand with poverty (*amor ingenii neminem umquam divitem fecit*, 83.9; *nescio quo modo bonae mentis soror est paupertas*, 84.4). Here, Seneca presents the more radical idea concerning the relationship between wealth and wisdom, and Petronius presents the standard cliché. The overall connections suggest that both authors are testing old and new ideas and that the attitudes toward wealth in the *Satyricon* and *De vita beata* are part of a serious, probing look at the relationship between money and the self.

Alleviating the fear of losing wealth in the *Epistles* and claiming that wealth can display the soul's virtues in *De vita beata* do not mark the extent of Seneca's thought on the economic world. Seneca's *De beneficiis*, which is by far his lengthiest work, sets forth what he calls a "law for life," explicating the proper manner in which to exchange money, goods, and services (1.4.2).[135] Gift exchange and commercial, or monetary, exchange play important roles in *De beneficiis*.[136] One of the core themes of this treatise is an idealization of the elite individual who has the power to designate to which system each transaction belongs. Favors can elide social hierarchies; money can enforce them. Petronius skillfully reveals the problem with Seneca's ideal of choice and suggests that Seneca's desire for a rigid separation between the two forms is untenable.[137] The point of contact between Seneca and Petronius lies in the question whether a slave can perform a benefit.

As scholars have noted, Seneca and Trimalchio speak similarly concerning the common humanity of slaves (*"servi sunt." immo homines*, Ep. 47.1; *et servi homines sunt*, Sat. 71.1).[138] Seneca encourages Lucilius to dine with his slaves. Trimalchio invites them to sit down with his other guests. This invitation does not lead Encolpius to engage in any humanitarian ideas, however; he says that the cook who reclines next to him is like his master and combines food with literature. Encolpius notes that this cook still reeks of the kitchen and continually imitates the (unknown) tragedian Ephesus (70.12–13). Before the dinner begins, however, Encolpius is less offended by Trimalchio's slaves. In fact, he comes to the rescue of one who is threatened with being beaten and is doubly rewarded for his act of kindness. Before we investigate this passage, let us look at how slaves and others of low status fit into Seneca's theory of exchange.

In contrast to other Stoic theories, Seneca states that slaves can perform benefits for their masters:

> Nevertheless, it has been asked by some, such as Hecaton, whether a slave is able to perform a favor for his master. For there are some who distinguish certain acts as favors, certain ones as duties, and certain ones as menial tasks; they say that a favor is what a stranger gives (a stranger is someone who can do nothing without censure), a duty is performed by a son or a wife or by those people whom ties of relationship stir up and order to bear aid, a menial task is performed by a slave, whose condition has placed him so that nothing of the things he can offer can make a claim on his superior.
>
> Moreover, he who denies that a slave sometimes performs a favor for his master is ignorant of the rights of human beings; for what matters is the soul of the person who gives, not his status. Virtue is not shut off from anybody; it lies open to all, it admits all, it invites all, both freeborn and freedmen and slaves and kings and exiles. It chooses neither home nor census status, it is content with a naked human being.... If a slave does not give a favor to his master, then one could not give one to his king, nor a soldier to his leader. If one is held by absolute power, why does the specific type of that power matter? (*Ben.* 3.18.1–3)[139]

De beneficiis has been critiqued for being impractically high-minded in its support of the Stoic paradox that to accept a favor gladly is to have repaid it (2.31.1). Nevertheless, Stoic "high-mindedness" may serve a social purpose.[140] As Seneca notes, the exchange of favors occurs between two souls (2.34.1). He writes that the souls of slaves remain free; only their bodies are bought and sold (3.20.2). Furthermore, Seneca's focus on the Stoic paradox and his denial of the importance of money and concrete acts of reciprocity may serve to open the door to include slaves in the society of human fellowship.[141] Indeed, in the section quoted above, Seneca is particularly concerned with all forms of subordination and power (*imperium*) that exist between soldiers and generals, kings and subjects, as well as between masters and slaves. Is Seneca suggesting to his elite audience that their subordination under the emperor should cause them to look around and consider the plight of those below them? Is this a concrete example of the ideals of Stoic cosmopolitanism and universal citizenship working in the real world of Roman society?

Lest we think that Seneca is a revolutionary in his thought, several points must first be borne in mind. He is not the first to make the claim that a slave can give and receive favors. During the middle republican period, Cato the Elder says so in his treatise on agriculture.[142] Writing during the reign of Tiberius, Valerius Maximus also includes several memorable deeds performed by slaves for their masters. In addition, Moses Finley and Keith Bradley have argued that Seneca's ideas on the common humanity of slaves likely did little to alleviate their suffering, and in fact his ideas can be seen insidiously to reinforce their position of servitude. Miriam Griffin takes a considerably more positive view of Seneca's advice on the proper treatment of slaves. Why did Seneca spend so much intellectual energy on the topic if he did not wish to improve the plight of slaves? she asks.[143] Later in *De beneficiis*, it seems clear that Seneca's claim that slaves can perform favors is a by-product rather than the primary concern of his development of the ideal of noncommercial giving and receiving of gifts. After giving several examples of slaves performing favors for their masters, Seneca states that he only made this point to back up his main argument, that sons can perform benefits for their fathers: "These things had to be said for the purpose of crushing the insolence of humans who are dependent upon fortune and to claim for slaves the right of granting favors in order that it might also be claimed for sons" (3.29.1).

Yet if, at least on a theoretical level, Seneca demonstrates the socially leveling power of the exchange of favors, he also demonstrates how exchange can reinforce social hierarchies. If you do not wish to be indebted to someone of ill-repute, you simply do not have to accept his favor. There are times, Seneca admits, when there is no choice. How can you maintain your social distance in such a situation? In such cases commercial exchange will be necessary. In book 2, Seneca mentions what he refers to as a frequently debated topic, whether Brutus should have accepted Caesar's clemency and then plotted to kill him. He quickly becomes impatient with this topic and turns to one that he finds more pressing. Moving from the unquestioned elite of Roman society, Seneca confronts the problem of status dissonance. How does one handle a person whose money may qualify him as a member of the elite but whose reputation removes him from the community? After offering his opinion on the relationship between Brutus and Caesar, Seneca writes:

> This is more worthy of some debate: what must a captive do when a man who prostitutes his body and disgraces his mouth has promised his ransom money.

Will I allow myself to be saved by an impure man? After being saved, then what thanks shall I give? Will I live with this obscene person? Will I not live with my savior? Let me tell you what I have decided. Even from such a person I would accept the money upon which my life depends. I will receive it as a loan, however, not as a favor; I will pay him back the money, and if a situation arises for me to save him when he is in danger, I will save him. I will not descend into friendship, which joins similar people, nor will I count him as a savior, but as a moneylender, to whom I know that I must give back what I have received. (*Ben.* 2.21.1–2)[144]

Later in *De beneficiis* Seneca admits that sometimes the two categories cannot be so easily separated. Why, for example, do we feel gratitude toward our teachers even though we have paid them? Strictly speaking, only a commercial relationship should exist between students and teachers, but Seneca states that teachers give more than they are paid for; hence social ties of gratitude are created in this relationship (6.15.1–2). Although Seneca is willing to admit that these categories can be combined, on the whole his theory of exchange is based on choice. His elite audience should be able to decide when a gift counts as a benefit and when it simply counts as a commercial exchange. He tries to grant his readers the power both to level social hierarchies and to reinforce them at will. In Petronius we find an example of a slave performing a benefit, but Petronius demonstrates that these two types of exchange, favors and commercial, are impossibly intertwined.

Trimalchio's former status as his master's head treasurer is prominently displayed in the mural that decorates the outer wall of his house. The gifts of his own *dispensator*, Cinnamus, are prominently shown on the doorposts to the triclinium. These gifts stress status and calculation. Emphasizing Trimalchio's status as a *sevir* of Augustus, they are placed next to two tables that illustrate the course of the moon, the planets, and the stars. Lucky and unlucky days are marked off (30.1–4). In addition, an inscription that declares Trimalchio's self-sufficiency reads: "On December 30th and 31st our Gaius eats out" (30.3). Encolpius and his companions soon meet this Cinnamus, who sits in a nearby little room counting gold coins. He briefly interrupts his work to perform a great benefit for our heroes. The narrative runs as follows:

> Filled with these pleasures, when we tried to enter the dining room, one of the slaves, who had been placed in charge of this duty shouted, "With the right foot!" Without a doubt we were a bit worried, lest one of us cross the threshold

contrary to the rule. But as we were trying to keep in step, a slave who had been stripped bare for a beating fell at our feet and began to ask that we save him from punishment; the crime on account of which he was imperiled was not great, he said; the treasurer's clothes had been stolen from him in the bathhouse, clothes that had hardly been worth ten sesterces. Therefore, we moved our right feet back and begged the treasurer, who was counting gold coins in a little room, to release the slave from punishment. He haughtily lifted his face and said, "It's not the loss so much as the negligence of that most worthless of slaves that bothers me. He lost my dinner clothes, which a certain client had given me for my birthday. Tyrian purple without a doubt, but already washed once. What about it, then? I give him to you."

We were obliged for so great a favor, and when we entered the dining room that same slave on whose behalf we had spoken ran up to us, and giving thanks to our kindness he planted innumerable kisses on us as we stood there stupefied. "In short," he said, "you will know right away to whom you granted a favor. The master's wine is the thanks of the servant." (*Sat.* 30.5–31.2)[145]

Even our brief look at the two systems of exchange in *De beneficiis* can help to elucidate the concepts that underlie this passage. We see two examples of slaves performing a benefit. Encolpius and his companions freely acknowledge the greatness of Cinnamus' favor and their obligation to him. The cycle continues as the rescued slave runs up in order to formally thank them and immediately offer a gift in return, presumably by promising to serve them Trimalchio's best wine. In addition to these almost textbook examples of the exchange of favors between slave and free, Cinnamus offers important insights on the slippery relationship between favors, money, personal sentiment, and status. Although he himself is a slave, he looks down upon these freeborn guests (*superbus ille*). He rates the physical suffering of a slave below the value of ten sesterces. Then he moves from the realm of value and monetary loss to more abstract concepts. He claims that he has only ordered the slave beaten because of his negligence. This garment has sentimental value; it was a birthday present from one of his clients. This claim of sentimentality also moves to the realm of strict status differentiation. Despite his servile status, Cinnamus is apparently also a patron who must be honored by his clients. Yet his use of the word *cliens* suggests that Cinnamus does not know how to handle his position as a social superior properly. As Richard Saller points out, the word *cliens* is infrequently used by literary authors, because of the "social inferiority and degradation implied by the word."[146] Nevertheless, Cinnamus has even grander aspirations. His regal status is demonstrated by the garment, "Tyrian purple without a doubt." "But it's already been washed once," he concludes, implying that this act has irrevocably decreased its value. After offering this worthless slave as a gift, he then presumably returns to counting gold coins, the one object whose value remains stable and easily quantifiable. The ideal of slaves performing benefits gets lost in a morass of hybridity and inversion. Cinnamus is the servile master of quantification and calculation, yet he also envisions himself as easily moving up the social ladder from his position as a simple owner of a slave, to that of a patron, to that of a purple-clad potentate. His gift of the slave is entirely forgotten, as is the slave's promise to serve his benefactors Trimalchio's best wine.

Petronius is not the only imperial author to critique Seneca's strict separation between forms of exchange. Tacitus focuses precisely on the artificiality of this division in his narrative of Seneca's attempt to retire from Nero's court.[147] In book 14 of his *Annales* Tacitus creates a dramatic conversation between the emperor and his subject that is based on several key points from Seneca's *De beneficiis*. In an attempt to undo the bonds that have been forged between them, Seneca focuses on the material nature of Nero's gifts. He states that Nero has piled upon him honor and wealth without moderation (14.53). Nero has surrounded Seneca with "countless money" (*innumeram pecuniam*), gardens, suburban villas, and fields that yield great profit (*tam lato faenore exuberat*, 14.53.5). Seneca draws attention to his humble origins and protests that his moderate soul is neither deserving nor able to handle such a financial and social change. He argues that one born to equestrian status in the provinces should not be counted among the leading men of Rome. He is only a parvenu, and his *novitas* should not shine among the established elite and those who far surpass him in distinction. Seneca cannot bear his wealth any longer, so he wants to give it back to Nero. His estate should be managed by the imperial procurators and received back into Nero's own fortune (14.54.2). Tacitus' Seneca implicitly removes Nero's *munera* from the system of gift exchange by claiming that his only defense for accepting them in the first place is that he could not refuse them (14.53.5). As Seneca himself states in *De beneficiis*, a gift must be freely given and freely received to qualify as a favor (2.18.7, 3.28). Thus, Tacitus' Seneca sets Nero up as a tyrant rather than a beneficent princeps who willingly takes part in the system of gift exchange among friends.[148] Furthermore, by his continual focus on the tangible and monetary value of

Nero's gifts, Seneca attempts to portray them as part of a commercial rather than a gift-based exchange. All Seneca has to do is return the gifts, and he will be free from any further bonds with Nero. The two can call it even.

Tacitus provides Nero with a response that drips with philosophical irony. Nero accepts Seneca's point that he has given him merely material objects—gardens, profitable investments, and villas—all of which are liable to fortune (14.55.4). Seneca's gifts, such as Nero's oratorical ability, are eternal. Seneca's education of Nero is priceless, ineffable; the money Nero gives to Seneca is the sole means, albeit insufficient, for Nero to show his gratitude. To Seneca's horror, Nero claims that the tally will never be even. Nero undermines Seneca's statement that his low status renders him undeserving of such wealth by stating that he is ashamed to see freedmen richer than his teacher. The *amicus principis* must have more money than Trimalchio and his ilk. Finally, Nero cuts to the core of Seneca's self-image and the nature of their relationship: if Seneca were allowed to return his money, the odium would fall on Nero. All would claim that Nero was excessively greedy, while praising Seneca's moderation (*continentia*). A philosopher should not gain glory for himself by heaping infamy upon a friend (14.56.2). Nero concludes by embracing and kissing his former tutor. Seneca can only offer his gratitude (*Seneca . . . grates agit*, 14.56.3), thereby following his own advice for life under a tyrant. In *De ira*, Seneca tells of an old courtier who claimed that he achieved the rare feat of growing old while attending upon kings "by receiving injury and saying 'thank-you'" (2.33.2).

Seneca's philosophical ideas of the role of money and gift exchange in the social world are taken in opposite directions by Petronius and Tacitus. Trimalchio's dinner, which itself is a paradigmatic example of gift exchange, begins with a comic conflation of ideas at the bottom of society.[149] At the other end of the social spectrum, Tacitus presents the problematic position of the emperor within this system and turns Petronius' servile comedy into an imperial drama of irony and dissimulation. Both of his characters have learned their Senecan scripts. Tacitus' Nero can respond extemporaneously to Seneca thanks to his teacher's gift of eloquence. Tacitus' Seneca can only respond by quoting a well-known utterance recorded in one of his dialogues about how a courtier needs to display false gratitude in order to survive.

Epilogue

We must now take leave of our two travelers in the knowledge that because both the *Satyricon* and Seneca's *Epistles* have come down to us in incomplete form, we will never know what conclusions they scripted for themselves. The *Satyricon* ends with a cliffhanger. Yet given the episodic nature of the surviving fragments, as well as the first-person narrative, it seems safe to assume that Encolpius at least escapes from Croton's legacy hunters and continues on with his travels.[1] Whether he is able to develop any deeper wisdom about himself and others is also a matter of speculation.

The potential for travel to lead to revelation and discovery is a theme that continues throughout Seneca's *Epistles*. His journey through the Crypta Neapolitana is followed by his consideration in the next letter of the Platonic concepts of being and the forms.[2] It seems as if Seneca's travels have led him through the cave to enlightenment. Nevertheless, these famous Platonic theories are rejected; they cannot improve the self (*Ep.* 58.25–26). Seneca prefers to look to the tradition of Plato's biography for inspiration (*Ep.* 58.30). Thus, Seneca travels again.[3] He opens letter 70 by saying that he is seeing Lucilius' native Pompeii again after a long time (70.1).[4] In letter 77 he is back in Puteoli (likely the home of Trimalchio) watching the arrival of boats carrying mail from Alexandria. Seneca describes himself as happily lazy and not following the crowd down to the shore to get news about his estates as quickly as possible. Here we see Seneca looking back on his former, less enlightened self, who was unable to brook any delay in learning about the status of his family, friends, and finances (77.1–3).[5] In the final letters, Seneca restlessly visits his own villas, which, as John Henderson points out, are on sites famous from the early days of Roman history: Nomentum (*Ep.* 104), home to Seneca's fabulously expensive and successful vineyards, and Alba (*Ep.* 123). He advises Lucilius to take care of his health at his country estate at Ardea (*Ep.* 105.1).[6]

In letter 123, the penultimate of the letters that survive, Seneca writes of arriving at his Alban villa to find that nothing has been prepared for him to eat (123.1). Instead of growing angry at his cook and his baker, and instead of refreshing himself with food, Seneca turns to writing and self-dialogue (123.1). He will not eat until hunger commands (*imperat*, 123.2). He comes to the realization that a great step on the way to freedom is developing a good-natured stomach that can endure rough treatment (*magna pars libertatis est bene moratus venter et contumeliae patiens*, 123.3). Although they speak about the problem from different directions, one from surfeit and the other from lack, here Trimalchio and Seneca achieve a level of common ground. Control of the body and its metabolic functions are also a necessary part of achieving "freedom."

If we can believe Tacitus, both Seneca and Petronius received their death sentences from Nero while traveling. In Tacitus' account, there is a tension between Seneca's self-presentation and Tacitus' ultimate control of the narrative. Tacitus says that he does not preserve Seneca's final dictations to his scribes, because they have already been published (*Ann.* 15.63.3). This omission silences Seneca's final moments of eloquence. Seneca's first attempt at suicide links him with Cato. Yet unlike the republican hero, who reopened his wounds after the first attempt was thwarted, Seneca picks another exemplar for his second attempt. According to Tacitus, Seneca had also planned to model his death on that of Socrates. Why else would he have hemlock lying around the house?[7] To some degree he may have achieved this goal, as the oldest image of Seneca to survive from antiquity is a double herm of the two philosophers.[8] Yet Tacitus' narrative does not simply link Seneca's death with that of his ideals, Cato and Socrates. Rather, like Seneca's own polygeneric corpus, his death cycles through various possibilities and ends with an echo of Trimalchio's villa, as Seneca finally expires in the heat of his private bathhouse.[9]

Whatever his final wishes, thanks to a large degree to Tacitus, Seneca also remains linked with Petronius and Nero. While this is a triad he likely would not have chosen, this third triumvirate from ancient Rome continues to wield a powerful influence. Although it probably has been centuries since a person has been described as "Senecal" and a specific writing style has been referred to as the "Senecan amble," Seneca's philosophical allegiance is still part of common parlance.[10] As Anthony Long has demonstrated, Hellenistic and Roman philosophical schools still define character types today. Nothing similar can be said about other philosophical movements. Long writes, "If we call someone today a Stoic or an Epicurean, we are making a comment on an ethical outlook by calling attention to highly general characteristics that imply certain basic attitudes to life and exclude others. The terms presuppose consistency on the part of the person they are applied to. We don't expect someone who is stoical on Monday to be cynical or epicurean or skeptical on Tuesday."[11] Petronius is one of the few ancient authors whose works serve as the basis for both modern films and novels.[12] Henryk Sienkiewicz developed Tacitus' portrait of Petronius into one of the central characters of his novel *Quo Vadis*.[13] Although he is only once mentioned by name in F. Scott Fitzgerald's *The Great Gatsby*, so strong was his influence on the work that Fitzgerald considered calling his novel *Trimalchio in West Egg*.[14] As Edward Champlin has pointed out, Nero is one of the most powerfully influential figures from classical antiquity, who holds more interest for modern readers than even Alexander the Great.[15]

For all these men's familiarity and contemporary resonance, one of the primary goals of this work has been to focus on one of the more idiosyncratic aspects of the literature of the early empire: the drive to create and reveal the self through language. Looking back on the language of his baroque predecessors from his place at the center of the Enlightenment, Voltaire is said to have commented, "We no longer live in an age where one addresses one's arm or one's soul."[16] The task of this book, particularly in part 1, has been to shed light on the literary age par excellence of self-address and to elucidate how this figure boiled down a combination of rhetoric, philosophy, drama, prose fiction, and politics into a means for shaping the self. The final lines of Seneca's tragedy *Phaedra* graphically illustrate the links between the rhetorical figure of self-apostrophe and self-command and the attempts to reassemble and refigure the mangled body of Hippolytus. Theseus first commands the chorus to help find his son's body parts, then turns to himself:

> Embrace his limbs and whatsoever remains of your child, o wretched man, warm them by bringing them close to your grieving breast. Father, set the scattered limbs of the mangled body in order and restore the separated parts to their place. Here was the location of his strong right hand, here the left must be placed, a hand so skilled at controlling the horses' reigns: I recognize the marks of his left side. How great a part of him is still absent from our tears! Trembling hands, remain firm for this sad task, and, my thirsty cheeks, stop the great flood of tears, while the father counts up the limbs of his child and fashions a body. (*Pha.* 1254–65)[17]

Theseus' combination of self-apostrophe and self-command with his gruesome attempts to create a body out of gathered pieces (*corpus fingit*) resonates with ancient oratorical theory and Seneca's own discussion of literary creation. Building on the corporeal metaphor, Quintilian writes that without figures of speech a speech is just a corpse; it takes figures to animate it: "Figures are the motion and the performance of speech; without them it lies flat like a body lacking a spirit to move it" (9.2.4).[18] Seneca writes in letter 84 that "whatever has been collected from reading, let the pen make into a body (*ut quidquid lectione collectum est stilus redigat in corpus*, 84.2). This letter's discussion of writing as a process that mimics bees gathering honey in a field is turned into a gruesome reality at the end of *Phaedra*, as Theseus and his servants gather up Hippolytus' scattered remains and vainly try to remake them into a complete body. The *Satyricon* also continually assembles different *ficta*, different options for literary and self-creation (e.g., *ficta severitate*, 132.16). The text as we now have it ends with bodily destruction as a form of survival and transformation. Eumolpus' "final" writing will presumably help his companions escape the legacy hunters in Croton. At the same time, his legatees believe that if they publicly cut up Eumolpus' body and can get their stomachs to "follow the command" so that they can consume it, they will transform themselves into wealthy heirs.

Karl Marx famously added to Hegel's claim that great historical facts and people occur twice by adding, "the first time as tragedy, the second as farce."[19] Our analysis of Seneca and Petronius has demonstrated how this repetition can also happen with ideas. The role of self-address and self-command is turned from philosophical therapy into tragic monologues in Senecan drama and then parodied by Petronius. The presentation of Nero's soul-revealing utterance in *De clementia* is turned into Claudius' and Trimalchio's deadly and windy insides. Our investigation ended by moving away from language to considering how both Seneca and Petronius problematize the role of the body and economics as a means to reveal the soul and one's social status. We have also seen how this interplay between tragedy and comedy is taken up by later authors when they consider the end of the Julio-Claudian period. Tacitus turns Seneca's ideal separation of commercial exchange and gift exchange into the first act of Seneca's attempts to distance himself from Nero. Suetonius turns self-address and self-command into one of Nero's final histrionic acts. Beneath this literary and philosophical repetition and transformation, we can find intellectual common ground between Seneca and Petronius. The two address similar questions about culture, *imperium*, and wealth. Both consider the role of language as creative and destructive of the self, as able to conceal and reveal what lies within. Both focus on the literary nature of self-fashioning and the role of imitation and the creation of memorable scripts. An investigation of the problematic links between political autocracy and self-autocracy also underlies the works of Seneca and Petronius. Both used to their relationship to Nero to gain the freedom to profit financially and experiment with new forms of literary creation in Latin. As Seneca was leaving his privileged position and Petronius was entering his, they both created their masterpieces of "autobiographical" narrative. For modern readers there is a similar message and impetus at the core of the works of these authors. Seneca and Petronius call on us to turn to self-questioning and self-reflexivity, to evaluate our ideas of high and low culture, our pretentions and feelings of self-importance, as well as our own blindness and willful self-delusion. These problems can be approached in a variety of ways, but the call to self-investigation is succinctly put by the question the freedman Hermeros poses to the freeborn scholar Ascyltus, "What are you laughing at?" (*Sat.* 57.2).

Notes

Introduction

1. There is also another series of letters by Seneca from Campania, *Ep.* 70–87, perhaps documenting a later trip; see Ker 2009a, 345n49. On Seneca's problematic relationship to travel, see Lavery 1980; and Montiglio 2006. For an analysis of Seneca's travels to various villas, see Tosi 1974–75 and Henderson 2004; on Seneca's trip through the Crypta Neapolitana, see Henderson 2006. On the location of the *Satyricon*, see K. Rose 1971; Sullivan 1968b, 46–47; and D'Arms 1981, 105.

2. On the difficulties of deciphering Petronius' full name, see Rankin 1965, 233n3; and Courtney 2001, 5–7. Tacitus writes, "de C. Petronio pauca supra repetenda sunt" (*Ann.* 16.18.1). Pliny the Elder mentions a T. Petronius (*HN* 37.20), as does Plutarch (*Mor.* 60e). Macrobius calls him "Arbiter" (*In Somn.* 1.2.8). Several manuscripts refer to him as "Petronii Arbitri Satyricon," but as Courtney (2001, 7) points out, *Arbiter* is a slave name that becomes the cognomen of a freedmen. It may have been transferred to his name by an identification with the Tacitus passage. The author of the *Satyricon* has also been identified as the consul suffect for May–September 62 CE, T. Petronius Niger; see K. Rose 1971, 50. Against this identification see Courtney 2001, 7 and n1; and Griffin 1984, 272n3. For an overview of the problems in determining authorship, see Prag and Repath 2009, 5–10. For a full list of the ancient and medieval testimonia, see Müller's 4th edition (1995), which is primarily used throughout. For the Latin text of Seneca's letters and dialogues, I follow primarily Reynolds 1965 and 1977. Unless otherwise indicated, all translations are my own.

3. There are several more connections between Seneca's first group of letters from Campania and the *Satyricon*. Specific locations in Campania are mentioned by Seneca in *Ep.* 49.1, 51.1, 53.1, 55.2, 55.7 (2x), 55.8, and 57.1 and by Petronius in *Sat.* 53.2, 53.5, 53.10, and frag. 16 Bücheler; ballplayers in the local baths, in *Ep.* 56.1 and *Sat.* 27.2–3; villas as homes of the dead, in *Ep.* 55.4, 6 and *Sat.* 72.10–73.1, 78.4–5 and throughout the *Cena*; references to Ulysses and Aeneas, in *Ep.* 53.3 (quoting Verg., *Aen.* 6.3, 3.277), *Ep.* 53.4 and 56.12–13 (quoting *Aen.* 2.726–29), *Ep.* 56.15, and *Sat.* 39.3 (Trimalchio quoting *Aen.* 2.44). In the later sections of the *Satyricon*, Encolpius frequently uses Odyssean motifs, such as Ulysses and the Cyclops, *Sat.* 97.4–5, 98.5, 101.5; the Sirens, *Sat.* 127.5; and Cicre and Polyaenus, *Sat.* 127.7. Another key point of contact between both *oeuvres* is economic themes, on which see chapter 6 below.

4. For chaos as the key theme of the *Satyricon*, see Zeitlin 1971. For Petronius as the "immoral immoralist" compared with Seneca the "immoral moralist," see Rudich 1997. For an overview of the various recent attempts to provide an overarching interpretation of the *Satyricon*, see Schmeling 1994; and Rimell 2002, 1–5.

5. On the *Satyricon*'s relationship to Pliny the Elder's encyclopedic *Natural History*, see Connors 1998, 145–46; yet it can also be related to the imperialistic cataloging drive of Seneca's *Natural Questions*, on which see chapters 3 (Encolpius and Hostius Quadra) and 5 (winds inside the earth and winds inside the human body; dangers of digging inside the earth in tension with the need to understand human insides).

6. See the essays in Volk and Williams 2006 and Bartsch and Wray 2009.

7. For an overview of the debate about the newness of Seneca's concept of the self, see Bartsch and Wray 2009, 3–19.

8. See, e.g., Foucault 1986, 61–68; Wistrand 1990; Edwards 1997; M. Wilson 1997; and Ker 2009b.

9. See Goldhill 1995; McGlathery 1998; and P. A. Miller 1998.

10. William James, quoted in Douglas 1966, 165.

11. Sullivan 1968b, 211–12; see also 255. See as well Bagnani 1954, 69; Walsh 1974, 190; Sullivan 1985, 160–61, 172–79; and Panayotakis 1995, 195–96. On Petronius' Epicureanism, see Raith 1963.

12. For a list of studies of the parallels between Seneca and Petronius on which Sullivan bases his analyses, dating from as early as the mid-nineteenth century, see Sullivan 1968b, 195n1.

13. Sullivan 1968b, 125–39. On Seneca's Maecenas as an indictment of Petronius, see Byrne 2006b.

14. Sullivan 1968a, 465.

15. Sullivan 1968b, 194.

16. Sullivan 1968b, 256; 1968a, 467.

17. Walsh 1974.

18. Sullivan 1968a, 462–63.

19. Smith 1975, 219.

20. Courtney 2001, 216–17. He cites, for example, the description of Julius Proculus in *Sat.* 38.12 in tandem with Sen., *Ben.* 2.27.1. As examples of passages that are used "without prejudice" Courtney cites *Sat.* 29.6, 46.8, 73.2, 78.5–6, 80.3–4, and 125.4 without indicating the references to Seneca.

21. M. Rose 1993, 47–48.

22. Bakhtin 1984, 11.

23. Stallybrass and White 1986, 5–6. For further insights into reading "opposed" authors, see Barthes 1976 on Sade and Loyola; and Horkheimer and Adorno 1972 on Sade and Kant.

24. Elsner 2007, 196.

25. On Seneca's innovative use of reflexive language, see Traina 1974, 14–19; Armisen-Marchetti 1989, 252–60; Cancik 1998; and Bartsch 2006, 246–47.

26. Courtney 1991, 19–20; 2001, 107; Panayotakis 2009, 60–61.

27. See, however, the warnings of Smith (1975, 218) against seeing this as a direct borrowing.

28. F. Jones 1991, 119.

29. Edwards 1997, 23–28. See also Bartsch 2006, 216–29, on Seneca's metamorphosis of the Stoic and Roman concept of the *persona* from something natural and authentic to something that is unnatural and inauthentic.

30. Compare also this letter's discussion of how reality returns to the actors after the play concludes (*Ep.* 80.7–8) with Petronius' poem on the same topic (*Sat.* 80.9).

31. I am convinced, but do not insist on the idea, that Tacitus' Petronius is in fact the author of the *Satyricon*. Rankin's statement (1965, 233) that "there is no longer any serious doubt that the writer of the *Satyricon* is the same man as that whom Tacitus described with such attention and vividness in Book XVI" may be hyperbolic. Martin (1975, 1999) would date the *Satyricon* to the Flavian era. A recent article by Daviault (2001) evaluates and supports Martin's arguments. See also Laird 2007, esp. 163n43.

32. On the rejection of "philosophical flummery," see Rankin 1965, 245. On the parody of Seneca, see Highet 1941, 194 and n49; Syme 1958, 538; Griffin 1986b, 199; Woodman 1998, 206; and Hill 2004, 247–51. Sandy (1969, 301–2) argues that Petronius' "natural" death echoes the main theme of the *Satyricon*. For Hill (2004, 239), Petronius' death's "deliberate inconsequentiality . . . strikes at the foundations of Roman ideals of the self." Edwards (2007, 158–59) makes several suggestions and claims that Petronius parodies Seneca or that he plays his role. She also argues (2007, 177–78) that Petronius' death is a rejection of Platonic and Stoic tradition for Epicureanism. She makes the intriguing suggestion that the death of Tacitus' Petronius is Epicurean and that it is modeled on Lucretius' claim in *De rerum natura* (3.398–99) equating death with leaving the banquet of life. This image is also found in Seneca's letters, however; see *Ep.* 77.8 and 98.15.

33. See Sandy 1969; and Courtney 2001, 9: "More subjective, though not without weight, is the feeling shared by many that the mental picture which we would be inclined to form of the author perfectly fits the character portrayed by Tacitus."

34. Tresch 1965, 173, quoted in Woodman 1998, 217.

35. Griffin 1984, 164.

36. *tum ipsi cum Pompeia Paulina uxore et amicis duobus epulanti mandata imperatoris edidit* (15.60.4); *iniit epulas* (16.19.2).

37. On the "paradoxes" Tacitus employs in narrating Petronius' death, see Bertrand-Dagenbach 1992, esp. 604, where he contrasts the ease of Petronius' death with Seneca's difficulty dying.

38. See J. Wilson 1990, 462–63: "Of all the accounts of suicides contained in Tacitus' discussion of the Pisonian conspiracy, cutting the legs is recorded only in the case of Seneca."

39. In contrast, Edwards (2005 and 2007, 111) argues that Seneca's body is well prepared for death and that his ability to endure pain reflects traditional Roman ideals of manliness.

40. Tacitus states that even before Seneca and Paulina slit their wrists together, Seneca "softens" after he embraces her: (*complectitur uxorem et paululum adversus praesentem fortitudinem mollitus*, 15.63.1).

41. While Petronius opens and closes his veins as he wishes, Paulina is forced by Nero's soldiers to close hers (*obligant brachia, premunt sanguinem, incertum an ignarae*, 15.64.1; *sed incisas venas, ut libitum, obligatas aperire rusum*, 16.19.2).

42. On the programmatic relationship of Petronius' list to the *Annales* as a whole, see Haynes 2010.

43. See Griffin 1986b, 199.

44. Dyson (1970, 78) argues that Tacitus mocks Seneca by having him die such a protracted death, which cycles through various options. Ker (2006, 24) suggests that these options recall Seneca's polygeneric corpus.

45. Socrates characterizes philosophy as training for death at *Phd.* 67c–d, a statement that is repeated by Cicero (*Tusc.* 1.74–75). Yet Cicero also exclaims that philosophy is a "guide for living" (*Tusc.* 5.25). On the dual role of philosophy as "learning how to live" and "learning how to die," see P. Hadot 1995, 82–101. On Petronius, see Arrowsmith 1966, 326.

46. On death in ancient Rome in general, see Edwards 2007; on Seneca, see Ker 2009a.

47. Most 1992.

48. See Cic., *De or.* 3.96; and Quint., *Inst.* 9.2.2–4.

49. Mayer 2005, 146.

CHAPTER ONE: Senecan Philosophy and the Psychology of Command

1. Socrates' disciple Antisthenes claimed that philosophy gave him the ability to converse with himself. See P. Hadot 1995, 91 and 118n94, for several examples from Diogenes Laertius of philosophers linking self-address with the cultivation of virtue. Self-address in literature could be used by philosophers as an explication of psychological theories. See, e.g., Plato's explanation (*Resp.* 390d and 441b and *Phd.* 94d–e) of Odysseus' commands to his "barking heart" (*Od.* 20.16–21). For a brief overview of philosophical self-address, see Leo 1908, 111–12.

2. "una Hannibalem hiberna solverunt et indomitum illum nivibus atque Alpibus virum enervaverunt fomenta Campaniae: armis vicit, vitiis victus est."

3. "nobis quoque militandum est, et quidem genere militiae quo numquam quies, numquam otium datur: debellandae sunt in primis voluptates, quae, ut vides, saeva quoque ad se ingenia rapuerunt."

4. "si faceremus quod fecit Hannibal, ut interrupto cursu rerum ommisoque bello fovendis corporibus operam daremus, nemo non intempestivam desidiam, victori quoque, nedum vincenti, periculosam, merito reprehenderet: minus nobis quam illis Punica signa sequentibus licet, plus periculi restat cedentibus, plus operis etiam perseverantibus."

5. Scipio Africanus wisely spent his exile in Liternum (51.11). Seneca describes his visit to this Spartan villa in letter 86. For an analysis of this visit see Henderson 2004, 53–61, 93–170.

6. For an account of Seneca's development of Fortune as an adversary, see Asmis 2009.

7. "si voluptati cessero, cedendum est dolori, cedendum est labori, cedendum est paupertati; idem sibi in me iuris esse volet ambitio et ira; inter tot adfectus distrahar, immo discerpar."

8. In the following section Seneca compares Alexander the Great's statement about his plans for conquering Asia with what Philosophy says (*Ep.* 53.10).

9. "incredibilis philosophiae vis est ad omnem fortuitam vim retundendam. nullum telum in corpore eius sedet; munita est, solida; quaedam defetigat et velut levia tela laxo sinu eludit, quaedam discutit et in eum usque qui miserat respuit." On the history of late antique and medieval personifications of philosophy, see Most 1996.

10. In this letter Seneca once again reevaluates the meaning of heroism. He cuts right to the core of the Roman ideal of *pietas* by condemning Aeneas for fearing for "his

companion and his burden" as he fled the sack of Troy (*Aen.* 2.726–29; *Ep.* 56.12–13). Cf. Motto and Clark 1970.

11. "Alexander Persas quidem et Hyrcanos et Indos et quidquid gentium usque in oceanum extendit oriens vastabat fugabatque, sed ipse modo occiso amico, modo amisso, iacebat in tenebris, alias scelus, alias desiderium suum maerens, victor tot regum atque populorum irae tristitiaeque succumbens; id enim egerat ut omnia potius haberet in potestate quam adfectus. o quam magnis homines tenentur erroribus qui ius dominandi trans maria cupiunt permittere felicissimosque se iudicant si multas [pro] milite provincias obtinent et novas veteribus adiungunt, ignari quod sit illud ingens parque dis regnum: imperare sibi maximum imperium est." Following the editorial convention for Greek and Latin texts, angled brackets signify what should be added to the text, and square brackets, what likely should be deleted.

12. "quem magis admiraberis, quam qui imperat sibi, quam qui se habet in potestate? gentes facilius est barbaras impatientesque arbitrii alieni regere, quam animum suum continere et tradere sibi."

13. Inwood 1985, 170; see also 111.

14. Roller 2001, 66.

15. M. Wilson 1997, 63. Wilson singles out *Ep.* 96.5 as the paradigmatic example: "To live, my Lucilius, is to be a soldier" (*vivere, Lucili, militare est*).

16. As Edwards (1993, 197) points out, "Self-control legitimated the power of the elite in a way that wealth alone could never do." We shall look at the role of wealth in chapter 6.

17. See, e.g., *Ep.* 31.11, 46.6.

18. "adice nunc quod nihil honeste fit nisi cui totus animus incubuit atque adfuit, cui nulla parte sui repugnavit. ubi autem ad malum acceditur aut peiorum metu, aut spe bonorum ad quae pervenire tanti sit devorata unius mali patientia, dissident inter se iudicia facientis: hinc est quod iubeat proposita perficere, illinc quod retrahat et ab re suspecta ac periculosa fugiat; igitur in diversa distrahitur. si hoc est, perit gloria; virtus enim concordi animo decreta peragit, non timet quod facit."

19. Roller 2001, 104.

20. Brunt 1988, 312, comments on Scipio's quotation: "In other words, a man was most free when he had the fullest right to enforce his own will." See also J. Richardson 1991, 9, which notes that even during the republic Roman *imperium* "always had the possibility of tyrannical power."

21. For an analysis of Cicero's speeches in support of extraordinary commands, see Steel 2001, 113–61.

22. See Steel 2001, 132–33 and nn50, 51, for a bibliography on the topic. But cf. Sallust's brief discussion of the *virtus* of kings and generals at *Cat.* 2.3.2: "But if the *virtus* of kings and generals were equally strong in peace and in war, human affairs would be more even and constant, and they would not be carried one way and then the other, nor would you see everything changed and mixed up" (*quod si regum atque imperatorum animi virtus in pace ita ut in bello valeret, aequabilius atque constantius sese res humanae haberent, neque aliud alio ferri neque mutari ac misceri omnia cerneres*).

23. "nunc denique incipiunt credere fuisse homines Romanos hac quondam continentia, quod in nationibus exteris incredible ac falso memoriae proditum videbatur. nunc imperii vestri splendor illis gentibus lucem adferre coepit."

24. "nulla est enim tanta vis quae non ferro et viribus debilitari frangique possit. animum vincere, iracundiam cohibere, victo temperare, adversarium nobilitate, ingenio, virtute praestantem non modo extollere iacentem sed etiam amplificare eius pristinam dignitatem, haec qui faciat, non ego eum cum summis viris comparo, sed simillimum deo iudico."

25. The notion of conquering one's *animus* can be seen already in Plaut., *Trin.* 310. For the command of the *animus*, see Cic., *Rep.* 3.37; Sall., *Cat.* 1.2; and Sall., *Iug.* 1.3.

26. Bartsch 2006, 184.

27. As recognized already by Aristotle, panegyric must mask protreptic rhetoric, *Rh.* 1367b35. For an overview of republican and early imperial Latin panegyric, see S. Braund 1998.

28. It has been argued that Seneca is trying to shape Nero into a Stoic philosopher-king. See Mortureux 1989, 1682; and S. Braund 1998, 72.

29. "severitatem abditam, at clementiam in procintu habeo; sic me custodio tamquam legibus quas ex situ ac tenebris in lucem evocavi, rationem redditurus sim. alterius aetate prima motus sum alterius ultima; alium dignitati donavi, alium humilitati; quotiens nullam inveneram misericordiae causam, mihi peperci."

30. See Edwards 1997, 31–32, on the "interiorizing" of dialogue in Seneca's *Epistles*. Edwards draws particular attention to *Ep.* 26.7 and 27.1, where "Seneca presents himself as the addressee of his own advice" (32). See also *Polyb.* 9.1; *Ben.* 3.38.3, 7.2.2, 7.21.2; and *Ep.* 8.6, 68.6–7, 94.46–48, 98.11–12.

31. While exiled in Corsica, Seneca practiced writing speeches for emperors on controlling their emotions. Toward the end of the *Consolatio ad Polybium*, Seneca scripts a long speech for Claudius outlining how several Roman generals and emperors, including himself, have conquered their grief after the loss of a loved one (14.2–16.3).

32. On the ambiguous role of the mirror in the care of the self, see Bartsch 2006, 15–56; see also 23–24 on the connections between self-speculation and self-dialogue.

33. On Seneca's use of *voluptas* in this passage, see Bartsch 2006, 183–91. Seneca himself defends using this word in a Stoic sense in *Ep.* 59.1–2.

34. Indeed, in letters 94 and 95 Seneca continually plays on the Latin words for "exercise," "discipline," and "army" (*exercitatio, exercere, exercitus*); see also *Ep.* 53.9 and 56.15, discussed above.

35. It is tempting to think that Seneca alludes to Nero in his opening critiques, in particularwhen he says that "there are many who have set fire to cities" (*multi inveniuntur qui ignem inferant urbibus*, 94.61).

36. "insanus amor magnitudinis falsae . . . infinita scilicet cupido crescendi."

37. "gloria et ambitio et nullus supra ceteros eminendi modus."

38. Cf. Foucault's discussion of the nature of power as possibly a "reversal of Clausewitz's assertion that war is politics continued by other means. If political power puts an end to war, this by no means implies that it suspends the effects of war or neutralizes the disequilibrium revealed in the final battle" (2005b, 514–15).

39. In the *Satyricon* this postbellum world is dramatically portrayed in Croton. As Eumolpus finishes his poem on the civil war, he and his companions look down on the city of Croton, which is experiencing the same stasis. Instead of political and military strife, the factionalism in Croton is economic.

40. "omne hoc quod vides, quo divina atque humana conclusa sunt, unum est; membra sumus corporis magni. natura nos cognatos edidit, cum ex isdem et in eadem

gigneret . . . ex illius imperio paratae sint iuvandis manus. ille versus et in pectore et in ore sit: 'homo sum, humani nihil a me alienum puto.' "

41. "hoc est illud punctum quod inter tot gentes ferro igne dividitur? O quam ridiculi sunt mortalium termini! ultra Istrum Dacos non exeat, imperium Haemo Thraces includant; Parthis obstet Euphrates; Danuvius Sarmatica ac Romana disterminet, Rhenus Germaniae modum faciat, Pyrenaeus medium inter Gallias et Hispanias iugum extollat, inter Aegyptum et Aethiopas harenarum inculta vastitas iaceat. si quis formicis det intellectum hominis, nonne et illae unam aream in multas provincias divident? cum te in illa vere magna sustuleris, quotiens videbis exercitus subrectis ire vexillis et, quasi magnum aliquid agatur, equitem modo extrema cingentem, modo ulteriora explorantem, modo a lateribus adfusum, libet dicere: 'it nigrum campis agmen.' formicarum iste discursus est in angusto laborantium. quid illis et vobis interest nisi exigui mensura corpusculi?" Hine's (1996) text only puts the first sentence in quotations. Here I follow the punctuation of Corcoran's Loeb (1971) edition and give the entire passage as the soul's self-address.

42. See Lucr. 2.19, on the sweet joys of looking down on the political world from a distance. Scipio Aemilianus, in book 6 of Cicero's *De republica*, claims that he is ashamed of the size of the empire but nevertheless will struggle to defend and expand it in order to gain his place in the eternal celestial regions. After his funeral, Lucan's Pompey also journeys up to the translunar regions, laughs at his insignificant body, and then returns to the breast of Brutus and the mind of Cato (*BC* 9.1–18). On the tradition of the "view from above," see P. Hadot 1995, 238–50; on this theme in Seneca's *Q Nat.*, see Hine 2006, 43–47.

43. On the tension between the active and the contemplative life in Seneca, see Momigliano 1969.

44. Just prior to this passage, Seneca writes a passage of self-praise for Lucilius, outlining how he remained true to his philosophy despite the dangers he faced under Caligula and Claudius (*Q Nat.* 4a.pref.14–17). On how this passage may also be a summary of Seneca's own life, see Motto 2001, 113; and Hine 2006, 47.

45. At *Q Nat.* 3.pref.5–10 Seneca condemns spending time in the study of history. One's goal should not be to subjugate others, but to subjugate the self: "Countless people have had cities and entire populations under their power; only the smallest number have had themselves" (*innumerabiles sunt qui populos, qui urbes habuerunt in potestate, paucissimi qui se*, 10).

46. Cf. Seneca's problematic praise of Sicily at *Marc.* 17.2–5, discussed in Bartsch 2007, 83–85.

47. "hanc ego habeo sub meo iure provinciam quae maximarum urbium exercitus et sustinuit et fregit, cum inter Carthaginem et Romam ingentis belli praemium iacuit; quae quattuor Romanorum principum, id est totius imperi, vires contractas in unum locum vidit aluitque; <quae> Pompeii fortunam erexit, Caesaris fatigavit, Lepidi transtulit, omnium cepit; quae illi ingenti spectaculo interfuit ex quo liquere mortalibus posset quam velox foret ad imum lapsus e summo, quamque diversa via magnam potentiam fortuna destrueret. uno enim tempore vidit Pompeium Lepidumque ex maximo fastigio aliter ad extrema deiectos, cum Pompeius alienum exercitum fugeret, Lepidus suum."

48. As Hine (2006, 42) demonstrates, the *Natural Questions* is structured around an unresolved tension: "On the one hand there is a grand vision of the cosmos and its

splendor, in comparison to which empires and imperial power, including Rome's, recede into insignificance ... but at the same time the work is firmly anchored in the Roman world, drawing widely on information about the natural world that was garnered from all corners of the Empire and from beyond."

49. In contrast to Seneca's portrayal of Nero's expedition as a disinterested search for truth, Pliny the Elder (*HN* 6.181, 12.19) and Dio Cassius (63.8.1–2) state that it was a reconnaissance mission to prepare for an invasion of Ethiopia. See Hine 2006, 63n88, for an overview of the bibliography on the expedition.

50. Seneca praises Nero for trying to find the source of the Nile: "Nero Caesar, as he is a great lover of all the other virtues, so he is especially a lover of the truth" (*ut aliarum virtutum ita veritatis in primis amantissimus*, Q *Nat.* 6.8.3). He describes the appearance of a comet in 60 CE as occurring "during the most happy principate of Nero" (*Neronis principatu laetissimo*, 7.21.3); Seneca also quotes a line of Nero's poetry, calling it "most elegant" (*disertissime*, 1.5.6). See Hine 2006, 63–67, on whether Seneca's praise of Nero is genuine.

51. There have been various interpretations of Seneca's views on the proper relationship of the self to the external world. Most scholars have focused on Seneca's minimization of political life at Rome. For example, Nussbaum (1994, 354–55) focuses on how Stoic reason remains free from political constraint and argues that Seneca sets a "countersociety over against Roman society" (on *Ep.* 44). Roller (2001, 64–126, discussed above) argues that Seneca's primary goal is to privilege Stoic ethics above traditional Roman ideals; and Bartsch (2006, 236) argues that Seneca's "'community' largely consists of characters who are dead, imaginary, or divine." See also Asmis 2009. Edwards (1997) demonstrates how Seneca relates daily practices of Roman life to individual psychology. Elsewhere (2007, 94) she argues that Seneca's praise of republican heroes such as Mucius Saevola and Cato may be closer to traditional Roman ideals of physical toughness than previously thought. Critiquing Foucault's vision of the care of the self as excessively aesthetic and socially isolating, P. Hadot (1995, 208) stresses the cosmopolitan aspect of Seneca's thought. Citing *Ep.* 66.6, he notes that Seneca exhorts Lucilius to "place himself in the entirety of the universe" (*toti se inserens mundo*).

52. See Bartsch 2006, 245: "One's progress toward normative Stoic virtue depends on the assumption of a set of guiding values that Seneca himself claims are no longer to be found within the community, but only in the writings of philosophers and the conduct of long dead exemplars—men whom one must select as one's dialogic partners and watching judges." One wonders, however, whether the Romans ever exclusively valued the habits and figures of contemporary society as guides for conduct. The celebration of the tradition of the ancestors (*mos maiorum*), for example, would seem to mitigate valuing contemporary society highly.

53. "nam mundus quoque cuncta complectens rectorque universi deus in exteriora quidem tendit, sed tamen introsum undique in se redit. idem nostra mens faciat: cum secuta sensus suos per illos se ad externa porrexerit, et illorum et sui potens sit. hoc modo una efficietur vis ac potestas concors sibi et ratio illa certa nascetur, non dissidens nec haesitans in opinionibus comprensionibusque nec in persuasione, quae cum se disposuit et partibus suis consensit et, ut ita dicam, concinuit, summum bonum tetigit. nihil enim pravi, nihil lubrici superest, nihil in quo arietet aut labet; omnia faciet ex imperio suo nihilque inopinatum accidet, sed quidquid agetur in bonum exibit facile et parate et sine tergiversatione agentis; nam pigritia et haesitatio pugnam et inconstan-

tiam ostendit. quare audaciter licet profitearis summum bonum esse animi concordiam; virtutes enim ibi esse debebunt ubi consensus atque unitas erit: dissident vitia."

54. Cf. Aegisthus' question to his *animus* during his opening monologue in Seneca's *Agamemnon*: "Why do you turn your back, my soul?" (*quid terga vertis, anime?*). This play is discussed in chapter 2.

55. Inwood 1985, 47.

56. For a full list of such usages, see Inwood 1985, chap. 1, esp. p. 16: "Aristotle also uses imperatival language in describing how action issues from a combination of desire and belief. Again, his remarks are unsystematic, but in several places he associates imperatival force and language with desire." Inwood cites *Eth. Nic.* 1147a25, 1147a29 and *De an.* 432b26–433a3 as examples.

57. On translating *animus* as "soul" as opposed to "mind," see Nussbaum 1994, 317n2. On the soul, specifically the *hegemonikon* as the self for the Stoics, see Long 2001, 248: "Cleanthes allegedly called man 'soul alone'" (citing *SVF* 1.538); and Reydams-Schills 2005, 15–16. For passages on the *hegemonikon*, see Long and Sedley 1987, 53H and 53K–M.

58. The abilities to use articulate language and to give or withhold assent to impressions were seen by the Stoics as the defining characteristics of humanity. Furthermore, the entire processes of perception and action were theorized as functioning through language. See Annas 1992, 74–75, discussing Diog. Laert. 7.49 = *SVF* 2.52. The impressions that were received by the *hegemonikon* were thought to be propositions, or *lekta*, incorporeal "sayables." See Long 2001, 273; Long and Sedley 1987, 33D, 33F; and Sen., *Ep.* 117.13 = Long and Sedley 1987, 33E.

59. Translation from Inwood 1985, 62.

60. "quid sit adsensio dicam. oportet me ambulare: tunc demum ambulo cum hoc mihi dixi et adprobavi hanc opinionem meam."

61. Annas 1992, 96.

62. Long and Sedley 1987, 2:200.

63. Mele (1992, 292–93) argues that desire is not sufficient to generate action: "We have fleeting desires, relatively weak desires, and even some very strong desires, to do any number of things that we do not do, largely because we decide or intend to do something else."

64. Translation from Inwood 1985, 62.

65. See Inwood 1985, 62: "For although the proposition is a true statement about what he should do, it does not necessarily follow that he will act. Knowing what to do provides no guarantee by itself that one will act. Aristotle recognized this. . . . There is no reason why the Stoics should not have seen the same distinction and realized its importance."

66. "animus noster modo rex est, modo tyrannus: rex cum honesta intuetur, salutem commissi sibi corporis curat et illi nihil imperat turpe, nihil sordidum; ubi vero inpotens, cupidus, delicatus est, transit in nomen detestabile ac dirum et fit tyrannus. tunc illum excipiunt adfectus inpotentes et instant." For a full investigation of this letter, see chapter 6.

67. Inwood 2000, 52–55. He cites *Ira* 2.12 on 54–55: "What we would without hesitation describe as an act of will, and indeed think of as paradigm instances of willpower, are here portrayed as self-directed commands in pursuit of moral self-control and character improvement. Here we have mental events, acts of 'will,' despite the ab-

sence of the obvious label that connects readily to modern lexical correspondences. For Seneca, then, it is self-directed commands that are acts of 'will.'"

68. Cf. Inwood 2000, 53–54: "The language of self-command is used in two different modes. Sometimes Seneca uses explicitly reflexive language (e.g., *Ira* 2.12.4) where the command is both given and accepted by either the agent or some significant psychological part of the agent; and at other times one part of the soul gives an order either to another part or to the agent as a whole (e.g., *Ira* 3.32). In either mode the effect is the same. Seneca is in most cases isolating a mental event that has an important, if not decisive bearing on action and ascriptions of responsibility."

69. "atqui nihil est tam difficile et arduum quod non humana mens vincat et in familiaritatem perducat adsidua meditatio, nullique sunt tam feri et sui iuris adfectus ut non disciplina perdomentur. quodcumque sibi imperavit animus optinuit."

70. Indeed, in this passage Seneca continues the idea of the language of our psychology and notes that when "the mind declares endurance upon itself," it can overcome all impediments (*sibi ipsa mens patientiam indiceret*, 2.12.4).

71. "quemadmodum totum corpus animo deservit et, cum hoc tanto maius tantoque speciosius sit, ille in occulto maneat tenuis et in qua sede latitet incertus, tamen manus, pedes, oculi negotium illi gerunt, illum haec cutis munit, illius iussu iacemus aut inquieti discurrimus, cum ille imperavit, sive avarus dominus est, mare lucri causa scrutamur, sive ambitiosus iam dudum dextram flammis obiecimus aut voluntarii terram subsiluimus."

72. "That we have a soul, by the command of which we are driven forward or called back, all will admit" (*habere nos animum, cuius imperio et impellimur et revocamur, omnes fatebuntur*, *Q Nat*. 7.25.2).

73. In addition, Seneca writes about the command of other virtues associated with the soul: reason (*Ep.* 66.32), wisdom (85.32), and moderation (*temparantia*) (88.29).

74. B. Williams 1997, 211, responding to Sorabji 1997b, 205.

75. Pleasure commands as well; see *Ep.* 92.25–26.

76. Cf. Seneca's advice to Polybius that when he feels grief for his dead brother, he should "think of Caesar" (*Caesarem cogita*, *Polyb.* 7.1).

77. See Newman 1989, 1493, on the rhetorical nature of *meditatio* and how one is free to choose phrases from Seneca's text, by virtue of its characteristic pointedness, to repeat: "The *sententiae* provided the bones of the *meditatio*, but Seneca did not always specify the exact phrases to be used while meditating. Instead, he left such details to the imagination of his correspondent."

78. "tunc illos et paenitentia coepti tenet et incipiendi timor subrepitque illa animi iactatio non invenientis exitum, quia nec imperare cupiditatibus suis nec obsequi possunt."

79. Inwood (1985, 17) notes that Aristotle shied away from giving the passions a command of their own; he had a "strong preference for attributing imperatival force to rational desire alone, as though reluctant to dignify irrational desire with the position of 'commander' in the soul."

80. Inwood 1993, 157. For an overview of Seneca's Stoic orthodoxy, see Rist 1989.

81. Inwood 1985, 138. He continues, "Anyone, they thought, who is not blinded by theoretical blinkers must recognize that sometimes there are two warring elements in the soul. The Stoics' move to negate this evidence is not in the end

fully satisfying except (or perhaps even) to those who share their theoretical commitments."

82. Atherton 1988.

83. "nullum sequitur florem orationis neque dilatat argumentum; minutis interrogantiunculis quasi punctis quod proposuit efficit." See also *Brut.* 114, 119; *De or.* 2.153, 3.65; and Krostenko 2001, 134–37.

84. Cicero says in *Parad. Stoic.* (1–3) that he is particularly impressed by Cato's persuasive abilities. As Atherton (1988, 402) notes, "Cato's success is all the more remarkable because the philosophy he popularizes is generally unpopular, and because his style of discourse, the style he uses in the Senate is not calculated to please."

85. Atherton 1988, 401.

86. The general was Calpurnius in Sicily during the First Punic War; see also Livy 22.60.11.

87. Newman 1989, 1475.

88. Sorabji 1997b, 204–5.

89. Sorabji 1997b, 209.

90. Newman 1989, 1482.

91. "omnes sensus perducendi sunt ad firmitatem; natura patientes sunt, si animos illos desît corrumpere, qui cotidie ad rationem reddendam vocandus est."

92. There is considerable debate about whether Seneca's example of self-investigation in *De ira* 3.36 contributes anything new to the idea of the self. Inwood (2009, 56) and Gill (2009, 83) argue that it does not, but cf. Nussbaum 1994, 425, and Ker 2009b.

93. See Mischel and Mischel 1977 for an analysis of modern techniques for increasing self-control, which are remarkably like Seneca's. Mischel and Mischel write, for example, that "self-instructions and intention statements are likely to be important aspects of the individual's plans and the hierarchical organization of his self-regulatory behavior" (47).

94. Other examples are: "I will command my sense of shame" (*imperabo pudori meo, Ben.* 5.20.7); "The soul must be commanded" (*animo imperandum est, Ep.* 18.3); and "If you will command [the pleasures] rather than serve them" (*si illis imperabis quam si servies, Ep.* 116.1).

95. M. Wilson 1997, 61–62. He also states that for Seneca, philosophy is an "imperial art, not a medical one" (65).

96. It may seem curious that Cato, the "perfect Stoic" in Seneca's eyes, would need to use a technique of self-control to get himself to perform his self-defining action. Perhaps this apostrophe is used to demonstrate Cato's full commitment to the deed. Modern philosophy treats the question of seemingly extraneous exercises of self-control. Mele (1987, 72) classifies such cases as instances of "downhill self-control," when one's motivation to exercise self-control is even greater than one's desire to act.

97. On the lack of historical evidence for Cato's dying words and the subsequent tradition of creative invention of them, see Tandoi 1965, 330–33; and Goar 1987, 38–39. "Cato's last words" became a standard declamatory exercise that even the Stoic Persius cannot bear to remember reciting as a lad (3.44–47).

98. See also *Ep.* 24.6–8.

99. Goar 1987, 40.

100. Bonner 1949, 71–83.

101. Bonner 1949, 160–67. Bonner's conclusion is most revealing of his attitude toward his topic: "Few now can spare time for the effusions of Latro, Cestius, Arellius Fuscus, Gallio and their lesser contemporaries" (167).

102. Bonner 1949, 167.

103. Anderson 1995, 78. Anderson generously concludes that declamation does not present the "inverse of the moral world" (90).

104. See also Quint., *Inst.* 2.10.1–15, 10.5.17; Tac., *Dial.* 33.4–5; Juv. 7.166–70; and Sen., *Controv.* 7.pref.7, 9.pref.1, all cited in F. Jones 1991, 113.

105. Conte 1996, 45.

106. Conte 1996, 84. According to Conte, "With Encolpius a whole literary culture is under fire, the culture that transformed these great moments into spectacular and melodramatic themes" (90).

107. Elsner 1993, 30. On critics' resistance to the possibility of ironically self-aware characters in the *Satyricon*, see Rimell 2002, 7 (on Encolpius), and 2007b (on Trimalchio). In a similar vein, several scholars have begun to look for the real-world social importance of Roman declamation. See Beard 1993; Bloomer 1997; and Gunderson 2003.

108. Vickers 1982, 15–16.

109. "aversus quoque a iudice sermo, qui dicitur apostrophe, mire movet, sive adversarios invadimus: 'quid enim tuus ille gladius, Tubero, in acie Pharsalica?' sive ad invocationem aliquam convertimur: 'vos enim iam ego, Albani tumuli atque luci,' sive ad invidiosam inplorationem: 'o leges Porciae legesque Semproniae!'"

110. There are other examples of address to the *animus* in the declamations. See also the case of the "torture of the poor man" (*tormenta pauperis*) preserved in the longer declamations of Pseudo-Quintillian. The pauper, a free man, wants to be tortured in court so that he can bear witness against the rich man who killed his son. In his speech arguing for this right, the pauper imagines how he will steel himself during the torture: "Among the fires and the whips it will suffice me, if I say, 'This is your enemy, my soul, who repeatedly defamed us'" (7.6). Here again, although there is not an outright command to his *animus*, the pauper's self-apostrophe is the means by which he will endure the torture and continue with his case. Further examples include: "Where are you leading me my soul? Where are you dragging me, my passions?" (*quo me ducis, anime? quo me trahis, adfectus?*, [Quint.], *Minor dec.* 315.22); and "Make haste to bewail this present sorrow, my soul, make haste" (*festina<s> ad complorationem praesentis doloris, anime, festinas*, [Quint.], *Maior dec.* 14.2).

111. "servatque immobile corpus,/seque probat moriens atque haec in pectore volvit:/'saecula Romanos numquam tacitura labores/attendunt, aevumque sequens speculatur ab omni/orbe ratem Phariamque fidem: nunc consule famae./fata tibi longae fluxerunt prospera vitae:/ignorant populi, si non in morte probaris,/an scieris adversa pati. ne cede pudori/auctoremque dole fati: quacumque feriris,/crede manum soceri. spargant lacerentque licebit,/sum tamen, o superi, felix, nullique poetestas/hoc auffere deo. mutantur prospera vita,/non fit morte miser. videt hanc Cornelia caedem/Pompeiusque meus: tanto patientius oro,/claude dolor, gemitus: gnatus coniunxque peremptum,/si mirantur, amant.'"

112. Bramble 1982, 535.

113. W. R. Johnson 1987, 79.

114. W. R. Johnson 1987, 81.

115. Ormand 1994, 48.

116. W. R. Johnson (1987, 80) argues that in his speeches Pompey is presented as *"miles gloriosus*, now bellowing of his preeminence, now whining in resentment and self-pity." For Johnson this pattern extends from Pompey's first speech in book 2 to his final public speech (8.262–327). On Pompey's failure to persuade his troops, in part because of his frequent apostrophes to the absent Caesar, see Fantham 1992, 181; Ormand 1994, 44–46; and Roller 2001, 31–32.

117. On how the narrator's frequent apostrophes make him an engaged and individualized character in Lucan's *De bello civili*, see Bartsch 1997, 95, 100; and Leigh 1997, 48.

118. Cf. Seneca's claim in *De vita beata* that the uncorrupt man is the artist or creator (*artifex*) of his life (8.3). On the use of this term in Seneca, see Bartsch 2009, 209–12.

119. Warmington 2000, 85.

120. See Dingel 1974 for a sustained argument that Seneca's tragedies negate his philosophy.

121. Letter 99 is an example of how Senecan philosophy avoids the charge of "lethal high-mindedness," which B. Williams (1997) attributes to it.

122. "clarius cum audiuntur gemunt, et taciti quietique dum secretum est, cum aliquos videre, in fletus novos excitantur; tunc capiti suo manus ingerunt (quod potuerant facere nullo prohibente liberius), tunc mortem comprecantur sibi, tunc lectulo devolvuntur: sine spectatore cessat dolor."

CHAPTER TWO: Self-Address in Senecan Tragedy

1. Apostrophes to the *animus*, which are the main focus of this chapter, number twenty-five in Seneca's tragedies, as Viansino (1993, 370) points out; see also Tarrant 1976, 194–95.

2. I am concerned here with self-command in Senecan tragedy as part of what Foucault identifies as the "arts of existence" or "techniques of the self" in classical and Hellenistic philosophy. Foucault (1984, 10–11) defines these techniques as "intentional and voluntary actions by which men not only set themselves rules of conduct but also seek to transform themselves, to change themselves in their singular being, and to make their life into an *oeuvre* that carries certain aesthetic values and meets certain stylistic critieria." As Foucault (1986, 46) demonstrates, "taking care of one's soul" achieved a particular fullness in the philosophy of Seneca; see also 48–68 for a general discussion of *askesis* in Seneca and elsewhere. I focus on the relationship between self-address, self-control or self-creation, and the passions that exists in Seneca's tragedy. Of course, the linguistic basis of self-construction in literature and philosophy is not unique to Seneca. Gill (1996, 183), for example, argues that Greek self-address is ultimately based on the norms of communication in society and of interpersonal dialogue. According to Gill, characters such as Medea address themselves only because of their exceptional isolation. In his analysis of the development of the modern concept of self, Taylor (1989, 183) also notes the importance of language: "The self is both made and explored with words; and the best for both are the words spoken in the dialogue of friendship. In default of that, the debate with solitary self comes limping far behind." The key difference between Taylor and Seneca has to do with the specific nature of the

language of the self. Seneca is concerned with this "limping" and solitary form of self-construction and self-exploration. It is not based on a dialogue of interpersonal debate. For Seneca, the language of the self is *imperatival*.

3. The ideas expressed here are based on Turner's (1969) theories on the relationship between structure and antistructure; see esp. 49, 97.

4. See *Ira* 2.3.4–5, 2.4.1–2; Gill 1983, 138–39; and Inwood 1993, 181.

5. See Gill 1983, 138–42, and Nussbaum 1994, 379, on Chrysippus; and Inwood 1993, 165–81, on Seneca's developments in *De ira*. See also Plut., *Mor.* 446f–447a = *SVF* 3.459.

6. See *Ira* 1.8 and 1.17, discussed in Tarrant 1976, 194. As Seneca says, "Delay is the greatest remedy for anger" (*Ira* 2.29.1).

7. On one level, Seneca's portrayal of the passions in his tragedies contradicts the orthodox Stoic notion that the passions reject planning and control. On the Stoic dichotomy between the passions and control, see Nussbaum 1994, 397; on Chrysippus' definition of the passions as an "excessive impulse," see Gill 1983, 143. Chrysippus compares the passions to a runner whose legs are out of control. Seneca intensifies this basic comparison and likens the irrevocable and out-of-control effect of the passions on the *animus* to falling off a cliff (*Ira* 1.7.4). From the tragedies' initially unorthodox portrait, Seneca develops a nuanced idea of the structure and maintenance of the passions that is ultimately based on Stoic theories of therapy. See Gill 1997, 227–28, on the fundamental humanity, virtue, and rationality that lie at the core of Phaedra's and Medea's passions. The portrayal of consistency of vice and criminal self-control in Seneca's tragedies is an important precedent for modern literary and philosophical discussions. See Mele 1992, 289, on the links between weakness of will (*akrasia*) and self-control; and Shattuck 1996, 229–99, on the portrayal of self-control in the Marquis de Sade.

8. The nature of the relationship between Senecan philosophy and tragedy remains one of the most vexed questions in Senecan criticism. Dingel (1974, 14, 18) argues that the two must remain separated. He claims that the tragedies must be understood as strictly "poetic" and may even "negate" Stoic principles. He claims (58) that Seneca consciously tried to distance himself not just from his own tragic output but from the entire genre. See also Armisen-Marchetti 1989, 347–65, on the difficulties inherent in linking the two bodies of work. In a series of works, Schiesaro also argues for a critical separation of the two genres. Schiesaro 1994 argues most forcefully for separation. Schiesaro 1997 takes a more sympathetic view of philosophical readings of the tragedies. Most recently, Schiesaro (2003, 6) argues against political and moralistic interpretations of Atreus. Perhaps the most forceful arguments for a Stoic reading of Senecan tragedy are in Nussbaum 1993, 148 (critiqued by Schiesaro 1997, 108–9), and 1994, esp. 448–53, where Nussbaum connects *Medea* explicitly to the Stoic theory of the passions.

9. On the early Stoic goal of life formulated by Zeno as "living consistently [with nature]," see Inwood 1985, 105. For discussions of the possible meanings of this dictum, see Striker 1991; and more recently Schofield 2003, 239–46. Other important discussions of the virtue of consistency in Seneca include *Ep.* 52.1–2, 66.9, 13, 67.10, 74.30–34, and 92.3. Elsewhere, e.g., in *VB* 9.4, Seneca describes Stoic virtue as *concordia animi*. On the links between the Stoic ideal of *constantia* and Seneca's tragedies, see Tietze 1987. Tietze concludes that Seneca's characters are "*characerismoi* of *inconstan-*

tia" (141); my focus, however, is on the characters' ability successfully to battle *inconstantia*. See also Motto 2001, 79–87.

10. The opening of letter 120 contains an important contribution to Seneca's overall analysis of psychology and action. As Roller (2001, 77–83) has demonstrated in his analysis of *gratia* in *De beneficiis*, Seneca moves the focus of the socially binding practices of gift-giving and bestowing and returning favors from the act itself to the will of the agent. Seneca thus reevaluates human action and locates virtue in the psychological state behind the act rather than in its success or failure. The act itself frequently is elided, as Roller points out. In letter 120, however, Seneca advises Lucilius to change his focus continually between the internal (the agent's psychology) and the external (the act itself) (120.8–9). Lucilius must look for consistency and concord between the two.

11. Discussions of psychological fluctuation are numerous throughout Seneca's philosophy. *Tranq.* 1 provides a lengthy description of the difficulties that even a *proficiens* like Serenus faces in controlling his *animus*. See also *Tranq.* 2.7, 2.10, 10.6; and *Ep.* 16.3, 23.8, 34.4, 35.4, 69.1.

12. "et modo parum illis severus est Curius, parum pauper Fabricius, parum frugi et contentus vilibus Tubero, modo Licinum divitîs, Apicium cenis, Maecenatem delicis provocant."

13. "modo uxorem vult habere, modo amicam, modo regnare vult, modo id agit ne quis sit officiosior servus."

14. "sic maxime coarguitur animus inprudens: alius prodit atque alius et, quo turpius nihil iudico, inpar sibi est."

15. For an analysis of theatrical metaphors in Seneca, see Hijmans 1966. Hijmans (242) pays particular attention to the significance of the verb *agere* in Seneca's philosophy.

16. See Edwards 1997, 34, on the conclusion of letter 120. In this passage Seneca seems to be expressing his own concept of the "persona theory." See Cic., *Off.* 1.97–98, 1.115; and Epict., *Diss.* 1.2.5–8. This passage in Seneca also denies the statement by the early Stoic Ariston of Chios, that the wise man knows how to play many roles; he can be both Thersites and Agamemnon (*SVF* 1.351). On the changing concept of *persona* in Seneca, see Bartsch 2006, 216–29.

17. "hoc ergo a te exige, ut qualem institueris praestare te, talem usque ad exitum serves; effice ut possis laudari, si minus, ut adgnosci."

18. "de aliquo quem here vidisti merito dici potest 'hic qui est?': tanta mutatio est."

19. On the concept of Neronian theatricality, see Bartsch 1994. An analysis of the age of Nero in terms of the "rhetoricized mentality" is provided in Rudich 1997. Rosenmeyer (1989, 47–52) discusses the theatricality of Stoicism in general.

20. As Elsner (1993, 2007) argues, Neronian authors, in particular Petronius, take an ironic, self-aware, and critical stance toward contemporary society.

21. As Too (1994, 219–22) points out, in the *Epistles* there is a contradictory slippage between ideas of movement and ideas of stability in Seneca's metaphors describing the state of the *sapiens*. This conflict comes out in the tragedies too. Medea and Atreus in particular must *transform* themselves into their ideal, consistent selves. Self-transformation and *constantia* are intimately linked.

22. It remains unclear whether Seneca envisions an authentic "real" self for one to play. On the apparent shifting of authorial selves in the *Epistles*, see Too 1994, 215–16;

and Edwards 1997, 33–34. In letter 120, playing one role is an act of choice (*institueris*), presentation (*praestare*, rather than *esse*) and performance (*unum hominem agere*). Despite the existential urgency with which this letter ends, Seneca takes away existential certainty. Remove the mask, and a Rousseauistic inner "real" human is not there; what remains is a choice to play one role. Yet this choice to remain consistent in one role and the difficulties inherent in making and especially maintaining it are at the heart of Senecan tragedy. Bartsch (2006, 227) argues, however, that in Seneca "the emphasis on the false *persona* is sustained. The idea is that one can drop the public mask from people to see who they really are."

23. Dupont 1995, chap. 5, is titled "La construction du héros par lui-même." Dupont begins her discussion of this topic by focusing on the opening and concluding images of the characters on stage; see esp. 123–25.

24. Atreus' own psychological preparation for this act of vengeance is investigated below.

25. "causa natalis tui,/Aegisthe, venit. quid pudor vultus gravat?/quid dextra dubio trepida consilio labat?/quid ipse temet consulis torques rogas,/an deceat hoc te? respice ad patrem: decet." The edition used is Zwierlein's Oxford Classical Text; translations are my own.

26. Both father and son use the vocative *Aegisthe* (49, 233), focus on Aegisthus' incestuous birth (48–49, 233), and base their apostrophes on a series of rebuking questions and commands.

27. "clausa iam melior via est./licuit pudicos coniugis quondam toros/et sceptra casta vidua tutari fide;/periere mores ius decus pietas fides/et qui redire cum perit nescit pudor."

28. "da frena et omnem prona nequitiam incita:/per scelera semper sceleribus tutum est iter./tecum ipsa nunc evolve femineos dolos,/quod ulla coniunx perfida atque impos sui/amore caeco, quod novercales manus/ausae, quod ardens impia virgo face/Phasiaca fugiens regna Thessalica trabe:/ferrum, venena—vel Mycenaeas domos/coniuncta socio profuge furtiva rate./quid timida loqueris furta et exilium et fugas?/soror ista fecit: te decet maius nefas."

29. Tarrant 1976, 196.

30. "quod tempus animo semper ac mente horrui/adest profecto, rebus extremum meis./quid terga vertis, anime? quid primo impetu/deponis arma? crede perniciem tibi/et dira saevos fata moliri deos:/oppone cunctis vile suppliciis caput,/ferrumque et ignes pectore adverso excipe,/Aegisthe: non est poena sic nato mori."

31. Still another crux here concerns the dramatic unity of this act. Why, after repeatedly commanding herself to kill Agamemnon, does Clytemnestra suddenly and inexplicably change her mind after Aegisthus' entrance monologue (*amor iugalis vincit*, 239)? Tarrant (1976, 193) provides a full discussion of the connection between these scenes: "The sudden change of attitude is not depicted and so can have no dramatic reality. The proper conclusion appears to be that the Clytemnestra-Nutrix dialogue and the following scene between Clytemnestra and Aegisthus are presented by Seneca as independent dramatic units, each with its own sets of premises which are made clear in the opening lines." Ultimately, Tarrant takes an analyst's viewpoint. Citing the connections between Thyestes' apostrophe to his son and Aegisthus' self-apostrophe, Tarrant (15–16) argues that the Clytemnestra-Nutrix scene was written separately and added in later. Yet by this very repetition of opening monologues of apostrophe and command,

Seneca appears to be investigating the process of self-shaping and the struggle for consistency of action and *animus*. Clytemnestra's radical reversals can perhaps be related to Seneca's descriptions of psychological dissonance and existential uncertainty that conclude letter 120. There are two other examples of self-address and self-command in *Agamemnon*. At the climax of the play, Cassandra orders herself not to fear the murder of Agamemnon (867–69); as Electra wonders what to do with her brother Orestes, she commands her *animus* not to fear the approaching stranger (915–16).

32. Bonner 1949, 167. Self-address in Seneca's tragedies has not received much critical comment. It is condemned by Leo (1908, 108) as simply the "overuse of a rhetorical figure." Boyle (1997, 18–19) offers a positive interpretation of Seneca's overall "rhetorical" and baroque aesthetic, but when he discusses self-apostrophe, he can only appeal to tradition and calls it a "formula" (157). In her recent study of apostrophe in Senecan tragedy, Billerbeck (1998) treats only address to mute personae and does not breach the topic of self-apostrophe. Senecan self-apostrophe thus bears out Culler's famous analysis of the critical "embarrassment" that apostrophe causes (1981, 135–54). As Culler argues, scholars have either ignored this figure or simply declared it to be a "traditional" formal aspect of poetry, without paying attention to apostrophe's functional significance in a text.

33. Inwood 2000, 53.

34. Inwood 2000, 55.

35. Inwood 2000, 54.

36. See Seneca's discussion of the two types of tears, discussed at the conclusion of the previous chapter. One type we allow to fall, the other we command (*permittamus illis cadere, non imperemus*, Ep. 99.16).

37. Tarrant's analysis of Clytemnestra's opening address to her *animus* has become a point of reference for commentators on several Senecan tragedies; see, e.g., Coffey and Mayer 1990, 101, 144, on *Phaed.* 112, 592. Other commentators dutifully catalogue the parallels: Boyle 1994, 190, and Töchterle 1994, 164, on *Oed.* 35, 589, 933, 597 952, 624, 1024; Hine 2000, 119, on *Med.* 41. Citing *Med.* 895, Tarrant (1976, 195) cautiously admits that self-address and self-command may have philosophical significance, stating that with these apostrophes Seneca "may be alluding to the assent of the *animus* required to make an instinctive impulse . . . a voluntary act."

38. Tarrant 1976, 194.

39. Tarrant 1976, 194.

40. Thyestes commands himself to enjoy the feast (935), but *dolor* commands (*iubes*) him to act otherwise (942–44). As we have seen, Seneca also gives *dolor* an imperative quality; see *Helv.* 18.9.

41. The idea of self-fashioning as a process of creating a consistent and recognizable self lies at the core of Seneca's letter 31; see also 120.22. Letter 31 begins with Seneca's triumphant declaration (*agnosco Lucilium meum*, 31.1) and continues with a command to Lucilius to continue with this psychological *impetus* (*sequere illum impetum animi*; cf. *Med.* 895: *sequere felicem impetum*). The goal of this letter is to demonstrate to Lucilius the link between psychological consistency, self-fashioning, and the divine, as Seneca makes clear by quoting *Aen.* 8.364–65. Similarly, by the end of the play, Atreus' consistency and recognition enable him to walk "equal to the stars" (885) and even be superior to the gods (*dimitto superos*, 888).

42. Schiesaro 2003, 105.

43. Thus, Atreus seems paradoxically to fulfill the philosophical tenets of *Ep.* 120.4–14, in which Seneca advises Lucilius to observe carefully the psychology and actions of those around him. See Davis 2003, 65–66, for an excellent treatment of how Atreus paradoxically fulfills Stoic ideals.

44. Schiesaro 2003, 106.

45. My point here is that Seneca's ideas of psychology and therapy are at work in his plays. Other studies focus on modern psychoanalytic theories. In his reading of Senecan tragedy, Schiesaro (2003) employs Freudian and post-Freudian interpretations of literature and the unconscious. See Segal 1986 for a Lacanian-based reading of *Phaedra*.

46. The opening prologue seems to suggest that the irresistible force of the Fury is controlling the action of this play, commanding Tantalus to infect the house with madness; see lines 101–21. Nevertheless, like Clytemnestra and Aegisthus, Atreus must progress through his own process of self-construction to ensure that he is able to command and control his passions in order to carry out his vengeance. A similar problem of the Furies' effect on the agency of Senecan characters comes up in *Medea*. At the end of the play, Medea seems to hallucinate and envision the onset of the Furies and the ghost of her brother. Despite these hallucinations and visions, she continues to command herself to action and to perfect her infanticidal revenge. Indeed, even in her final "madness," she commands her brother to drive away the Furies (967–68) and leave her to herself (*mihi me relinque*, 969). In Seneca's plays, it is only in *Hercules* that we see the Furies blinding an agent to act unknowingly. In the prologue, Juno commands the Furies to drive Hercules mad. In this play, Seneca's portrayal of Hercules' murder of his wife and children (955–1053) reveals a type of occurrent, raving madness familiar in Greek tragedies, as outlined by Padel (1992, 163–81; 1995). See also Gill 1997, 218–21, for a discussion of the differences between "Greek-type" madness and Senecan "akratic self-surrender," which Gill demonstrates characterizes Phaedra and Medea.

47. Self-address in Seneca's tragedies has been largely misunderstood. Rosenmeyer (1989, 177–81) provides an extended discussion and argues that in their monologues, Senecan characters attempt to deflect language away from themselves. He notes that Atreus' opening monologue in particular "starts with a rebuke to himself, and then, via the nominative *iratus Atreus*, glides off into directives addressed to a cosmic armed force that includes his own *animus* (192) as one of its soldiers" (181). Thus, according to Rosenmeyer, this peculiar brand of Senecan *Schreirhetorik* reveals the instability of the agent. Yet as we have seen, self-address, especially when directed to the *animus*, is the means by which Senecan characters attempt to fight their psychological fluctuation and achieve stability and consistency. Thus, by addressing their *animus*, *mens*, passions, or even themselves in the second or third person, Senecan characters are not attempting to deflect agency and responsibility from themselves. In fact, the situation is precisely the opposite: self-directed commands to the *animus* or another psychological part lie at the very core of Seneca's theory of agency and responsibility (see Inwood 2000, 53–55). On the role of self-naming in Seneca's tragedies, see Segal 1982; and Fitch and McElduff 2002, 24–27. See also Gill's (1996, 29–41) important reevaluation of Adkins' analysis of personal agency and impersonal verbs. Agency and responsibility are not determined by the mere presence of a first-person verb or pronoun.

48. "age, anime, fac quod nulla posteritas probet,/sed nulla taceat. aliquod audendum est nefas/atrox, cruentum, tale quod frater meus/suum esse mallet—scelera non ulcisceris,/nisi vincis."

49. On self-directed commands, see Mele 1987, 69–74, and 1992, 286–87; on the links between desire and action in modern philosophy, see Mele 1992, 292–93.

50. For Atreus' self-directed commands, see 241–43 (with a demand to look to paternal models) and 270. See also 505 and 507, as Atreus demands that his *ira* remain under control so that he can carry out his plan. In this scene (491–507), as Atreus praises himself for capturing his brother and nephews, Atreus reveals that his plan will not be successful unless he knows how to control his *ira* (*cum sperat ira sanguinem, nescit tegi—/tamen tegatur*, 504–5). Atreus gives a new and paradoxical meaning to the idea of "restraining rage," to quote the title of an important recent book on the topic (Harris 2001). Self-address and self-command are also the means that Atreus uses to stop the psychological wavering and hesitation that afflict him as he perfects his plan for Thyestes' cannibal feast: "my soul, why are you afraid again and subside before the deed? It must be dared, come on" (*anime, quid rursus times/et ante rem subsidis? audendum est, age*, 283–84). Atreus must check and correct himself as he decides whether to make his sons, Agamemnon and Menelaus, privy to his crime: "you are acting badly, you retreat, *animus*: if you spare your own children, you also spare his" (*male agis, recedes, anime: si parcis tuis,/parces et illis*, 324–25). Once his plan is fully developed, Atreus can proceed without any further psychological difficulty. The final figure of Atreus, the product of his own demands for consistency, is at last recognized (1006) and praised (885–89, 1096–97). Cf. Seneca's closing advice to Lucilius in *Ep.* 120.22.

51. Wilamowitz-Mollendorff 1919, 162, discussed in Schiesaro 2003, 18.

52. "per viscera ipsa quaere supplicio viam,/si vivis, anime, si quid antiqui tibi/remanet vigoris; pelle femineos metus/et inhospitalem Caucasum mente indue."

53. In Seneca's *Troades*, Andromache commands her *dolor* to reveal (falsely) the death of Astyanax to Ulixes (*fatere quos premis luctus, dolor*, 595).

54. Fyfe 1983, 82. Fyfe acknowledges that Medea "uses her own speeches to build confidence and self-motivation," but according to her (79), the real power of Medea's language is "made more evident in her magical incantation (740–848)." Throughout *Medea*, Seneca brings ritual language and the language of self-command together, and he emphasizes the power and efficacy of the latter. Medea begins her opening monologue with a prayer to the gods and ends with commands directed at herself (1–55). After Medea's incantation and successful murder of Creon and his daughter, Medea must monitor and command herself in order to discover still more extreme methods of punishment (895–905). As she prepares to kill her second child, Medea commands her *animus* with the ritual cry given at sacrifices, *hoc age* (976; see also 905). On this gruesome shift of ritual command to self-command, see Costa 1973, 120.

55. See also lines 754 (*evocavi*) and 769 (*nostris cantibus*). Significantly, Medea is the only one of Seneca's tragic characters who is able to command the universe around her. The others attempt to order the cosmos to react to their suffering, only to have the response be silence. For example, after Atreus' revelation of his crimes Thyestes' appeals to the earth (1006–9) and Jupiter (1077) go unheeded. For a full treatment of the question of Stoic *sympatheia* in Seneca's tragedies, see Rosenmeyer 1989.

56. On the unity of passions and *animus* in Senecan tragedy, see Nussbaum 1994, 451–52. As Nussbaum points out, several critics and translators have in the past been

perplexed by the rapid shifts that Senecan characters make in naming their emotions. She argues that such passages "should not be normalized. For it is not surprising that love, anger and grief are this close, if the Stoics are right about what the passions are. Medea's passionate love, her anger, her grief are all identical with judgments that ascribe high and non-replaceable value to Jason" (452).

57. See Foley's (1989) analysis of the great monologue of Euripides' Medea as encompassing a conflict between a masculine self and a "feminine, maternal self" (62). For a comparison of the psychological aspects of Medea's final monologue in Euripides and in Seneca, see Gill 1987, 25–37.

58. "cor pepulit horror, membra torpescunt gelu / pectusque tremuit. ira discessit loco / materque tota coniuge expulsa redit."

59. Thus, in stark contrast to Clytemnestra and Phaedra, who explicitly state that the "better path" is closed to them (*Ag.* 109–13, *Pha.* 177–80), Medea, at least briefly, feels that it is possible for her to spare her children and act in accordance with virtue.

60. Here Medea's language comes closest to Cato's in *De providentia*. For further connections between Seneca's Medea and Cato, see W. R. Johnson 1988, 87–88. Mele (1992, 282–83) provides an excellent general discussion of the paradoxical link that exists between *akrasia* and self-control: "Some exercises of self-control apparently are not performed in the service of a better or best judgment." This certainly describes the nature of self-command for Medea, Clytemnestra, Aegisthus, and Atreus.

61. A parallel to this command to be taken over by forces of madness can be found in the opening scene of *Hercules*. Juno commands the Furies to take her over and drive her mad first in order that they may later afflict Hercules with blinding madness. Juno rebukes herself and then addresses the Furies (108–11).

62. On the development of Medea's infanticide as motivated by guilt and as a means of self-punishment, see Gill 1997, 215–18.

63. "quid repens affert sonus? / parantur arma meque in exitium petunt. / excelsa nostrae tecta conscendam domus / caede incohata. perge tu mecum comes. / tuum quoque ipsa corpus hinc mecum aveham. / nunc hoc age, anime: non in occulto tibi est / perdenda virtus; approba populo manum."

64. Furthermore, Medea paradoxically links control of the passions with political power. She claims that her final performance before Jason brings back her ancestral royal status (982–84). For an analysis of the theme of regression and the obsession with recapturing the past that dominates Medea, see Schiesaro 2003, 208–14.

65. For other examples of self-apostrophe and self-command immediately before action, see *Agamemnon*, where both Cassandra (867–71) and Electra (913–17) order themselves to change their disposition and not feel fear in the immediate situation. Perhaps the finest example of a Senecan character ordering herself immediately before acting is Phaedra's aside after she returns to consciousness and orders herself to confess to Hippolytus (592–99). For an important discussion of the postclassical development of the technique of aside and general differences between Senecan and fifth-century Attic tragedy, see Tarrant 1978, 242–46.

66. "ex vulnere ipso sanguinem calidum in tua / defundere ora debui, ut viventium / biberes cruorem—verba sunt irae data / dum propero."

67. On this unity of virtue and vice, see Braden 1970, 14n3: "The dramatic point is not that good people think this way and bad ones think that way, but that everyone in

sight is thinking much the same way, and there is this result. Hence Hercules can perform as both hero and villain without appreciably changing his personality."

68. For a classic statement of the argument that Senecan tragedy "negates" Senecan philosophy, see Dingel 1974. More recently, Schiesaro (1997, 109–11) argues for the "impossibility of Stoic tragedy."

69. Greenblatt (1980, 210) describes a similar phenomenon at work in Christopher Marlowe's Seneca-influenced plays. Marlowe's characters cannot escape the system against which they are rebelling, and hence they can only repeat and reinforce its structures: "Marlowe's protagonists rebel against orthodoxy, but they do not do so just as they please; their acts of negation not only conjure up the order they would destroy but seem at times to be themselves conjured up by that very order." For an excellent analysis of Seneca in the Renaissance, see Braden 1985.

CHAPTER THREE: Self-Address in the *Satyricon*

1. See Bodel 1994.
2. Highet 1941.
3. Schmeling 1994–95. See also Schmeling 1995; Veyne 1964; Beck 1973; and Rimell 2002, 2007a, 2007b. For the classic reading of the interplay between *actor* and *auctor* in Apuleius, see Winkler 1985. Inwood (2009, 63–64) makes the provocative suggestion that Seneca's focus on first-person "self-assertion" in his philosophical writings may have encouraged Augustine to write his own spiritual autobiography in the *Confessions*.
4. On the rise of prose fiction during the Neronian period, see Bowersock 1994, 22. Inwood (2007b, xii) writes that although Seneca's letters may originally have been part of a genuine correspondence between him and Lucilius, "it is now widely agreed that Seneca's letters in their present form . . . are creations of the writer's craft." See also Inwood 2007a; Griffin 1992, app. B; and M. Wilson 2001. On Seneca's "epistoliterarity" and his use of mimesis in his travel letters, see Henderson 2004 and 2006, to which this chapter is much indebted. Seneca's letters likely represent the introduction of a new genre to Latin literature, the philosophical letter.
5. *Ep.* 64.7–8. On this metaphor, see Hijmans 1976, 1; on the economics of Senecan composition, see Ker 2006.
6. Seneca himself plays with the authorial stance of narrating the simple truth (*haec ita vera*) at the start of the *Apocolocyntosis*. On similar declarations about describing "reality" in Juvenal (1.85–86) and Martial (10.4.7–10), see Conte 1996, 191. On the topos of Cato as reader, see Conte 1996, 194; Phaed. 4.7.21–22; and Mart. 1.pref.
7. On Petronius' self-conscious parody of moralizing topoi, see Elsner 1993 (reworked and expanded in Elsner 2007); and Rimell 2002, 7, which asks, "Can we claim that Encolpius is simply stupid (and therefore 'inferior') and not ever or always self-consciously posing as a clown, empowered by ironic self-mockery and by his audience's necessary inability to tell when they are being manipulated or fooled?"
8. The critical reception of the *Satyricon* over the past several decades relates the interplay between fiction and reality. Although Eric Auerbach famously included an analysis of Petronius in chapter 2 of *Mimesis* (1953), literary critics today see the *Satyricon* as a thoroughly anti-mimetic work; see, e.g., F. Jones 1991; Panayotakis 1995; Conte 1996; and Courtney 2001, 221. Social historians, on the other hand, have become

increasingly willing to mine this text, an attitude well summarized by Hopkins 1993, 6: "Serious historians of the ancient world have often undervalued fiction, if only . . . because by convention history is concerned principally with the recovery of truth about the past. But for social history—for the history of culture, for the history of peoples' understanding of their own society—fiction occupies a privileged position." See, e.g., D'Arms 1981, 97–120; Bowersock 1994; Finley 1999, 36, 50–51; Bodel 2003; and Verboven 2009.

9. Petronius, frag. 16 Bücheler, mentions the mountain passage: *satis constaret eos nisi inclinatos non solere transire cryptam Neapolitanam.*

10. Seneca here is likely referring to the *prima praeludentia* of emotion, which he discusses at length in *Ira* 2.4.1–2. The significance of these involuntary reactions is discussed further in chapter 6.

11. For a full analysis of this letter, see Henderson 2006. Seneca describes the Crypta Neapolitana as a long, dark prison (*nihil illo carcere longius, nihil illis facibus obscurius, quae nobis praestant non ut per tenebras videamus, sed ut ipsas*, 57.2). On passages in Seneca and Epictetus that describe the body as a prison for the soul, see Bartsch 2005, 77–78.

12. "'molestum est quod puer hospiti placet. quid autem? non commune est quod natura optimum fecit? sol omnibus lucet. luna innumerabilibus comitata sideribus etiam feras ducit ad pabulum. quid aquis dici formosius potest? in publico tamen manant. solus ergo amor furtum potius quam praemium erit? immo vero nolo habere bona nisi quibus populus inviderit. unus, et senex, non erit gravis; etiam cum voluerit aliquid sumere, opus anhelitu prodet.' haec ut infra fiduciam posui fraudavique animum dissidentem, coepi somnum obruto tunicula capite mentiri."

13. Sullivan 1968b, 194–96, citing *Ep.* 73.6–8. For a full list of parallels, see Habermehl 2006, 325–29.

14. Eumolpus, however, is unimpressed and does not wish to know the cause of Encolpius' anger, but rather manages to shut him out so that he can have his way with Giton (94.7).

15. The relationship between physical scars and the scars on the souls of those ruled by the passions, particularly the tyrant, is discussed further in chapter 5. The interplay between bodily and psychological scars is signaled as Giton binds up Eumolpus' physical wound (98.7) and then Encolpius asks him to leave his soul without the scar of anger (99.2).

16. Who this poet is remains unknown. Baehrens conjectures that *ingenia inmansueta* is the start of the verse and prints it in *FPR* 359, frag. 25. The connection that Seneca and Petronius make between climate and psychology was an old theme. As Ferrari (2009, 411) notes, "As early as the Hippocratic treatise *Airs, Waters, Places* shows, it was intellectually respectable to believe that climate and geography could influence the characters of a whole people."

17. *qualis ille somnus post recognitionem sui sequitur, quam tranquillus, quam altus ac liber* (*Ira* 3.36.2); *coepi somnum obruto tunicula capite mentiri* (*Sat.* 100.2).

18. Goldhill (1995) states at the outset of his work, "It is not by chance, I shall argue, that it is the *narratives* of the novels (and works like Plutarch's *Amatorius*) that are treated most inadequately by Foucault. The engagement required by these allusive, ironic, and highly self-reflexive texts produces not only problematic history, but also a problematizing frame for the homiletic texts with which Foucault is most concerned" (xii).

19. McGlathery 1998, 206.
20. P. Miller 1998.
21. On the philosophical and medical implications of Catallus' poem 76, see Booth 1997. See also the lament of Attis (*miser a miser, querendum est etiam atque etiam, anime*, 63.61), which inverts the Stoic ideal. Here Attis commands his *animus* to lament. Encolpius' self-address in which he worries about rivals for Giton's affections is also reminiscent of the elegiac lover, specifically Catullus in his poems to Juventius. Echoing Encolpius' concerns, Catullus' poems to this "young boy" frequently involve threatening rivals (e.g., in 15) or deprecating potential suitors (e.g., 24, 99). In the Catullan corpus, desire for Juventius is paired with money, as Catullus insults his rivals' solvency, while Juventius appears to be passed around like a coin, as Wray (2001, 73) demonstrates. So Giton passes between Encolpius and Ascyltus and is almost divided up like one of their possessions. When Ascyltus comes looking for Giton, he offers a reward of a thousand gold coins (97.2), which Eumolpus is happy to collect (*"mille" inquit "nummos inveni,"* 98.2). Eumolpus, however, is the actual poet involved in this love triangle. When he first sees Giton, he promises to praise the boy in his poems (*ego laudes tuas carminibus implebo*, 94.2) and thus takes on the role of Catullus in poem 48. Eumolpus is also asked to take on the role of the Catullan blame poet. Bargates addresses him as *poetarum disertissime* (perhaps a reference to Catullus 49.1, *disertissime Romuli nepotum*) and asks him to write insulting poems directed at his wife (96.6–7).
22. On the relationship between Theocritus and Catullus, see Wray 2001, 93–95. For lyric self-address to the soul (*thymos*), see Archilochus, frag. 128.1 West; and Theognis, lines 695, 877, 1029 West. This theme is already found throughout the *Iliad* (e.g., 11.403; 17.90; 18.5, 20, 343; 21.53) and the *Odyssey* (e.g., 5.298, 355, 407, 464). In Latin poetry after Catullus, Dido twice addresses herself (*perdita*, 4.541; *infelix Dido*, 4.596). Propertius addresses his *animus* (2.10.11) and addresses himself (*Properti*, 2.8.17). Ovid's Medea engages in a lengthy monologue addressed to herself concerning her love for Jason (*Met.* 7.11–71). See also Auhagen 2007, 176–77.
23. Nussbaum 1994, 439–83.
24. Quoted in Nussbaum 1994, 439. In *Ep.* 116.5–6, Seneca also discusses the problem of whether the wise man will marry. In *Ep.* 104.1–5 he discusses how his wife, Paulina, continually urges him to take care of his health. Seneca claims that her very breath hangs upon his, so he will begin to look after himself in the way that he looks after her (*nam cum sciam spiritum illius in meo verti, incipio, ut illi consulam, mihi consulere*, 104.2).
25. For a summary of interpretations of this monologue, see Bartsch 2006, 109n168. Bartsch notes that Hostius' speech has been compared to that of the hero of epic or drama. She states that it also "calls to mind Stoic self-dialogue."
26. In his study of the theme of impotence in the *Satyricon* and of classical literature in general, McMahon (1998) attributes Encolpius' cure to his ability to talk to others about his problem. According to McMahon, Encolpius is an atypical character because he is not ashamed of his impotence. He does not hide his problem but rather freely admits it to others, such as Giton (129.1). However, while Encolpius is unafraid to admit his problem to others, when he engages in self-dialogue he initially doubts the propriety of his speech.
27. Toward the end of the surviving fragments, Encolpius calls their ruse among the *captatores* a "tragedy" (*tragoediam*, 140.6). On the relationship between tragedy and

comedy in defining prose fiction (*plasmata*), see Bowersock 1994, 16–18. For examples of the "*Fugitive Millionaire*-mime," see Panayotakis 1994, 458–59 and n. 3.

28. "'quid' aiebam 'si callidus capatator exploratorem in Africam miserit mendaciumque deprehenderit nostrum? quid, si etiam mercennarius praesenti felicitate lassus indicium ad amicos detulerit totamque fallaciam invidiosa proditione detexerit? nempe rursus fugiendum erit et tandem expugnata paupertas nova mendicitate revocanda. dii deaeque, quam male est extra legem viventibus: quicquid meruerunt, semper expectant.'"

29. *Od.* 12.184. It is also significant that Circe teaches Odysseus how to hear the Sirens' song (12.39–54), as Connors (1998, 40) and Rimell (2002, 145 and n118) point out. Petronius likely refers to this fact when he describes Circe's voice as the "concord of the Sirens" (127.5). Seneca also refers to Circe's advice to Odysseus' crew as a possible means to help him live above the Neapolitan bathhouse (*Ep.* 56.15).

30. On this epic scene's "translation" into Latin, see Connors 1998, 41–42; and Rimell 2002, 145–47.

31. On the necessity and dangers of using the mirror for philosophical or erotic self-speculation, see Seneca's account of Hostius Quadra (*Q Nat.* 1.16); and Bartsch 2006.

32. His self-questioning about true pleasure takes the form of a poem about the false nature of dreams and their effect on the *animus*, which may suggest Epicurean influence (128.6). Indeed, the relationship between false dreams and love forms the crux of Lucretius' *De rerum natura*, book 4. For an analysis of the complex interplay between simulacra, dreams, and eros in Lucretius, see Nussbaum 1994, 140–91. Epicurus' theory of dreams is also referenced by Eumolpus. In an attempt to keep Encolpius and Giton from being discovered, Eumolpus cites Epicurus' condemnation of the belief in the prophetic power of dreams and divine voices (104.2). Within the context of the *Satyricon*, this claim is in fact wrong. The prophecies given to Lichas and Tryphaena by Priapus and Neptune are correct (104.3). In his poem defending his text against the Catos of the world, Encolpius calls Epicurus the "father of truth" (132.15.7), while presenting a trivialized version of the philosophy's goal. It may seem tempting to adopt the view that Petronius himself was an Epicurean and that this text reflects this viewpoint against Senecan Stoicism. Nevertheless, it is more likely that the references to Epicureanism reflect the *Satyricon*'s general engagement with philosophy as a problematic means for gaining access to the truth.

33. Dimondo 2007, 191. Petronius is not alone in composing innovative epistles, as Seneca's epistles are the first philosophical letters in Latin.

34. Schmeling (1994–95, 223) points out that this confession of guilt resembles parts of the Tibullan corpus (3.5.7–14 and 1.2.81–84). Is confession actually a pack of lies? After his unsuccessful self-address and Cato poem, Encolpius turns to prayer and then to the magic of Proselenus. He prays on bended knee to the *numen adversum*, confessing his purity. Here he claims that he is innocent of the crimes he confessed in his letter to Circe (133.3.6–9).

35. Petronius may be playing with themes of the Ovidian lover as a soldier and the Senecan idea of the philosopher as soldier.

36. On the Vergilianisms in this section of the *Satyricon*, see Murgatroyd 2000, 349–50. Another Vergilian reference may be added: although the number of unsuccessful attempts is different, Encolpius' three failed attempts to act on his desire are

akin to Daedalus' two failed attempts to sculpt Icarus' fall on the walls at the temple of Cumae. In an apostrophe to Icarus, Vergil claims that he would have had a great part in the work if *dolor* had allowed it: "twice he had tried to shape the fall in gold, twice the father's hands fell" (6.31–33). Dehon (2001) provides an analysis of the phrase *figidior rigente bruma* (132.8.5). For an analysis of how this poem's Sotadean meter, the meter often associated with *cinaedi*, reads dactylic hexameter backwards, see Connors 1998, 30–33.

37. "'quid dicis' inquam 'omnium hominum deorumque pudor? nam ne nominare quidem te inter res serias fas est. hoc de te merui, ut me in caelo positum ad inferos traheres? ut traduceres annos primo florentes vigore senectaeque ultimae mihi lassitudinem imponeres? rogo te, mihi apodixin <non> defunctoriam redde.'"

38. "illa solo fixos oculos aversa tenebat,/nec magis incepto vultum sermone movetur/quam lentae salices lassove papavera collo."

39. See Walsh 1970, 42. For lists of examples of precedents, beginning with Aristophanes, see Adams 1982, 29–34; and Richlin 1992, 116–20. Murgatroyd (2000), however, is "not fully convinced by claims of Ovidian inspiration" (346n2) and provides an analysis of the "significant novelty" in Petronius (346).

40. Slater 1990, 128, building on Zeitlin 1971, 71. Collignon (1892, 131) is shocked by the "singular impudence" of Petronius' use of Vergil. See also Sullivan 1968b, 218–19; Walsh 1970, 44; Panayotakis 1995, 174; Rimell 2002, 155–56, 165–66; and Auhagen 2007, 174.

41. As Motto and Clark (1993) point out, Vergil is the author most frequently cited by Seneca. Yet Seneca is not averse to rendering paradoxical interpretations of his poetry, most notably in *Ep.* 56.12–13. Here he claims that the famous lines that define *pietas* for the Romans—Aeneas leading his father, son, and the Penates out of Troy—do not define the wise man. He critiques Aeneas because he fears for "his companion and his burden" (*Aen.* 2.729).

42. Auhagen (2007, 174) notes that Petronius demonstrates clearly that Encolpius is speaking these words aloud to himself, rather than simply thinking them (*inquam*, 132.9, 12).

43. Other examples are, "The soul must be hardened by means of a great amount of training and exercise" (*Ep.* 82.16); and "All possibilities must be considered, and the soul must be hardened against anything that may happen" (*Ep.* 91.7).

44. As Bartsch (2005; 2006, 164–82) has pointed out, for the Stoics of the Roman period, Seneca and Epictetus in particular, the body is conceived of as soft and vulnerable, whereas only the soul must remain firm. Petronius does not simply take Senecan philosophy and apply it to the body. His characters echo Seneca's language of psychological health and hardness, or lack thereof, as well. After Encolpius' evening of caring for body and soul, Chrysis asks him if he has regained his "good mind" (*bonam mentem*, 131.3). At the opening of *De tranquillitate animi*, for example, Serenus confesses that the "weakness of his good mind follows him in all things" (1.15). The phrase *bona mens* can be found frequently throughout the pages of Seneca. See, e.g., *Ep.* 16.1, 17.1, 23.1, 27.8, 28.6, 37.1 41.1, 44.2, 50.5, 7, 53.9, 56.6; see also Long 2006, 364–65, and Ker 2009a, 151. On this phrase in Petronius, see Conte 1996, 22.

45. See also Gell., *NA* 17.5.5.

46. "'quid autem ego' inquam 'mali feci, si dolorem meum naturali convicio exoneravi? aut quid est quod in corpore humano ventri male dicere solemus aut gulae capitique

etiam, cum saepius dolet? quid? non et Ulixes cum corde litigat suo, et quidam tragici oculos suos tamquam audientes castigant? podagrici pedibus suis male dicunt, chiragrici manibus, lippi oculis, et qui offenderunt saepe digitos, quicquid doloris habent in pedes deferent.'"

47. See also Sen., *Ep.* 120.15–16, for a list of "typical" complaints about bodily ailments.

48. Encolpius may be on to something. Scientific studies suggest that swearing may help reduce pain. See *Scientific American*, 12 July 2009, http://www.scientificamerican.com/article.cfm?id=why-do-we-swear; and "Swearing can help relieve pain, study claims," 18 April 2011, http://www.telegraph.co.uk/science/8458163/Swearing-can-help-relieve-pain-study-claims.html.

49. Of course, Petronius' account of "real people" addressing their afflicted body parts is a topos from satire, as Auhagen (2007, 175n10) points out. She cites several examples from Horace: *Sat.* 1.9.32 and *Epist.* 1.2.52 (*podagrici*); *Sat.* 2.7.15 and *Epist.* 1.1.31 (*chiragrici*); and *Sat.* 1.1.120, 1.5.49 (*lippi*). Senecan characters do not simply address their souls; body parts are frequently addressed and commanded as well. See, e.g., Theseus in Seneca's *Phaedra* (1254–68), which is discussed in the book's epilogue.

50. Vickers 1982, 16.

51. Collignon 1892, 53; Raith 1963, 44; Sullivan 1968b, 98–102. Courtney (1991, 13) presents arguments for both sides. As Connors (1998, 72n57) points out, Tacitus' declaration that Petronius appeared to be simple and frank (*speciem simplicitatis, Ann.* 16.18.2) has been taken as support for reading this poem as the intervention of the author.

52. Beck 1973, 50–53; Slater 1990, 123, 165–66; Panayotakis 1995, 175–76; Conte 1996, 188–94; Connors 1998, 72n57.

53. *Sat.* 132.16 is only preserved by the L manuscript tradition. The bulk of section 132 and the start of 133 are found in both traditions, L and O.

54. On the links between the opening and final fragments, see Rimell 2007a, 2007b.

55. Bakhtin 1984, 317.

56. On the technical, legal contrast between a *legatum* and *hereditas*, see Champlin 1991, 88: "a legacy is merely a gift of some value taken out of the inheritance; an inheritance is everything."

57. See also Seneca's discussion of the writing of wills in *Ben.* 4.11.4–6. During the *Cena*, wills play a significant role. After declaring that "slaves are people too," Trimalchio has a copy of his will read to prove that he will free them and so that his *familia* will love him as much now as when he is dead (71.1–5). Trimalchio first inherited a "senator's fortune" when his master made him co-heir with Caesar (76.2). The Greek fortuneteller Serapa told Trimalchio that he would soon receive an inheritance (77.2). When the day's *acta* at Trimalchio's estates were read, he learned that he had been disinherited in a formal codicil (*cum elogio*) by some of the keepers of his estates (*saltuarii*, 53.9). On the phrase *cum elogio*, see Smith 1975, 144; and Champlin 1991, 12. The freedman Phileros notes that the recently dead Chyrsanthus was angry at his brother and left his patrimony to someone outside the family (43.5).

58. Fedeli 1987.

59. Hopkins 1983, 239.

60. See Hopkins 1983, 235–47.

61. See Champlin 1991, 201–2.

62. See esp. Pliny the Elder's denunciations in *HN* 14.5 and 20.160.

63. See also *Ben.* 4.20.3, where Seneca declares that a person who sits beside the bed of a sick friend and has in his soul hope of profit turns from a dutiful friend to a *captator* dropping his fishhook.

64. On the practice of reading one's will in public, see Champlin 1991, 24, citing both Augustus (Suet., *Aug.* 14.2) and Trimalchio (*Sat.* 71.3–4) as examples.

65. In contrast, Philomela pretends to entrust her children to Eumolpus so that they can learn from him and gain an intellectual inheritance.

66. Uncomfortable with Eumolpus' honesty in his will, Conte (1987) proposes emending *devoverint* to *devorarint*. Thus the passage would read: "As they devoured the (knowledge) of my spirit, so they should consume my body." This emendation and its accompanying rationale are not accepted by Slater (1990, 133), Bowersock (1994, 137n37), or Rimell (2002, 167n15). Eumolpus' outspokenness may represent the Roman cultural notion that in writing a will, freedom of speech and judgment were allowed. See Champlin 1991, 11–12. As Champlin notes (6–7), this idea was parodied by Lucian: "The Romans tell the truth only once in their lives, in their will" (*Nigr.* 30).

67. Bowersock (1994, 134–38) argues that Eumolpus' "new testament" is a parody of the Christian Eucharist. Critiqued by Courtney 2001, 211–12.

68. In fact Trimalchio (56.4–6) references a line from this speech about the impropriety of eating sheep and wearing wool. See Ov., *Met.* 15.115–26.

69. By implication, the cannibalistic feast of Tereus is also present. In the section immediately preceding the reading of Eumolpus' will, Philomela entrusts her children to Eumolpus with the hope that their sexual favors will win her a place in his will (140.1–3). In order to inherit from him, Philomela sacrifices her children, and thus by implication she references the act her literary namesake inflicted on Tereus. See Ov., *Met.* 6.424–674.

70. See Sen., *Thy.* 1067–68. Seneca's Atreus laments that his brother "tore apart his children with his impious mouth, but he did so unknowingly, and they did not know as well" (*scidit ore natos impio, sed nesciens, / sed nescientes*). Although Atreus is angry that his brother did not know he was eating his children, he does delight in playing with his brother's ignorance. On Atreus' linguistic power over his brother in this scene, see Meltzer 1988; and Mader 1998. Similarly in the *Metamorphoses* (6.652) Tereus does not at first know the contents of his feast. After he finishes, he calls for his son Itys to be brought to him.

71. In this sense, Eumolpus' heirs more closely echo the Cyclopean feast.

72. "Ille sine sensu iacet in monumento, et valent verba ipsius" (*Enarr. in ps.* 21 2.30, quoted in Champlin 1991, 5).

73. As Pliny the Younger writes, "Wills are commonly believed to be a mirror of one's character" (*creditur vulgo testamenta hominum speculum esse morum, Ep.* 8.18.1). See Champlin 1991, 10.

74. First, however, Seneca notes that when writing wills, we are removed from "hope and fear and that most slothful of vices, pleasure" (*depravat spes ac metus et inertissimum vitium, voluptas, Ben.* 4.11.5).

75. Bramble 1974, 1. As Bramble notes, making metaphors real is a crucial facet of the satires of Petronius' contemporary Persius. See also Edwards 1993, 179n14, on "nobility consumed," *comesta nobilitate*.

76. For an analysis of the psychological links between money and human filth, see Freud 1959; and Laporte 2000, 39–43. On this theme in Petronius, see Arrowsmith 1966; Rankin 1969, 384; and Conte 1996, 104–39. Just as Chrysanthus was prepared (*paratus fuit*), so at the end of the *Satyricon* Gorgias is prepared to follow the tenets of Eumolpus' will (*Gorgias paratus erat exsequi*, 141.5).

77. *Continentia* may have been used by Claudius to refer to the act of holding in or repressing bodily functions; see Suet., *Claud.* 32.1.

78. We have already seen how the *captatores*' cannibalism turns Croton into the inverse of a Pythagorean city. Petronius may also be referencing the paradoxical political theories of the early Stoics Zeno and Chrysippus, who were pilloried for the claims in their *politeai* that under necessary circumstances the wise man may commit cannibalism and incest without blame. For the tentative suggestion that Petronius is attacking Seneca's Stoicism via a presentation of the infamous political ideas of its founders in this scene, see Rankin 1969, 382. For an analysis of the significance of these early Stoic theories as a response to Plato's representation of the desires of the tyrant in the *Republic*, see Hook 2005.

79. See Bowersock 1994, 130. Rankin (1969, 382–83) questions whether Petronius is relying exclusively on Herodotus and also draws a connection to the culturally relativist views of the fifth-century sophists.

80. Bartsch (2009, 197–200) points out that willful misprision and confession of the truth are often combined in Senecan therapy.

81. Ker (2009b, 184) notes that *De ira* is defined by a similar movement from the barbarian world (3.14–15), to the Roman (3.18.1–3.19.5), to the soul of the individual (3.36). See also Nussbaum 1994, 402.

82. The mention of the siege of Numantia is significant. Along with the defeat of Carthage in 146 BCE, the Romans frequently saw the defeat of Numantia in 133 BCE as the start of their moral decline at home.

83. Courtney 2001, 212–13. For Saguntum and Petelia, see Val. Max. 6.6.2. For Numantia, see Val. Max. 7.6.2. As Courtney notes, Petronius changes Valerius' undifferentiated "many" (*complures*) into mothers and Valerius' dead (*trucidatorum*) into their children.

84. The so-called *porcus Troianus*, according to Macrobius (*Sat.* 3.13.3) a well-known dish since the time of the republic.

85. On the theme of entrapment in the *Satyricon*, see Rimell 2007a and 2007b.

86. See Rimell 2002, 135–39.

87. "quid est homo? quolibet quassu vas et quolibet fragile iactatu. non tempestate magna ut dissiperis opus est: ubicumque arietaveris, solueris." On the metaphor of self as vessel, see also Epict., *Diss.* 4.5.12, 4.13.12.

88. On the different interpretations of this maxim, see Bartsch 2006, 24–26.

89. As Bartsch (2006, 204) points out, Cicero's interpretation of the *nosce te* in *Tusc.* 1.52 is based on that of *Alcibiades* 1, which may not in fact have been written by Plato. On the importance of this text in the development of Hellenistic and Roman models of the care of the self, see Foucault 2005a.

90. See also *Tusc.* 5.70, where Cicero defines the goal of the Delphic maxim to be the mind's perceiving itself as joined with the divine mind.

91. In fact, Seneca only mentions the *animus* briefly at the end of this section (11.5). Toward the end of the dialogue, he mentions that great *ingenia* do not wish to delay in the body and bear with difficulty being enclosed in its narrowness (23.2).

92. This image resonates with Seneca's equation of the length of one's life with the contents of an amphora; see *Ep.* 1.5, 24.20, 108.26 and Ker 2009a, 161–67.

93. *et amphoras copiosas gypsatas, ne effluant vinum* (71.11); *statim allatae sunt amphorae vitreae diligenter gypsatae* (34.6).

94. On Epicurus' discovery that the human vessel corrupts all the goods that flow into it, cf. Lucr. 6.14–23.

95. This story is also recounted by Pliny the Elder, who places the incident during the reign of Tiberius. He also comments that even though this art of creating unbreakable glass was destroyed in order to keep the value of precious metal intact, during Nero's principate two small glass cups known as *petroti* (stoneware) were sold for six thousand sesterces (*HN* 36.195). See also Dio Cass. 57.21.7.

96. On the possible obscene connotations of *vas*, see Smith 1975, 157; and Adams 1982, 41–42. Hermeros' use of the masculine form for the neuter *vas* or *vasum* is an example of the unclassical "dialect" of Petronius' freedmen, in which second-declension neuter singular nouns drop out, e.g., *totus caelus* (39.6), *lorus* (57.8), *fatus meus* (77.2).

97. See also Seneca's comparison of Socrates' cup of hemlock with the elaborate drinking vessels of the wealthy in *Prov.* 3.12–13.

98. It must be remembered, however, that Cicero's portrayal of Tubero's feast is likely colored by the speech's larger goal of critiquing the misplaced Stoic austerity of Cato the Younger. See Richardson-Hay 2009, 72.

99. There is also a philosophical tradition of describing the soul as a leaky vessel; see Pl., *Grg.* 492e7–494a5. This idea is picked up by Lucretius (3.935–39, 3.1002–10) and Seneca (*Ep.* 99.5). On these images in Lucretius, see Reinhardt 2002 and 2004.

100. *Matella* is a word that Seneca apologizes for using at *Ben.* 3.26.2. It is another term of abuse used by Hermeros to describe Ascyltus: he calls him "a mouse in a chamber pot" (*mus in matella*, 58.9).

101. Note the verbal parallels between this scene and the final fragment: *recustantem* (64.6), *ne recusent* (141.4), *de stomachi tui recustatione* (141.6); *panemque semesum* (64.6), *liberorum suroum tenerent semesa in sinu corpora* (141.11).

102. At another feast, Habinnas' wife, Scintilla, ate some bear meat and almost threw up her guts (*paene intestina sua vomuit*, 66.5).

103. The phrase "leaky vessel of human life" is a reference to Seneca's sympathetic portrait of humanity as a leaking ship in *De ira* 2.10.8. See Nussbaum's discussion of this passage as an important indication of Seneca's acceptance of human frailty and imperfection (1994, 419–26).

104. Scarborough (1970) gives an overview of the Roman view of Greek medicine and doctors in general.

105. "si potes, proice omnem ex toto dolorem, si minus, introrsus abde et contine, ne appreat."

106. "Puto multos potuisse ad sapientiam pervenire, nisi putassent ne pervenisse, nisi quaedam in se dissimulassent, quaedam opertis oculis transiluissent. non est enim quod

magis aliena <nos> iudices adulatione perire quam nostra. quis sibi verum dicere ausus est?" We can also contrast Trimalchio's and Serenus' calls for a bold confession of the truth with Gorgias' advice to his listeners to "close their eyes" (*operi modo oculos*, 141.7).

107. As Davis (2003, 53–55) demonstrates, Seneca's Atreus blurs the lines separating humanity, divinity, and bestiality. The site of this scene may be important. Seneca tells us (*Ep.* 108.17–23) that he studied under the Pythagorean Sotion and enjoyed being a vegetarian until his father made him stop.

108. Epictetus offers similar advice. See *Diss.* 2.4.26; and the discussions of Long (2001, 284–85) and Bartsch (2009, 194–200).

109. The content of this letter also bears close resemblance to themes in the *Satyricon*. Seneca opens by lamenting the excesses of Saturnalia (*December est mensis*, *Ep.* 18.1–4; *io Saturnalia, rogo, mensis December est?*, *Sat.* 58.2). He closes by imagining Lucilius' demand for a "payment" of philosophical wisdom gleaned from Seneca's reading: "'First,' you say, 'pay back what you owe'" ("*prius*" inquis "*redde quod debes,*" *Ep.* 18.14). Cf. Hermeros, "No one has said to me in the forum: 'pay back what you owe'" (*nemo mihi in foro dixit: "redde quod debes,"* 57.5).

110. "subsilire in caelum ex angulo licet: exurge modo 'et te quoque dignum/finge deo.' finges autem non auro vel argento. non potest ex hac materia imago deo exprimi similis; cogita illos, cum propitii essent, fictiles fuisse." Cf. Seneca's praise of Tubero's "earthenware vessels" (*vasa fictilia*, *Ep.* 95.72–73) and Hermeros' insult *vasus ficilis* (*Sat.* 57.8), discussed above. It should be noted that the adjective *fictilis* is etymologically related to the verb *fingere*.

CHAPTER FOUR: Political Speech in *De clementia*

1. See Adam 1970, 12–20; Mortureux 1989, 1656–58; Griffin 1992, 143–44; S. Braund 1998, 73n51; and S. Braund 2009, 24–30.

2. On the paucity of representations of *clementia* on Julio-Claudian coins, see Wallace-Hadrill 1981, 310, which suggests that this "virtue" may have been seen as "too despotic." In contrast, see Konstan 2005.

3. On the general Roman "intolerance" for this word, during both the republic and empire, see Cic., *Rep.* 2.47–49; Tac., *Ann.* 3.56.2; and Plin., *Pan.* 55.7. Elsewhere, Seneca advises his readers to abstain from adopting the attitude of kings with regard to others, such as slaves (*Ep.* 47.20) and friends (*Ben.* 6.34.1). Diogenes Laertius records that the Stoics considered the best form of government to be a mixture of democracy, kingship, and aristocracy (7.131 = *SVF* 3.700 = Long and Sedley 1987, 67U). On Seneca's use of the terms *reges* in tandem with *principes* in *De clementia*, see Griffin 1992, 141–48, which concludes that Seneca was likely trying to point out to his audience that they should avoid hairsplitting over terminology. See also Leach 1989, 218n43.

4. See also Cic., *Rep.* 2.47; and Griffin 1992, 145. As the Declaration of Independence notes, "A Prince, whose character is thus marked by every act which may define a Tyrant is unfit to be the ruler of a free people."

5. Among the grievances listed against the king of England, the Declaration of Independence pays particular attention to the king's judicial abuses, noting, for example, "He has refused his Assent to Laws, the most wholesome and necessary for the public good.... He has obstructed the Administration of Justice, by refusing his

Assent to Laws for establishing Judiciary Powers. He has made Judges dependent on his Will alone, for the tenure of their offices, and the amount and payment of their salaries."

6. For the influence of *De clementia* on medieval and Renaissance Italian thought, see Stacey 2007.

7. On the notion of empire as a body of geographic space that is also embodied in the emperor, see J. Richardson 1991, 2009.

8. On the importance for the Stoics of the proper use of appearances, see Epict., *Diss.* 1.1.7; and Nussbaum 1994, 327. See also Sen., *Ep.* 120.9; and the further discussion below in this chapter.

9. Nussbaum 1993. See also Staley 2010; and Goldberg 1997, which notes that Senecan tragedy moves the dramatic focus from spectacle to language.

10. On the historiographers' accounts of Nero's oppressive gaze from the stage, see Bartsch 1994, 1–35. Pliny the Younger writes of Domitian's oppressive gaze (*Pan.* 33.1–4); the good emperor Trajan, on the other hand, allows himself to be watched back (*Pan.* 51.4). See Bartsch 1994, 32–33.

11. Cf. Seneca's Medea, who also looks to her own mythical exemplar for inspiration.

12. Stacey (2007, 38–45) makes the intriguing suggestion that the Nero speaking in the opening monologue of *De clementia* is Seneca's presentation of the idealized Nero created through the rhetorical technique of *fictiones personarum* (Quint., *Inst.* 9.2.29). On Seneca's claim that the emperor is not wearing a mask, Stacey writes: "'No one can wear a *persona* for long' is a statement not only of high drama but of the deepest possible irony, for a *persona* is precisely what Seneca appears to have pressed upon Nero through the fiction of impersonation" (45). On the inability to wear a mask for long, cf. Petron., *Sat.* 80.9; and Lucr. 3.58. On the changing idea of the philosophical *persona* in Seneca, see Bartsch 2006, 216–29. Suetonius famously states that Nero had masks made up to look like himself or his lovers (*Ner.* 21.3). See also Juvenal's critiques of Nero's performances (*Sat.* 8.215–21); and the comments of Bartsch (1994, 49–50) and Cowan (2009).

13. "fastigio tuo adfixus es . . . multa contra te lux est, omnium in istam conversi oculi sunt; prodire te putas? oreris." For the possible pharaonic influence of the image of the ruler with his face toward the sun, see Grimal 1971, 207–11.

14. "ille est enim vinculum per quod res publica cohaeret, ille spiritus vitalis quem haec tot milia trahunt nihil ipsa per se futura nisi onus et praeda, si mens illa imperii subtrahatur. 'rege incolumi mens omnibus una, / amisso rupere fidem.'"

15. In the *Republic*, for example, Plato focuses on the drones: 552c, 554b, 554d–e, 559c–d, 564b–565c. See also Varro, *Rust.* 3.16.6: "They are like human communities, because in the hive there is a king and dominion and fellowship" (*haec ut hominum civitates, quod hic est rex et imperium et societas*).

16. "praeterea insignis regi forma est dissimilisque ceteris cum magnitudine tum nitore."

17. Aristotle's analysis of bees in *Historia animalium* differs considerably from Seneca's. For example, Aristotle notes that the sex of the leaders is unknown, that the kings or rulers have a stinger but do not use it and thus some people mistakenly think they do not have a stinger at all. He also notes that there are several leaders in the hive, not just one (553a26–b19). See also Plin., *HN* 11.52. For a list of other appearances of the trope of the king bee, see Griffin 1992, 145n7.

18. The contrast between Nero's youthful beauty and Claudius' deformity is a major theme of the song of Apollo in *Apocolocyntosis* 4.

19. "quemadmodum totum corpus animo deseruit et, cum hoc tanto maius tantoque speciosius sit, ille in occulto maneat tenuis et in qua sede latitet incertus."

20. A similar point is expressed at Sen., *Q Nat.* 7.25.1–2: "That we have a soul by the command of which we are driven on or called back, all will admit. Nevertheless, what the soul is, that controller and lord of us, no one will be able to explain to you any more than they could explain where it is" (*habere nos animum, cuius imperio et impellimur et revocamur, omnes fatebuntur. quid tamen sit animus ille rector dominusque nostri, non magis quisquam tibi expediet quam ubi sit*). See also Plato's account of the difficulties in treating the soul in and of itself, apart from the body encrusted around it (*Resp.* 611c).

21. On the struggle between aristocrats and emperors to define the nature and limits of Roman autocracy during the Julio-Claudian period, see Roller 2001, and esp. 213–87 for the methods by which aristocrats attempted to model the emperor. Roller focuses on the competing master-slave and father-son metaphors to define the relationship between the emperor and his subjects. This topic was also important for late republican politics as well; see, e.g., Cic., *Deiot.* 15, and Philodemus' treatise, likely from the early 50s BCE, *On the Good King According to Homer*. On the possible political purposes of this work, see Harris 2001, 208.

22. Cf. Arist., *Pol.* 1285a27: the king "rules by law over willing subjects."

23. On the development of the concept and representations of imperial *clementia*, see Dowling 2006. On its differentiation from Greek ideas of "mildness," see Griffin 1992, 148–49.

24. "clementia est temperantia animi in potestate ulciscendi vel lenitas superioris adversus inferiorem in constituendis poenis . . . itaque dici potest et inclinatio animi ad lenitatem in poena exigenda." On virtue as a condition of the soul, see Cic., *Inv. rhet.* 2.159 (*virtus est animi habitus*); and Sen., *Ep.* 113.7 ("'what is justice?' . . . the soul holding itself in a certain manner" [*"iustitia quid est?" inquit. animus quodam modo se habens*]), as well as *Ep.* 106.3–5, 108.11–13.

25. For an analysis of the emperor's display of his virtues, particularly on coins, see Wallace-Hadrill 1981; and Noreña 2001.

26. On the Stoics' notorious and unfortunate low opinion of animals as irrational, guided only by impulse and unable to use language, see Annas 1992, 59–61, 89–91. Cleanthes apparently said that a pig's soul was like salt, to keep its flesh fresh until eaten (*SVF* 1.516; see also *SVF* 2.722–23). On instinct in animals, see Sen. *Ep.* 121; and on dumb beasts contrasted with rational humans, *Ep.* 124.15.

27. On the Stoic scale of beings, see Annas 1992, 50–56. Epictetus makes several statements about how the ability to use judgment in evaluating appearances differentiates humans from animals, *Diss.* 1.6.12–20; see also 2.18.24–26 and 4.5.17–21, the latter referring to Nero.

28. On the importance of judgment (*iudicum*) for the Stoics, see S. Braund 2009, 389. Similarly, Seneca argues in *De ira* that anger does not simply occur as a result of a natural or uncontrollable impulse; rather, it is the product of judgment (*impetu an iudicio*, 2.1.1).

29. "sic haec immensa multitudo unius animae circumdata illius spiritu regitur, illius ratione flectitur pressura se ac fractura viribus suis, nisi consilio sustineretur."

30. Annas 1992, 81.

31. The critique of Claudius' judicial practices is a core theme of the *Apocolocyntosis*. See, e.g., the ironic dirge that Claudius hears on his way to Hades, "Weep for the man, than whom no one could more quickly learn about legal cases after having heard only one side, and often neither. What judge will now hear plaintiffs the whole year through?" (*deflete virum, quo non alius/potuit citius discere causas,/una tantum parte audita,/saepe neutra. quis nunc iudex/toto lites audiet anno?*, 12.3.19–23).

32. "summa enim prudentia altissimi viri et rerum naturae peritissimi maluerunt velut incredible scelus et ultra audaciam positum praeterire quam, dum vindicant, ostendere posse fieri; itaque parricidae cum ea lege coeperunt, et illis facinus poena monstravit; pessimo vero loco pietas fuit postquam saepius culleos vidimus quam cruces. in qua civitate raro homines puniuntur, in ea consensus fit innocentiae et indulgetur velut publico bono." Suetonius also records the frequency of Claudius' punishment of parricides (*Claud.* 34.1); contrast Augustus' treatment of those accused of the crime (Suet., *Aug.* 33.1).

33. "non tamen volgo ignoscere decet; nam ubi discrimen inter malos bonosque sublatum est, confusio sequitur et vitiorum eruptio; itaque adhibenda moderatio est, quae sanabilia ingenia distinguere a deploratis sciat."

34. See also *VB* 13.4 on the need to establish a distinction between the various pleasures (*voluptates*); and *Ep.* 120.8.

35. On the importance of judgment and differentiation of virtues and vices in *De clementia*, see also Griffin 1992, 148–71; and S. Braund 1998, 71–72.

36. *est enim vitium pusilli animi ad speciem alienorum malorum succidentis* (2.5.1); *misericordia est aegritudo animi ob alienarum miseriarum speciem* (2.5.4).

37. See also Petronius' mention of those who have similar problems with their eyes (*lippi*, 132.14).

38. Seneca had already touched on this topic. In his *Consolatio ad Polybium*, written from exile, Seneca notes that Claudius' freedman Polybius cannot act the way he chooses, because everyone investigates and looks into his soul (6.1).

39. In addition, Seneca encourages the emperor, "You are able to boldly declare this out loud, that everything that has come into your guardianship has been held safe, that you have taken nothing from the republic either by force or by fraud" (1.1.5). He also praises Nero's magnanimous boast that he has not spilled a single drop of human blood (1.11.3).

40. On the connections between *De ira* and *De clementia*, see Mazzoli 2003.

41. As Edwards (1997, 38) notes, following Foucault, Seneca frequently uses metaphors from social life to describe the relationship one should cultivate with oneself. This internalization does not imply a wholesale rejection of the external world, however. Seneca's *meditatio* also looks out into the world, as Nussbaum (1994, 426) demonstrates, "Thus, this most private part of *De ira* is also extremely public, central to its prescription for public action." Nussbaum also remarks that "Seneca's prescription for public life depends on getting each individual to recognize the deficiencies of his or her own soul" (405).

42. On the possible Egyptian influence on this passage, see Fears 1975, 493.

43. "quid enim est memorabilius quem eum, cuius irae nihil obstat, cuius graviori sententiae ipsi qui pereunt adsentiuntur, quem nemo interpellaturus est, immo, si vehementius excanduit, ne deprecaturus est quidem, ipsum sibi manum inicere et potestate sua in melius placidiusque uti hoc ipsum cogitatnem: 'occidere contra legem nemo

non potest, servare nemo praeter me'?" See also the opening of Nero's monologue ("I am the judge of life and death for entire races" [*ego vitae necisque gentibus arbiter*, 1.1.2]); and the comments of S. Braund 2009, 161: "Seneca draws a distinction between *iudex* and *arbiter* at *Ben.* 3.7.5 which underlines the aptness of *arbiter* as applied to the absolute ruler: in the Roman legal system a *iudex* was bound by the terms of the praetor's formula when he gave his verdict, whereas an *arbiter* enjoyed freedom of decision. The emperor in practice was the ultimate legal authority in the empire."

44. *tradetur ista animi tui mansuetudo diffundeturque paulatim per omne imperii corpus, et cuncta in similitudinem tuam formabuntur* (2.2.1).

45. "nam dictator Caesar summis oratoribus aemulus; et Augusto prompta ac profluens, quae<que> deceret principem, eloquentia fuit. Tiberius artem quoque callebat qua verba expenderet, tum validus sensibus aut consulto ambiguus. etiam C. Caesaris turbata mens vim dicendi non corrupit. nec in Claudio, quotiens meditata dissereret, elegantiam requireres. Nero puerilibus statim annis vividum animum in alia detorsit: caelare, pingere, cantus aut regimen equorum exercere; et aliquando carminibus pangendis inesse sibi elementa doctrinae ostendebat." The rhetorical abilities and literary pursuits of the emperors are reoccurring themes throughout Suetonius' imperial biographies, e.g., *Tib.* 70–71, *Calig.* 53 (containing the famous critique of Seneca's style), and *Claud.* 3, 41–42.

46. For a list of passages praising Caesar's rhetorical abilities, see Furneaux 1907, 156–57. Quintilian claims that if Caesar had had the time for the forum, he would have been Cicero's sole rival. He also connects Caesar's *animus*, his style of speech, and his style of waging war (*Inst.* 10.1.114); see also Tac., *Dial.* 21.5.

47. Syme (1958, 700–703) suggests that Tacitus' Tiberian speeches may make use of the emperor's actual words as preserved in the public records of the Senate. In an effort to test this hypothesis, N. Miller (1968) provides a study of "solitaries," i.e., words attributed to Tiberius that appear only once in the surviving works of Tacitus. Miller's findings are strongly critiqued by Wharton (1997). Brunt (1977, 97) comments on Suet., *Tib.* 24.2: "When he at last accepted imperium, he did so with the reservation, apparently recorded *verbatim*: *dum veniam ad id tempus, quo vobis aequum possit videri dare vos aliquam senectuti meae requiem.*" The Latin may be translated as follows: "until I come to the time when it might seem right for you to grant some repose to my old age").

48. The statements about Caligula's and Claudius' eloquence despite their "disturbed minds" stand in stark contrast to Seneca's analysis of their speaking abilities. At the conclusion of *De ira*, book 1, Seneca condemns Caligula's "epic utterance." Claudius' lack of eloquence is a major theme in the *Apocolocyntosis*.

49. The later emperors appear to have followed Nero's precedent of "borrowing eloquence." Tacitus states that Otho's valedictory address was written by Galerius Trachalus (*Hist.* 1.90.2). As Haynes (2003, 5) states, "Otho's ability to speak in his own voice . . . dwindle[s] throughout the course of book one." Cf. Suetonius' comments on Domitian: "Letters, orations and edicts he fashioned by another's talents. His speech, however, was not inelegant and sometimes was characterized by noteworthy remarks" (*Dom.* 20).

50. See Stacey 2007, 44: "Seneca makes no attempt to theorize princely eloquence—to argue, for example, that the emperor's rhetorical ability no less than his virtue should excel that of his subjects. But eloquence was still a crucial index of political intelligence among the Roman aristocracy."

51. Thus, we are left in the paradoxical position of realizing the importance placed on the speech of a ruler, as Tacitus' *seniores* make clear, but knowing that we can rarely be sure what an emperor said on a given occasion. See, e.g., Auerbach's analysis (1953, 33–40) of the speech of the soldier Percennius, which foments revolt at the start of Tacitus' *Annales* (1.16): "The grand style of historiography requires grandiloquent speeches, which as a rule are fictitious. Their function is graphic dramatization (*illustratio*) of a given occurrence, or at times the presentation of great political or moral ideas; in either case they are intended as the rhetorical bravura pieces of the presentation" (39). See also Laird 1999, 127–52. Epigraphy can be of some help to us. Some inscriptions recording emperors' speeches survive. The Lyons Tablet, which preserves Claudius' address to the Senate, is a famous example. Remarkably, the surviving text contains a self-apostrophe and a self-command by the emperor: "Now is the time, Tiberius Caesar Germanicus, to reveal to the senators where your oration is heading" (*tempus est iam Ti. Caesar Germanice detegere te patribus conscriptis quo tendat oratio tua*). Cf. Tacitus' version of this speech in *Ann.* 11.24. On the emperor's philological and oratorical habits, see Billerbeck 1990; on Claudius' speech, see 199–200.

52. As testament to the continued positive interpretation of Caesar's crossing, we need look no further than the Jeep Rubicon.

53. "cunctanti ostentum tale factum est. quidam eximia magnitudine et forma in proximo sedens repente apparuit harundine canens; ad quem audiendum cum praeter pastores plurimi etiam ex stationibus milites concurrissent interque eos et aeneatores, rapta ab uno tuba prosilivit ad flumen et ingenti spiritu classicum exorsus pertendit ad alteram ripam. tunc Caesar: 'eatur,' inquit, 'quo deorum ostenta et inimicorum iniquitas vocat. iacta alea est,' inquit."

54. The punishment of Claudius at the end of the *Apocolocyntosis* may reference this tradition as well. Claudius will never be able to "cast the dice," as they fall through the bottom of his perforated box (14.4–15.1). According to Suetonius, Claudius flagrantly broke the law against dicing (*Claud.* 5, 33.2); see Eden 1984, 135.

55. In the Neronian period, the "dice of fate" are referred to to explain Caesar's actions. In his account of the civil war, Lucan states that once in Greece, Caesar desires a decisive battle with Pompey and that he decides that the dice of fate will choose who will be destroyed (*BC* 6.7–8). Petronius' *Satyricon* contains its own poetic version of the civil war. As the poetaster Eumolpus narrates events, before Caesar crosses the Rubicon, he declares that since the Senate is denying him his rightful honor and in fact punishing him, after so many victories, he will let fortune be the judge and let the dice fall (*iudice Fortuna cadat alea*, 122.174). Cf. Seneca's description of the great risk (*magnam aleam*) run by the Roman people while it remained uncertain which direction Nero's noble character would take (*Clem.* 1.1.7).

56. Caesar comes under attack frequently in *De officiis*; see 1.26, 112; 2.27–29.

57. Cic., *Off.* 3.82, quoting Eur. *Phoen.* 524–25.

58. On the difficulties of using anecdotes as historical evidence, see Saller 1980. While anecdotes may not reveal "the way it really was," Saller concludes that they "can be valuable evidence for the attitudes and ideologies of peoples . . . a full scale study should lead to a better appreciation of the importance of anecdotes in the Roman 'structures mentales' with their characteristic moral authoritarianism. The number of occasions on which Romans appealed to anecdotal *exempla* of men who had been dead

59. Cf. the repeated vignettes of Cato's final words invented by Seneca (e.g., *Prov.* 2.10 and *Ep.* 24).

60. Suetonius includes what he calls Caesar's excuse; Pompey's explanation; Cato's plans to impeach Caesar; and Asinius Pollio's account, which Suetonius states is "more probable" (*probabilius, Iul.* 30.4). Here again, however, we run into the problem of Caesar's supposed exact words. According to Pollio, as Caesar looked over his slaughtered and scattered enemies on the battlefield of Pharsalus, he said, "They wanted this; I, Gaius Caesar, would have been found guilty despite my great deeds if I had not sought aid from my army" (30.4).

61. This problem continued. According to our sources, the appearance of Domitian deceived the Romans. His modest blush led people to believe that he was going to be a good princeps. See Tac., *Hist.* 4.40; Suet., *Dom.* 18.2; Plin. *Pan.* 48.4; and Wallace-Hadrill 1982, 42. For Seneca's take on the difficulties in interpreting the moral significance of a blush, see chapter 6.

62. See also how Pliny contrasts Trajan and the tyrant Domitian: "What I have just now heard, what I have just now come to learn, is not 'the princeps is above the laws' but 'the laws are above the princeps'" (*quod ego nunc primum audio, nunc primum disco, non est "princeps super leges" sed "leges super principem,"* Pan. 65.1). On this passage, Brunt (1977, 109) comments, "This implies not merely that Domitian had in practice set the laws at naught (so Pliny held) but that he had been heard to say, or others had said on his behalf that he stood above them."

63. "ut de clementia scriberem, Nero Caesar, una me vox tua maxime compulit, quam ego non sine admiratione et, cum diceretur, audisse memini et deinde aliis narrasse, vocem generosam, magni animi, magnae lenitatis, quae non composita nec alienis auribus data subito erupit et bonitatem tuam cum fortuna tua litigantem in medium adduxit. animadversurus in latrones duos Burrus praefectus tuus, vir egregius et tibi principi natus, exigebat a te, scriberes in quos et ex qua causa animadverti velles; hoc saepe dilatum ut aliquando fieret, instabat. invitus invito cum chartam protulisset traderetque, exclamasti: 'vellem litteras nescirem!' o dignam vocem quam audirent omnes gentes, quae Romanum imperium incolunt quaeque iuxta iacent dubiae libertatis quaeque se contra viribus aut animis attollunt! o vocem in contionem omnium mortalium mittendam, in cuius verba principes regesque iurarent! o vocem publica generis humani innocentia dignam, cui redderetur antiquum illud saeculum! nunc profecto consentire decebat ad aequum bonumque expulsa alieni cupidine, ex qua omne animi malum oritur, pietatem integritatemque cum fide ac modestia resurgere et vitia diuturno abusa regno dare tandem felici ac puro saeculo locum."

64. Tacitus notes that at the beginning of his first full year as princeps, Nero displayed his leniency by restoring Plautius Laternus to the Senate and by pledging his *clementia* in frequent speeches, which Seneca made public (*Ann.* 13.11). As noted by Syme (1958, 336) and O'Gorman (2000, 149–50), this passage likely refers to the publication of *De clementia*.

65. *quam vellem nescire litteras*, according to Suetonius. In this section, Suetonius also claims that when the Senate voted Nero thanks, he responded, "When I will have deserved it" (*agenti senatui gratias respondit: "cum meruero,"* Ner. 10.2).

66. On the state following the example of the ruler, see Cic., *Leg.* 3.30–32; and S. Braund 2009, 387.

67. "diutius me morari hic patere, non ut balandiar auribus tuis (nec enim hic mihi mos est, maluerim veris offendere quam placere adulando); quid ergo est? praeter id, quod bene factis dictisque tuis quam familiarissimum esse te cupio, ut quod nunc natura et impetus est fiat iudicium, illud mecum considero multas voces magnas sed detestabiles, in vitam humanam pervenisse celebresque vulgo ferri, ut illam: "oderint dum metuant," quoi Graecus versus similis est qui se mortuo terram misceri ignibus iubet, et alia huius notae. ac nescioquomodo ingenia immania et invisa materia secundiore expresserunt sensus vehementes et concitatos; nullam adhuc vocem audii ex bono lenique animosam." For the final sentence, I adopt the reading and translation of S. Braund (2009, 142–43); on the difficulties in interpreting this passage, see 391.

68. Seneca also quotes and discusses "great-souled" utterances throughout his philosophy, e.g., *Polyb.* 11.1–3; *Prov.* 5.5; *Constant.* 5.6–7; *VB* 24.4; and *Ep.* 107.11–12, 108.35, 110.18.

69. The interpretation and translation of this phrase has vexed scholars. Basore's Loeb edition (1928, 435) translates it as I do; Malaspina's (2001, 387) Italian commentary understands these words similarly as well: "Until that moment when I heard you, Nero." S. Braund (2009, 392) notes, "He is saying that the wicked generally have a monopoly on passionate remarks . . . until now, when his good prince Nero has uttered a *vox animosa*." Cooper and Procopé (1995, 159), on the other hand, render the passage, "I have yet to hear from a good and gentle person an utterance that was at all spirited," apparently believing that Seneca is still waiting to hear one and that Nero's does not qualify.

70. On the lengthy, complicated history of interpretations of Sulla as a merciful general or a cruel tyrant, see Dowling 2000. Accounts of this massacre are given in Livy, *Per.* 88; Val. Max. 9.2.1; Dio Cass. 35.109.5–9; and Plut., *Sull.* 30. Only Seneca records Sulla's comment about the executions.

71. "quis tamen umquam tyrannus tam avide humanum sanguinem bibit quam ille, qui septem milia civium Romanorum contrucidari iussit et, cum in vicino ad aedem Bellonae sedens exaudisset conclamationem tot milium sub gladio gementium, exterrito senatu: 'hoc agamus,' inquit, 'P.C.; seditiosi pauculi meo iussu occiduntur'?" On Sulla's words, S. Braund (2009, 300) comments: "Curiously, Seneca's three instances of *pauculi* are all in direct speech, *Vit. Beat.* 17.2, *Apo.* 3.3."

72. Seneca is not the only writer to contrast Nero with Sulla. The anonymous poet of the *Einsiedeln Ecologues*, likely written during the early part of Nero's reign, also connects the two (2.32–34). See Dowling 2000, 334–35.

73. At *De ira* 1.12.1–2, Seneca also states that one's father and mother can be avenged without anger. See Nussbaum 1994, 414–15.

74. The line was perhaps parodied by Tiberius, who according to Suetonius (*Tib.* 59.2) said, "Let them hate, provided that they approve" (*oderint dum probent*). See also S. Braund 2009, 302–3.

75. See also Aristotle's discussion in *Eth. Nic.* 1123a34–1125b.

76. The Stoic tradition came down on the side of Socrates as embodying the true meaning of greatness; see *SVF* 3.264, 265, 269, 270. The later Stoics would add Cato the Younger to this tradition.

77. See also Cicero's definition of *magnanimitas* in *Tusc.* 4.61. This concept appears frequently in *De clementia*: 1.5.5 (2x), 1.11.3, 1.20.3 (2x), 2.1.1, 2.5.5. See also the many references to this concept in the fragments of the early Stoics, *SVF* 3.264, 265, 269, 270, 274, 275; and S. Braund 2009, 223–24.

78. See Mazzoli 1991, 178–208, for an overview of Seneca's discussions of greatness of soul.

79. Seneca claims that freedom is the ability to endure insult at *Constant.* 19.2.

80. Cf. Seneca's characterization of Claudius in the *Apocolocyntosis* as an empty gourd full of wind and excrement.

81. Seneca critiques a falsely impressive and "spirited" utterance of Alexander the Great (*Ben.* 2.16.1). He also discusses how to interpret the spirited (*animose*) utterances of philosophers (*VB* 24.4).

82. As S. Braund (2009, 302–3) points out, Gell., *NA* 13.2.2 "claims Accius read the play to Pacuvius who died long before Sulla."

83. See also Cic., *Sest.* 102 and *Phil.* 1.34.

84. On the significance of Cicero's concept of decorum for Stoicism, see Sherman 2005, 52–58.

85. "si Aeacus aut Minos diceret 'oderint dum metuant' aut 'natis sepulcro ipse est parens' indecorum videretur, quod eos fuisse iustos accepimus, at Atreo dicente plausus excitantur, est enim digna persona oratio."

86. Seneca explicitly links the horrors of Sulla's cruelty with those of Caligula in *Ira* 3.18.1–4. On the role of Caligula in Seneca's dialogues, see Wilcox 2008. According to Tacitus, Tiberius prophetically declared that Caligula would be another Sulla: "He predicted that he would have all the vices of Sulla and none of his virtues" (*omnia Sullae vitia et nullam eiusdem virtutem habiturum praedixit, Ann.* 6.46.4). See Dowling 2000, 333–35.

87. Cf. *Apocol.* 5, where Claudius identifies himself as a Caesar by quoting a line of Homer to Hercules.

88. Cf., e.g., *Ira* 3.16.3; and Hdt. 4.84.

89. On the complex nature of suicide during the late republic and the early empire, see Griffin 1986a and 1986b; Plass 1995; Hill 2004; and Edwards 2007.

90. Nussbaum 1994, 431–32.

91. Seneca offers a different reason at *Constant.* 18.2–4, but one that deals with Caligula's speech. According to Seneca, the tribune Chaerea had a weak voice (*languidus sono*, 18.3) that did not match the bravery of his deeds. Caligula continually mocked him by giving to him erotic passwords, such as *Venus* or *Priapus*. As a result, Chaerea was the first of the conspirators to strike, and with one blow he cut off Caligula's head so that he would never have to ask for the password again.

92. The series of would-be assassins is listed by Livia at *Clem.* 1.9.6, and also by Suetonius (*Aug.* 19).

93. "rursus silentio interposito maiore multo voce sibi quam Cinnae irascebatur: 'quid vivis, si perire te tam multorum interest? quis finis erit suppliciorum? quis sanguinis? ego sum nobilibus adulescentulis expositum caput in quod mucrones acuant; non est tanti vita, si, ut ego non peream, tam multa perdenda sunt.'" Augustus' other self-address occurs at 1.9.4. Compare the phrase "more angry at himself than with Cinna" (*sibi quam Cinnae irascebatur*) with Seneca's narration of Cato's death. When he stabs himself for the second time, Cato is "more angry at himself than at Caesar" (*Ep.* 24.8).

94. Seneca frequently reminds his readers of the earlier, bloodstained life of Octavian before he took the name Augustus (1.9.1, 1.11.1–2).

95. On Seneca's possibly un-Stoic political hopefulness at the start of Nero's reign, see Nussbaum 2009 on the *Apocolocyntosis*.

96. C. Jones (2000) demonstrates that more of Nero's words and writings survive in Greek than in Latin. In this language as well, Nero's development seems to parallel his development in Latin. According to Jones, Nero's early Greek pronouncements appear to have required "borrowed eloquence." A letter written to the city of Rhodes in 55 CE is written in a "flat and non-descript" style, and a similarly datable letter to the city of Ptolemais "suggests a young, untried prince mouthing words drafted by a secretary" (456). From the period after Seneca's "retirement" in 62 CE, Nero appears to have found his voice in Greek as well. In a speech announcing the "liberation" of the province of Achaea in 67 CE, Nero adopts the grand, egoistic style of a tyrant (458).

97. Although it is generally agreed that *De clementia* was written in 55 or 56 CE, as S. Braund (1998, 71n46) points out, "Whether or not it precedes the murder of Britannicus early in 55, is hotly disputed among scholars." See also Griffin 1992, 133–34 and app. A.3.

98. "facit quasdam sententias sola geminatio, qualis est Senecae in eo scripto quod Nero ad senatum misit occisa matre, cum se periclitatum videri vellet: 'salvum me esse adhuc nec credo nec gaudeo.'" The next examples are of better *sententiae* written by Cicero.

99. On the emperor's jokes, see Plass 1988, 8–11, 121, 153; cf. Haynes 2003, 6–11. On jokes in Suetonius, see Edwards 2000, xxv.

100. See Furneaux 1907, 306. Cf. the reports that Nero praised his mother's beauty while looking over her corpse (Tac., *Ann.* 14.9.1).

101. Tacitus notes that it is uncertain whether the fire was started by chance or by Nero's deliberate act (*forte an dolo principis incertum*, *Ann.* 15.38.1).

102. The tragedy of Nero's reign and Seneca's inability to control the emperor are the subject of the *praetexta* drama *Octavia*, likely written by an imitator of Seneca during the early Flavian period. Nero's orders for the assassination and return of the heads of Plautus and Sulla are his first lines (437–38). After Nero gives this command to his prefect in the play, he and Seneca begin a debate on the value of imperial clemency, which treats the example of Augustus (477–91) and references *De clementia* (esp. 1.11.1). In this drama, Nero is then allowed to voice his counterargument and interpretation of Julius Caesar, Augustus, and the fantasy and futility of command based on mercy (492–532).

CHAPTER FIVE: Soul, Speech, and Politics in the *Apocolocyntosis* and the *Satyricon*

1. Swift 1996, 62. For further connections between the satire of Jonathan Swift and the *Apocolocyntosis*, see Nussbaum 2009, 110–11.

2. Like Swift, the narrators of the *Apocolocyntosis* and the *Satyricon* both claim to be using simple, unadorned language to present the "simple truth." Seneca opens his satire by adopting the stance of a historian, claiming that he will truthfully report what happened in heaven on 13 October (*nihil nec offensae nec gratiae dabitur. haec ita vera*, 1.1). Near the end of the surviving fragments of the text the *Satyricon* is defined as a

"work of new simplicity" that "reports with a clear style what people do" (*damnatisque novae simplicitatis opus? / sermonis puri non tristis gratia ridet, / quodque facit populus, candida lingua refert*, 132.15.2–4).

3. As Ker (2006, 31) suggests, however, the *Apocolocyntosis* may occupy a more central position and "can be taken as a symptomatic example of Seneca's polygeneric writing: for all its uniqueness, the work's prosimetric form captures the underlying aspiration of the entire corpus."

4. For an outline of the verbal links between the *Apocolocyntosis* and the *Satyricon*, see Altamura 1959. On the political function of the *Apocolocyntosis* and its links with *De clementia*, see Nauta 1987, 76; Leach 1989; Griffin 1992, 129–33; and Braund and James 1998.

5. It may be that Seneca had tuberculosis in his youth and never fully recovered. See Griffin 1992, 42–43; and Inwood 2007b, 329.

6. See Braund and Gold 1998, 255.

7. As Relihan (1993, 75–77) points out, Claudius' journey through the three realms of the cosmos places him in a select group of ancient travelers.

8. Claudius was married to his niece Agrippina. See Sen., *Apocol.* 8.2; and Eden 1984, 102, citing Tac., *Ann.* 12.3.2, 12.4.1, 12.8.1, 13.1.2, and Suet., *Claud.* 24.3, 27.2, 29.1.

9. On the problematic status of disabled bodies in classical myth and literature, see Vlahogiannis 1998, 19–20, which notes that there "was an ambiguous and indeed contradictory discourse that privileged the disabled into positions of status and power: on the one hand, heroes and protagonists are marginalized, debased and disempowered by their disability, on the other they are protected, empowered and privileged by their unnatural state." On Brutus, see p. 24.

10. Hercules fears a "blow from a fool" (7.3), the Britons already worship Claudius as a god and "pray to meet with a well-disposed fool" (8.3). According to Suetonius, Nero often joked that Claudius had "ceased to play the fool" (*morari*) among mortals (*Ner.* 33.1). Apparently, Nero lengthened the first syllable when speaking, turning the Latin *morari* (to linger) into a neologism based on the Greek *môros*.

11. As Braund and James (1998, 307) point out, the age of Saturn was seen as the age of equality between humans but also the time when laws were first created. They write that "Claudius would have been an embodiment of such a dialectic." See also Verg., *Aen.* 8.319–22.

12. On the importance of "famous last words" in the literary tradition of the early empire, see Connors 1994.

13. While Claudius was alive, Seneca praised the healing power of his eloquence and also scripted a lengthy speech by him to Polybius; see *Polyb.* 14.2–16.4.

14. "et ille quidem animam ebulliit, et ex eo desiit vivere videri. expiravit autem dum comoedos audit, ut scias me non sine causa illos timere. ultima vox eius haec inter homines audita est, cum maiorem sonitum emisisset illa parte, qua facilius loquebatur: 'vae me, puto, concacavi me.' quod an fecerit, nescio; omnia certe concacavit."

15. The *Apocolocyntosis*, likely written in late 54 CE, was the comic precursor to *De clementia*, which was composed during the years 55–56 CE. The dating follows Griffin 1992, 395–411.

16. There is a theatrical motif in Claudius' death scene. Seneca notes that the emperor died while listening to comic actors (*expiravit dum comoedos audit*, 4.2). Cf. Cal-

igula's angry challenge to Jupiter for disturbing the performance of some pantomimes (*Ira* 1.20.8).

17. Edwards 1993, 191–92, on Cic., *Phil.* 2.63.

18. Mader 2003, 636. See also Meltzer 1988, 314 and passim on Thyestes' belch and on the role of "black humor" throughout the play, respectively.

19. See chapter 2.

20. Braund and James 1998.

21. "illa purulenta et quae tantum non ex ipso igne in os transferuntur iudicas sine noxa in ipsis visceribus extingui? quam foedi itaque pestilentesque ructus sunt, quantum fastidium sui exhalantibus crapulam venterem! scias putrescere sumpta, non concoqui." Earlier in this passage, Seneca may be alluding to some of the characteristic dining habits of Claudius (mushrooms) and Nero (water chilled by snow, *Ep.* 95.24–25). Claudius was fond of mushrooms and may have died from eating a poisoned one (Suet., *Claud.* 44.2). According to Suetonius, Nero praised mushrooms as "food of the gods." This became a proverbial expression in Greek, as Suetonius states (*posthac proverbio Graeco, Ner.* 33.1). Dio Cass. (61.35) records Nero's remark, claiming that it is "not unworthy of record." This section also contains Seneca's brother Gallio's quip that Claudius was taken to heaven on a hook and is our source for the title *Apocolocyntosis* as well. See also Juv. 5.147. Modern historians doubt whether poison mushrooms really were the cause of Claudius' death; see Rudich 1993, 1. Nero was famous for drinking snow-cooled water (see Suet., *Ner.* 48.3 and Pliny *HN* 31.40), a practice condemned again by Seneca at *Q Nat.* 4b.13.6–11; see also *Ner.* 27.2 on ice-cold baths. On the "decoction of Nero" as a literary metaphor for the period, see Gowers 1994.

22. For a list of other Latin passages about belching revelers, see Mader 2003, 635–36.

23. Goldhill 1995, 20. As Goldhill points out (17), in the *Republic* (388e) Plato is ready to censure Homer for portraying the gods overcome by laughter at the limping and panting Hephaestus (*Il.* 1.599–600). In the *Laws* (667e) Plato does try to grant a place for "play" in the regulation of the city. Seneca, by contrast, wishes to encourage laughter at the limping and panting Claudius.

24. See also Arist., *Rh.* 1398b10, and *Pol.* 1336b, discussed in Goldhill 1995, 18–19.

25. Cf. Plato's claim at *Resp.* 388e that violent laughter can lead to a violent change of mood. Seneca also notes that people who laugh vigorously also quickly become vigorously angry e (*observa, videbis eosdem intra exiguum tempus acerrime ridere et acerrime rabere, Ep.* 29.7).

26. Nevertheless, Cicero thoroughly appreciated and mastered the use of humor in his oratory and political invectives; see Corbeill 1996. As Corbeill demonstrates, Cicero used laughter as a means of social control to exclude those individuals he viewed as valuing themselves over the collective ideals of the community. This method of social stigmatization of "deviant" individuals became increasingly problematic under the triumvirs, and as Corbeill suggests (215–17), one of Cicero's jokes may have ended the young Octavian's siding with the Senate against Antony (*Fam.* 11.20.1). Cicero's *De oratore* contains a lengthy analysis of the use of jokes (2.217–90). Cicero's interlocutor, Julius Caesar Strabo, is careful to advise limits to the type and timing of oratorical humor; see, e.g., 2.238, 2.244, 2.247. The ancient Law of Twelve Tables made insult and slander an offense punishable by death (table 7.1a), cited with approval in *Rep.* 4.12.

27. "ipsumque genus iocandi non profusum nec immodestum, sed ingenuum et facetum esse debet. ut enim pueris non omnem ludendi licentiam damus, sed eam quae ab honestatis actionibus non sit aliena, sic in ipso ioco aliquod probi ingenii lumen eluceat. duplex omnino est iocandi genus, unum inliberale petulans flagitiosum obscenum, alterum elegans urbanum ingeniosum facetum . . . facilis igitur est distinctio ingenui et inliberalis ioci. alter est si tempore fit, ut si remisso animo, <gravissimo> homine dingus, alter ne libero quidem, si rerum turpitudo adhibetur et verborum obscenitas."

28. Indeed, as Smith (1975, 125) points out, Trimalchio is the paradigmatic "disgusting man," according to Theophrastus' *Characters* (20.6).

29. In his commentary, Smith (1975, 125) cautions against taking Trimalchio's remarks as a parody of Claudius.

30. For an analysis of Cicero's letter, see Richlin 1992, 18–26. As she notes, *cacare*, used twice by Seneca in *Apocol.* 4.2, is one of the seven main obscenities in Latin. As she well notes (231n25), this list corresponds to the comedian George Carlin's list of the seven words you'll never hear on television.

31. "quid <quod> ipsa res modo honesta, modo turpis? suppedit, flagitium est; iam erit nudus in balneo, non reprehendes."

habes scholam Stoicam: *ho sophos euthurrhêmonêsei*. quam multa ex uno verbo tuo! te adversus me omnia audere gratum est; ego servo et servabo (sic enim adsuevi) Platonis verecundiam. itaque tectis verbis ea ad te scripsi quae apertissimis agunt Stoici. sed illi etiam crepitus aiunt aeque liberos ac ructus esse oportere. honorem igitur Kalendis Martiis.

tu me diliges et valebis."

32. Later in this treatise, Seneca censures the obscene habits and language of Mamercus Scaurus and asks why Providence allowed him to be consul (*Ben.* 4.31.3–5). This story, of course, begs the question why, if Seneca is so offended by this obscenity, he narrates it at all? See also *Ben.* 2.21.1–2.

33. See also Hermeros' insult, "mouse in a chamber pot" (*mus in matella*, *Sat.* 58.9). When telling the remarkable story of a Spartan slave who killed himself rather than attend to his master's chamber pot, Seneca uses the circumlocution *vas obscenum* (*Ep.* 77.14).

34. In the *Handbook*, Epictetus advises against excessive laughter (*Ench.* 33.4). As Nussbaum (2009, 87–89) points out, however, laughter and mockery, particularly as a means to reform standard sympathetic interpretations of tragic characters, are common throughout Epictetus' works.

35. Cooper and Procopé 1995, 50n17. As they point out, Seneca may have learned of this philosophical pairing from his teacher Sotion. On the laughing Democritus, see Cic., *De or.* 2.235.

36. See Cic., *Tusc.* 4.12–15; Diog. Laert. 7.116; and Graver 2007, 195.

37. Especially in letters 106 and 113.

38. In letter 29 Seneca discusses his friend Marcellinus, who enjoys poking fun at the hypocrisy of philosophers. Seneca admits that Marcellinus' critiques cause him to laugh (29.7).

39. On the self-correcting laughter of the Stoics, see Nussbaum 2009, 86–91. Nussbaum concludes, however, that the laughter of the *Apocolocyntosis* is not Stoic, because it is too concerned with the emotion of hope and puts too much stake in the unstable vicissitudes of the political world. According to Nussbaum, a movement toward Stoic

detachment can be found in Claudius' death scene: get out of the political world; it is covered in the emperor's feces.

40. On the emperor's two funerals, one for his body, the other for his *imago*, see Dupont 1989.

41. In his edition, Eden (1984, 5n10) also considers this to be a possibility. See also Beard and Henderson 1998, 196.

42. As Nauta (1987, 93–95) states, the *Apocolocyntosis* uses laughter to "test new boundaries in a playful setting" and to create a new communal "in group" and excludes Claudius from it. Cf. Corbeill's (1996) discussion of the political role of laughter in the writings of Cicero. For further analysis of the audience's laughter during Claudius' funeral oration, see Plass 1988, 121, critiqued by Haynes 2003, 10. The first divine consecration was a topic for ridicule, as Cicero attacks Antony's "piety" as a priest of Julius Caesar (*Phil.* 2.110). Gradel (2002, 56–57) writes that the triumvirs waited until 40 BCE to officially enact Caesar's divine honors. It appears that Nero quickly lost interest in following Augustus' precedent in using his father's apotheosis for his own propaganda. He soon dropped the title "son of a god" (*divi filius*) from his coins; see Griffin 1984, 98.

43. For an analysis of this attack on Cato's Stoicism, see Craig 1986.

44. Seneca's ostentatious wealth, desire for praise for his eloquence, and frequency of writing poems are also among the charges.

45. On the significance of the adverb *palam* in the context of criticizing a tyrant, see Ahl 1984, 193.

46. Sutton (1985, 346) also includes non-Western and early modern dramatic practices, Japanese Nō plays followed by kyogen, and Elizabethan tragedy followed by jigs.

47. Bakhtin 1981, 53.

48. Bahktin 1981, 58; see also Huizinga 1950, 177–78.

49. Discussed in Stallybrass and White 1986, 13.

50. Eden (1984, 129) comments: "By arrogating judicial functions to himself, Claudius had encouraged the rapacity of barristers, who by dishonesty and collusion made flagrantly unlawful profits. The *lex Cincia* of 204 BCE . . . (Tac. *Ann.* 11.5.3) was ignored, and in spite of Senatorial opposition, Claudius did not enforce it but tacitly abrogated it by imposing an upper limit of 10,000 HS on fees (*Ann.* 11.5–7). In the first year of Nero's reign barristers' fees were regulated (Suet. *Nero* 17) and out of court bargaining was made illegal (*Ann.* 13.5.1)."

51. As Eden (1984, 97) points out, *causidici* is a pejorative term; see Cic., *De or.* 1.46.202; and Tac., *Dial.* 1.1.

52. Compare how the *iurisconsulti* step "from the shadows" (*e tenebris*, 12.2) with Nero's opening claim in *De clementia* that he has called the laws "from the shadows" (*ex situ ac tenebris*, 1.1.4).

53. On the two versions of Saturnalia at work in the *Apocolocyntosis*, see Braund and James 1998, 302–4. The Saturnalia was originally confined to 17 December. According to Dio Cassius (60.25.8), Claudius officially extended it to five days. On the festival in general, see Balsdon 1969, 124. On the ambiguous attitude of the Roman elite toward this holiday, see Edwards 1993, 194–95. Seneca gives his own critique of the "month-long holiday" at *Ep.* 18.1–4.

54. It is generally accepted that the *Apocolocyntosis* was written for the Saturnalia of 54 CE, i.e., just over two months after Claudius' death; see Eden 1984, 3–4, 14 (arguing

that Seneca performed it). The intended audience remains a matter of debate. Grimal (1978, 107–19), Leach (1989), and Braund and James (1998) see it as part of Seneca's political program and argue, as I do here, that it is to be counted along with *De clementia*. In contrast, Nauta (1987, 75) argues: "It is highly implausible that the *Apocolocyntosis* was meant for the ears (or eyes) of either Senate or People." Baldwin (1964) argues that this text was not for the people and was likely not written by Seneca, but cf. Reeve 1984, supporting Senecan attribution. Toynbee 1942 argues for a date of 60 CE.

55. See Plaza 2000, 131–42. On the role of the manumission tax in the *Satyricon*, see Kleijwegt 2002.

56. On freedmen's pride in their social standing, see Plaut., *Poen.* 515–28, 533–40; and W. Fitzgerald 2000, 88.

57. Pace Braund and James 1998, 301, which takes this phrase to describe Claudius' "unprecedented appearance."

58. Translation from Eden 1984, 37.

59. Hom., *Od.* 1.170, Telemachus to Athena disguised as Metes. Seneca may be misquoting Homer slightly here. As Eden (1984, 85) points out, in place of Seneca's "what kind" (*poiê*) the manuscripts of Homer read "where then" (*pothi toi*). On the role of citation in the *Apocolocyntosis*, see Schmitzer 2000; and O'Gorman 2005.

60. On how this passage likely makes fun of Claudius' birth, as well as his introduction of the Aedui into the Senate, see D. Braund 1980.

61. "ego eram qui tibi ante templum tuum ius dicebam totis diebus mense Iulio et Augusto. tu scis quantum illic miseriarum ego contulerim, cum causidicos audirem diem et noctem. in quod si incidisses, valde fortis licet tibi videaris, maluisses cloacas Augeae purgare: multo plus ego stercoris exhausi. sed quoniam volo . . ."

62. One wonders whether Claudius is granted this ability only because he had planned this speech beforehand. As we have seen, Tacitus claims that Claudius could be eloquent so long as he spoke on things that he had thought out beforehand (*nec in Claudio, quotiens meditata dissereret, elegantiam requireres, Ann.* 13.3.2).

63. See Eden 1984, 96–97, citing Suet., *Claud.* 14, 23.1; and Dio Cass. 60.4.3.

64. Leach (1989, 200, 210–15), following Momigliano (1961, 76–77), argues that Augustus' speech may mark the end of the audience's sympathy with Claudius.

65. See Suet., *Claud.* 39.1.

66. Eden (1984, 81) calls Claudius' unintelligible speech a "leit-motiv." See *Apocol.* 5.2, 5.3, 6.2, 7.2, 4, 11.3, 14.2; Suet., *Claud.* 4.6, 30; and Dio Cass. 60.2.2.

67. "Claudius animam agere coepit nec invenire exitum poterat.
tum Mercurius, qui semper ingenio eius delectatus esset, unam e tribus Parcis seducit et ait: 'quid, femina crudelissima, hominem miserum torqueri pateris? . . . fac quod faciendum est: "dede neci, melior vacua sine regnet in aula."'"

68. Thomas 1988, 162–63.

69. "erit alter maculis auro squalentibus ardens—/ nam duo sunt genera: hic melior insignis et ore/ et rutulis clarus squamis; ille horridus alter/ desidia latamque trahens inglorius alvum./ ut binae regum facies, ita corpora plebis."

70. As Braund and Gold (1998, 247) note, there is a "profound interconnectedness of satire and the material body." On the politics of bodily appearance in *De clementia* and the *Apocolocyntosis*, see Braund and James 1998, esp. 286–87.

71. "insigne visum est earum Caesaris litterarum initium; nam his verbis exorsus est: 'quid scribam vobis, patres conscripti, aut quo modo scribam aut quid omnino non

scribam hoc tempore, di me deaeque peius perdant quam perire me cotidie sentio, si scio.' adeo facinora atque flagitia sua ipsi quoque in supplicium verterant. neque frustra praestantissimus sapientiae firmare solitus est, si recludantur tyrannorum mentes, posse aspici laniatus et ictus, quando ut corpora verberibus, ita saevitia, libidine, malis consultis animus dilaceretur. quippe Tiberium non fortuna, non solitudines protegebat quin tormenta pectoris suasque ipse poenas fateretur." On this passage's connections to Plato, see Haynes 2003, 181. Suetonius also quotes the beginning of Tiberius' letter (*Tib.* 67.1).

72. At *Ep.* 76.32 Seneca writes that the proper way to judge a person is to judge him naked, to strip away his body and look into his soul. *Ep.* 102.24–27 provides a vivid description of death as stripping the body away from the soul.

73. See also *Clem.* 1.22.2, where Seneca notes that the more frequently people are punished, the less serious the mark of punishment is.

74. On the difficulties in interpreting the significance of this scar, see S. Braund 2009, 335–36. Cf. fragment 91.5 of Seneca's *De amicitia*: "true friendship ought to be healed without a scar" (*praeterea sinceram amicitiam decet, ut sine cicatrice sanetur*). In his consolations to Marcia and to his mother, Seneca refers to the scars of psychological wounds; see *Marc.* 1.5 and *Helv.* 15.4. Seneca also notes, however, that the weak mind flees from scars (*VB* 5.3). The brave soul counts its scars and obeys the commands of the universal *imperator* (*VB* 15.5–6). For other uses of *cicatrix* by Seneca, either metaphorical or literal, see *Ben.* 6.26.2; *Ep.* 2.3; *Q Nat.* 3.15.6; and *Tro.* 123. Walters (1997, 37–40) discusses the ambiguous status of scars in Roman society.

75. There are two other references to the "scars" caused by jealousy over Giton. Encolpius says, "O hateful crime . . . that I love you although I have been abandoned, and although there was a great wound in this breast, I do not have a scar" (*"o facinus" inquam "indignum, quod amo te quamvis relictus, et in hoc pectore, cum vulnus ingens fuerit, cicatrix non est,"* 91.6); see also 113.8.

76. Richlin 1997, 32–33.

77. The actual marking is described at 103.4. On what letters Eumolpus may have written, see Habermehl 2006, 378–79. On stigma in general, see C. Jones 1987. Seneca inveighs against the practice of branding slaves at *Ira* 3.3.6. Elsewhere, however, he is less charitable, stating that an ungrateful guest should not simply have been branded but should have had the words carved into his chest (*Ben.* 4.37.3–4).

78. Normally, sailors would shave their heads as a vow to the gods during a storm. For a list of significant parallel passages, see Habermehl 2006, 380–81.

79. *Od.* 19.361–507. Earlier, Encolpius uses an Odyssean technique to hide Giton from Ascyltus (97.5, 98.5). Lichas is called the Cyclops (101.5), and the ship his cave (101.7). See Rimell 2002, 118–19; 2007b, 114, 130–31; and Conte 1996, 53–55. Lichas uses an appropriate means for identifying Encolpius, whose name can be translated as "the crotch" or "the groin"; see Habermehl 2006, 412. On "Odysseus' scar," see Auerbach 1953, 3–23, which is the chapter before his analysis of the *Satyricon*. Odysseus is not far from Plato's mind when he describes the judgment of marks on the soul in *Grg.* 526d.

80. Note the link between psychological disturbance and breathing trouble. Encolpius has a "palpitating soul" (100.4), and Giton gasps for breath (101.1). Similarly, Encolpius tells himself that if Eumolpus ever makes a move on Giton, the old man's panting will betray him (100.1).

81. As Rimell (2007a, 69) points out, Trimalchio declares that the most difficult profession (*artificium*) is writing (*litteras*), followed by medicine and money changing (56.1): "Trimalchio implies here that writers also have a privileged knowledge of interiors, and this passage helps us to understand more fully how the host is constructing himself as a (powerful, elite, canny) writer in the *Cena*. As the symposiarch, he alone (together with his side-kick slave-artist Daedalus) knows what his complicated layered dishes contained before the awestruck diners." See also Rimell 2002, 193.

82. Like Claudius, Trimalchio is also a "tyrant" whose departure allows his guests to speak freely (41.9–10). On Trimalchio's imperial pretensions, see Rimell 2007a, 74–75.

83. "'credite mihi, anathymiasis in cerebrum it et in toto corpore fluctum facit. multos scio sic periisse, dum nolunt sibi verum dicere.' gratias agimus liberalitati indulgentiaeque eius, et subinde castigamus crebris potiunculis risum."

84. See also Seneca's advice for philosophical self-address, "You will become accustomed to speaking and hearing the truth" (*adsuesces et dicere verum et audire, Ep.* 68.6).

85. Courtney 2001, 100–101.

86. Smith 1975, 128.

87. Toohey 2004, 209; see also Toohey 1997.

88. The second-century CE medical writer Galen was famously hostile to the Stoics. Nevertheless, the development of Stoicism may owe much to early medical texts. See Gill 2006, 11–12; Gundert 2000; and von Staden 2000. On the medical metaphor as one of the defining tropes of Hellenistic philosophy, see Nussbaum 1994; on this theme in Seneca's letters, see Edwards 1999. Seneca claims that he owes his life more to philosophy than to the advice of doctors (*Ep.* 76.3); he contrasts the healing prescriptions of medicine and philosophy (*Ep.* 78.5; see also *Clem.* 1.17.1–2).

89. See Colvin 2005. For a critique of this concept, see Plut., *Comm. not.* 1084f–1085b.

90. Translation from Long and Sedley 1987, 1:315.

91. Long and Sedley 1987, 2:313. See also Sen., *Ep.* 113.23 (= *SVF* 2.836), and Long and Sedley's (1987) important commentary on this passage at 2:316. For the early Stoics' discussions of *anathymiasis*, see *SVF* 1.501, 2.652, 2.196; and the analysis of Colvin 2005.

92. See Celsus, *Med.* 2.29; and Rimell 2007b, 110.

93. It is interesting that Trimalchio may have been reading *De tranquillitate animi*. Despite this dialogue's rather sober title, it ends with Seneca recommending the restorative powers of drinking and the loosening of rational restraint. According to Seneca, even Socrates, Cato, and Scipio knew how to have a good time (17.4). Seneca also celebrates the gifts of Bacchus (17.8).

94. Here again the title may be significant. Several explanations of the meaning of *Apocolocyntosis* have been suggested. One translation, "Pumpkinification," meets with the objection that Claudius is never turned into a gourd. Athanassakis (1974), however, argues that Claudius is indeed transmogrified at the text's end. The translation "Deification of an Empty Gourd" is another interpretation of the title's significance. See the discussions of Eden (1984, 1–4) and Braund and James (1998, 298–301), who point out that in true carnivalesque fashion, Claudius is portrayed as an empty vessel full of food and excrement. Cf. Shakespeare's similar characterizations of Falstaff, ana-

lyzed in Bristol 1985, 204–5. The portrayal of Claudius as an empty vessel would also further connect him to an important motif in Seneca's philosophy and in the *Cena*; see chapter 3.

95. Yet the very interdependence of these texts suggests that the two political forms structure and are dependent on each other as well. On how the relationship between high and low, exalted and base, structures society, Stallybrass and White write (1986, 3): "The vertical extremities form all further discursive elaborations. If we can grasp the system of extremes which encode the body, the social order, psychic function and spatial location, we thereby lay bare a major framework of discourse within which any further 'redress of balance' or judicious qualification must take place. In our study therefore we have focused upon the symbolic extremities of the exalted and the base . . . we have tried to see how high discourses, with their lofty style, exalted aims and sublime ends are structured in relation to the debasements and degradations of low discourse."

96. See Edwards 1993, 191–92.

97. On how a dual view of purity and disgust defines the understanding of human insides, see W. I. Miller 1998, 58.

98. See Rohde 1894, 555.

99. See Long 2001, 55; and on Stoicism's debts to and differentiations from Platonic psychology, see Gill 2006, 4–46.

100. On this hierarchy, see Long and Sedley 1987, 47P. It must be noted, as Gill (2006, 31–32) points out, that in higher beings these levels of *pneuma* "build or supervene on each other within a single entity. Hence, in human beings and other animals the structure of bones is the work of *hexis*, organic growth and nutrition derive from *phusis*, and functions such as impression, impulse, and movement belong to psyche."

101. Long 2001, 249; the entire chapter (224–49) is helpful for understanding the Stoic view of the relationship between body and soul.

102. For an explanation of Platonic, Aristotelian, Epicurean, and Stoic views of the soul and its relationship to the body, see Long 2001, 225–26.

103. "nunc me putas de Stoicis dicere, qui existimant animam hominis magno pondere extriti permanere non posse et statim spargi, quia non fuerit illi exitus liber? ego vero non facio: qui hoc dicunt videntur mihi errare. quemadmodum flamma non potest opprimi (nam circa id diffugit quo urgetur), quamadmodum aer verbere atque ictu non laeditur, ne scinditur quidem, sed circa id cui cessit refunditur, sic animus, qui ex tenuissimo constat, deprehendi non potest nec intra corpus effligi, sed beneficio subtilitatis suae per ipsa quibus premitur erumpit. quomodo fulmini, etiam cum latissime percussit ac fulsit, per exiguum foramen est reditus, sic animo, qui adhuc tenuior est igne, per omne corpus fuga est."

104. See Henderson 2006.

105. On the links between Seneca's own difficult death in Tacitus and Dio Cassius and Claudius' in the *Apocolocyntosis*, see Ker 2009a, 84.

106. Seneca's sickness is no laughing matter: "Do you think I'm cheerful writing this to you because I have escaped? I would be acting as ridiculously, if I were delighted in this result of quasi good health, as anyone who thinks he has won his case when he is released on bail" (*hilarem me putas haec tibi scribere quia effugi? tam ridicule facio, si hoc fine quasi bona valitudine delector, quam ille, quisquis vicisse se putat cum vadimonium distulit, Ep.* 54.3).

107. In the next letter, Seneca describes himself as still trying to regain his good health by shaking his body to loosen up the bile in his throat or to thin out his breath (*Ep.* 55.2). This advice is also found in Celsus, *Med.* 2.15, as Henderson (2004, 71–72) points out.

108. Annas 1992, 54: "According to the Stoics, growth and what we would call the metabolic functionings are not due to soul, but to nature."

109. On the relationship between *anima* and *animus* in Latin, see the respective entries in the *Thesaurus Linguae Latinae*. In letter 57 Seneca differentiates between the two. When describing the theory he does not agree with, he uses *anima* (57.7); when explicating the soul's ability to survive, he uses *animus* (57.8).

110. There is a focus on death by suffocation in Seneca's philosophy. Seneca writes about his friend Cornelius Senecio, who while having dinner at his house suddenly is unable to breathe and dies (*Ep.* 101.3). On how this death relates to Seneca, see Ker 2009a, 165–66. Seneca also describes a heroic captive German who, before fighting beasts in the arena, asks to relieve himself and then suffocates himself by shoving a toilet sponge down his throat, thus combining some of the key themes of this chapter—death, defecation, and breathing (*Ep.* 70.20). See also Sen., *Prov.* 6.9; *Ep.* 120.15–16; and Inwood 2007b, 329.

111. "vexari te destillationibus crebris ac febriculis, quae longas destillationes et in consuetudinem adductas sequuntur, eo molestius mihi est quia expertus sum hoc genus valetudinis, quod inter initia contempsi—poterat adhuc adulescentia iniurias ferre et se adversus morbos contumaciter gerere—deinde succubui et eo perductus sum ut ipse destillarem, ad summam maciem deductus." Seneca almost let himself die, but then, after thinking about the effect it would have on his aged father, he "commanded himself to live" (*Ep.* 78.2).

112. I follow the dating of Griffin 1992, 395–411. On the possible links between the *Satyricon* the roughly contemporary Roman "encyclopedias of knowledge," see Rimell 2007b, 110: "The *Satyricon*'s Neronian over-consumption might be construed as a further symptom and expression of the universalizing drive epitomized by Pliny's *Natural History* or Seneca's *Natural Questions*." On the links between Petronius and Pliny, see Connors 1998, 145–46.

113. The fear of being buried alive, discussed in letter 57, is also brought up at *Q Nat.* 6.1.8–9; see Inwood 2005, 179.

114. See Inwood 2005, 182–83; and G. Williams 2006. In book 5, when discussing terrestrial winds, Seneca mentions the theory that the earth's wind is produced in a manner similar to the manner in which wind is produced in the human body (*Q Nat.* 5.4.2); see G. Williams 2005b, 424–25. For other descriptions of the earth as a living being, see *Q Nat.* 3.15.1–2, 6.14.2.

115. Human beings have turned the terrestrial winds into a deadly force as well, most notably in the pursuit of empire; see *Q Nat.* 5.18.4–16, and G. Williams 2005b, 442–47. Trimalchio's *anathymiasis* can be brought into the context of meteorology. Aristotle thought that winds were caused by exhalations (*anathymiaseis*) of the earth's particles into the atmosphere (*Mete.* 360a). This theory discussed by Seneca at *Q Nat.* 5.4.3; see also G. Williams 2005b, 424. Seneca discusses the "gulf breezes," which in Greek are called *encolpias* (*Q Nat.* 5.8.1).

116. "diximus solere post magnos terrarum motus pestilentiam fieri, nec id mirum est. multa enim mortifera in alto latent: aer ipse qui, vel terrarum culpa vel pigritia et

aeterna nocte torpescens [gravis . . . est], vel corruptus internorum ignium vitio, <gravis haurientibus est>, cum e longo situ emissus est, purum hunc liquidumque maculat ac polluit insuetumque ducentibus spiritum adfert nova genera morborum." See also Seneca's mention of other places in Italy where deadly exhalations are emitted (*Q Nat.* 6.28.1). Puteoli, where the *Cena* likely takes place, was one area. Another list can be found at Plin., *HN* 2.207–8.

117. "sed ut ad propositum revertar, accipe argumentum magnam vim aquarum in subterraneis occuli fertilem foedorum situ piscium; si quando erupit, effert secum immensam animalium turbam, horridam aspici et turpem ac noxiam gustu. certe cum in Caria circa Idymum urbem talis exiluisset unda, perierunt quiquemque illos ederant pisces, quos ignoto ante eam diem caelo novus amnis ostendit."

118. Cf. *Ep.* 94.56: "Nature has placed gold and silver under our feet and has made everything that tramples and oppresses us be trampled underfoot and pressed down" (*pedibus aurum argentumque subiecit calcandumque ac premendum dedit quidquid est propter quod calcamur ac premimur*).

119. G. Williams (2005b, 421) writes: "Man's *rectus spiritus* . . . befits his upright stature (*hominem ad sidera erectum*) which is itself designed by divine theology to elevate his gaze so that he can contemplate *natura ipsa* in all her celestial wonder. But, in their descent into the dark depths, the miners not only reverse this uplifting tendency towards celestial illumination: their moral as well as their physical uprightness is also lost (*incurvavit* 5.15.3)."

120. "ante Philippum Macedonum regem fuere qui pecuniam in altissimis usque latebris sequerentur et recto spiritu liberoque in illos se demitterent specus in quos nullum perveniret noctium dierumque discrimen. a tergo lucem relinquere quae tanta spes fecit? quae tanta necessitas hominem ad sidera erectum incurvavit et defodit, et in fundum telluris intimae mersit, ut erueret aurum non minore periculo quaerendum quam possidendum?"

121. See, e.g., "retreat into yourself" (*recede in te ipsum*, *Ep.* 7.8); "withdraw into yourself" (*in te ipse secede*, *Ep.* 25.6); "one must flee and retreat into the self" (*fugiendum ergo et in se recedendum est*, *Q Nat.* 4a.pref.20); "retreat into the self" (*in se recedendum est*, *Tranq.* 17.3); and "the soul must be called back into itself from all external things" (*utique animus ab omnibus externis in se revocandus est*, *Tranq.* 14.2). For the idea of "digging out" hidden virtue from the self, see *VB* 3.1.

122. See, e.g., *Q Nat.* 1.pref.13–14.

123. "Nature lifted our faces to the sky and whatever she made that is magnificent and marvelous she wished to be seen by those who can look up" (*illa vultus nostros erexit ad caelum et quidquid magnificum mirumque fecerat videri a suspicientibus voluit*, *Ep.* 94.56); see G. Williams 2006, 127.

124. See, e.g., Sall., *Cat.* 1.1; Ov., *Met.* 1.84–86; and Sen., *Ep.* 92.30.

125. See also *Clem.* 1.3.5, which says that the multitude is ruled by Nero's spirit (*illius spiritu regitur*).

126. "December est mensis: cum maxime civitas sudat. ius luxuriae publice datum est; ingenti apparatu sonant omnia, tamquam quicquam inter Saturnalia intersit et dies rerum agendarum; adeo nihil interest ut <non> videatur mihi errasse qui dixit olim mensem Decembrem fuisse, nunc annum."

127. As Branham (2002, 180) points out, "Trimalchio is the lord of misrule, the old king—and this is what makes him comic—who is eagerly awaiting his own uncrowning,

which he enacts in a mock ritual. Trimalchio's determined attempt to enjoy his own funeral, to witness his own exit and read his own epitaph, is a comically literal version of Bakhtin's idea."

CHAPTER SIX: Writing, Body, and Money

1. "C. Pompeius Trimalchio Maecenantianus hic requiescit. huic severatis absenti decretus est. cum posset in omnibus decuriis Romae esse, tamen noluit. pius, fortis, fidelis, ex parvo crevit; sestertium reliquit trecenties, nec umquam philosophum audivit. vale: et tu."

2. Sullivan 1968b, 150; Baldwin 1984; Byrne 1999, 2006a, 2006b. D'Arms (1981, 111–15) argues that Trimalchio's refusal to accept higher offices at Rome speaks to his "equestrian pretensions" and can be linked to Maecenas' refusal as well; see *Eleg. Maec.* 1.31–32. Schoonhoven (1980, 39–66) provides an overview of the debate concerning whether the *Elegiae in Maecenantem* were written to defend Maecenas against Seneca's attack. *Maecenantius* is not given as part of Trimalchio's name in the inscription Encolpius reads on one of the doorposts at the entrance to the triclinium (30.2).

3. Seneca continues that Maecenas' cloak gave him the appearance of a runaway slave in a pantomime (*non aliter quam in mimo fugitivi divitis solent*, Ep. 114.6). As Byrne (2006a, 33) points out, Trimalchio's shaved head "brings to mind the appearance of a slave or newly freed ex-slave."

4. Baldwin 1984; Byrne 2006a, 43–44.

5. These lines are preserved by Isidore of Seville (*Etym.* 19.32.6). Cf. Trimalchio's poem (*Sat.* 55.9–14). It is generally agreed that Trimalchio is not quoting Publilius; see Smith 1975, 148. The template for these lines, if there is one, remains a matter of debate. Smith (1975) argues for Varro. His view is critiqued by Baldwin (1984, 402). Courtney (1991, 19–20; 2001, 107) and Panayotakis (2009, 60–61) see these lines as a parody of Seneca, who occasionally quotes Publilius' maxims.

6. Byrne 2006a, 31.

7. Byrne 2006b.

8. Abbott 1907; Smith 1975, 220–24; Horsfall 1989a, 75. For example, Trimalchio quotes Vergil, declares that philology should be studied even while eating, and then uses the "wrong" form to describe the heavens (*caelus hic*, 39.3–5). Echion's discussions with Agamemnon about his son's education are a particularly famous example (46). As Laird (1999, 254) cautions, we must remember that Encolpius, not Petronius, presents the freedmen's language.

9. As Edwards (2009) notes, Seneca uses slaves and freedmen to highlight the striving for, and achievement of, freedom, which is the philosopher's goal. See Sen. *Ep.* 44.6, 80.4–5; see also Joshel 1992. For an analysis of "freedmen's art," as well as Trimalchio's problematic status as its ultimate practitioner, see Hackworth-Peterson 2006, reviewed by Hughes 2007.

10. See Smith 1975, 199, citing Tac., *Agr.* 4.3; see also Billerbeck 1990, 191. According to Suetonius, Agripinna did not allow Seneca to teach Nero philosophy, warning that it was contrary to the interests of one who was going to rule (*sed a philosophia eum mater avertit monens imperaturo contrariam esse*, Suet. *Ner.* 52).

11. Rimell 2007b, 126.

12. P. Hadot 1995, 86.

13. P. Hadot 1995, 109.

14. Foucault 1994, 417, 420–21, 425–27, discussed and summarized in P. Miller 2004, 220–21, and Rimell 2007a, 75–77. See also Dupont 1997.

15. "illud admoneo, auditionem philosophorum lectionemque ad propositum beatae vitae trahendam, non ut verba prisca aut ficta captemus et translationes inprobas figurasque dicendi, sed ut profutura praecepta et magnificas voces et animosas quae mox in rem transferantur." As Graver (1998, 625n52) notes, Seneca has typically been criticized for not following his own stylistic advice. On Seneca's theory and practice, see Leeman 1965, 277–78; Cizek 1972, 298–322; Too 1994; and Bartsch 2009.

16. Cf. Seneca's praise of Agrippa's use of a *sententia* from Sallust (*Ep.* 94.46 = Sall., *Iug.* 10.6). Thus in the *Epistles*, Augustus' two main men, Agrippa and Maecenas, serve as a diptych illustrating how to use literature to shape and reveal the self.

17. "quid enim ad rem pertinet an tu quiescere velis? fortuna tua non vult. quid si illi etiam nunc permiseris crescere? quantum ad successus accesserit accedet ad metus. volo tibi hoc loco referre dictum Maecenatis vera in ipso eculeo elocuti: 'ipsa enim altitudo attonat summa.' si quaeris in quo libro dixerit, in eo qui Prometheus inscribitur. hoc voluit dicere, attonita habet summa."

18. "est ergo tanti ulla potentia ut sit tibi tam ebrius sermo? ingeniosus ille vir fuit, magnum exemplum Romanae eloquentiae daturus nisi illum enervasset felicitas, immo castrasset. hic te exitus manet nisi iam contrahes vela, nisi, quod ille sero voluit, terram leges."

19. Paradoxically, Seneca's portrayal of the "life" of Maecenas is likely a limited and limiting fiction, as Graver 1998, 607, and Byrne 2006b, 83–95, demonstrate.

20. "poteram tecum hac Maecenatis sententia parem facere rationem, sed movebis mihi controversiam, si novi te, nec voles quod debeo <nisi> in aspero et probo accipere. ut se res habet, ab Epicuro versura facienda est." According to Suetonius, Nero also preferred "fresh coin" (*nummum asperum*, *Ner.* 44.2); see also Crawford 1970, 45–46.

21. See Graver 1998, 620: "'Unbeltedness' is near to being the exact opposite of masculinity. . . . As a point of dress the absence of cincture equals defiance of convention and also unreadiness for action, in particular the ability to wear a weapon. Applied to writing, the term suggests a lack of structure and consequent ineffectiveness as a vehicle for thought." On the idea of *discinctus*, see *Eleg. Maec.* 1.21–26; and see, in general, Richlin 1992, 92; Edwards 1993, 90; and Corbeill 1996, 160n82.

22. "'debilem facito manu,/debilem pede coxo,/tuber adstrue gibberum,/lubricos quate dentes:/vita dum superest, benest;/hanc mihi, vel acuta/si sedeam cruce, sustine.' . . . huic putes umquam recitasse Vergilium: 'usque adeone mori miserum est?'" Seneca's interpretation here could be an example of his tin ear when it came to the nuances of poetry. As Byrne (2006a, 33–34) notes, Maecenas' poem could be ironic. In *Carm.* 2.17, Horace refers to Maecenas' fear of death, but this too, as Byrne (2006a 34n14) points out, could also be an example of Horace's "humorous handling of their friendship."

23. Of course, there was a strong current of thought that argued that written style did not mirror character; see Graver 1998, 608–9. For statements contradicting Seneca, see, e.g., Catull. 16; Ov., *Tr.* 2.363–60; and Sen., *Controv.* 6.8. In contrast, see Bramble 1974, 23. On "literature as a revelation of personality" in early modern and modern works, see Abrams 1953, 226–62.

24. Seneca does not appear to be alone in his investigations of bad writing. Pliny the Elder wrote eight books on "Dodgy Latin" during the last years of Nero's reign, according to his nephew, the younger Pliny (*dubii sermonis octo: scripsit sub Nerone novissimis annis, Ep.* 3.5.5). Henderson (2002, 281n25) suggests that the ideas expressed in Pliny's books would have been similar to those expressed in Seneca's letter 114.

25. Cf. *Clem.* 1.13.5, where Seneca notes that if Nero is merciful, then what people say about him in public will be the same as in private. There will be no need for political doublespeak. Seneca's Atreus deconstructs this ideal as follows: "True praise can often happen to even a humble man, false praise only to a powerful one" (*laus vera et humili saepe contingit viro, / non nisi potenti falsa, Thy.* 211–12). On this contrast, see Bartsch 1994, 175–77.

26. Graver (1998, 612–14) provides a helpful analysis of the possible meanings of *ingenium* in this passage, specifically how its meaning can move between "literary/oratorical ability" and "soul."

27. "vide ut 'alveum lyntribus arent versoque vado remittant hortos.' quid? si quis 'feminae cinno crispat et labris columbatur incipitque suspirans, ut cervice lassa fanantur nemoris tyranni.' 'inremediabilis factio rimantur epulis lagonaque temptant domos et spe mortem exigunt.' 'genium festo vix suo testem.' 'tenuisve cerei fila et crepacem molam.' 'focum mater aut uxor investiunt.'" For proposals of different emendations and breaks in the citations, see Summers 1908; and Graver 1998, 619n34.

28. The tradition of critiquing Maecenas' writing may have begun with Augustus himself. In his concluding remarks about the first emperor's personal *oratio*, Suetonius notes that Maecenas' "scented curls" were singled out for critique (*Aug.* 86.2). According to Suetonius, Augustus also attacked Mark Antony's writing style as "proof" of his insanity (86.2).

29. See Graver 1998; on the rhetoric of gender in Seneca's letters, see Habinek 1998, 144–46; on Seneca's distortions of the historical Maecenas, see Byrne 2006b.

30. See Velleius Paterculus (2.88) for general comments on Maecenas and also his praise of Maecenas while serving as regent in 31 BCE for executing Lepidus the Younger for conspiring against Octavian. According to Velleius, Maecenas put down this coup "with great swiftness and with no disturbance either to political affairs or to the people" (*mira celeritate nullaque cum perturbatione aut rerum aut hominum*, 2.88.3).

31. "maxima laus illi tribuitur mansuetudinis: pepercit gladio, sanguine abstinuit, nec ulla alia re quid posset quam licentia ostendit."

32. See also Graver 1998, 612.

33. For other analyses of things people say revealing their soul in the *Dialogues*, see, e.g., *Brev.* 12.6–9; *Tranq.* 14.3–9; and *Ira* 2.5.4, 3.23.8.

34. "talis est oratio Maecenatis omniumque aliorum qui non casu errant sed scientes volentesque. hoc a magno animi malo oritur: quomodo in vino non ante lingua titubat quam mens cessit oneri et inclinata vel prodita est, ita ista orationis quid aliud quam ebrietas nulli molesta est nisi animus labat. Ideo ille curetur: ab illo sensus, ab illo verba exeunt, ab illo nobis est habitus, vultus, incessus. illo sano ac valente oratio quoque robusta, fortis, virilis est: si ille procubuit, et cetera ruinam sequuntur.

rege incolumi mens omnibus una est:
    amisso rupere fidem.

rex noster est animus; hoc incolumi cetera manent in officio, parent, obtemperant: cum ille paulum vaccillavit, simul dubitant. cum vero cessit voluptati, artes quoque eius actusque marcent et omnis ex languido fluvidoque conatus est.

quoniam hac similitudine usus sum, perseverabo. animus noster modo rex, modo tyrannus: rex cum honesta intuetur, salutem commissi sibi corporis curat et illi nihil imperat turpe, nihil sordidum; ubi vero inpotens, cupidus, delicatus est, transit in nomen detestabile ac dirum et fit tyrannus. tunc illum excipiunt adfectus inpotentes et instant; qui initio quidem gaudet, ut solet populus largitione nocitura frustra plenus et quae non potest haurire contrectans."

35. See Thomas 1988, 185. Thomas comments that this comparison is deeply troubling. Vergil states that the bees' devotion to their king is even more fanatical than that of the traditional exemplars of non-Roman subservience and obsequiousness—North Africa, Egypt, and the Near East (*G*. 4.210–11). The implications for Seneca's use of this passage are perhaps even more troubling in *De clementia*.

36. This point is also mentioned by Trimalchio at *Sat.* 56.6. Bettini (1991, 197–246) offers an elaborate schema of how winged creatures—bees, moths, wasps, and bats—are used as metaphors for the soul in antiquity. He takes as his starting point another passage from Vergil, the simile at *Aen.* 6.706–9 comparing the souls flying near the river Lethe to bees in a flowery summer meadow.

37. Seneca's word choice is significant. Rather than using a word with negative Stoic connotations, such as *pleasure* (*voluptas*), Seneca writes that the soul feels "joy" (*gaudet*) when the passions first creep in. As we have seen, joy (*gaudium*) is one of the Stoic "good emotions" (*eupathaeiai*); see Diog. Laert. 7.116, Cic., *Tusc.* 4.12–15, and Graver 2007, 195.

38. See B. Williams 1973; Lear 1998; Evrigenis 2002; and Ferrari 2003, 2009.

39. See Pl., *Resp.* 434d–435b, 441c–445e, 544d–e, and the discussion of the transformations throughout book 8.

40. Cf. Auerbach's (1953, 28) analysis of this temporal adverb in the speeches of Petronius' freedmen.

41. On the dangerous corrupting power of the masses at public *munera* in particular, see *Ep.* 7. At the start of *De vita beata*, Seneca urges his brother to flee from the crowd. His definition of the *vulgus* is not class based, however; it is made up of courtiers as well as slaves (*vulgum autem tam chlamydatos quam coronatos voco*, 2.2).

42. Lear 1998, 219–46.

43. "aspice veteraria nostra et plena multorum saeculorum vindemiis horrea: unum putas videri ventrem cui tot consulum regionumque vina cluduntur? aspice quot locis terra vertatur, quot millia colonorum arent, fodiant: unum videri putas ventrem cui et in Sicilia et in Africa seritur?"

44. Rimell 2002, 30, 71–72, 176–77, 203–5. On food and drink as literary critical metaphors in Persius and other classical texts, see Bramble 1974, 45–59.

45. "mellitos verborum globulos et omnia dicta factaque quasi papavere et sesamo sparsa. qui inter haec nutriuntur non magis sapere possunt quam bene olere qui in culina habitant."

46. "sic eloquentiae magister, nisi tamquam piscator eam imposuerit hamis escam, quod scierit appetituros esse pisciculos, sine spe praedae moratur in scopulo."

47. For another reference to the *Libri moralis philosophiae* in the *Epistles*, see 106.2.

48. In another letter, Seneca writes that our continued foolishness (*stultitia*) is in part the result of not "drinking in with open breasts the words of the wise" (*non satis credimus nec apertis pectoribus haurimus, Ep.* 59.9).

49. See also Henderson 2004, 46.

50. On literature as nectar or honey, see Bramble 1974, 52. On the importance of the apian metaphor for literary imitation during the Renaissance, see Pigman 1980.

51. See also *Ep.* 2.2–4, 46.1, 59.9.

52. See also what Seneca imagines these seafood-loving epicures to say: "It's difficult to have our luxuries one by one; let them all at once be placed together and turned into the same flavor" (*gravest luxuriari per singula; omnia semel et in eundem saporem versa ponantur, Ep.* 95.27).

53. "in quem sic pretiosa congerimus tamquam recepta servantem. sine fastidio implendus est; quid enim ad rem pertinent quid accipiat, perditurus quidquid acceperit? . . . at mehercules ista sollicite scrutata varieque condita, cum subierint ventrem, una atque eadem foeditas occupabit. vis ciborum voluptatem contemnere? exitum specta."

54. See also *VB* 9.4, stating that the stomachs of beasts are bigger than humans', and 20.5, stating that the goal of eating and drinking is not simply to fill up and empty the belly.

55. "tam insatiabliem nobis natura alvum dedit, cum tam modica corpora dedisset, ut vastissimorum edacissimorumque animalium aviditatem vinceremus? minime; quantulum est enim quod naturae datur! parvo illa dimittitur. non fames nobis ventris nostri magno constat sed ambitio." As Edwards (2007, 172–74) points out, the conclusion of this letter, as well as *Ep.* 122.4, links eating with death and thus can be connected with one of the master tropes of the *Satyricon*.

56. Cf. Ovid's Pythagoras at *Met.* 15.116–19.

57. See Sen., *Ep.* 88.44: *Zenon Eleates omnia negotia de negotio deiecit*.

58. In doing so, Trimalchio also points out his imperial pretensions as well, as Starr (1987) demonstrates.

59. Trimalchio also gives a witty reply to the opening of Agamemnon's declamation, "A rich man and a poor man were enemies." He asks, "What is a poor man?" (*quid est pauper?*, 48.5).

60. As Marchesi (2005, 324–28) notes, Trimalchio frequently interrupts the freedmen's servile and fable-based language in order to demonstrate his own "knowledge" of high literature; see 39.1 and 47.1.

61. These two points beg the question, does Encolpius himself know Greek?

62. Long 2001, 228–29; see also Graver 2007, 19.

63. On the theory of "total mixture" (*krasis di' holon*), see *SVF* 2.366–36; Long 2001, 230; and Bartsch 2005, 77.

64. Gill 2006. See also Reydams-Schils 2005, 42; and Sherman 2005, 28–62. On the Stoic view of the body compared with the later orthodox Christian view, see Brown 1988, 26–27, 77–78.

65. See Reydams-Schils 2005, 37n47. Reydams-Schils also notes that the Roman Stoics frequently stress the conflict between body and soul, but she cautions that their notion of the self remains "fundamentally anti-Platonic" (42).

66. Bartsch 2005, 76–77.

67. See Seneca's initial praise of Maecenas' line about not caring whether his corpse is mutilated (*Ep.* 92.34–35, discussed above), as well as, for example, *Ep.* 65.16–22. At *VB*

3.3, Seneca notes that we should care for the body, but not to the extent that we become overly anxious about it.

68. Bartsch 2005, 78–79.

69. For a refutation of the claim that Seneca is in fact a dualist, see Inwood 1993.

70. See also *Ep.* 50.6: "What is the soul but air holding itself in a certain state?" (*quid enim est aliud animus quam quodam modo se habens spiritus?*). Seneca also notes, however, that one of the key questions we must pursue is whether or not the soul is a body (*utrum corpus sit an non sit, Ep.* 88.34).

71. Encolpius also wears *phaecasia* (82.3), or elegant, white shoes stereotypically sported by Greek priests, gymnasiarchs, and philosophers; Fortunata wears a gilded pair (67.4). See also Sen., *Ben.* 7.21.1; and, for a discussion of other relevant passages, Habermehl 2006, 50–51.

72. Seneca states that it is the task of philosophy to "measure" the soul (*Ep.* 88.13) and enquire about it (*Ep.* 90.29). Yet he also admits that we do not know what it is (*quid sit animus, ubi sit, qualis sit aut unde nesciamus, Ep.* 121.12).

73. Corbeill 2004, 2.

74. Corbeill 2004, 2–4.

75. As Corbeill (2004, 10–11) notes, "For Tacitus, the accession of Tiberius and the introduction of a new political order have prompted the rise of a new cosmic order, a new perception of the increasingly inscrutable relationship between truth and the body."

76. See also *Ep.* 52.12; and Gleason 1999, 75. On the appearance of virtue and vice in everyday life, see *VB* 7.3. In the *Satyricon*, Chrysis claims to be able to judge a person's character from his or her face (126.3).

77. Some modern psychologists have devoted their research to the physical, especially facial, manifestations of emotions. See esp. Izard 1971; and Ekman 1980.

78. "ut scias autem non esse sanos quos ira possedit, ipsum illorum habitum intuere; nam ut furentium certa indicia sunt audax et minax vultus, tristis frons, torva facies, citatus gradus, inquietae manus, color versus, crebra et vehementius acta suspiria, ita irascentium eadem signa sunt: flagrant ac micant oculi, multus ore toto rubor exaestuante ab imis praecordiis sanguine, labra quatiuntur, dentes comprimuntur, horrent ac surriguntur capilli, spiritus coactus ac stridens, articulorum se ipsos torquentium sonus, gemitus mugitusque et parum explanatis vocibus sermo praeruptus et conplosae saepius manus et pulsata humus pedibus et totum concitum corpus magnasque irae minas agens, foeda visu et horrenda facies depravantium se atque intumescentium— nescias utrum magis detestabile vitium sit an deforme.

cetera licet abscondere et in abdito alere: ira se profert et in faciem exit, quantoque maior, hoc effervescit manifestius."

79. On Seneca's possible break from traditional Stoic physiognomy, see Graver 1998, 612–13. On the place of physiognomy in the ancient world, see Evans 1969; and T. Barton 1994b. On the Stoic idea of the perceptibility of the vices and virtues, see *SVF* 3.85 = Long and Sedley 1987, 60R.

80. "ut horror frigida adspersis, ad quosdam tactus aspernatio; ad peiores nuntios surriguntur pili et rubor inproba verba suffunditur sequiturque vertigo praerupta cernentis."

81. "et ut scias quemadmodum incipiant adfectus aut crescant aut efferantur, est primus motus non voluntarius, quasi praeparatio adfectus et quaedam comminatio;

alter cum voluntate non contumaci, tamquam oporteat me vindicari cum laesus sim, aut oporteat hunc poenas dare cum scelus fecerit; tertius motus est iam inpotens, qui non si oportet ulcisci vult sed utique, qui rationem evicit." See also 2.3.5.

82. Sorabji 2000, 66–92. See also Inwood 1993 and 1995b, 76, where Inwood notes, "In addition to adding the notion of 'will' to the Stoic tradition, Seneca also rethought to some important degree the earlier Stoic conception of assent—this rethinking is expressed in the early pages of *De Ira* book two, in his discussion of the 'preliminary passions.'" Graver (1999) downplays Seneca's contribution and argues that the concept of the pre-emotions belongs to earlier Greek thought.

83. See Cooper and Procopé 1995, 45n4.

84. Cf. Seneca: "This is not the pain of sadness, but a bite: you make it sadness" (*non est dolor iste sed morsus: tu illum dolorem facis, Ep.* 99.14).

85. For an analysis of this passage in terms of the history of the "pre-emotions" (*propatheai*), see Graver 2002, 124–27.

86. See also Seneca's warning at *Ep.* 103.2 against trusting the faces of men. Elsewhere, however, in order to help remove the fear of poverty, he invites Lucilius to compare the faces of the rich and the poor. According to Seneca, the poor appear to be happier (*Ep.* 80.6).

87. "sed de illo in quem fortuna ius perdidit: huius quoque ferietur animus, mutabitur color. quaedem enim, mi Lucili, nulla effugere virtus potest; admonet illam natura mortalitatis suae. itaque et vultum adducet ad tristia et inhorrescet ad subita et caligabit, si vastam altitudinem in crepidine eius constitutus despexerit: non est hoc timor, sed naturalis adfectio inexpugnabilis rationi." See also *Constant.* 10.4; and *Ep.* 71.29, 74.31–32. Epictetus also makes brief mention of the first movements (*Diss.* 3.24.108) and in a fragment claims that the wise man's body can be involuntarily affected (Gell., *NA* 19.1 = frag. 9 Schenkl). See also Sorabji 2000, 69.

88. Other passages in the *Epistles* in which the bodily reactions of the wise man are discussed include 71.27–29, 72.5, 74.31, and 85.29; in contrast, see 116.4, where Seneca says that the wise man can stop his tears and pleasures whenever he wishes.

89. Pace C. Barton 1999.

90. On the ideological significance of walking and on physiognomy in general in republican Rome, see Corbeill 2002.

91. Cf. Seneca's characterization of the ideal form of exchange of *beneficia*: it takes place between souls (2.34.1).

92. "vulgum autem tam chlamydatos quam coronatos voco; non enim colorem vestium, quibus praetexta sunt corpora aspicio. oculis de homine non credo, habeo melius et certius lumen, quo a falsis vera diiudicem: animi bonum animus inveniat."

93. On the notion of the inadequacy of vision in the *Natural Questions*, see Inwood 2005, 180, 189–91.

94. As Seneca writes at the end of the *Natural Questions*, "That very one who manages these things, who founded them, who made the foundations secure and placed them around himself, who is the greater and better part of his own work, escapes the eyes; he must be seen by thought . . . he does not give any access except to the soul" (*ipse qui ista tractat, qui condidit, qui totum hoc fundavit deditque circa se, maiorque est pars sui operis ac melior, effugit oculos: cogitatione visendus est . . . nec ulli dat aditum nisi animo*, 7.30.3–4).

95. For other examples of the vision of the soul in the *Epistles*, see 71.14, 71.24, and 94.19.

96. Asmis 2009, 127. See *Ep.* 44.5–6; and Edwards 2009.

97. As Edward Said (1993, 23) notes about the modern age of imperialism in Conrad's *Heart of Darkness*, the business of empire is turned into the empire of business. This transition is illustrated in the *Satyricon*: after Eumolpus' recitation of the "civil war," he looks upon the city of Croton and asks a passerby what type of business is conducted there (*quodve genus negotiationis praecipue probarent*, 116.3).

98. Yet as Erskine (1996) points out, from as early as the second century BCE the Romans were characterized by the Greeks as being excessively avaricious and greedy. Social and economic historians are generally more sympathetic to Trimalchio's attitudes toward wealth. See, e.g., D'Arms 1981; Finley 1999, 36; and Harris 2006, 20n174, 22.

99. Mayer 2005, 146.

100. Auerbach 1953, 30.

101. Conte 1996, 116.

102. Bodel 2003, 278.

103. See Wallace-Hadril 1981; and Noreña 2001.

104. Mabbott 1941; Crawford 1970, 47. On Nero's monetary reforms, see Griffin 1984, 197–98; and Harris 2006, 20–21.

105. Cf. Caelius' famous insult referring to Clodia as a "two-bit Clytemnestra" (*quadrantaria Clytemnestra*) in Quint., *Inst.* 8.6.53.

106. Cf. Hermeros' invective against Ascyltus: "He is some slave who runs away under cover of darkness, who is not worth his own piss . . . and yet he laughs. What reason does he have to laugh? Did his father pay money for him when he was born?" (*larifuga nescio quis, nocturnus, qui non valet lotium suum . . . ridet. quid habet quod rideat? numquid pater fetum emit lamna?*, 57.3–4). On the difficulties in interpreting the last line, see Smith 1975, 155.

107. On the importance of *fides* for conducting business transactions, see Cic., *Off.* 3.44–70; on its importance for making oaths, see 3.104. See also Edwards 1993, 183. In *De officiis*, Cicero approvingly quotes a proverb of the "country folk" on how to describe a trustworthy person: someone with whom you can play the game of *morra* in the dark (3.77–78; see also *Fin.* 2.52 and *Div.* 2.85). Similarly, Ganymede describes the old aedile Safinius as "upright, trustworthy, a friend to a friend, with whom you'd boldly play *morra* in the dark" (*sed rectus, sed certus, amicus amico, cum quo audacter posses in tenebris micare*, 44.7). On the links between popular morality and high philosophy, see Morgan 2007.

108. He also doubts the genuineness of Ascyltus' equestrian ring (*nisi si me iudicas anulos buxeos curare, quos amicae tuae involasti*, 58.10). Seneca praises *fides* as the "most holy good of the human breast, which can be forced by no necessity toward deceit and can be corrupted by no reward: 'burn,' it says, 'cut, kill: I shall not betray, but the more pain seeks out my secrets, so much deeper shall I hide them'" (*fides sanctissimum humani pectoris bonum est, nulla necessitate ad fallendum cogitur, nullo corrumpitur praemio: "ure," inquit "caede, occide: non prodam sed quo magis secreta quaeret dolor, hoc illa altius condam," Ep.* 88.29). Cf. his citation of the gladiatorial oath to Encolpius' description of the oath to deceive the inhabitants of Croton (*Sat.* 117.5).

109. On Trimalchio's use of the language and imagery of fables, see Marchesi 2005, 327–26. Cf. his insult to Fortunata, "But she puffs herself up like a frog" (*at inflat se tamquam rana*, 74.13).

110. Generally, the freedmen of the *Satyricon* define themselves not as "men" (*viri*) but as human beings (e.g., *homo inter homines*, 39.4). By describing his *virtus*, the qualities that make a man (*vir*), Trimalchio appropriates both the masculine ideal of the Roman elite and that of Stoicism. On the contrast between *homo* and *vir* and the links between manhood and *virtus* in Roman culture, see Edwards 1993, 20, 185.

111. For Seneca on *frugalitas*, see *Polyb.* 3.5; and *Ep.* 5.5, 58.32, 87.5, 88.30, and 115.3, where it is one of the virtues he wishes the "eye of the soul" could see in the *animus* of the good man.

112. On the connections between the *Symposium* and the *Satyricon*, see Cameron 1969; and Conte 1996, 120–21. On the influence of the *Phaedrus* on Roman writers of the late republic and early empire, see Bartsch 2006, 70–103, esp. 84n82, and 102nn144, 145.

113. See also *SVF* 3.650–53; and Cic., *Tusc.* 4.72. On early Stoic theories of love, see Schofield 1991, 28–32 and appendices B and C; and Nussbaum 2002, 78–79. On Cicero's critique of these theories, see Bartsch 2006, 100–101.

114. Trimalchio does suggest, however, that his master encouraged him to learn *philologia* so that he could become "a human being among humans" (*homo inter homines*, 39.4).

115. Seneca too could not escape accusations regarding his sexual behavior. See *VB* 27.5; and Dio Cass. 61.10.4, discussed in Bartsch 2006, 167.

116. We discover later the boy's name, Croesus, as well as the dirty condition of his teeth (*sordidissimis dentibus*, 64.6). On Trimalchio's former status as a *deliciae*, see Pomeroy 1992. On the presentation of sex in the *Satyricon*, see Gill 1973; T. Richardson 1984; and C. Williams 1999.

117. "qua sapientia, quibus philosophorum praeceptis intra quadriennium regiae amicitiae ter milies sestertium paravisset? Romae testamenta et orbos velut indagine eius capi, Italiam et provincias immenso faenore hauriri." See also Juv. 10.16; and Dio Cass. 61.10.2.

118. See Levick 2003. For an overview of Seneca's attitudes toward wealth, see Griffin 1992, 286–314.

119. Veyne 2003, 9–14.

120. Edwards 1993, 172–206.

121. Ker 2006, 40.

122. Ker 2006, 35, drawing attention to *Ira* 3.36.2 and Plin., *Ep.* 7.31.2. For a general discussion of Seneca's metaphor of the self as commodity, see Bartsch 2009, 204–8.

123. Rosivach 1995; Henderson 2004, 49–50. See, e.g., *Ep.* 24.17, "I shall become a poor man: I shall be one among many" (*pauper fiam: inter plures ero*); and *Ep.* 62.3, 88.11, 98.10. Seneca admits, however, that he sometimes feels embarrassed when he "practices poverty" in public (*nondum audeo frugalitatem palam ferre, Ep.* 87.5). Seneca also speaks out against wealth, esp. in *Ep.* 87.26–41; he refers to *paupertas* as the origin of the Roman *imperium* (87.41).

124. On the economics of Seneca's relationship to Lucilius, see Habinek 1998, 141–42.

125. See also *Ep.* 19.10 and 118.1.

126. Seneca also discusses how wealth can display greatness of soul in the *Epistles*; see *Ep.* 18.11, 20.10–11, and 86.3. In letter 104 he praises his vineyards at Nomentum for curing his soul (104.6). This estate was famously profitable. See Columella, *Rust.* 3.3; Plin., *HN* 14.51; and Ker 2006, 24.

127. In this dialogue, Seneca makes a distinction between the hard "uphill" virtues of poverty and the "downhill" virtues of wealth: "Since there is this division, I prefer to use those that can be exercised in relative tranquility rather than those whose practice requires blood and sweat" (*cum hoc ita divisum sit, malo has in usu mihi esse quae exercendae tranquillius sunt quam eas quarum experimentum sanguis et sudor est, VB* 25.7–8). In the *Epistles*, however, Seneca stresses the Stoic concept of the unity of the virtues; see *Ep.* 66.13. Unlike in *De vita beata*, he also claims that he prefers the harsh goods to the mild ones; see *Ep.* 66.49.

128. "quid autem dubii est quin haec maior materia sapienti viro sit animum explicandi suum in divitiis quam in paupertate, cum in hac unum genus virtutis sit non inclinari nec deprimi, in divitiis et temperantia et liberalitas et diligentia et dispositio et magnificientia campum habeat patentem?" Seneca notes that wealth, like other "indifferents," such as good heath, cannot be taken away without causing ruin to the principal good (*quaedam enim, etiam si in summam rei parva sunt [ait] et subduci sine ruina principalis boni possunt, VB* 22.3). Cf. his discussion of the ruin (*ruina*) that is caused when the emperor is taken away (*Clem.* 1.4.2) and when the soul of the individual is corrupted (*Ep.* 114.22). See also *VB* 25.2, where Seneca says he would prefer to display the state of his soul while wearing a toga rather than with naked shoulders.

129. Asmis 1990, 254. At *Ep.* 104.27 Seneca states that Socrates was poor; at *Ep.* 58.32 he praises Plato's *frugalitas*.

130. Seneca begins his discussion of wealth by voicing the criticisms of those who "bark against philosophy" (*qui philosophiam conlatrant*, 17.1). As noted in the introduction, several of these critiques may also be directed against Trimalchio; see *VB* 17.2, 21.1, 27.4. Seneca's answer is that the philosopher admits his faults and tries to live as he ought to (17.3, 18.2, 20.2). Trimalchio, however, only seems interested in bettering himself economically, e.g., trying unsuccessfully to invest money (53.4). Once he leaves the world of business, he lends out money through his freedmen (76.9).

131. Griffin 1992, 309. As Griffin also points out (399nF), the fact that name of the dedicatee, Seneca's brother, is given, not as *Novatus*, but as *Gallio*, his adopted name, shows that *De vita beata* must have been written after 52 CE.

132. Griffin 1992, 307–9.

133. Asmis 1990, 254.

134. For an analysis of Plato's critiques of the Sophists for selling wisdom, see Tell 2009. Schofield (2006, 250–81) discusses Plato's views on money.

135. This topic is also taken up in letter 81 of the *Epistles*; see also *VB* 24.3, where Seneca says that the house of a wealthy man provides a great opportunity for the giving of benefits.

136. See Roller 2001, 131–34. Roller writes that "gift-exchange and commodity-exchange are entirely compatible: they can and do exist side-by-side in many societies, including Roman elite society" (133).

137. Seneca's idealization of the writing of wills and the granting of legacies as the paradigmatic example of disinterested giving (*Ben.* 4.11.4–6) is given the lie in the *Satyricon*. As we have seen, the surviving fragments close with the cannibalistic tenets of Eumolpus' will (*Sat.* 141.2). Trimalchio makes clear why he has his will read during dinner: "I make all these things public," he declares, "so that my family will love me as much now while I am alive as when I am dead" (71.3). On the social power that wills offered to the living, see Champlin 1991, 22–28.

138. See Sullivan 1968b, 219; critiqued by Smith 1975, 218.

139. "quamquam quaeritur a quibusdam, sicut ab Hecatone, an beneficium dare servus domino possit. sunt enim, qui ita distinguant, quaedam beneficia esse, quaedam officia, quaedam ministeria; beneficium esse, quod alienus det (alienus est, qui potuit sine reprehensione cessare); officium esse filii, uxoris, earum personarum, quas necessitudo suscitat et ferre opem iubet; ministerium esse servi, quem condicio sua eo loco posuit, ut nihil eorum, quae praestat, imputet superiori.

praeterea servum qui negat dare aliquando domino beneficium, ignarus est iuris humani; refert enim, cuius animi sit, qui praestat, non cuius status. nulli praeclusa virtus est; omnibus patet, omnes admittit, omnes invitat, et ingenuos et libertinos et servos et reges et exules; non eligit domum nec censum, nudo homine contenta est. . . . si non dat beneficium servus domino, nec regi quisquam suo nec duci suo miles; quid enim interest, quali quis teneatur imperio, si summo tenetur?"

140. The word *high-mindedness* is taken from MacMullen's (1986, 521) critique of this treatise. On Seneca's move away from the republican ideal of concrete forms of reciprocity, see Roller 2001, 79–82.

141. In *De beneficiis*, Seneca focuses on the Stoic paradox that "to receive a favor gladly is to have repaid it" (2.30.2), advises against "sordid calculation" (4.11.1), and metaphorically calls a favor "a loan that cannot be repaid" (4.12.1). Yet he also reveals the level of wealth with which he is accustomed to dealing. At the end of book 4, he mentions that Zeno lent 500 denarii to a man he knew to be insolvent. His friends advised him against performing this favor. Zeno gave the money anyway because it was only a trifling amount, or as the saying goes, an amount that "can be spent on a disease" (*in morbo consumat*, 4.39.1–2). This story is printed as *SVF* 1.16. To give this amount some comparative context, a legionary soldier was paid only 250 denarii per year, with deductions for food, etc., as Cooper and Procopé (1995, 307n85) point out.

142. "Let him give thanks in return for a favor, so that he will be willing to do right to others" (*pro beneficio gratiam referat, ut aliis recte facere libeat*, Cato, *Agr. Orig.* 5.2). See also Val. Max. 6.8.

143. The critiques of Finley and Bradley are summarized and defended in Griffin 1992, 515.

144. "illud magis venire in aliquam disputationem potest, quid faciendum sit captivo, cui redemptionis pretium homo prostituti corporis et infamis ore promittit. patiar me ab impuro servari? servatus deinde quam illi gratiam referam? vivam cum obsceno? non vivam cum redemptore? quid ergo placeat, dicam. etiam a tali accipiam pecuniam, quam pro capite dependam, accipiam autem tamquam creditum, non tamquam beneficium; solvam illi pecuniam et, si occasio fuerit servandi periclitantem, servabo; in amicitiam, quae similes iungit, non descendam, nec servatoris illum loco numerabo sed feneratoris, cui sciam reddendum, quod accepi."

145. "his repleti voluptatibus cum conaremur in triclinium intrare, exclamavit unus ex pueris, qui supra hoc officium erat positus: 'dextro pede.' sine dubio paulisper trepidavimus, ne contra praeceptum aliquis nostrum limen transiret. ceterum ut pariter movimus [dextros] gressus, servus nobis despoliatus procubuit ad pedes ac rogare coepit, ut se poenae eriperemus: nec magnum esse peccatum suum, propter quod periclitaretur; subducta enim sibi vestimenta dispensatoris in balneo, quae vix fuissent decem sestertiorum. rettulimus ergo dextros pedes dispensatoremque in oecario aureos numerantem deprecati sumus, ut servo remitteret poenam. superbus ille sustulit vultum

et 'non tam iactura me movet' inquit 'quam neglegentia nequissimi servi. vestimenta mea cubitoria perdidit, quae mihi natali meo cliens quidam donaverat, Tyria sine dubio, sed iam semel lota. quid ergo est? dono vobis eum.'

obligati tam grandi beneficio cum intrassemus triclinium, occurrit nobis ille idem servus, pro quo rogaveramus, et stupentibus spississima basia impegit gratias agens humanitati nostrae. 'ad summum, statim scietis' ait 'cui dederitis beneficium. vinum dominicum ministratoris gratia est.'"

146. Saller 1982, 9.

147. On the connections between this invented dialogue and Seneca's works, see Grimal 1967. See also *SVF* 3.691 for Stoic theories about accepting wealth from a ruler.

148. On the role of the emperor in the system of exchange in *De beneficiis*, see Inwood 1995a; Roller 2001, 129–212; and Griffin 2003a, 2003b.

149. Roller (2001, 129–73) discusses the role dinner parties as object of exchange.

Epilogue

1. See Schmeling 1991.

2. See Henderson 2006, 124.

3. The inconveniences of mud and dust that Seneca experiences on his journey through the Crypta Neapolitana appear again (*Ep.* 57.2), this time as a metaphor for the difficulties one will experience on the journey of life (*omnia ista in longa vita sunt, quomodo in longa via et pulvis et lutum et pulvia*, *Ep.* 96.3).

4. As Henderson (2004, 37–41) points out, the later travel narratives echo events from the earlier ones (*Ep.* 49–57). Thus letter 70 recalls letter 49, and *Ep.* 122.15–16 describes another noisy downstairs and is reminiscent of letter 56.

5. Long 2006, 375–76.

6. Henderson 2004, 41–42.

7. "He asked his friend Statius Annaeus to bring forth the poison that had been previously prepared, by which those who are condemned in public court at Athens are killed" (*orat provisum pridem venenum quo d<am>nati publico Atheniensium iudicio extinguerentur promeret*, *Ann.* 15.64.3).

8. Usually dated to the third century CE, the herm is now in Berlin; see Griffin 1992, 369n2.

9. See Dyson 1970, 78; and Ker 2006, 24.

10. The adjective *Senecal* is from Guise's description of Claremont in George Chapman's "anti-revenge tragedy," *The Revenge of Bussy D'Ambois* (1609–10): "In short, this Senecal man is found in him:/ He may with heaven's immortal powers compare,/ To whom the day and fortune equal are./ Come fair or foul, whatever chance can fall,/ Fixed in himself, he still is one to all" (4.4.1–46). Williamson (1951) discusses the "Senecan amble."

11. Long 2006, 3.

12. See Schmeling 1995, 151; and Rimell 2002, 1–2, for a list of the *Satyricon*'s contemporary influence. On the film *Fellini-Satyricon*, see Paul 2009.

13. In Sienkiewicz's novel (1905, 22), Petronius publishes the *Satyricon* anonymously. When he sees a copy for sale in the bookstalls, he gives it to Marcus Vinitius and recommends that he read the feast of Trimalchio closely.

14. See F. Scott Fitzgerald 1995, 207; and 2000.

15. Champlin 2003, 235. To offer one recent example, the potent image "While Rome Burns," by Anita Kunz, served as the cover of the 22 January 2007 *New Yorker* magazine.

16. Quoted in Starkie 1968, 102.

17. "complectere artus, quodque de nato est super,/miserande, maesto pectore incumbens fove./disiecta, genitor, membra laceri corporis/in ordinem dispone et errantes loco/restitue partes: fortis hic dextrae locus,/hic laeva frenis docta moderandis manus/ponenda: laevi lateris agnosco notas./quam magna lacrimis pars adhuc nostris abest!/durate trepediae lugubri officio manus,/fletusque largos sistite, arentes genae,/dum membra nato genitor adnumerat suo/corpusque fingit."

18. See also Cicero's discussion of the ornate style at *De or.* 3.96; and Fantham 1972, 168.

19. Marx 1978, 594.

Bibliography

Abbott, F. F. 1907. "The Use of Language as a Means of Characterization in Petronius." *Classical Philology* 2:43–50.
Abrams, M. 1953. *The Mirror and the Lamp: Romantic Theory and the Critical Tradition.* Oxford.
Adam, T. 1970. *Clementia Principis: Der Einfluss hellenistischer Fürstenspiegel auf den Versuch einer rechtlichen Fundierung des Principats durch Seneca.* Stuttgart.
Adams, J. N. 1982. *The Latin Sexual Vocabulary.* Baltimore.
Ahl, F. 1984. "The Art of Safe Criticism in Greece and Rome." *American Journal of Philology* 105:174–208.
Alston, W. P. 1977. "Self-Intervention and the Structure of Motivation." In Mischel 1977, 65–102.
Altamura, D. 1959. "Apokolokyntosis et Satyricon." *Latinitas* 7:43–54.
Anderson, G. 1995. "*Ut ornatius et uberius dici posset*: Morals into Epigram in the Elder Seneca." In Innes, Hine, and Pelling 1995, 75–91.
Annas, J. 1992. *Hellenistic Philosophy of Mind.* Berkeley and Los Angeles.
———. 1993. *The Morality of Happiness.* Oxford.
Armisen-Marchetti, M. 1989. *Sapientiae Facies: Étude sur les images de Sénèque.* Paris.
Arrowsmith, W. 1966. "Luxury and Death in the *Satyricon*." *Arion* 5:304–31.
Asmis, E. 1990. "Seneca's *On the Happy Life* and Stoic Individualism." In *The Poetics of Therapy: Hellenistic Ethics in its Rhetorical and Literary Context*, edited by M. C. Nussbaum, 219–56. Edmonton, AB.
———. 2009. "Seneca on Fortune and the Kingdom of God." In Bartsch and Wray 2009, 115–38.
Athanassakis, A. N. 1974. "Some Evidence in Defense of the Title *Apocolocyntosis* for Seneca's Satire." *Transactions of the American Philological Association* 104:11–22.
Atherton, C. 1988. "Hand over Fist: The Failure of Stoic Rhetoric." *Classical Quarterly* 38:392–427.
Auerbach, E. 1953. *Mimesis: The Representation of Reality in Western Literature.* Translated by W. R. Trask. Princeton, NJ.
Auhagen, U. 2007. "Tragödienparodie bei Petron, 132.9–14." In Castagna and Lefèvre 2007, 173–83.
Bagnani, G. 1954. *Arbiter of Elegance: A Study of the Life and Works of C. Petronius.* Toronto.
Bakhtin, M. M. 1981. *The Dialogic Imagination: Four Essays.* Translated by C. Emerson and M. Holquist. Austin.
———. 1984. *Rabelais and His World.* Translated by H. Iswolsky. Bloomington, IN.

Baldwin, B. 1964. "Executions under Claudius: Seneca's *Ludus de morte Claudii.*" *Phoenix* 18:39–48.

———. 1981. "Seneca and Petronius." *Acta Classica* 24:133–40.

———. 1984. "Trimalchio and Maecenas." *Latomus* 43:402–3.

Balsdon, J. P. 1969. *Life and Leisure in Ancient Rome*. New York.

Barthes, R. 1976. *Sade/Fourier/Loyola*. Translated by R. Miller. Baltimore.

Barton, C. 1999. "The Roman Blush: The Delicate Matter of Self-Control." In Porter 1999, 212–34.

Barton, T. 1994a. "The *Inventio* of Nero: Suetonius." In Elsner and Masters 1994, 48–66.

———. 1994b. *Power and Knowledge: Astrology, Physiognomics, and Medicine under the Roman Empire*. Ann Arbor, MI.

Bartsch, S. 1994. *Actors in the Audience: Theatricality and Doublespeak from Nero to Hadrian*. Cambridge, MA.

———. 1997. *Ideology in Cold Blood*. Cambridge, MA.

———. 2005. "Eros and the Roman Philosopher." In *Erotikon: Essays on Eros Ancient and Modern*, edited by S. Bartsch and T. Bartscherer, 59–83. Chicago.

———. 2006. *The Mirror of the Self: Sexuality, Self-Knowledge, and the Gaze in the Early Roman Empire*. Chicago.

———. 2007. "Wait a Moment *Phantasia*: Ekphrastic Interference in Seneca and Epictetus." *Classical Philology* 102:83–95.

———. 2009. "Senecan Metaphor and Stoic Self-Instruction." In Bartsch and Wray 2009, 188–220.

Bartsch, S., and D. Wray, eds. 2009. *Seneca and the Self*. Cambridge.

Basore, J. 1928. *Seneca: Moral Essays I*. Cambridge, MA.

Beard, M. 1993. "Looking (Harder) for Roman Religion: Dumezil, Declamation and the Problems of Definition." In *Mythos in mythenloser Gesellschaft: Das Paradigma Roms*, edited by F. Graff, 41–64. Stuttgart.

Beard, M., and J. Henderson. 1998. "The Emperor's New Body: Ascension from Rome." In *Parchments of Gender: Deciphering Bodies in Antiquity*, edited by M. Wyke, 191–219. Oxford.

Beck, R. 1973. "Some Observations on the Narrative Technique of Petronius." *Phoenix* 27:42–61.

———. 1979. "Eumolpus *Poeta*, Eumolpus *Fabulator*: A Study of Characterization in the *Satyricon*." *Phoenix* 33:239–53.

Bertrand-Dagenbach, C. 1992. "La mort de Pétrone et l'art de Tacite." *Latomus* 51:601–5.

Bessone, F. 1993. "Discorsi dei liberti e parodia del simposio platonico nella *Cena Trimalchionis*." *Materiali e Discussioni per l'Analisi dei Testi Classici* 30:63–86.

Betensky, A. 1978. "Neronian Style, Tacitean Content: The Use of Ambiguous Confrontations in the *Annals*." *Latomus* 37:419–35.

Bettini, M. 1991. *Anthropology and Roman Culture: Kinship, Time, Images of the Soul*. Translated by J. Van Sickle. Baltimore.

Billerbeck, M. 1990. "Philology at the Imperial Court." *Greece and Rome* 37:191–203.

———. 1998. "Apostrophes de rôles muets et changements implicates d'interlocuteur: Deux observations sur l'art dramatique de Sénèque." *Pallas* 49:101–10.

Bishop, J. 1985. *Seneca's Daggered Stylus: Political Code in the Tragedies.* Meisenheim, Germany.

Block, E. 1982. "The Narrator Speaks: Apostrophe in Homer and Vergil." *Transactions of the American Philological Association* 112:7–22.

Bloomer, M. 1997. "A Preface to the History of Declamation: Whose Speech? Whose History?" In Habinek and Schiesaro 1997, 199–215.

Bodel, J. 1994. "Trimalchio's Underworld." In *The Search for the Ancient Novel*, edited by J. Tatum, 237–59. Baltimore.

———. 2003. "*Omnia in nummis*: Money and the Monetary Economy in Petronius." In *Moneta, mercanti, banchieri: I precedenti greci e romani dell'euro*, edited by G. Urso, 270–82. Pisa.

Bonner, S. F. 1949. *Roman Declamation in the Late Republic and Early Empire.* Liverpool.

Booth, J. 1997. "All in the Mind: Sickness in Catullus 76." In Braund and Gill 1997, 150–68.

Bowersock, G. W. 1994. *Fiction as History: Nero to Julian.* Berkeley and Los Angeles.

Boyle, A. J., ed. 1994. *Seneca's "Troades."* Leeds.

———. 1997. *Tragic Seneca: An Essay in the Theatrical Tradition.* New York.

Braden, G. 1970. "The Rhetoric and Psychology of Power." *Arion* 9:5–41.

———. 1985. *Renaissance Tragedy and the Senecan Tradition: Anger's Privilege.* New Haven, CT.

Bramble, J. 1974. *Persius and the Programmatic Satire.* Cambridge.

———. 1982. "Lucan." In *The Cambridge History of Classical Literature*, vol. 2, edited by E. J. Kenney and W. Clausen, 533–57. Cambridge.

Branham, R. B. 2002. "A Truer Story of the Novel?" In *Bakhtin and the Classics*, edited by R. B. Branham, 161–86. Evanston, IL.

Braund, D. C. 1980. "The Aedui, Troy, and the *Apocolocyntosis*." *Classical Quarterly* 30:420–25.

Braund, S. 1998. "Praise and Protreptic in Early Imperial Panegyric: Cicero, Seneca, Pliny." In *The Propaganda of Power: The Role of Panegyric in Late Antiquity*, edited by M. Whitby, 53–76. Leiden.

———, ed. 2009. *Seneca: De Clementia.* Oxford.

Braund, S., and C. Gill, eds. 1997. *The Passions in Roman Thought and Literature.* Cambridge.

Braund, S., and B. Gold. 1998. Introduction to "Vile Bodies: Roman Satire and Corporeal Discourse," edited by Braund and Gold, 247–56. Special issue, *Arethusa* 31.

Braund, S., and P. James. 1998. "*Quasi Homo*: Distortion and Contortion in Seneca's *Apocolocyntosis*." In "Vile Bodies: Roman Satire and Corporeal Discourse," edited by S. Braund and B. Gold, 295–311. *Arethusa* 31.

Bristol, M. 1985. *Carnival and Theater: Plebeian Culture and the Structure of Authority in Renaissance England.* New York.

Brown, P. 1988. *The Body and Society: Men, Women and Sexual Renunciation in Early Christianity.* New York.

Brunschwig, J., and M. C. Nussbaum, eds. 1993. *Passions and Perceptions: Studies in Hellenistic Philosophy of Mind; Proceedings of the Fifth Symposium Hellenisticum.* Cambridge.

Brunt, P. A. 1977. "Lex de Imperio Vespasiani." *Journal of Roman Studies* 67:95–116.
———. 1988. *The Fall of the Roman Republic and Related Essays*. Oxford.
Byrne, S. N. 1999. "Maecenas in Seneca and Other Post-Augustan Authors." In *Veritatis Amicitiaeque Causa: Essays in Honor of Anna Lydia Motto and John R. Clark*, edited by S. N. Byrne and E. P. Cueva, 21–40. Wauconda, IL.
———. 2006a. "Maecenas and Petronius' Trimalchio Maecenatianus." *Ancient Narrative* 6:31–49.
———. 2006b. "Petronius and Maecenas: Seneca's Calculated Criticism." In *Authors, Authority, and Interpreters in the Ancient Novel: Essays in Honor of Gareth L. Schmeling*, edited by S. N. Byrne, E. P. Cueva, and J. Alvares, Ancient Narrative Supplementum 5, 83–111. Groningen.
Cameron, A. 1969. "Petronius and Plato." *Classical Quarterly* 19:367–70.
Cancik, H. 1998. "Persona and Self in Stoic Philosophy." In *Self, Soul and Body in Religious Experience*, edited by A. I. Baumgarten, J. Assmann, and G. G. Stroumsa, 335–46. Leiden.
Castagna, L., and E. Lefèvre, eds. 2007. *Studien zu Petron und Seiner Rezeption / Studi su Petronio e sulla sua fortuna*. Berlin.
Champlin, E. 1991. *Final Judgments: Duty and Emotion in Roman Wills, 200 B.C.–A.D. 250*. Berkeley and Los Angeles.
———. 2003. *Nero*. Cambridge, MA.
Cizek, E. 1972. *L'époque de Néron et ses controverses idéologiques*. Leiden.
Claus, D. B. 1981. *Toward the Soul: An Inquiry into the Meaning of* ψυχή *before Plato*. New Haven, CT.
Coffey, M., and R. Mayer, eds. 1990. *Seneca: Phaedra*. Cambridge.
Collignon, A. 1892. *Étude sur Pétrone: La critique littéraire, l'imitation et la parodie dans la "Satyricon."* Paris.
Colvin, M. 2005. "Heraclitus and Material Flux in Stoic Psychology." *Oxford Studies in Ancient Philosophy* 28:257–72.
Connors, C. 1994. "Famous Last Words: Authorship and Death in the *Satyricon* and Neronian Rome." In Elsner and Masters 1994, 225–36.
———. 1998. *Petronius the Poet: Verse and Literary Tradition in the "Satyricon."* Cambridge.
Conte, G.-B. 1987. "Petronius, *Sat*. 141.4." *Classical Quarterly* 37:529–32.
———. 1994. *Genres and Readers: Lucretius, Love Elegy, Pliny's "Encyclopedia."* Translated by G. W. Most. Baltimore.
———. 1996. *The Hidden Author*. Berkeley and Los Angeles.
Cooper, J., and J. F. Procopé, eds. and trans. 1995. *Seneca: Moral and Political Essays*. Cambridge.
Corbeill, A. 1996. *Controlling Laughter: Political Humor in the Late Roman Republic*. Princeton, NJ.
———. 2002. "Political Movement: Walking and Ideology in Republican Rome." In *The Roman Gaze: Vision, Power, and the Body*, edited by D. Fredrick, 182–215. Baltimore.
———. 2004. *Nature Embodied: Gesture in Ancient Rome*. Princeton, NJ.
Corcoran, T. H. 1971. *Naturales Questiones*. 2 vols. Cambridge, MA.
Costa, C. D. N., ed. 1973. *Seneca: Medea*. Oxford.
———. 1995. "Rhetoric as a Protreptic Force in Seneca's Prose Works." In Innes, Hine, and Pelling 1995, 107–15.

Courtney E. 1991. *The Poems of Petronius*. Atlanta.
———. 2001. *A Companion to Petronius*. Oxford.
Cowan, R. 2009. "Starring Nero as Nero: Poetry, Role-Playing and Identity in Juvenal 8.215–21." *Mnemosyne* 62:76–89.
Craig, C. P. 1986. "Cato's Stoicism and the Understanding of Cicero's Speech for Murena." *Transactions of the American Philological Association* 116:229–39.
Crawford, M. 1970. "Money and Exchange in the Roman World." *Journal of Roman Studies* 60:40–48.
Culler, J. 1981. *The Pursuit of Signs: Semiotics, Literature and Deconstruction*. Ithaca, NY.
D'Arms, J. 1981. *Commerce and Social Standing in Ancient Rome*. Cambridge.
Daviault, A. 2001. "Est-il encore possible de remettre en question la datation Néronienne du *Satyricon* de Pétrone?" *Phoenix* 55:327–42.
Davis, P. J. 2003. *Seneca: Thyestes*. London.
Dehon, P.-J. 1993. "Une parodie de Sénèque chez Pétrone (*Satiricon*, CIX, 9, SP. 1–2)." *Revue des Études Latines* 71:33–36.
———. 2001. "A Skilful Petronian Simile: *Frigidior rigente bruma* (*Sat.* 132.8.5)." *Classical Quarterly* 51:314–18.
de Romilly, J. 1984. *Patience mon coeur: L'essor de la psychologie dans la literature greque classique*. Paris.
De Vivo, A., and E. Lo Cascio. 2003. *Seneca uomo politico e l'età di Claudio e di Nerone*. Bari, Italy.
Dickey, E. 1996. *Greek Forms of Address: From Herodotus to Lucian*. Oxford.
———. 2002. *Latin Forms of Address: From Plautus to Apuleius*. Oxford.
Dimondo, R. 2007. "Presenze elegiache nel *Satyricon*." In Castagna and Lefèvre 2007, 183–95.
Dingel, J. 1974. *Seneca und die Dichtung*. Heidelberg.
Dominik, W. J., ed. 1997a. *Roman Eloquence: Rhetoric in Society and Literature*. New York.
———. 1997b. "Style Is the Man: Seneca, Tacitus and Quintilian's Cannon." In Dominik 1997a, 50–70.
Douglas, M. 1966. *Purity and Danger: An Analysis of the Concepts of Pollution and Taboo*. London.
Dowling, M. B. 2000. "The Clemency of Sulla." *Historia* 49:303–40.
———. 2006. *Clemency and Cruelty in the Roman World*. Ann Arbor, MI.
Dupont, F. 1989. "The Emperor-God's Other Body." In *Fragments for a History of the Human Body, Part Three*, edited by M. Feher, 397–419. New York.
———. 1995. *Les monstres de Sénèque: Pour une dramaturgie de la tragédie romaine*. Paris.
———. 1997. "*Recitatio* and the Reorganization of the Space of Public Discourse." In Habinek and Schiesaro 1997, 44–60.
Dyson, S. 1970. "The Portrait of Seneca in Tacitus." *Arethusa* 3:71–84.
Eden, P. T., ed. 1984. *Seneca: Apocolocyntosis*. Cambridge.
Edwards, C. 1993. *The Politics of Immorality in Ancient Rome*. Cambridge.
———. 1997. "Self-Scrutiny and Self-Transformation in Seneca's Letters." *Greece and Rome* 44:23–37.
———. 1999. "The Suffering Body: Philosophy and Pain in Seneca's *Letters*." In Porter 1999, 252–68.
———. 2000. *Suetonius: Lives of the Caesars*. Oxford.

———. 2005. "Archetypally Roman? Representing Seneca's Ageing Body." In *Roman Bodies: Antiquity to the Eighteenth Century*, edited by A. Hopkins and M. Wyke, 13–22. London.

———. 2007. *Death in Ancient Rome*. New Haven, CT.

———. 2009. "Free Yourself! Slavery, Freedom and the Self in Seneca's *Letters*." In Bartsch and Wray 2009, 139–59.

Ekman, P. 1980. *The Face of Man: Expressions of Universal Emotions in a New Guinea Village*. New York.

Eliot, T. S. 1932. "Seneca in Elizabethan Translation." In *Selected Essays, 1917–1932*, 51–90. New York.

Elsner, J. 1993. "Seductions of Art: Encolpius and Eumolpus in a Neronian Picture Gallery." *Proceedings of the Cambridge Philological Society* 39:30–47.

———. 2007. *Roman Eyes*. Princeton, NJ.

Elsner, J., and J. Masters, eds. 1994. *Reflections of Nero: Culture, History and Representation*. Chapel Hill, NC.

Ernout, A., ed. 1993. *Pétrone: Le Satiricon*. Paris.

Erskine, A. 1990. *The Hellenistic Stoa*. Berkeley and Los Angeles.

———. 1996. "Money-Loving Romans." *Papers of the Leeds International Latin Seminar* 9:1–11.

Evans, E. C. 1969. "Physiognomics in the Ancient World." *Transactions of the American Philological Association* 59:1–101.

Evrigenis, I. D. 2002. "The Psychology of Politics: The City-Soul Analogy in Plato's *Republic*." *History of Political Thought* 23:590–610.

Fantham, E. 1972. *Comparative Studies in Republican Latin Imagery*. Toronto.

———. ed. 1992. *Lucan: De Bello Civile, Book II*. Cambridge.

Fears, J. R. 1975. "Nero as Vicegerent of the Gods in Seneca's *De Clementia*." *Hermes* 103:486–96.

Fedeli, P. 1987. "Petronio: Crotone o il mondo alla rovescia." *Aufidius* 1:3–34.

Ferrari, G. R. F. 2003. *City and Soul in Plato's "Republic."* Sankt Augustin, Germany.

———. 2009. "Williams and the City-Soul Analogy (Plato, *Republic* 435e and 544d)." *Ancient Philosophy* 29:407–13.

Finley, M. I., ed. 1987. *Classical Slavery*. London.

———. 1999. *The Ancient Economy*. Berkeley and Los Angeles.

Fitch, J. G., and S. McElduff. 2002. "Construction of the Self in Senecan Drama." *Mnemosyne* 55:18–40.

Fitzgerald, F. Scott. 1995. *The Great Gatsby*. New York.

———. 2000. *Trimalchio: An Early Version of "The Great Gatsby."* Edited by J. West. Cambridge.

Fitzgerald, W. 2000. *Slavery and the Roman Imagination*. Cambridge.

Foley, H. 1989. "Medea's Divided Self." *Classical Antiquity* 8:61–85.

Foucault, M. 1984. *The Foucault Reader*. Edited by Paul Rainbow. New York.

———. 1985. *The Use of Pleasure: The History of Sexuality, Volume 2*. Translated by Robert Hurley. New York.

———. 1986. *The Care of the Self: The History of Sexuality, Volume 3*. Translated by Robert Hurley. New York.

———. 1994. *Dits et écrits: 1954–1988*. Edited by D. Defert and F. Ewald. Vol. 4. Paris.

———. 2005a. *The Hermeneutics of the Subject: Lectures at the College de France, 1981–1982.* Translated by G. Burchell. New York.

———. 2005b. "Power/Knowledge." In *Political Philosophy: The Essential Texts*, edited by S. Cahn, 511–24. Oxford.

Freud, S. 1959. "Character and Anal Eroticism." In *The Standard Edition of the Complete Psychological Works of Sigmund Freud*, translated by J. Strachey, 9:168–75. London.

Freudenberg, K., ed. 2005. *The Cambridge Companion to Roman Satire.* Cambridge.

Furneaux, H. 1907. ed. *The "Annals" of Tacitus.* Vol. 2, Books XI–XVI. Oxford.

Fyfe, H. 1983. "An Analysis of Seneca's *Medea*." In *Seneca Tragicus*, edited by A. J. Boyle, 77–93. Berwick, Australia.

Garnsey, P. 1981. "Independent Freedmen and the Economy of Roman Italy under the Principate." *Klio* 63:359–71.

Giangrande, G. 1968. "On the Use of the Vocative in Alexandrian Epic." *Classical Quarterly* 18:53–59.

Gill, C. 1973. "The Sexual Episodes in the *Satyricon*." *Classical Philology* 68:172–85.

———. 1983. "Did Chrysippus Understand Medea?" *Phronesis* 28:136–49.

———. 1987. "Two Monologues of Self-Division: Euripides *Medea* 1021–80 and Seneca *Medea* 893–977." In *Homo Viator: Classical Essays for John Bramble*, edited by M. Whitby, P. Hardie, and M. Whitby, 24–37. Bristol, England.

———. 1996. *Personality in Greek Epic, Tragedy and Philosophy: The Self in Dialogue.* Oxford.

———. 1997. "Passion as Madness in Roman Poetry." In Braund and Gill 1997, 213–41.

———. 2006. *The Structured Self in Hellenistic and Roman Thought.* Oxford.

———. 2009. "Seneca and Selfhood: Integration and Disintegration." In Bartsch and Wray 2009, 65–83.

Gleason, M. 1999. "Elite Male Identity in the Roman Empire." In *Life, Death and Entertainment in the Roman Empire*, edited by D. S. Potter and D. J. Mattingly, 67–84. Ann Arbor, MI.

Goar, R. J. 1987. *The Legend of Cato Uticensis from the First Century B.C. to the Fifth Century A.D.* Brussels.

Gold, B. 1998. "The House I Live in Is Not My Own: Women's Bodies in Juvenal's Satires." In "Vile Bodies: Roman Satire and Corporeal Discourse," edited by Braund and Gold, 369–86. Special issue, *Arethusa* 31.

Goldberg, S. M. 1997. "Melpomene's Declamation (Rhetoric and Tragedy)." In Dominik 1997a, 166–81.

Golden, M., and P. Toohey, eds. 1997. *Inventing Ancient Culture: Historicism, Periodization and the Ancient World.* London.

Goldhill, S. 1995. *Foucault's Virginity: Ancient Erotic Fiction and the History of Sexuality.* Cambridge.

Gowers, E. 1993. *The Loaded Table: Representations of Food in Roman Literature.* Oxford.

———. 1994. "Persius and the Decoction of Nero." In Elsner and Masters 1994, 131–50.

Gradel, I. 2002. *Emperor Worship and Roman Religion.* Oxford.

Graver, M. 1998. "The Manhandling of Maecenas: Senecan Abstractions of Masculinity." *American Journal of Philology* 119:607–32.

———. 1999. "Philo of Alexandria and the Origins of the Stoic *Propatheiai.*" *Phronesis* 44:300–325.
———. 2002. *Cicero on the Emotions: Tusculan Disputations 3 and 4.* Chicago.
———. 2007. *Stoicism and Emotion.* Chicago.
Greenblatt, S. 1980. *Renaissance Self-Fashioning: From More to Shakespeare.* Chicago.
Griffin, M. T. 1984. *Nero: The End of a Dynasty.* London.
———. 1986a. "Philosophy, Cato and Roman Suicide: I." *Greece and Rome* 33:64–77.
———. 1986b. "Philosophy, Cato and Roman Suicide: II." *Greece and Rome* 33: 192–202.
———. 1992. *Seneca: A Philosopher in Politics.* Oxford.
———. 2003a. "*De Beneficiis* and Roman Society." *Journal of Roman Studies* 93:92–113.
———. 2003b. "Seneca as a Sociologist: *De Beneficiis.*" In De Vivo and Lo Cascio 2003, 89–121.
———. 2005. "Seneca and Pliny." In *The Cambridge History of Greek and Roman Political Thought*, edited by C. Rowe and M. Schofield, 532–58. Cambridge.
Grimal, P. 1967. "Le discours de Sénèque dans les *Annales* de Tacite." *Giornale Italiano di Filologia* 20:131–38.
———. 1971. "Le *De Clementia* et la royauté solaire de Néron." *Revue des Études Latines* 49:205–17.
———. 1978. *Sénèque ou la conscience de l'empire.* Paris.
Gunderson, E. 2003. *Declamation, Paternity, and Roman Identity: Authority and the Rhetorical Self.* Cambridge.
Gundert, B. 2000. "Soma and Psyche in Hippocratic Medicine." In Wright and Potter 2000, 13–35.
Habermehl, P. 2006. *Petronius, "Satyrica" 79–141: Ein philologisch-literarischer Kommentar: Bd. 1: "Sat." 79–110.* Berlin.
Habinek, T. 1998. *The Politics of Latin Literature: Writing, Identity, and Empire in Ancient Rome.* Princeton, NJ.
Habinek, T., and A. Schiesaro, eds. 1997. *The Roman Cultural Revolution.* Cambridge.
Hackworth-Peterson, L. 2006. *The Freedman in Roman Art and Art History.* Cambridge.
Hadot, I. 1969. *Seneca und die griechisch-römische Tradition der Seelenleitung.* Berlin.
Hadot, P. 1995. *Philosophy as a Way of Life: Spiritual Exercises From Socrates to Foucault.* Translated by M. Chase. Oxford.
Hankinson, R. J. 1991. "Galen's Anatomy of the Soul." *Phronesis* 36:197–233.
Harris, W. V. 2001. *Restraining Rage: The Ideology of Anger Control in Classical Antiquity.* Cambridge, MA.
———. 2006. "A Revisionist View of Roman Money." *Journal of Roman Studies* 96:1–24.
Haynes, H. 2003. *The History of Make-Believe: Tacitus on Imperial Rome.* Berkeley and Los Angeles.
———. 2010. "The Tyrant Lists: Tacitus' Obituary of Petronius." *American Journal of Philology* 131:69–100.
Henderson, J. 2002. "Knowing Someone through their Books: Pliny on Uncle Pliny (*Epistles* 3.5)." *Classical Philology* 97:256–84.

———. 2004. *Morals and Villas in Seneca's "Letters": Places to Dwell.* Cambridge.
———. 2006. "The Journey of a Lifetime." In Volk and Williams 2006, 124–46.
Henry, D., and B. Walker. 1963. "Tacitus and Seneca." *Greece and Rome* 10:98–110.
———. 1985. *The Mask of Power: Seneca's Tragedies and Imperial Rome.* Chicago.
Highet, G. 1941. "Petronius the Moralist." *Transactions of the American Philological Association* 72:176–94.
Hijmans, B. L. 1966. "Drama in Seneca's Stoicism." *Transactions of the American Philological Association* 97:237–51.
———. 1976. Inlaboratus et Facilis: *Aspects of Structure in Some Letters of Seneca.* Leiden.
Hill, T. 2004. *Ambitiosa Mors: Suicide and the Self in Roman Thought and Literature.* New York.
Hine, H. M. 1995. "Seneca, Stoicism and the Problem of Moral Evil." In Innes, Hine, and Pelling 1995, 93–106.
———, ed. 1996. *L. Annaei Senecae Naturalium Quaestionum Libros.* Stuttgart.
———, ed. 2000. *Seneca: Medea.* Warminster, England.
———. 2006. "Rome the Cosmos, and the Emperor in Seneca's *Natural Questions*." *Journal of Roman Studies* 96:42–72.
Hirzel, R. 1895. *Der Dialog: Ein literar-historischer Versuch.* Leipzig.
Holzberg. N. 1995. *The Ancient Novel: An Introduction.* London.
Hook, B. 2005. "Oedipus and Thyestes Among the Philosophers: Incest and Cannibalism in Plato, Diogenes, and Zeno." *Classical Philology* 100:17–40.
Hopkins, K. 1983. *Death and Renewal.* Cambridge.
———. 1993. "Novel Evidence for Roman Slavery." *Past and Present* 138:3–27.
Horkheimer, M., and T. W. Adorno. 1972. *Dialectic of Enlightenment.* Translated by J. Cumming. New York.
Horsfall, N. 1989a. "'The Uses of Literacy' and the *Cena Trimalchionis*: I." *Greece and Rome* 36:74–89.
———. 1989b. "'The Uses of Literacy' and the *Cena Trimalchionis*: II." *Greece and Rome* 36:194–209.
Hughes, L. 2007. Review of *The Freedman in Roman Art and Art History*, by Lauren Hackworth-Peterson. *Bryn Mawr Classical Review.* bmcr.brynmawr.edu/2007/2007-07-54.html.
Huizinga, J. 1950. *Homo Ludens: A Study of the Play-Element in Culture.* Boston.
Hutchinson, G. O. 1993. *Latin Literature from Seneca to Juvenal: A Critical Study.* Oxford.
Innes, D., H. Hine, and C. Pelling, eds. 1995. *Ethics and Rhetoric: Classical Essays for Donald Russell on His Seventy-Fifth Birthday.* Oxford.
Inwood, B. 1985. *Ethics and Human Action in Early Stoicism.* Oxford.
———. 1993. "Seneca and Psychological Dualism." In Brunschwig and Nussbaum 1993, 150–83.
———. 1995a. "Politics and Paradox in Seneca's *De Beneficiis*." In *Justice and Generosity: Studies in Hellenistic Social and Political Philosophy*, edited by A. Laks and M. Schofield, 241–65. Cambridge.
———. 1995b. "Seneca in his Philosophical Milieu." *Harvard Studies in Classical Philology* 97:63–76.

———. 2000. "The Will in Seneca the Younger." *Classical Philology* 95:44–60.
———. 2005. *Reading Seneca: Stoic Philosophy at Rome*. Oxford.
———. 2007a. "The Importance of Form in Seneca's Philosophical Letters." In *Ancient Letters: Classical and Late Antique Epistolography*, edited by R. Morell and A. Morrison, 133–48. Oxford.
———, ed. and trans. 2007b. *Seneca: Selected Philosophical Letters*. Oxford.
———. 2009. "Seneca and Self-Assertion." In Bartsch and Wray 2009, 39–64.
Izard, C. E. 1971. *The Face of Emotion*. New York.
Johnson, W. A. 2000. "Toward a Sociology of Reading in Classical Antiquity." *American Journal of Philology* 124:593–627.
Johnson, W. R. 1987. *Momentary Monsters: Lucan and His Heroes*. Ithaca, NY.
———. 1988. "Medea Nunc Sum: The Close of Seneca's Version." In *Language and the Tragic Hero: Essays on Greek Tragedy in Honor of Gordon M. Kirkwood*, edited by P. Pucci, 85–95. Atlanta.
Jones, C. P. 1987. "Stigma: Tattooing and Branding in Graeco-Roman Antiquity." *Journal of Roman Studies* 77:139–55.
———. 2000. "Nero Speaking." *Harvard Studies in Classical Philology* 100:453–62.
Jones, F. M. 1991. "Realism in Petronius." In *Groningen Colloquia on the Novel, 4*, edited by H. Hofmann, 105–19. Groningen.
Joshel, S. R. 1992. *Work, Identity, and Legal Status of Rome: A Study of the Occupational Inscriptions*. Norman, OK.
Kaster, R. A. 2001. "The Dynamics of *Fastidium* and the Ideology of Disgust." *Transactions of the American Philological Association* 131:143–89.
Ker, J. 2006. "Seneca, Man of Many Genres." In Volk and Williams 2006, 19–41.
———. 2009a. *The Deaths of Seneca*. Oxford.
———. 2009b. "Seneca on Self-Examination: Re-Reading *On Anger* 3.36." In Bartsch and Wray 2009, 160–87.
Kleijwegt, M. 2002. "'*Cum vicensimariis magnam mantissam habet*' (Petronius *Satyricon* 65.10)." *American Journal of Philology* 123:275–86.
Kneale, J. D. 1991. "Romantic Aversions: Apostrophe Reconsidered." *ELH: English Literary History* 58:141–65.
Konstan, D. 2005. "Clemency as a Virtue." *Classical Philology* 100:337–56.
Krostenko, B. A. 2001. *Cicero, Catullus and the Language of Social Performance*. Chicago.
Kurke, L. 1999. *Coins, Bodies, Games, and Gold: The Politics of Meaning in Archaic Greece*. Princeton, NJ.
Laird, A. 1999. *Powers of Expression, Expressions of Power: Speech Presentation and Latin Literature*. Oxford.
———. 2007. "The True Nature of the *Satyricon*?" In *The Greek and Roman Novel: Parallel Readings*, edited by M. Paschalis, S. Frangoulidis, S. Harrison, and M. Zimmerman, Ancient Narrative Supplementum 8, 151–67. Groningen.
Laporte, D. 2000. *History of Shit*. Translated by N. Benabid and R. el-Khoury. Cambridge, MA.
Larmour, D. H. J., P. A. Miller, and C. Platter, eds. 1998. *Rethinking Sexuality: Foucault and Classical Antiquity*. Princeton, NJ.
Lavery, G. B. 1980. "Metaphors of War and Travel in Seneca's Prose Works." *Greece and Rome* 27:147–57.

Leach, E. W. 1989. "The Implied Reader and the Political Argument in Seneca's *Apocolocyntosis* and *De Clementia.*" *Arethusa* 22:197–230.
Lear, J. 1998. *Open Minded: Working Out the Logic of the Soul.* Cambridge, MA.
Leeman, A. D. 1965. *Orationis Ratio.* Amsterdam.
Leigh, M. 1997. *Lucan: Spectacle and Engagement.* Oxford.
Leo, F. 1878. *De Senecae Tragoediis Observationes Criticae.* Berlin.
———. 1908. *Der Monolog im Drama: Ein Beitrag zur griechisch-römischen Poetik.* Berlin.
Levick, B. 2003. "Seneca and Money." In De Vivo and Lo Cascio 2003, 211–28.
Long, A. A. 1986. *Hellenistic Philosophy: Stoics, Epicureans, Sceptics.* Berkeley and Los Angeles.
———. 1991. "Representation of the Self in Stoicism." In *Companions to Ancient Thought 2: Psychology,* edited by S. Everson, 102–20. Cambridge.
———. 2001. *Stoic Studies.* Berkeley and Los Angeles.
———. 2006. *From Epicurus to Epictetus: Studies in Hellenistic and Roman Philosophy.* Oxford.
Long, A. A., and D. Sedley, eds. 1987. *The Hellenistic Philosophers.* 2 vols. Cambridge.
Mabbott, T. O. 1941. "Epictetus and Nero's Coinage." *Classical Philology* 36:398–99.
MacMullen, R. 1966. *Enemies of the Roman Order: Treason, Unrest and Alienation in the Empire.* Cambridge.
———. 1986. "Personal Power in the Roman Empire." *American Journal of Philology* 107:512–24.
Mader, G. 1998. "*Quod nolunt velint*: Deference and Doublespeak at Seneca, *Thyestes* 334–335." *Classical Journal* 94:31–47.
———. 2003. "Thyestes' Belch (Seneca, *Thy.* 911–12)." *Classical Quarterly* 53:634–36.
Malaspina, E., ed. 2001. *L. Annaei Senecae: "De Clementia libri duo"; Prolegomeni, testo critico e commento.* Alessandria, Italy.
Marchesi, I. 2005. "Traces of a Freed Language: Horace, Petronius, and the Rhetoric of Fable." *Classical Antiquity* 24:301–30.
Martin, R. 1975. "Quelques remarques concernant la date du *Satyricon.*" *Revue des Études Latines* 55:182–224.
———. 1999. *Le "Satyricon" de Pétrone.* Paris.
Marx, K. 1978. "The Eighteenth Brumaire of Louis Bonaparte." In *The Marx-Engels Reader,* edited by R. Tucker, 594–617. New York.
Mayer, R. 2005. "Sleeping with the Enemy: Satire and Philosophy." In Freudenburg 2005, 146–59.
Mazzoli, G. 1991. "Seneca e la poesia." In *Sénèque et la prose Latine,* edited by P. Grimal, 177–210. Geneva.
———. 2003. "Seneca *De Ira* e *De Clementia*: La politica negli specci della morale." In De Vivo and Lo Cascio 2003, 123–38.
McGlathery, D. 1998. "Reversals of Platonic Love in Petronius' *Satyricon.*" In Larmour, Miller, and Platter 1998, 204–27.
McMahon, J. 1998. *Paralysin Cave: Impotence, Perception and the Text in the "Satyrica" of Petronius.* Leiden.
Mele, Alfred R. 1987. *Irrationality: An Essay on Akrasia, Self-Deception and Self-Control.* Oxford.
———. 1992. "Akrasia, Self-Control and Second-Order Desires." *Nous* 26:281–302.

Meltzer, G. 1988. "Dark Wit and Black Humor in Seneca's *Thyestes*." *Transactions of the American Philological Association* 118:309–30.
Miller, N. P. 1968. "Tiberius Speaks." *American Journal of Philology* 89:1–19.
Miller, P. A. 1998. "Catullan Consciousness, the 'Care of the Self,' and the Force of the Negative in History." In Larmour, Miller, and Platter 1998, 171–203.

———. 2004. *Subjecting Verses: Latin Love Elegy and the Emergence of the Real.* Princeton, NJ.
Miller, W. I. 1998. *The Anatomy of Disgust.* Cambridge.
Mischel, T., ed. 1977. *The Self: Psychological and Philosophical Issues.* Totowa, NJ.
Mischel, T., and H. N. Mischel. 1977. "Self-Control and the Self." In Mischel 1977, 31–63.
Momigliano, A. 1961. *Claudius: The Emperor and His Achievement.* Translated by W. D. Hogarth. New York.

———. 1969. "Seneca between Political and Contemplative Life." In *Quatro Contributo alla Storia deli Studi Classica e del Mondo Antico*, 239–56. Rome.
Montiglio, S. 2006. "Should an Aspiring Wise Man Travel? A Dilemma in Seneca's Thought." *American Journal of Philology* 127:553–87.

———. 2009. "'My soul, consider what you should do': Psychological Conflicts and Moral Goodness in the Greek Novels." *Ancient Narrative* 8:1–34.
Morford, M. 1973. "The Neronian Literary Revolution." *Classical Journal* 68:210–15.
Morgan, T. 2007. *Popular Morality in the Early Roman Empire.* Cambridge.
Mortureux, B. 1989. "Les idéaux stoïciens et les premières responsibilités politiques: Le 'De Clementia.'" In *Aufstieg und Niedergang der römischen Welt*, 2.36.3:1641–85. Berlin.
Most, G. W. 1992. "*Disiecti membra poetae*: The Rhetoric of Dismemberment in Neronian Poetry." In *Innovations of Antiquity*, edited by R. Hexter and D. Selden, 91–419. London.

———. 1996. "Reading Raphael: 'The School of Athens' and its Pre-Text." *Critical Inquiry* 23:145–82.
Motto, A. L. 2001. *Further Essays on Seneca.* Frankfurt am Main.
Motto, A. L., and J. Clark. 1968. "*Paradoxum Senecae*: The Epicurean Stoic." *Classical World* 62:37–42.

———. 1970. "*Epistle 56*: Seneca's Ironic Art." *Classical Philology* 65:102–5.

———. 1971. "*Et terris iactatus et alto*: The Art of Seneca's *Epistle* LIII." *American Journal of Philology* 92:217–25.

———. 1988. *Senecan Tragedy.* Amsterdam.

———. 1993. *Essays on Seneca.* Frankfurt am Main.

———. 1997. "Seneca's Visionary Drama." *Listy Filologické* 70:34–41.
Müller, K., ed. 1995. *Petronius: "Satyricon" Reliquiae.* 4th ed. Munich.
Murgatroyd, P. 2000. "Petronius, *Satyricon* 132." *Latomus* 59:346–53.
Nauta, R. R. 1987. "Seneca's *Apocolocyntosis* as Saturnalian Literature." *Mnemosyne* 40:69–96.
Newman, R. J. 1989. "*Cotidie Meditare*: Theory and Practice of the *Meditatio* in Imperial Stoicism." In *Aufstieg und Niedergang der römischen Welt*, 2.36.3:1473–1517. Berlin.
Nicolet, C. 1991. *Space, Geography and Politics in the Early Roman Empire.* Ann Arbor, MI.
Noreña, C. 2001. "The Communication of the Emperor's Virtues." *Journal of Roman Studies* 91:146–68.

Nussbaum, M. C. 1978. *Aristotle's "De Motu Animalium."* Princeton, NJ.
———. 1993. "Poetry and the Passions: Two Stoic Views." In Brunschwig and Nussbaum 1993, 97–149.
———. 1994. *The Therapy of Desire: Theory and Practice in Hellenistic Ethics.* Princeton, NJ.
———. 2002. "Eros and Ethical Norms: Philosophers Respond to a Cultural Dilemma." In *The Sleep of Reason: Erotic Experience and Sexual Ethics in Ancient Greece and Rome*, edited by M. C. Nussbaum and J. Sihvola, 55–94. Chicago.
———. 2009. "Stoic Laughter: A Reading of Seneca's *Apocolocyntosis.*" In Bartsch and Wray 2009, 84–115.
O'Gorman, E. 2000. *Irony and Misreading in the "Annals" of Tacitus.* Cambridge.
———. 2005. "Citation and Authority in Seneca's *Apocolocyntosis.*" In Freudenberg 2005, 95–108.
Ormand, K. 1994. "Lucan's *Auctor Vix Fidelis.*" *Classical Antiquity* 13:38–55.
Osgood, J. 2007. "The *Vox* and *Verba* of an Emperor: Claudius, Seneca and *Le Prince Ideal.*" *Classical Journal* 102:329–53.
Padel, R. 1992. *In and Out of Mind: Greek Images of the Tragic Self.* Princeton, NJ.
———. 1995. *Whom Gods Destroy: Elements of Greek and Tragic Madness.* Princeton, NJ.
Panayotakis, C. 1994. "A Sacred Ceremony in Honor of the Buttocks." *Classical Quarterly* 44:458–67.
———. 1995. *Theatrum Arbitri: Theatrical Elements in the "Satyrica" of Petronius.* Leiden.
———. 2009. "Petronius and the Roman Literary Tradition." In Prag and Repath 2009, 48–64.
Paul, J. 2009. "*Fellini-Satyricon*: Petronius and Film." In Prag and Repath 2009, 198–217.
Pigman, G. W. 1980. "Versions of Imitation in the Renaissance." *Renaissance Quarterly* 33:1–32.
Plass, P. 1988. *Wit and the Writing of History: The Rhetoric of Historiography in Imperial Rome.* Madison.
———. 1995. *The Game of Death in Ancient Rome: Arena Sport and Political Suicide.* Madison.
Plaza, M. 2000. *Laughter and Derision in Petronius' "Satyrica": A Literary Study.* Stockholm.
Pomeroy, A. J. 1992. "Trimalchio as *Deliciae.*" *Phoenix* 46:45–53.
Porter, J. I., ed. 1999. *Constructions of the Classical Body.* Ann Arbor, MI.
Prag, J., and I. Repath, eds. 2009. *Petronius: A Handbook.* Malden, MA.
Raith, O. 1963. *Petronius: Ein Epikureer.* Nuremberg.
Rankin, H. D. 1965. "On Tacitus' Biography of Petronius." *Classica et Mediaevalia* 26:233–45.
———. 1969. "Eating People Is Right: Petronius 141 and a Topos." *Hermes* 97: 381–84.
Reeve, M. D. 1984. "Apotheosis . . . Per Saturam." *Classical Philology* 79:305–7.
Reinhard, T. 2002. "The Speech of Nature in Lucretius' *De Rerum Natura* 3.931–71." *Classical Quarterly* 52:291–304.
———. 2004. "Readers in the Underworld: Lucretius *De Rerum Natura* 3.912–1075." *Journal of Roman Studies* 94:27–46.

Relihan, J. C. 1993. *Ancient Menippean Satire*. Baltimore.
Reydams-Schils, G. 2005. *The Roman Stoics: Self, Responsibility, and Affection*. Chicago.
Reynolds, L. D., ed. 1965. *L. Annaei Senecae Ad Lucilium Epistulae Morales*. Oxford.
———, ed. 1977. *L. Annaei Senecae Diologorum Libri Duodecem*. Oxford.
Richardson, J. S. 1991. "*Imperium Romanum*: Empire and the Language of Power." *Journal of Roman Studies* 81:1–9.
———. 2009. *The Language of Empire: Rome and the Idea of Empire from the Third Century BC to the Second Century AD*. Cambridge.
Richardson, T. W. 1984. "Homosexuality in the *Satyricon*." *Classica et Mediaevalia* 35:105–27.
———. 1986. "Further on the Young Trimalchio." *Phoenix* 40:201.
Richardson-Hay, C. 2009. "Dinner at Seneca's Table: The Philosophy of Food." *Greece and Rome* 56:71–96.
Richlin, A. 1992. *The Garden of Priapus: Sexuality and Aggression in Roman Humor*. Oxford.
———. 1997. "Towards a History of Body History." In Golden and Toohey 1997, 16–35.
Rimell, V. 2002. *Petronius and the Anatomy of Fiction*. Cambridge.
———. 2007a. "The Inward Turn: Writing, Voice and the Imperial Author in Petronius." In *Seeing Tongues, Hearing Scripts*, edited by V. Rimell, Ancient Narrative Supplementum 7, 61–85. Groningen.
———. 2007b. "Petronius' Lessons in Learning—the Hard Way." In *Ordering Knowledge in the Ancient World*, edited by J. König and T. Whitmarsh, 108–32. Cambridge.
Rist, J. M. 1989. "Seneca and Stoic Orthodoxy." In *Aufstieg und Niedergang der römischen Welt*, 2.36.3:1993–2012. Berlin.
Rohde, E. 1894. *Psyche: Seelencult und Unsterblichkeitsglaube der Griechen*. Freiburg im Breisgau.
Roller, M. B. 2001. *Constructing Autocracy: Aristocrats and Emperors in Julio-Claudian Rome*. Princeton, NJ.
Rose, K. F. C. 1967. "Trimalchio's Accountant." *Classical Philology* 62:258–59.
———. 1971. *The Date and Author of the "Satyricon."* Leiden.
Rose, M. A. 1993. *Parody: Ancient, Modern, and Post-Modern*. Cambridge.
Rosenmeyer, T. 1989. *Senecan Drama and Stoic Cosmology*. Berkeley and Los Angeles.
———. 1990. "Decision Making." *Arion* 23:187–217.
Rosivach, V. J. 1995. "Seneca on Fear of Poverty in the *Epistulae Morales*." *Antiquité Classique* 64:91–98.
Rudich, V. 1993. *Political Dissidence under Nero: The Price of Dissimulation*. New York.
———. 1997. *Dissidence and Literature under Nero: The Price of Rhetoricization*. New York.
Ryberg, I. S. 1942. "Tacitus' Art of Innuendo." *Transactions of the American Philological Association* 73:383–404.
Said, E. 1993. *Culture and Imperialism*. New York.
Saller, R. 1980. "Anecdotes as Historical Evidence for the Principate." *Greece and Rome* 27:69–93.
———. 1982. *Personal Patronage under the Early Empire*. Cambridge.
Sambursky, S. 1987. *Physics of the Stoics*. Princeton, NJ.
Sandy, G. 1969. "Satire in the *Satyricon*." *American Journal of Philology* 90:293–303.

Scarborough, J. 1970. "Romans and Physicians." *Classical Journal* 65:296–306.
Schadewaldt, W. 1926. *Monolog und Selbsgesprach: Untersuchungen zur Formgeschichte der griechischen Tragodie*. Berlin.
Scheidel, W. 1993. "Slavery and the Shackled Mind: On Fortune-telling and Slave Mentality in the Graeco-Roman World." *Ancient History Bulletin* 7:107–14.
Schelling, T. C. 1984. "Self-Command in Practice, in Policy and in a Theory of Rational Choice." *American Economic Review* 74:1–11.
Schiesaro, A. 1994. "Seneca's *Thyestes* and the Morality of Tragic *Furor*." In Elsner and Masters 1994, 196–210.
———. 1997. "Passion, Reason and Knowledge in Seneca's Tragedies." In Braund and Gill 1997, 89–111.
———. 2003. *The Passions in Play: "Thyestes" and the Dynamics of Senecan Tragedy*. Cambridge.
Schifter, D. E., and I. Ajzen. 1985. "Intention, Perceived Control and Weight Loss: An Application of the Theory of Planned Behavior." *Journal of Personality and Social Psychology* 49:843–51.
Schmeling, G. 1991. "The *Satyricon*: The Sense of an Ending." *Rheinisches Museum für Philologie* 134:352–78.
———. 1994–95. "*Confessor Gloriosus*: A Role of Encolpius in the *Satyricon*." *Würzburger Jahrbücher für die Altertumswissenschaft* 20:207–24.
———. 1995. "*Quid Attinet Veritatem Per Interpretem Quaerere?*: *Interpretes* and the *Satyricon*." In *Roman Literature and Ideology: Ramus Essays for J. P. Sullivan*, edited by A. J. Boyle, 144–68. Bendigo, Australia.
Schmitzer, U. 2000. "Falsche und richtige Philologie: Die Homer-Zitate in Seneca, *Apocolo.* 5." *Rheinisches Museum für Philologie* 143:191–96.
Schnur, H. C. 1959. "The Economic Background of the *Satyricon*." *Latomus* 18:790–99.
Schofield, M. 1991. *The Stoic Idea of the City*. Cambridge.
———. 2003. "Stoic Ethics." In *The Cambridge Companion to the Stoics*, edited by B. Inwood, 233–56. Cambridge.
———. 2006. *Plato: Political Philosophy*. Oxford.
Schoonhoven, H., ed. 1980. "*Elegiae in Maecenatem*": *Prolegomena, Text, and Commentary*. Groningen.
Schraidt, N. 1939. "Literary and Philosophical Elements in the *Satyricon* of Petronius Arbiter." *Classical Journal* 35:154–61.
Segal, C. 1982. "*Nomen Sacrum*: Medea and Other Names in Senecan Tragedy." *Maia* 34:241–46.
———. 1984. "Senecan Baroque: The Death of Hippolytus in Seneca, Ovid, and Euripides." *Transactions of the American Philological Association* 114:311–25.
———. 1986. *Language and Desire in Seneca's "Phaedra."* Princeton, NJ.
Sharples, R. W. 1983. "'But Why Has My Spirit Spoken with Me Thus?': Homeric Decision Making." *Greece and Rome* 30:1–7.
Shattuck, R. 1996. *Forbidden Knowledge: From Prometheus to Pornography*. New York.
Shaw, W. D. 1999. *The Origins of the Monologue*. Toronto.
Sherman, N. 2005. *Stoic Warriors: The Ancient Philosophy behind the Military Mind*. Oxford.
Sienkiewicz, H. 1905. *Quo Vadis: A Tale of the Time of Nero*. Translated by S. Binion and S. Malevsky. New York.

Slater, N. 1990. *Reading Petronius*. Baltimore.
Smith, M. S., ed. 1975. *Petronius: Cena Trimalchionis*. Oxford.
Sorabji, R., ed. 1997a. *Aristotle and After*. London.
———. 1997b. "Is Stoic Philosophy Helpful as Psychotherapy?" In Sorabji 1997a, 97–209.
———. 2000. *Emotion and Peace of Mind: From Stoic Agitation to Christian Temptation*. Oxford.
Stacey, P. 2007. *Roman Monarchy and the Renaissance Prince*. Cambridge.
Staley, G. 2010. *Seneca and the Idea of Tragedy*. Oxford.
Stallybrass, P., and A. White. 1986. *The Politics and Poetics of Transgression*. Ithaca, NY.
Starkie, W. J. M., ed. 1968. *The "Acharnians" of Aristophanes*. Amsterdam.
Starr, R. 1987. "Trimalchio's Libraries." *Hermes* 115:252–53.
Steel, C. E. W. 2001. *Cicero, Rhetoric and Empire*. Oxford.
Striker, G. 1991. "Following Nature: A Study in Stoic Ethics." *Oxford Studies in Ancient Philosophy* 9:1–73.
Sullivan, J. P. 1968a. "Petronius, Seneca, and Lucan: A Neronian Literary Feud?" *Transactions of the American Philological Association* 99:453–67.
———. 1968b. *The "Satyricon" of Petronius: A Literary Study*. Bloomington, IN.
———. 1985. *Literature and Politics in the Age of Nero*. Ithaca, NY.
Summers, W. C. 1908. "On Some Fragments of Maecenas." *Classical Quarterly* 2:170–74.
Sutton, D. F. 1985. "The Satyr Play." In *The Cambridge History of Classical Literature*, vol. 1, edited by P. E. Easterling and B. M. W. Knox, 346–54. Cambridge.
Swift, J. 1996. *Gulliver's Travels*. Mineola, NY.
Syme, R. 1958. *Tacitus*. Oxford.
Tandoi, V. 1965. "Morituri Verba Catonis." *Maia* 17:315–39.
Tarrant, R. J., ed. 1976. *Seneca: Agamemnon*. Cambridge.
———. 1978. "Senecan Drama and its Antecedents." *Harvard Studies in Classical Philology* 82:213–63.
———, ed 1985. *Seneca's "Thyestes."* Atlanta.
———. 1995. "Greek and Roman in Seneca's Tragedies." *Harvard Studies in Classical Philology* 97:215–30.
Taylor, C. 1989. *The Sources of the Self: The Making of Modern Identity*. Cambridge.
Tell, H. 2009. "Wisdom for Sale? The Sophists and Money." *Classical Philology* 104:13–33.
Thomas, R. F. 1988. *Vergil: Georgics*. Vol. 2, *Books III–IV*. Cambridge.
Tietze, V. 1987. "The Psychology of Uncertainty in Senecan Tragedy." *Illinois Classical Studies* 12:135–41.
Töchterle, K., ed. 1994. *Lucius Annaeus Seneca: Oedipus*. Heidelberg.
Too, Y. L. 1994. "Educating Nero: A Reading of Seneca's *Moral Epistles*." In Elsner and Masters 1994, 211–24.
Toohey, P. 1997. "Trimalchio's Constipation: Periodizing Madness, Eros, and Time." In Golden and Toohey 1997, 50–65.
———. 2004. *Melancholy, Love, and Time: Boundaries of the Self in Ancient Literature*. Ann Arbor, MI.
Tosi, G. 1974–75. "La villa romana nelle *Epistulae ad Lucilium* di L. Anneo Seneca." *Aquileia Nostra* 45–46:217–26.

Toynbee, J. M. C. 1942. "*Nero Artifex*: The *Apocolocyntosis* Reconsidered." *Classical Quarterly* 36:83–93.
Tracy, V. A. 1980. "Aut captantur aut captant." *Latomus* 39:399–402.
Traina, A. 1974. *Lo stilo "drammatico" del filosofo Seneca.* Bologna.
Tresch, J. 1965. *Die Nerobücher in den Annalen des Tacitus.* Heidelberg.
Turner, V. 1969. *The Ritual Process: Structure and Antistructure.* Chicago.
Verboven, K. 2009. "A Funny Thing Happened on the Way to the Market: Reading Petronius to Write Economic History." In Prag and Repath 2009, 125–39.
Veyne, P. 1964. "Le 'je' dans le *Satyricon*." *Revue des Études Latines* 32:301–24.
———. 1969. "Vie de Trimalchion." *Annales* 16:213–47.
———. 1990. *Bread and Circuses: Historical Sociology and Political Pluralism.* Translated by B. Pearce. London.
———. 2003. *Seneca: The Life of a Stoic.* New York.
Viansino, G., ed. 1993. *Lucio Anneo Seneca: Teatro.* Milan.
Vickers, B., ed. 1982. *Rhetoric Revalued: Papers from the International Society for the History of Rhetoric.* Binghamton, NY.
Vlahogiannis, N. 1998. "Disabling Bodies." In *Changing Bodies, Changing Meanings: Studies on the Human Body in Classical Antiquity*, edited by D. Montserrat, 13–36. London.
Voelke, J.-P. 1973. *L'idée de volonté dans le Stoïcisme.* Paris.
Volk, K., and G. D. Williams, eds. 2006. *Seeing Seneca Whole: Perspectives on Philosophy, Poetry and Politics.* Leiden.
von Staden, H. 2000. "Body, Soul, and Nerves: Epicurus, Herophilus, Erasistratus, the Stoics and Galen." In Wright and Potter 2000, 79–117. Oxford.
Wallace-Hadrill, A. 1981. "The Emperor and His Virtues." *Historia* 30:298–323.
———. 1982. "*Civilis Princeps*: Between Citizen and King." *Journal of Roman Studies* 72:32–48.
Walsh, P. G. 1970. *The Roman Novel: The "Satyricon" of Petronius and the "Metamorphosis" of Apuleius.* Cambridge.
———. 1974. "Was Petronius a Moralist?" *Greece and Rome* 21:181–90.
Walters, J. 1997. "Invading the Roman Body: Manliness and Impenetrability in Roman Thought." In *Roman Sexualities*, edited by J. Hallet and M. Skinner, 23–43. Princeton, NJ.
———. 1998. "Making a Spectacle: Deviant Men, Invective, and Pleasure." In "Vile Bodies: Roman Satire and Corporeal Discourse," edited by Braund and Gold, 355–68. Special issue, *Arethusa* 31.
Warmington, B. H., ed. 2000. *Suetonius: Nero.* London.
Weaver, P. R. C. 1967. "Social Mobility in the Early Roman Empire: The Evidence of the Imperial Freedmen and Slaves." *Past and Present* 37:3–20.
Webster, T. B. L. 1965. "Self-Apostrophe in Menander." *Classical Review* 15:17–18.
Wenskus, O. 1994. "Der seekranke Odysseus: Seneca's 53. Brief." *Hermes* 122:479–84.
Wharton, D. B. 1997. "Tacitus' Tiberius: The State of the Evidence for the Emperor's *Ipsissima Verba* in the *Annals*." *American Journal of Philology* 118:119–25.
Wilamowitz-Mollendorff, U. von. 1919. *Griechische Tragödien.* Vol. 3. Berlin.
Wilcox, A. 2008. "Nature's Monster: Caligula as *exemplum* in Seneca's *Dialogues*." In *KAKOS: Badness and Anti-Value in Classical Antiquity*, edited by I. Sluiter and R. Rosen, 451–76. Leiden.

Williams, B. 1973. "The Analogy of the City and Soul in Plato's *Republic*." In *Exegesis and Argument: Studies in Greek Philosophy Presented to Gregory Vlastos*, edited by E. N. Lee, A. P. D. Mourelatos, and R. Rorty, 196–206. Leiden.

———. 1997. "Stoic Philosophy and the Emotions: Reply to Richard Sorabji," In Sorabji 1997a, 211–13.

Williams, C. A. 1999. *Roman Homosexuality: Ideologies of Masculinity in Classical Antiquity*. Oxford.

Williams, G. D. 2005a. "Interactions: Physics, Morality and Narrative in Seneca *Natural Questions 1*." *Classical Philology* 100:142–65.

———. 2005b. "Seneca on Winds: The Art of Anemology in *Natural Questions 5*." *American Journal of Philology* 126:417–50.

———. 2006. "Greco-Roman Seismology and Seneca on Earthquakes in *Natural Questions 6*." *Journal of Roman Studies* 96:124–46.

Williamson, G. 1951. *The Senecan Amble: A Study in Prose Form from Bacon to Collier*. London.

Wilson, J. P. 1990. "The Death of Lucan: Suicide and Execution in Tacitus." *Latomus* 49:458–63.

Wilson, M. 1987. "Seneca's Letters to Lucilius: A Revaluation." In *The Imperial Muse: Ramus Essays on Roman Literature of the Empire, to Juvenal through Ovid*, edited by A. J. Boyle, 102–21. Berwick, Australia.

———. 1997. "The Subjugation of Grief in Seneca's *Epistles*." In Braund and Gill 1997, 48–67.

———. 2001. "Seneca's Epistles Reclassified." In *Texts, Ideas and the Classics: Scholarship, Theory, and Classical Literature*, edited by S. J. Harrison, 164–88. Oxford.

Winkler, J. J. 1985. *Auctor and Actor: A Narratological Reading of Apuleius's "The Golden Ass."* Berkeley and Los Angeles.

Wistrand, M. 1990. "Violence and Entertainment in Seneca the Younger." *Eranos* 88: 31–46.

Woodman, A. J. 1998. *Tacitus Reviewed*. Oxford.

Wray, D. 2001. *Catullus and the Poetics of Roman Manhood*. Cambridge.

Wright, J. 1976. "Disintegrated Assurances: The Contemporary American Response to the *Satyricon*." *Greece and Rome* 23:32–39.

Wright, J. P., and P. Potter, eds. 2000. *Psyche and Soma: Physicians and Metaphysicians on the Mind-Body Problem from Antiquity to Enlightenment*. Oxford.

Zeitlin, F. I. 1971. "Petronius as Paradox: Anarchy and Artistic Integrity." *Transactions of the American Philological Association* 102:631–84.

Zwierlein, O., ed. 1986. *L. Annaei Senecae Tragoediae*. Oxford.

Index

Accius, 133–35
actors, 67, 119, 135
Aeacus, 135, 154, 156
Aegisthus, 62, 69–70, 72–73, 74, 83, 90, 223n54
Aeneas, 2, 94–95, 113, 215n3, 218n10, 239n31
Agamemnon (in Senecan tragedy), 69, 72
Agamemnon (scholar in the *Satyricon*), 53, 98, 183–84
Agrippa, 32, 33, 47, 265n16
Agrippina, 137, 146, 149, 254n8
Alexander the Great, 25–26, 32, 211, 252n81
anathymiasis, 17, 111–12, 161–63, 186, 188, 262n115
anima, 163–64, 167–68
animus. *See* soul
apodixis, 96
apostrophe, 15, 65, 69, 79, 83; and agency, 232n47, 234n65; to *animus*, 50–51, 55–56, 73, 76, 77, 81, 227n1, 231n37; to body, 211–12; as natural language, 97; Pompey's self-apostrophe, 56–58; Quintilian's definition of, 54
appearances, 11, 245n8; difficulty interpreting, 118, 121–25, 130, 156, 179, 193; of virtue and vice, 119, 124, 158, 164
Aristotle, 38–39, 44, 162, 220n27; on bees, 245n17; on greatness of soul, 133–34; on humor, 145
Ascyltus, 14, 108, 109, 187, 213, 271n106
asthma, 141, 166–67
Atreus, 16, 62, 63, 65, 69, 75–77, 83, 90, 243n107, 266n25; in Accius, 135; and cannibalism, 112, 144; surpassed by Eumolpus, 101; surpassed by Medea, 82

Auerbach, Erich, 194, 235n8, 249n51, 267n40
Augustine, 85, 101, 235n3
Augustus, 117, 127, 137; in *Apocolocyntosis*, 150, 153–54, 156, 164; and Maecenas, 177, 266n28
autobiography, 2, 9, 200, 213
autocracy, 2, 26, 117–18, 128, 130, 213
autocrats, 122, 130; individual as, 182–83; language and psychology of, 127–28, 133; language of, 125–30

Baiae, 1, 23–24, 32, 86, 166
Bakhtin, Mikhail, 8, 98, 150, 263n127
Bartsch, Shadi, 119, 188, 222n51, 242n88, 242n89
baths, 84, 86, 106, 109, 171, 210, 238n29
bees, 120–21, 122–23, 143, 155, 156, 180, 245n15, 245n17; discussed by Trimalchio, 186–87; as model for reading and writing, 184–85, 212, 268n50
belching, 144–45
blushing, 192, 250n61
body, 8, 14, 93, 97, 104, 110, 111; destroyed by passions, 182; fragility of, 107, 183, 239n44; hides *virtus*, 193; as literary work of art, 185; political relationship with soul, 118, 121, 125, 131, 139, 143, 156, 181; of slaves, 202
Brutus, Lucius Junius, 142
Brutus, Marcus Junius, 203
Burrus, 5, 131, 149

Caesar, Julius, 24, 30, 32–34, 36, 47, 117, 128–30, 149, 203

Caligula, 13, 127, 138; in *Apocolocyntosis*, 157, 158, 164; assassination of, 136, 252n91; as Atreus, 135
Campania, 12–13, 24, 84, 86, 87, 139, 166, 167–68, 184, 215n3
cannibalism, 69, 98–105, 109, 113
capital punishment, 122, 126, 131, 153–54, 156; of parricides, 123–24
captatores, 92, 98, 100–103, 112, 122, 207, 212, 235n27, 242n78; in Latin literature, 99; Seneca on, 100
carnival, 7–8, 17, 98, 99, 111, 142, 150, 164, 260n94
castration, 94–95
catarrh, 141, 167–68
Cato the Elder, 203
Cato the Younger, 2, 14, 17, 24, 28, 33–34, 49, 149, 243n98; compared with Senecan tragedy, 63, 69, 83, 234n60; last words and suicide, 50–52, 53, 59, 65, 73, 252n93; wealth of, 200
Catullus, 89, 91, 237n21, 237n22
Celsus, 162, 260n92
Chrysanthus, 102, 242n76
Chrysippus, 38, 197, 228n7, 242n78
Chrysis, 93, 94, 239n44, 269n76
Cicero, 29–30, 45, 99, 107, 109, 135; on Mark Antony, 144, 257n42; on Julius Caesar, 129–30; on first movements, 191; on humor, 145–46, 255n26; in *Satyricon*, 184; on soul's nature, 165–66; on Stoics' views of obscenity, 146
Cinnamus, 204–6
Circe, 91, 92–93, 94
civil war (Roman), 9, 33, 56–58, 105, 128–30, 220n39; Croton as, 92, 99; and Maecenas, 178
classical body, 164
Claudius, 17, 123–24, 127, 139, 242n77; archetypal nature of, 142; as empty gourd, 260n94; in Hades, 154, 156, 169; judgments of, 153–54; last words, 141–44, 160, 163–64; linked with Seneca, 161, 166, 168, 261n105; linked with Trimalchio, 161, 167–69, 212, 256n29; and Nero, 143; physical appearance of, 141–42, 156, 160, 180

Cleanthes, 162, 190
Clementia. See mercy
clients, 205–6
Clytemnestra, 16, 62, 65, 70–72, 83, 90
coins, 175, 195, 244n2, 246n25, 257n42, 265n20; gold, 204–5
comedy, 3, 12, 14, 139, 143, 164, 187, 207, 213
commands, 103; military, 26–27, 29, 47; of nature, 26, 33; of the passions, 41–47; of the soul, 36–41; self-directed, 27, 47–52, 60–61, 97, 211–12
Constantia, 13, 14; of Encolpius, 88, 91, 159; of Medea, 80–81; of Petronius, 13; in Senecan drama, 63, 65, 66, 67, 68, 73, 74, 83
constitution (political), 117, 122, 132
consumption, 33, 98, 101, 108, 112; and *continentia*, 105–13; and writing, 183–84
continentia, 16, 29, 102, 188, 242n77; and Claudius, 146; and consumption, 105–13; and control of emotions, 111; of Seneca, 207; in soul, 193; and Trimalchio, 161, 163
Corax, 92
cosmopolitanism, 33, 202, 222n51
cosmos, 33, 78, 169, 254n7
Croton, 91–92, 99, 100–101, 112, 207, 212, 220n39
cruelty, 123–25
Crypta Neapolitana, 1, 86, 166, 209, 236n9, 236n10
Culler, Jonathan, 231n32
cyclops, 89, 101, 259n79

debt, 175, 199
declamation, 50, 98; and apostrophe to *animus*, 54–56, 226n110; ruins great literature and rhetoric, 52–53, 73, 86
Declaration of Independence, 117–18, 244n4, 244n5
defecation, 17, 108, 143, 163
deliciae, 110, 272n116
Democritus, 147
dice, 128–29, 156, 249n54, 249n55
Dido, 95

Dio Cassius, 58, 138, 222n49, 261n105
disgust, 101, 103, 105, 256n28
doctors, 93, 110, 111, 243n104, 260n88
dolor, 43, 57, 60, 72, 231n40; of Encolpius, 97; of Medea, 78, 80, 82
Domitian, 245n10, 248n49, 250n61

earth, 141; air trapped within, 168; and human body, 169, 262n114; interior of, 166, 168–69
earthquakes, 167–68, 193
Edwards, Catharine, 11, 144, 198, 222n51
Egypt, 56, 245n13, 247n42
empire (Roman), 1, 2, 3, 8, 9, 14, 15, 17, 19, 23–26, 29, 31–36; and Claudius, 143, 159; destroyed by passions, 182–83; as macrocosm of the self, 56, 88, 169, 180–83; and Nero, 122, 123, 126, 131; and rhetoric, 51, 53, 104–5, 141, 211; role of money in, 194–95
Encolpius, 1, 2, 84, 103, 105, 106, 112, 147, 159, 207; anger and self-address of, 87–88; and care of the self, 94; finds Vergil offensive, 187; gives declamation against declamation, 52–53, 98, 183–84; impotence and self address of, 95–98; as narrator, 172; recognized by Lichas, 160; self-address and worry about discovery in Croton, 92; trapped on Lichas' ship, 160–61
epic (Greek), 51, 55, 128, 136, 250n79; used by Claudius, 155, 258n59
Epictetus, 99, 239n44, 242n87, 244n108, 245n8; on coins, 195; on laughter, 256n54
Epicureanism, 4, 5, 98, 144–45, 165, 185, 188
Epicurus, 175, 238n32, 243n94
Eucharist, 241n67
Eumolpus, 7, 10–11, 15; and *captatores*, 98–103, 105, 108, 112, 184, 212; in Croton, 92, 220n39; disguises Encolpius and Giton, 159–60; interest in Giton, 87–88, 91, 237n2; and Philomela, 98; poetic theory of, 184; on wealth, 201
eunuchs, 109, 171, 178

eupatheiai, 148, 267n37
exchange, 9, 85, 105, 108, 194, 199; commercial, 201, 203–4, 206–7; of gifts, 201, 203–4, 206–7; between souls, 202
extirpation, 40, 50, 104, 111, 136, 148

favors, 18, 201; and slaves, 202–6; in the *Satyricon*, 204–6
fiction, 3, 15, 86, 130, 212, 235n4, 237n28
Fides, 18; of Trimalchio and freedmen, 194, 195–96, 200, 271nn107–8
figures of speech (*figurae*), 2, 15, 44, 212; and passions, 97
Fingere, 15, 112–13, 244n110
"first movements," 18, 190–92, 236n10, 270n85, 270n87
Fitzgerald, F. Scott, 211
fluctuation, 27, 37, 44; in Senecan tragedy, 63, 65, 66, 69, 70, 75, 79, 81, 233n50; in the *Satyricon*, 111, 161, 163
Fortunata, 196, 269n71, 271n109
fortune, 12, 24–25, 92, 126, 200, 207
Foucault, Michel, 3, 220n38; on the ancient novel, 88–89; on the care of the self, 173, 216n8, 222n51, 227n2
freedmen, 4, 10, 151–52, 157, 258n56; bodies of, 18, 194; dialect of, 172, 195, 243n96, 264n8; and favors, 202; love of money, 9, 195–95, 200, 207
Freud, Sigmund, 232n45, 242n76
Frugalitas, 18; of boy slave, 196–97; in soul, 193, 272n111; of Trimalchio and freedmen, 194, 200
Furies, 80, 232n46, 234n61

Galen, 162–63, 260n88
Gill, Christopher, 188, 227n2, 228n7
Giton, 86–87, 91, 93, 94, 151; poses as slave, 151, 159–60, 195; trapped on Lichas' ship, 160–61
Goldhill, Simon, 89, 145, 236n18, 255nn23–24
Gorgias (character in the *Satyricon*), 102–4, 110, 111, 112, 243n106
Gorgias (Platonic dialogue), 157–58, 243n99

Graves, Robert, 142
greatness of soul, 130–39, 251n68, 252n81, 272n126
grotesque body, 8, 85, 98, 156, 164

Habinnas, 14, 107, 197, 243n102
Hadot, Pierre, 173
Hannibal, 24, 36, 105, 108
Hecaton, 199, 202
Hegel, Georg Wilhelm Friedrich, 8, 212
Hegemonikon, 38, 182
Henderson, John, 210, 235n4, 236n11
Heraclitus, 147; on the soul, 162
Hercules, 113, 232n46; in the *Apocolocyntosis*, 153, 156, 254n10
Hermeros, 108, 109, 243n96, 244n109; *fides* of, 195–96; insults Ascyltus, 187, 213, 271n106; insults Giton, 151, 195, 256n33
Herodotus, 102, 136
Hexis, 165
Hippolytus, 90, 211–12
Hopkins, Keith, 99, 235n8
Hostius Quadra, 90, 238n31

Imperium, 15, 23, 25, 26, 28, 47, 202, 213, 219n20; of Lucilius, 35; of self, 30, 32, 33, 36, 37, 40, 44; and self-address, 34; of stomach, 103, 112
impotence, 16, 91, 93, 237n26
indigestion, 16, 109
infanticide, 80–82, 104, 112, 241n69
Inwood, Brad, 26, 37–39, 44, 74, 235n3

Jason, 77–78, 82
Jews, 159
judgment, 123, 125, 139, 141, 246n28; of rulers, 154–60, 164, 178, 181
judicial system, 118, 123–24, 126; Claudius takes over, 142, 150–51, 153, 157, 257n50
Julio-Claudian dynasty, 58, 127, 128, 213
Juno, 90, 232n46, 234n61

Ker, James, 198, 235n5, 242n81, 242n92, 254n3, 261n105
"know thyself," 106–7, 242nn89–90

laughter, 8, 9, 144–52; and self-control, 145–48, 255n23, 255n25
legacy hunters. See *captatores*
Lekta, 223n58
Leonidas, 46–47
Lichas, 91, 159–60
Lucan, 56, 249n55; on death of Pompey, 56–58
Lucilius, 1, 23, 35, 51, 66, 69, 73, 148; advised on reading, 184; asks about literary style, 176; economic relationship, 198–99; encouraged to leave politics, 174; sickness of, 167; and slaves, 201; villas of, 210
Lucretius, 238n32, 243n94

Maecenas, 5, 17, 66, 266n28; condition of soul, 178–79; deceptive appearance of, 179; lack of belt, 175, 177, 178, 265n21; mercy of, 178; political ability of, 177, 266n30; on the body, 175–76; and Trimalchio, 171–72
magic, 91, 94
Marius, 24, 32, 33, 47
Marullus, 60–61
Marx, Karl, 212
McGlathery, Daniel, 89
Medea, 2, 16, 62, 63, 65, 69, 71; and infanticide, 112; and love, 90; appearance of, 190; power of language, 78, 233nn54–55; self-command of, 76–83; virtue of, 228n7
Meditatio, 40, 47–48, 85, 224n77; and cannibalism, 98, 102, 111; and *eros*, 86–98; and laughter, 147; of Nero, 125–26, 131; and self-address, 43, 48, 87; and sleep, 88, 91; and torture, 147–48
Melissa, 197
mens, 37, 75, 88
mercy, 31, 117, 119; of Augustus, 137; of Julius Caesar, 30, 203, 253n102; differentiated from pity, 125; of Maecenas, 178; separates king from a tyrant, 122–25
Messalina, 153
metaphors, 44–45; of bees, 156; of Claudius' tyranny, 164; economic, 85, 198–99; of entrapment, 160, 166; and figures of

speech, 212; improper use of, 174; literature as food, 183–84; made real, 101; in *meditatio*, 103, 112; political, 151, 158, 179; Seneca's use of for soul, 189; theatrical, 67; of vessels, 109

Miller, Paul Allen, 89

mirrors, 31, 93

money, 18, 102–3, 105, 106, 108, 207, 242n76; displays virtue, 18, 194; freedmen's love of, 9, 18, 194; as means of judging people, 195; and philosophical authority, 200–201; quantification of, 205–6

Nero, 1, 2, 5, 17, 211; ability to judge, 118–20, 125, 154, 158; adopts tyrannical language, 138–39; borrows eloquence, 127–28; and Claudius, 143, 164; coins of rejected, 195; magnanimous utterances of, 119, 123, 131, 133, 143, 154, 200; physical appearance of, 121, 156, 246n18; self-address of, 30–31; as soul of the empire, 40–41, 118, 121, 143, 156, 181; speaking Greek, 253n96; suicide and self-address of, 58–59; theatricality of age, 68, 119, 245n12; as vital spirit, 169, 263n125

Niceros, 187, 197

Nile, 35, 50, 222n49

Numantia, 28, 104, 112, 242n82

Nussbaum, Martha, 8, 90, 119, 222n51, 228n7; on the *Apocolocyntosis*, 253n1, 256n34, 256n39

Octavia, 253n102

Odysseus, 2, 96–97, 215n3, 218n1, 238n29; recognized by scar, 160; Seneca and Encolpius as, 84, 92–93; in *Troades*, 71, 233n53

Oedipus, 142

Otho, 248n49

Ovid, 91, 95, 99, 101, 153

parody, 2, 4, 6, 7, 85, 87, 111, 212, 241n67

passions, 16, 39, 65, 72, 74; command of, 41–47, 77; defeated by command of soul, 40; maintenance of, 62, 63–64, 82; as *populus Romanus*, 181, 182

Paulina, 13, 217n41, 237n24

personae, 11, 68, 119, 245n12

Petelia, 104

Petronius, 3–11, 172–73, 211, 213; death of, 11–13; on wealth, 200, 207

Phaedra, 71, 90, 228n7; appearance of, 190

Philomela, 98, 122, 241n61, 241n65

physiognomics, 18, 179, 197; critique of, 189–94, 269n79

Plato, 107, 145, 146, 158, 209, 218n1, 242n78; on bees, 245n15; city-soul analogy, 182; on the nature of the soul, 165, 246n20; theory of love, 197

pleasures, 23, 24, 55, 148; ability to command, 225n93; distinction between, 247n34; and Epicureanism, 145; of self-address, 30; sexual, 93; of tyrants, 122; at Trimalchio's house, 204; unable to enjoy, 182; of wills, 103

Pliny the Elder, 99, 215n1, 216n5

Pliny the Younger, 99, 245n10

Plocamus, 187

Plutarch, 44, 128–30, 145

pneuma, 162–63, 165, 188

Pompey, 24, 29, 32–34, 36, 47, 128; blush of, 192; death described by Lucan, 56–58

Priapus, 84, 94, 238n32

prima praeludentia. See first movements

prostitutes, 203–4

Publilius, 10, 172, 186, 264n5

Pythagoras, 100–101, 112

Quintilian, 54–55, 96, 138, 189, 212, 248n46

Quintus Fabius Maximus, 47

reading, 173; as spiritual nourishment, 183–89

reason, 64, 123, 133, 147–48, 193

rebellion, 118, 136–37, 138

recognition, 67, 69, 75, 82, 231n41; and scars, 159–60

republic (American), 117

republic (Roman), 28–30, 33, 117, 128, 132, 134, 135, 149, 246n21; founding of, 142; importance of body during, 192

revenge, 62, 63, 69, 76, 77, 82, 144
Rimell, Victoria, 183, 235n7, 240n54, 260n81
Roller, Matthew, 26, 28, 222n51
Rubicon, 128–30

Saguntum, 104
Sallust, 32, 47
sapiens. See wise man
Saturnalia, 8, 144–52, 244n109; Claudius as prince of, 142, 170; of Claudius and Trimalchio, 169; as date of the *Apocolocyntosis*, 257n54; as restoring order, 150–52; return under Nero, 169–70
Satyricon, 1–2, 5–7, 9–10; and *Apocolocyntosis*, 141, 252n2, 252n4; and appropriateness of language, 16, 96–98, 172; and bodily entrapment, 160–61; and civil war, 249n55, 271n97; and *De ira*, 87–88, 91, 95, 103–4; and *De tranquillitate animi*, 111, 161, 163, 243n106, 260n93; and *De vita beata*, 200–201; and doctors, 162–63; and Epicureanism, 98, 238n32; and favors, 204–6; and the *Iliad*, 93; and *Moral Epistles*, 1–2, 84, 209; and Ovid, 91, 95; and Plato, 197, 272n112; and Stoicism, 187–88; and Vergil, 94–96, 113–14, 187, 238n36
Schiesaro, Alessandro, 75–76, 228n8
Schmeling, Gareth, 85, 235n3, 238n34
Scipio Aemilianus, 28–29, 105, 221n42
self, 2, 15, 19; annihilation of, 14; care of, 3, 4, 14, 16, 17, 35, 88–89, 91, 94, 111, 126, 147, 198; command of, 2, 15, 23, 25–27, 62, 63, 64, 69, 72, 95, 97; construction of, 4, 14, 63, 98, 112, 113, 139, 173, 194, 211; court of, 2, 96, 126; deception of, 88, 91, 103; digging into, 169, 263n121; revelation of, 7, 17, 98, 141, 143, 173, 194, 211; shaping of, 7; as vessel, 15, 16, 106–13, 139, 243n103; and wealth, 201
self-reflexivity, 9
Senate, 132–33, 135, 192; and Agrippina, 149; and Claudius, 249n51; Nero's letter to, 138; on Olympus, 150, 153, 164; and Tiberius, 248n47
Senators, 10, 158, 240n57, 249n51

Seneca, Lucius Annaeus, 1; *Ad Helviam*, 43, 112; *Ad Marciam*, 106–7, 108; *Ad Polybium*, 111, 254n13; *Apocolocyntosis*, 4, 7, 8, 17, 127, 128, 139, 173, 180–81; as Cato, 14, 210; critiqued by Quintilian, 138; *De beneficiis*, 26, 100, 101, 103, 147, 201–4, 205, 206; *De clementia*, 4, 7, 17, 30–31, 40–41, 141, 142, 156, 158, 164, 170, 173, 177, 180–81, 212; *De constantia*, 148; *De ira*, 41–43, 47, 48, 87–88, 96, 103–4, 111, 131, 133, 136, 137, 147, 189–91, 207; *De matrimonio*, 90; *De providentia*, 50–51, 65, 69, 73; *De tranquillitate animi*, 43–44, 111, 147; *De vita beata*, 9–10, 36–37, 144–45, 193, 199–201, 227n118; on eating, 185–86; exile of, 43, 220n31; linked with Claudius, 161, 166–68, 261n105; linked with Trimalchio, 9–10, 161, 168, 198, 207, 210; on Maecenas in the *Moral Epistles*, 17–18, 171–81; *Moral Epistles*, 1, 5, 6, 17, 32–34, 39, 41, 45–46, 48–50, 51, 53, 59–61, 65–69, 85, 86, 97, 98–99, 100, 109, 113, 141, 144, 147, 167, 170, 184–85, 198–99, 209–10; *Natural Questions*, 7, 34–35, 41, 90, 141, 167–69, 193, 221n48; as Nero's speechwriter, 18, 31, 117, 128, 131, 137, 150, 153, 177; and Platonic forms, 209; self-parody of, 84, 85, 143, 148; sicknesses of, 48–48, 141, 166–67, 169, 254n5; as Socrates, 14, 210; on soul's material nature, 188–89; tragedy and philosophy of, 3, 65, 83, 95, 139, 190, 228n8, 235n68; and Vergil, 112–13, 120, 143, 155, 156, 174, 175–76, 180, 239n41; wealth of, 9, 198, 206; on wealth, 198–201, 207, 273n128
"Senecan Amble," 211
Seneca the Elder, 52–53, 55
Sibyl, 107
Sicily, 35, 106, 221n46
Sienkiewicz, Henryk, 211
slaves, 5, 107, 124, 159, 244n3; beating of, 205; and emperors, 154; and favors, 202–6; humanity of, 201–2; memorable death of, 49–50; and Trimalchio, 106, 146
Socrates, 49, 91, 134, 243n97; on the nature of the soul, 165; on wealth, 200, 273n129; on writing revealing character, 176

soul, 4, 8, 25, 66, 68, 97, 111, 242n91; as air, 165–66; cognate with stars, 169–70; command of, 16, 36–41, 44, 104, 245n20; consumes literature, 184; creates literature, 178–79, 185; of Encolpius, 93; as falsely great, 134; immortality of, 13; and *ingenium*, 176; as king or tyrant, 39, 179–83; of kings and tyrants, 121–22, 141, 156; material nature of, 17, 86, 141, 164, 166, 188; scars on, 87–88, 157–58, 159, 236n15, 259nn74–75; as self, 38; vision of, 193; and wealth, 199, 213
spectatorship, 50–51, 60, 66, 82, 119, 232n43, 245n10
Stoics, early, 38, 44–45; and animals, 246n26; on greatness of soul, 251n76, 252n77; on obscenity, 146; and physiognomy, 197; psychological dualism, 44; theory of best government, 244n3; theory of love, 197; theory of soul's material, 162–63, 165–66, 188–89; theory of total mixture, 268n63; theory of unified soul, 43–44, 233n56
Stoics, middle, 200
Suetonius, 58–59, 128–30, 131, 135, 137, 146, 213; on the fire at Rome, 139
suicides, 11–13, 49–51, 58–59, 73, 136, 137
Suillius, Publius, 198, 200
Sulla, 132–33, 134–35; blush of, 192; and Caligula, 252n86; and Nero, 251n72
Sullivan, J. P., 3, 5, 6, 87
Swift, Jonathan, 140–41, 253n2
syllogisms, 45–46
sympatheia, 233n55

Tacitus, 4, 5, 99; on death of Claudius, 146; on deaths of Seneca and Petronius, 11–14, 210–11; on imperial eloquence, 126–28; on Nero's actual words, 138–39; on Nero's eulogy for Claudius, 126–27, 148–49; on Seneca's attempt to retire, 206–7, 213; on Seneca's indulgence of Nero, 178; on Seneca's mocking of Nero, 149–50; on Tiberius' letter, 158
testamenta. *See* wills
theaters, 119
Theocritus, 89, 237n22

Theseus, 211–12
Thyestes, 69, 70, 71, 72, 75, 82, 101, 230n31
Tiberius, 127, 158, 189, 242n95, 251n74
Tigellinus, 12, 138, 149
tragedy, 2, 3, 4, 12, 14, 96–97, 139, 212, 213, 237n27
tragedy (Greek), 51, 55, 77, 129–30, 150, 232n46, 234n57
Trajan, 195
Trimalchio, 10, 14, 15, 84, 100, 105, 139; combines body and literature, 186–87; combines languages and genres, 187; digestive problems of, 110–12, 141, 146, 186; life as slave, 187; linked with Claudius, 161, 167–69, 212, 256n29; linked with Seneca, 9–10, 161, 168, 198, 207, 210; love of boys, 196–98; and Maecenas, 171–72; as philosopher, 187; self-sufficiency of, 106, 204; self-transformation of, 194, 196; tomb of, 5, 107–8, 171, 173; as tyrant, 105, 139, 260n82; *virtus* of, 196
truth, confession of, 86, 88, 92–93, 103, 110, 111, 161, 163, 187, 260n84
Tubero, 109, 242n98, 244n110
tyrants, 43, 105, 132, 136, 236n15; Claudius as, 141, 154; differentiated from kings, 117–18, 120, 121–22, 130; endless Saturnalia of, 170; how to live under, 136, 207; insides of, 165, 169; Nero as, 206–7

Ulixes. *See* Odysseus
Ulysses. *See* Odysseus

Valerius Maximus, 105, 203, 242n83
Varro, 245n15
vessels, 108, 110, 243n97; of earthenware, 108–9, 113; of glass, 108
vices, 6, 23, 24, 26, 32, 37, 131; of body, 183, 186; command of, 61, 72; consistency of, 63, 64, 65, 63, 228n7; curing of, 48; of inconsistency, 43, 65; of money, 198; of pity, 125; of pleasure, 145, 241n74; psychology of, 63, 64, 73, 83; of tyrant, 178; and virtues, 119, 122–25, 158, 174, 193

villas, 1, 32; of Seneca, 206, 210; as underworld, 84
Virtus, 27–28, 51, 68; hidden by body, 193; of Medea, 81; of Trimalchio and freedmen, 18, 194, 196, 200, 272n110; in war, 29
Voltaire, 211

wills, 15, 85, 98–100, 103, 212, 240n57; power of, 101, 108, 273n137; Seneca's pursuit of, 198

wine, 107, 110, 205
wise man, 66–67, 86, 88, 125; bodily reactions of, 192, 270n88; and wealth, 18, 199–200
writing, 173; as revelation of character, 175–81, 265n65; as spiritual nourishment, 183–89

Zeno, 45–46, 88, 197, 228n9, 242n78, 274n141; on the soul, 162